The Two Worlds of

William March

William March (Courtesy of the William S. Hoole Special Collections Library of the Amelia Gayle Gorgas Library, The University of Alabama)

The Two Worlds of

William
March

Roy S. Simmonds

THE UNIVERSITY OF ALABAMA PRESS

Quotations from published and unpublished material by William March are reprinted with permission of Harold Ober Associates on behalf of the copyright holders, the Trustees of the William E. Campbell (March) Trust U/W, Merchants National Bank of Mobile, Mobile, Alabama. Material from the Archives of Harold Ober Associates, held at Princeton University, is published with permission of Princeton University Library.

The author is grateful to the following publishers, authors, and literary agents for permission to reprint copyrighted material:

Albert Halper, for *Good-bye, Union Square*, by Albert Halper. Copyright © 1970 by Albert Halper. Reprinted by permission.

The Paris Review, for "The Art of Fiction: LXXIII," by John Gardner. Copyright © 1979 by The Paris Review Inc. Reprinted by permission.

Laurence Pollinger, Ltd., Simon & Schuster, Inc., and Lester & Orphen Dennys, Ltd., for *Ways of Escape*, by Graham Greene. Copyright © 1980 by Graham Greene. Reprinted by permission.

The Pushcart Press, for *The Little Magazine in America: A Modern Documentary History*, edited by Elliott Anderson and Mary Kinzie. Copyright © 1978 by *Triquarterly*. Reprinted by permission.

Saturday Review, for "Poor Pilgrim, Poor Stranger," by Robert Tallant. Copyright © 1954 by *Saturday Review*. All rights reserved. Reprinted by permission.

Library of Congress Cataloging in Publication Data

Simmonds, Roy S.
    The two worlds of William March.

    Bibliography: p.
    Includes index.
    1. March, William, 1893–1954. 2. Novelists, American—20th century—Biography. I. Title.
PS3505.A53157Z85   1983   813'.52 [B] 83-1100
ISBN 0-8173-0167-4

This book is dedicated to my good and valued friends William T. Going, Preston C. Beyer, and the late James Clinton Bolton. Without their immense assistance, continued encouragement, and wise counseling, this book would never have been written.

. . . everybody must seem crazy if you see deep enough into their minds.

The Looking-Glass

When I was younger, and lived in a gentler world, I occasionally wondered at the reason for witches, and for their repudiation of the human heritage. In those far-away, innocent days, I thought of them as silly, demented creatures, but as I grow older, I am not so sure, for sometimes it seems most pleasant to be able to mount a broomstick and ride off to an imaginary realm behind the clouds. No matter what that land of witches is like, it can hardly be crueler or more unbelievable than our own world—the frightening world in which we are asked to live out our days to their end.

"Warlock"

. . . man . . . is a frail, lost creature, too weak to walk unaided.

"This Heavy Load"

Contents

Preface

I first became interested in the life and work of William March as a result of my correspondence more than ten years ago with the brilliant young Canadian scholar and critic Lawrence William Jones. Jones came to England with his wife and baby daughter in the late summer of 1970 to take up a teaching post at Leicester University. We made several appointments to meet, but somehow or other events outside our control seemed always to intervene and frustrate us. Then his baby daughter became sick and did not recover until shortly before Christmas. We arranged to meet quite definitely early in the New Year. In the last letter he wrote to me on December 21, he announced that his wife and he were "scheming to get up to see y'all as soon as Santa has had his Day." In mid-January, I received a letter from Paris Leary, Lawrence's supervisor at Leicester, informing me that Lawrence had been killed in a car accident a few weeks before. Dr. Leary advised me that Lawrence's widow had already departed for Canada, leaving most of her husband's working papers behind at the university with instructions that I was to be given any of these I might wish to have.

Among the papers I collected from Leicester were Lawrence's initial research materials for a study of William March. At that time, I had read none of March's works, apart from a short story, "The Slate and the Sorrow," which had been reprinted in the anthology *The Esquire Treasury* in 1953. I was vaguely aware that March was the author of a war book titled *Company K* and of another novel, *October Island*, on which, in a letter earlier in 1970, Lawrence had told me he was planning to base a film scenario he wished to write. Lawrence's letters expressed the excitement he had felt upon "discovering" March, and some of this sense of excitement and curiosity had already rubbed off onto me. Reading through the material he had collected—and in particular a forty-three-page typescript memoir "Bill March" by the New Orleans journalist Clint Bolton—I determined to complete the work Lawrence had started and been so tragically prevented from completing.

These papers—the Bolton memoir, the Xerox copies of some of the short stories, the first rough working notes on some of the stories, the tentative beginnings of a checklist—formed the basis of my subsequent researches. I followed up the few leads Lawrence had established, writing to Bolton (and thus commencing an immensely enjoyable and stimulating dialogue by letter and tape which lasted until Bolton's death in the spring of 1980); to Edward Glover, March's London psychoanalyst; to William T. Going, the most distinguished and knowledgeable of all March scholars; and to Lillian Jackson, the trust officer of the Merchants National Bank of Mobile, the trustees of the William E. Campbell (March) Trust. From all, I received courtesy, assistance, and encouragement. As I began to fit together the jigsaw pieces of information that were providing me with a slowly emerging overview of the life and work of this fascinating human being and writer William Campbell/March, I knew that the principal work to which I would have to devote myself was the writing of his biography.

Although the Campbell trustees and the Campbell family were, to begin with, cooperative about my undertaking a critical survey of March's work, they were, unfortunately, not enthusiastic when I made known my intention to write a biography. It was put to me that March had once intimated that he wished for no biography to be written, and I was politely informed that no materials held by the bank, such as letters and manuscripts, would be made available to me in the furtherance of such a project. However, after reading my completed manuscript, the Campbell family kindly gave its full approval of the book, subject to the deletion of one short passage, and generously granted me permission to quote all the extracts I have used from March's unpublished letters.

The book is thus not exactly the work I would have wished to have written, its emphasis being on the literary career and rather less on the personal life. It will, I hope, nevertheless have the desired effect of sending those who read it—students, critics, and general readers alike—back to those works which constitute the legacy left to us by the man who admitted that he probably was never a professional writer in the accepted sense of the word, but whom the poet José Garcia Villa regards as "the greatest short story writer America has produced" and whom Alistair Cooke has described as "the unrecognized genius of our time."

Acknowledgments

During the ten-year gestation period of this book I have been constantly indebted to a vast number of people who have taken the time and the trouble to reply to my unsolicited letters. Without their generosity and kindness this book could never have been written. It was seldom that any letter I wrote remained unanswered, even if the recipient regretted that the lead I had followed up was abortive. The past decade has proved to me that the old-fashioned courtesies are as vitally practiced now as they ever were.

My gratitude, to begin with, goes to the late Lawrence William Jones for introducing me to the two worlds of William March. I hope that he would not have been too disappointed in the work I have attempted to complete on his behalf.

My greatest indebtedness is to the three people with whom I have constantly corresponded over the past ten years and who have been unstinting in giving their time, wisdom, and energies to my project as well as encouraging me during those periods when my own belief in what I was doing momentarily wavered: Preston C. Beyer for interviewing on my behalf March's brother and sister-in-law Peter and Gwen Campbell, March's art dealer and good friend Klaus Perls, and the poet José Garcia Villa; to the late James Clinton ("Clint") Bolton for his many reminiscences of March, for background information relating to the French Quarter of New Orleans, and for his comments and suggestions after reading the first draft of this book; William T. Going for generously providing me with information which he had gleaned for himself for his own projected, but regrettably unrealized, March biography, for also reading and commenting on the first draft of the book, and for his valued and valuable advice to a fledgling author tentatively trying out his wings. To these three, my eternal thanks.

Special gratitude is also due to Mary Holmes Sensabaugh, who made available to me her own research papers on March, which contained much important material I could have obtained from nowhere else; to the late Ruth Warren of the Special Collections Division, Mobile Public Library; to Abigail Ann Hamblen, who gave me valuable insights into March's work and graciously allowed me to read several of her unpublished essays on March; to Ellen Fay Peak, who also made important material available to me; to Nicholas S. McGowin, for many kindnesses and for his unswerving encouragement over the years; and to George H. Spies and Gordon R. Speck, who have both been wondrously indefatigable in their pursuit of remote March material on my behalf.

I am indebted to the following people for allowing either Preston Beyer or me to tape interviews with them: Peter and Gwen Campbell, the late Edward Glover, Klaus Perls, the late Clay Shaw, and José Garcia Villa. Other of March's friends who have been particularly generous and helpful in providing me with comprehensive written reminiscences are Kay Boyle, Arthur Calder-Marshall, Robert Clark, Joseph Dickinson, Lombard Jones, and David Mynders Smythe.

In addition to Peter and Gwen Campbell, I offer my sincere thanks to four other members of the Campbell-March families, namely Mr. and Mrs. Homer W. Jones, Jr., Dillon T. March, and Mrs. J. C. Maxwell. I also thank Lillian Jackson, formerly of the Merchants National Bank of Mobile, for her valuable assistance during the early days of my research; Garet V. Aldridge, vice-president and trust officer at the Merchants National Bank of Mobile; John Day Peake, Jr., vice-president and trust officer of the Merchants National Bank of Mobile; and Patricia Powell of Harold Ober Associates, March's literary agents during his later years.

To the many people who have contributed to greater or lesser degree to the writing of this book, I express my gratitude. I list their names alphabetically, for want of any better order, and pray forgiveness if I have inadvertently missed any name that should appear here: Betsy Amster of Random House, Inc.; Dallas Baillio, director of the Mobile Public Library; John P. Baker of the Research Libraries, New York Public Library; Linda Morrine Barber of *Mademoiselle*; Frances Barton, curator of Special Collections, The University of Alabama; William M. Beasley; W. J. Bedding, late of Walter Runciman & Co., Ltd., London; Lesley Benjamin, associate editor, *Paris Review*; Edmund Berkeley, Jr., Alderman Library, University of Virginia; Susan Bolotin of Random House, Inc.; Dorothy S. Boyle, manager, Program Records-Information, CBS Broadcast Group, New York; Ernest Brin of the Louisiana Division of the New Orleans Public Library; John Bush of Victor Gollancz, Ltd., London; Paul D. Byers; James P. Callan, Jr., executive secretary, Phi Kappa Sigma Fraternity, General Headquarters, Philadelphia; Gini Cammarata of *Redbook Magazine*; Ruth Collins, curator of Special Collections, The University of Alabama; Ron Coplen, librarian, Harcourt Brace Jovanovich, Inc.; Patricia Cork of Hughes Massie, Ltd., London; Tess Crager; Stephanie H. Craib;

Stephen G. Croom; Richard H. Crowder; David L. Darden, assistant dean, The University of Alabama; the late Marion Davenport; Carolyn A. Davis, the George Arents Research Library, Syracuse University; Peter de Vries; Stuart Dick, Special Collections, Morris Library, University of Delaware; Ellen S. Dunlap, Humanities Research Center, University of Texas at Austin; F. Irvin Dymond; Paul Engle; Elizabeth Fake, University of Virginia Library; Judith Falk of *Harper's Bazaar*; David Farmer, Humanities Research Center University of Texas at Austin; the late Martha Foley; Dudley Frasier; Donald Gallup, curator, Collection of American Literature, Beinecke Rare Book and Manuscript Library, Yale University; Donna Gillett Gehring, Department of Rare Books and Special Collections, University of Notre Dame; Livia Gollancz; Howard B. Gotlieb, director of Special Collections, Mugar Memorial Library, Boston University; Thomas Griffin; Robert E. L. Hall, University Publications Archives, McKeldin Library, University of Maryland; Albert Halper; Colin B. Hamer, Jr., Louisiana Division, New Orleans Public Library; Ann Hamilton, Birmingham-Southern College Library; Granville Hicks; Sam Hobson, M.D., New Orleans; David E. Horn, Archives of DePauw University, Greencastle, Indiana; Gregory A. Johnson, Manuscripts Department, Alderman Library, University of Virginia; Barbara Kulawiec, Burling Library, Grinnell College, Iowa; the late Marston LaFrance; Joyce H. Lamont, curator of Special Collections, The University of Alabama; Geoffrey T. Large, the National Magazine Co., Ltd., London; Margaret Laurens of Random House, Inc.; Paris Leary; Kenneth A. Lohf, curator, Butler Library, Columbia University; Robert Lowry; Malcolm M. MacDonald, director, The University of Alabama Press; William J. Maher, University Archives, University Library, University of Illinois at Urbana-Champaign; Anton C. Masin, Department of Rare Books and Special Collections, University of Notre Dame Memorial Library; Floyd McGowin; Richebourg Gaillard McWilliams; Wilbur E. Meneray, manuscript librarian, Tulane University Library; Charles L. Mo, registrar, New Orleans Museum of Art; Beatrice R. Moore; the late Harry T. Moore; Warren F. Nardelle, Sr., librarian, the Times-Picayune Publishing Corporation; G. M. Neufeld, head of the Reference Unit, History and Museums Division, U.S. Marine Corps, Washington, D.C.; Norman A. Nicolson; Jo Nordyke, *Prairie Schooner*, University of Nebraska; Arthur Plotnik of *Wilson Library Bulletin*; Mrs. Cameron Plummer, the Haunted Bookshop, Mobile; Gerald Pollinger; Jean F. Preston, Princeton University Library; Cynthia Reed of Little, Brown & Company; Barbara Reid; Michael Routh; Sarah Saunders of Holt, Rinehart & Winston; Mrs. G. Lewis Schaffer of the Memphis

Little Theater; David E. Schoonover, curator, Collection of American Literature, Beinecke Rare Book and Manuscript Library, Yale University; Pearl Schwarz; Gretchen Crager Sharpless; Frederick Silva; Brigadier General E. H. Simmons, Historical Division, Headquarters, U.S. Marine Corps, Washington, D.C.; William M. Sladen; A. O. Smith, Walter Runciman & Co., Ltd., London; E. Herdon Smith, Mobile; James Stern; Lois Cole Taylor; Paul E. Thune, registrar, Valparaiso University; Rita Vaughan of Harcourt Brace Jovanovich, Inc.; Edward F. Wegmann; Daniel A. Yanchisin, History and Travel Department, Memphis/Shelby County Public Library and Information Center; Robert J. Zietz, head of Special Collections, Mobile Public Library; and Elizabeth R. Ziman, U.S. Library, University of London Library.

For supplying me with Xerox copies of correspondence and other items from their files, I express my gratitude to the publishing houses of Holt, Rinehart & Winston; Little, Brown & Company; and Victor Gollancz, Ltd. My special thanks are due to Miss Livia Gollancz for allowing me personally to examine selected material from the files in the Gollancz office.

For providing me with Xerox copies of materials, I acknowledge my debt to the following libraries and institutions: William Stanley Hoole Special Collections Library, The University of Alabama; the Birmingham-Southern College Library; British Film Institute, Information and Library Department, London; Butler Library, Columbia University; Morris Library, University of Delaware; Roy O. West Library, DePauw University, Greencastle, Indiana; the Grinnell College Library, Iowa; Harvard University Library; University Library, University of Illinois at Urbana-Champaign; University of Iowa libraries; Kansas State University Library; McKeldin Library, University of Maryland; History and Travel Department, Memphis/Shelby County Library and Information Center; the University of Minnesota Library; Mobile Public Library; New Orleans Public Library; the Research Libraries, New York Public Library; Library of the University of North Carolina; Department of Rare Books and Special Collections, University of Notre Dame; Princeton University Library; the George Arents Research Library, Syracuse University; Humanities Research Center, University of Texas at Austin; the Beinecke Rare Book and Manuscript Library, Yale University.

To my editor, Joanne Ainsworth, of the Guilford Group, I owe a very personal debt of gratitude. Her wise suggestions have been both creative and helpful, and have resulted in many minor but essential improvements to my manuscript. Working with her has been a most rich and rewarding experience.

Particular acknowledgment is due to Professor Tetsumaro Hayashi, English Department, Ball State University, editor of the *Steinbeck Quarterly*, who was the first to encourage me to write and whose continuing interest and support has been an ever-present inspiration to me.

Finally, I give my thanks and my gratitude to my long-suffering wife and family who have had to bear with me during the past ten years. Their patience and understanding and, above all, their love have made my task that much the easier.

Abbreviations

Quotations from the works of William March are all from the U.S. first editions and are identified in text and notes by the following abbreviations:

BS	*The Bad Seed.*
CIATD	*Come in at the Door.*
CK	*Company K.*
LG	*The Looking-Glass.*
LW	*The Little Wife and Other Stories.*
99F	*99 Fables*, edited and with an introduction by William T. Going.
OI	*October Island.*
SLTS	*Some Like Them Short.*
TB	*Trial Balance.*
TT	*The Tallons.*
WMO	*A William March Omnibus*, with an introduction by Alistair Cooke.

The Two Worlds of

William
March

one

Early Years

Mobile, Alabama's only seaport and the most convenient Gulf port for the Panama Canal, Cuba, and South America, stands on the Mobile River at its entrance to the broad expanse of Mobile Bay. Several resort towns, such as Fairhope and Point Clear, are situated on the eastern side of the bay, and on the western shore lies Alabama Port. In the 1890s, the deep water channel, which made possible the eventual construction and development of extensive port installations and facilities, had not been dredged to anything near its present depth, and Mobile, while even then serving as a large port for cotton exports, had not assumed the status of its current commercial importance.

It was here in Mobile, at three o'clock in the afternoon, September 18, 1893, in a house at the northwest corner of Broad and Conti Streets, that the second child of John Leonard Campbell and Susan March Campbell was born with a complete caul.[1] The child was the first son of the proud parents. They named him William Edward Campbell. Under that name, he was destined to acquire respected recognition among Mobilians as an astute businessman. Later, he was to enjoy universal fame as the novelist and short-story writer William March, author of *Company K*, *The Looking-Glass*, and *The Bad Seed*.

Both of John Leonard's parents, William Robert Campbell and Margaret Crevey Campbell, were born in Scotland. They had several children, but Margaret died in 1857 near Sandyridge, Alabama, at the time of John Leonard's birth. William Robert was killed during the Civil War. John Leonard's elder brothers enlisted in the Confederate army and either died during the fighting or subsequently disappeared in the turmoil of the Reconstruction period. One of the daughters married and settled in Greenville, Alabama.

March was told by his mother that the maternal side of his family

1

descended from a most distinguished forebear—the celebrated Elizabethan philosopher and scientist Sir Francis Bacon, no less—but March seemingly gave little credence to this claim. His maternal great-grandfather, John Willis March, was born in England in 1806. Purportedly a younger son of the earl of March, he was something of a wild blade, and when eventually his escapades began to pose a decided threat to his well-being, he was sent to America by his family. He acquired U.S. citizenship in 1836. Shortly afterward, in Alabama, he met Lady Elizabeth Bacon, who had come over to America from Devon. They subsequently married and had three children: two sons, William, who was born in Mobile in 1839, and George, born in 1848, and a daughter, Emma, who died as a child. The elder son was twenty-nine when he married the twenty-two-year-old Mary Jane Baker, of Mobile County, on September 23, 1868. Their marriage was also blessed with three children, again two sons and a daughter. The daughter, Susan, the middle one of the offspring, was born in 1871. When Susan was seven and her younger brother only two, their mother contracted measles, presumably from one of the children, and died. Family legend, however, does not attribute Mary Jane's death to the disease itself but to the pneumonia to which she succumbed as a consequence of taking a cold bath "to drive the swelling in." Her bereaved husband remarried two years later, in 1880. His new bride was Susan Markham. She bore him five more children, three boys and two girls. William died in Mobile on May 12, 1902, when his grandson, the future author, was eight years old.[2] March remembered him as a venerable, white-haired gentleman, and, indeed, the grandfather was a prominent Methodist and played a leading role in the erection of the First Methodist Church in Mobile. His support of the church was not a virtue his grandson was to emulate. March had little time for organized religion and, while possibly not an atheist, was, as one member of the Campbell family has put it, "certainly no Billy Graham."[3]

In 1889, the God-fearing, landowning William March witnessed the marriage of his daughter Susan to John Leonard Campbell. There can be little doubt that in her family's eyes Susan had chosen to marry considerably beneath herself. At that time, John Leonard was, for want of a better word, the "captain" of a scow, which he navigated around the coast and back and forth across Mobile Bay. Whatever her family's opinion, Susan clearly thought herself extremely fortunate to have netted the affections of such a dashing and handsome seafaring man. She always referred to her husband as "Mr. Campbell."

After their marriage, the couple moved to Pensacola, Florida, living there and in various mill towns in Escambia County for the next sixteen or seventeen years. They were, from all accounts, poor and had to struggle to raise their large family. John Leonard found employment as a timber cruiser, traveling around the forests of Escambia County, estimating the lumber footage in a particular stand of trees and advising his employers whether or not it would be worthwhile to establish a sawmill in the area. Their first child, a daughter, Margaret Crevey, was born in 1891, two years earlier than her brother William. Altogether, John Leonard and Susan had eleven children, two of whom, John Leonard, Jr., and Louie, died in infancy. The first six children—Margaret, William, Robert, John Leonard, Jr. (1898), Mary Montgomery ("Marie," 1900), and George (1903)—were born while the Campbells were still living in Florida, the remaining five children—Richard Lamar (1908), Peter (1909), Louie (1911), Martha ("Patty," 1912), and Jere (1913)—being born after the family had moved to the small sawmill towns of Century and Lockhart in southern Alabama.

With the instability of John Leonard's childhood, orphaned as he was at such an early age, and—despite the early death of her own mother—the comparative stability of Susan's upbringing, coupled with her family's enhanced social status, there is little wonder that Susan is always referred to as the better educated of the two parents. She made it her business to teach her children to read and write before they began attending school. Obliged to live a somewhat nomadic existence because of the nature of John Leonard's duties, William obtained very little consistent education, and then mainly in small backwoods schools. Indeed, it was not until the turn of the century that any degree of state-organized education was introduced in the area. Even then, the schooling facilities left a great deal to be desired. It was not uncommon for the school in these sawmill towns to be a single-room building with one teacher in charge of seventy or more pupils. In such circumstances, the teacher could not possibly attend each day to the scholastic wants of all the pupils, so schooling inevitably became a somewhat haphazard operation. As likely as not, the pupils themselves would have to cut firewood in the schoolyard to keep the schoolroom warm during the winter months.

William's sixth-grade report card from School No. 1, Escambia County, Florida, still survives and records his monthly scholastic marks from November 1905 to June 1906. His end-of-term examination marks show that he achieved an average of 91 percent, compared with the general average for the grade of 91.3 percent. His best subject was history (97 percent), closely followed by reading (96 percent). He also attained high marks for spelling, grammar, and penmanship, and an average of 87 percent for composition. The report also records that he was an assiduous pupil, being absent for only a third of a day during the period, thus marking up an attendance record of 99.9 percent, that he was never tardy, and that he was awarded 93 percent for deportment.[4]

Opinions about March's childhood vary considerably. According to Alistair Cooke, "if his memories of childhood are to be believed, the small sawmill towns of Alabama and Florida sprouted as much melancholia as any crossroads in Faulkner's Mississippi."[5] In Lincoln Kirstein's view, March's childhood "warped him."[6] On the other hand, some friends gained the impression from the stories he told them that his childhood had been very happy.[7] Possibly the truth lies somewhere between the two extremes, as it does with most people. There can, however, be little doubt that the family's economic situation denied William the sort of environment in which he would have flourished as well as the opportunities to better himself, which, had they been present, he would have put to excellent advantage. In the opinion of Dr. Edward Glover, the eminent psychoanalyst, March was constantly fighting all his life to come to terms with a "very difficult" childhood, the result of his over-sensitive disposition.[8] It is unlikely, for example, that the young William, being the person he was, would have failed to note the comparison between the mode of life to which he was shackled in the sawmill towns and the more genteel existence enjoyed by his cousins in Mobile. Strongly and painfully aware of the dichotomy between the two life-styles, he would have rejected the sawmill and pined for the aesthetic. Certainly, when he underwent analysis with Glover in London in the mid-1930s, at a time when he was an extremely prosperous businessman, those childhood years were still very much on his mind. Additionally, he had not finally discovered his true relationship with or feelings toward the rest of the family. All these matters, apparently, took up considerable time in his analysis. Glover has recalled:

He was quite a precocious child, with a great capacity for observation. Nothing escaped his attention with regard to the interrelations within the family: the jealousies, the justices, and the injustices that occur. But they definitely had a traumatic effect on him. Many people spend their lives later trying to counter them. I think hat in justice to him it can be said that in view of the kind of family history he gave he did extremely well in doing so. But it left him, as many people—many children—are left when they grow up, rather lamed in emotional respects. His love systems, for example, which would have been tremendously important to him in his childhood, but which, rightly or wrongly in his view, were not present, still caused him trouble. Accordingly, he was half-afraid to embark on emotional relationships with people and half in dire need to do so.[9]

March's friends of later years cannot recall his telling them much about his family, and more than one of these friends has indicated that any reference he did make to his family was almost invariably either casual or cold. He once, in jest, made the extraordinary declaration that he would never dream of committing incest with any member of his family, giving as his principal reason the fact that they were "all so ugly."[10] Clearly, there is a strange ambivalence in March's attitude toward his parents and his siblings, so that a great deal of what he has said and written about them should be taken with a generous pinch of salt. It seemed to Robert Clark, the young artist who acted as March's companion-nurse during the last few weeks of the author's life, that March "felt cheated by being a member of a family which neither loved him nor recognized his deeper qualities."[11] March's brother Peter has admitted that William was different from his brothers and sisters, while maintaining that William nevertheless always kept in contact and that he was isolated from the family only in physical distance. This statement would seem to be borne out by the fact that right up to the end of his life March shared his good fortune with the less wealthy members of the family by way of regular allowances, sending $3,000 annually to each of sixteen of his brothers, sisters, nieces, and nephews. One of his long-time friends and former business associates has stated that March was always extremely fond of his mother and took care of her financially, particularly during those years following his father's death in 1921.[12] To Robert Clark, March rather bitterly recounted stories of his father's drinking habits; and yet—and here is that ambivalence again—March had earlier, in 1952, in a letter he wrote to screenwriter Dudley Nichols, recalled that he had always made a point of visiting the cinema whenever a film starring Preston Foster was showing. Some time went by, so he said, before he realized why he did this. It was because the actor reminded him of his father as he first remembered him.[13]

March's sister Margaret has agreed that their father did have something of a drinking problem. He did not drink constantly, but on those occasions when he did imbibe he tended to overindulge. Margaret also revealed that her father wrote verse, which was never published, and that he was fond of reading poetry. Another sister, Marie, recalled how, when he was slightly drunk, John Leonard would insist on all the family sitting at the dining table while he recited at length from the works of Edgar Allan Poe.[14]

The likelihood is that there was some measure of conflict between the young William and his father, and one can speculate how this may have arisen. John Leonard, being the sort of man he was, would hardly have approved of his eldest son's sensitive nature, nor would he have looked kindly upon William's early literary endeavors, especially as these were crowned with a modest element of success. There may even, on John Leonard's side, have been a modicum of jealousy creeping into the father-and-son relationship. Certainly, Margaret has attested that neither parent encouraged her brother in his childhood literary efforts. John Leonard died several years before March's first mature published work appeared, but it is clear that Susan, although she did not express an opinion as such, did not hold her son's writing in great esteem, notwithstanding the fact that she was, as his mother, naturally proud that his work had been published. The whole Campbell family, with the exception of Margaret and Peter, did not seem to be overly impressed by William's novels and short stories; it was not until his last book, *The Bad Seed*, came out in 1954 that they all became excited upon realizing that they had a best-selling novelist as a brother. Even then, appreciation that he was also a writer of the first order probably continued to escape them.

At the age of twelve, William produced an astonishing 10,000-line poem, which he grandly titled "Rhoesus Seeks for His Soul." The manuscript has long been lost, but thirty years or so later March claimed to remember the opening lines of this magnum opus, and they were reproduced in the June 1943 issue of the *Wilson Library Bulletin*:

> The fair young Rhoesus, wandering one day,
> Espied an ageing oak with branches bent,
> And stopping in his quick and youthful play
> He propped his limbs, and on his way he went.
> He went not far until a voice before
> Called softly to him through the deepening gloom:
> "Young Rhoesus, ask of me wealth, or more,
> And I shall give it to thee as a boom."[15]

The only member of the family in those days to take any interest in William's writing was Margaret, his brother Peter having not yet been born. Margaret's interest in her brother's work lasted the whole of her life. She encouraged and promoted his literary career whenever and however she could. Beginning with the publication of *Company K* in 1933, she compiled numerous scrapbooks of publication announcements and reviews of his books.[16]

The relationship between William and Margaret was a long and complicated one. In some respects, it seems that during those childhood years the sister assumed the role of second mother to William. They were extremely close. He shared most of his literary life with her, for she too had a superior intellect. He kept her advised of work in progress and the work he planned for the future, often asking her to act as hostess when, in the 1930s and 1940s, he threw his legendary cocktail parties in New York. In later years, sadly, a coolness developed between them. Many friends have indeed remarked that during the last years of his life March professed an intense dislike for his sister. Clearly, as an extension of the protective elder sister status she had enjoyed during their childhood and adolescence, she did attempt to continue running his personal life. She was careful, however, not to venture to direct or influence his writing in any way, for March most definitely wrote as he pleased and would brook no interference in that quarter. Perhaps, as with the father, an element of jealousy intruded into the brother-sister relationship. Margaret had herself long desired and planned to become a writer and she did write several stories, none of which was accepted for publication. Moreover, it is possible that William, on his side, always subconsciously resented the fact that his sister had been allowed to complete her education at high school in Pensacola, whereas his own education had been abruptly terminated; at the time he was ready to go to high school, the family moved to the south Alabama sawmill town of Lockhart, where the schooling in those days did not progress beyond the "intermediate department" he had already passed through. So he had to commence work instead, obtaining a post as filing clerk at the office of the Jackson Lumber Company in Lockhart.

Lockhart, Covington County, has been immortalized by March as Hodgetown, Pearl County, in his novel *The Tallons*. The early chapters of that book give a vivid impression of what life must have been like in that area of the country in those far-off days, when northern capitalists and speculators were still buying up vast tracts of pinelands in the South, mostly in Alabama and Mississippi, at a mere one or two dollars an acre. The timber resources were seemingly inexhaustible. The speculators moved in with their equipment and laid rail lines to connect with the larger railroads running up to the North and the ready markets waiting there. The felled timber was sawn up into marketable lumber on the spot. The companies hired local people or attracted outsiders, built settlements for the workers to live in with their families and provided company-operated commissaries so that they could recover most, if not all, of the wages they paid out. If the

operation was sufficiently large and likely to be spread over many
years, the companies would sometimes erect a schoolhouse, like the
ones March himself attended, and hire a teacher for the benefit of the
children. If there happened to be no church nearby, a separate building was provided for Sunday meetings. The community spirit in these
little towns was high, although life was drab and work was hard. A mill
might operate for ten hours a day, six days a week, and cut up to sixty
thousand to seventy thousand feet of timber a day. The wages were
depressed, so the workers were unable to afford luxuries, but at least
they were able to earn a livelihood of sorts. Once all the timber had
been felled and cut, the companies would move on to another location,
leaving the little towns they had brought into existence to remain as
permanent settlements.[17]

Whether or not Lockhart, as a sawmill town, was better than most
others is a matter that could only have been judged by the people
there at the time. In 1911, however, when the Campbell family was still
living there, the Alabama State Board of Immigration selected Lockhart for special mention in its promotional handbook, *Alabama's New
Era: A Magazine of Progress and Development.* The following account
has obvious affinities with the exaggerations and understatements
prevalent in present-day travel brochures:

> In the Yellow Pine district was found the typical lumber town of
> Lockhart. There is a fascination in the process of converting great forests
> into the "finished" product so indispensable to builders the world over.
> Few specifications for a building are now passed without including yellow
> pine. From the process of felling this pine in the forest and taking it down
> to the log pond where ten million feet are stored, to hearing the busy
> scream of the saws in the mill and visiting the comfortable quarters
> provided for the employees of the various mills, the visitor finds in
> Lockhart all the conditions of a model and interesting pine lumber town.[18]

At approximately the time the Campbell family moved to Lockhart,
William acquired for himself a degree of fame by winning a five-dollar
prize in a National Oats jingle contest. He also composed a short story,
titled "There Fate Is Hell," concerning "a rich man who died and was
tortured in the afterworld by his own earthly victims, who kept passing
by in endless procession, all the while chanting Greek choruses." The
period was, as he later termed it, his "proletarian phase," and he
embarked on a novel which he intended to be a "profound indictment
of prostitution."[19] His father apparently found the manuscript and
burned it, subsequently administering some extremely painful corpo-

ral punishment which resulted in the young crusader "sitting down carefully for some time."[20] Perhaps one should not be too beguiled by March's whimsical recollections of the incident. At the time, it undoubtedly would have had a traumatic effect on him and may account, at least in some part, for his feelings toward his father.

March was always to maintain that during his early years he had possessed an "unusually fine voice," which was later to be irreparably damaged by the "physical or the psychological effects" of his being gassed during World War I.[21] As a child, he was far more interested in music and acting than he was in writing, and apparently he was quite talented in these fields. In the tightly knit sawmill communities, the only entertainment available was that which the family units themselves provided, gathering in the schoolroom or in the church meetinghouse for afternoon recitations and socials and to put on skits, pageants, and plays. Young William loved dressing up, impersonating friends and neighbors. Knowing his aptitude for searching observation, one can imagine that these impersonations were both accurate and unrelenting. His most devoted audience was composed of his younger brothers and sisters. On one occasion, his mother was called next door to help out with a neighbor's child who was having convulsions. When she returned, she found William, attired in Margaret's long drawers, dancing on the dining-room table and acting out a story to an entranced group of siblings. Here can be seen the early manifestations of March's later practice, when he was an established author, of trying out his stories on anyone prepared to sit and listen to him.

During the Lockhart period of his life, William fell deeply in love with a girl named Bessie Riles. Her father had a good job in the lumber company and obviously nurtured high ambitions for his daughter, ambitions in which William, a mere clerk in the sawmill office, played no part. Mr. Riles made this clear to William. This adolescent love affair thus came to nothing, but, according to March's sister Marie, William never forgot Bessie and she figures in much of his work.[22]

When he was sixteen, William left Lockhart for Mobile. He never thereafter lived with his family. He had acquired early a determination to better himself and to compensate for his unfinished education. Possibly Mr. Riles's rejection of him as a possible future son-in-law spurred William into action, but it is more likely that the resolve was of a more long-standing and deeper nature than simply the aggrieved reaction of a disappointed suitor. If there was one thing March was never short of, it was a burning ambition.

At the time William arrived in Mobile, the wharves of Alabama Port were still under construction. The city itself was firmly on the way to becoming recognized as a thriving maritime, commercial, and industrial center. Until recently, all the land around Mobile had been covered with yellow pine forests, but by 1910 these forests had fallen under the onslaught of the lumbermen's axes and saws. The vast tracts of sand loam that remained were awaiting the influx of farmers from the North and West. Mobile was then a city of officially a little more than 50,000 souls. Taking into account those living within a one-mile radius of the city limits, however, the total population was nearer 70,000, all of whom enjoyed the benefits of telephone, gas, and electricity services and the comprehensive streetcar system Mobile boasted, the longest arm of which extended seven miles from the courthouse.

March obtained a post in a law office in downtown Mobile and entered a course of typing and bookkeeping at a business school. His sights, however, were set on a college education, but he quickly discovered that no college in Alabama would accept him without a high school diploma. Valparaiso University in Indiana, a self-governing coeducational college, did not, on the other hand, require the high school qualification. The school had a student body of six thousand, which was second in size to Harvard University. Indeed, Valparaiso was affectionately known all over the country as the "poor man's Harvard." William enrolled there for the school year 1913-14, pursuing a high school course of study and supporting himself with the money he had saved out of his salary from the Mobile law firm. In the early summer of 1914, his funds finally ran out and he left Valparaiso, but not before he had acquired the all-important high school qualification he needed to gain entry to the Alabama colleges.

Returning to Alabama, he worked throughout the summer to build up more funds and entered the law school of the University of Alabama in Tuscaloosa on September 9, 1914, as a special student shortly after his twenty-first birthday. He was invited to join the Phi Kappa Sigma fraternity two months later and was apparently popular on the campus. The 1915 edition of the university yearbook *Corolla* contains the following entry: "Bill is a silent lad from the low-cost-of-living University of Valparaiso. That won't-come-off smile looks more ministerial than legal, but you never can tell."[23] After a year at the university, he was again forced to drop out for lack of funds.

By this time, the Campbell family had moved from Lockhart to Tuscaloosa, the youngest child, Jere, being two years old. William's original idea was to work for a year and then resume his law studies. He returned to Mobile and started work in the law office of Greg Smith, but when the year was up, instead of returning to Tuscaloosa and the university, he decided to satisfy another of his ambitions, and one he shared with Margaret: to live in New York.

In the fall of 1916, therefore, he traveled to New York and took up residence in a rooming house on Lafayette Avenue, Brooklyn. He secured employment in the law offices of Nevins, Brett, and Kellog. In William's view, Nevins was one of the best lawyers in New York and considered to be the top authority on engineering law. William was not, however, directly answerable to Nevins, acting as a clerk and subpoena server under Philip Milledoler Brett. Brett's daughter remembers going to her father's office when she was a little girl and meeting his young assistant.[24] Brett kept track of March's business and literary careers and in later years remembered William quite fondly, but at the time, William himself was clearly not particularly enamored with the work he was doing. He also found that the cost of living in New York compared unfavorably with that in other places in which he had stayed, and there is evidence that he felt an occasional twinge of homesickness, if not for his family, at least for the South.

Life in the big city did have some compensations. He was able to satisfy his passion for the theater. In a letter dated May 22, 1917, to his sister Marie, he mentioned that he had seen several good shows in recent weeks, including "The Man Who Came Back" and "The Little Lady in Blue." The letter displays the touching concern of a twenty-three-year-old brother for his seventeen-year-old sister. He asked her to assure him that she did not mean what she said when she wrote that she was contemplating marriage that June. Protectively, almost cynically, in his role of a man of the world, he advised her to remain single and enjoy life for a few more years. He asked how she liked the new house the family had recently moved into on 26th Street, Tuscaloosa, and expressed the hope that he would be home for a visit at Christmas.[25]

When he wrote that letter to his sister, America had been at war with Germany for more than five weeks, and only four days earlier, on May 18, Congress had passed the conscription bill requiring all males between the ages of twenty-one and thirty to register. In an earlier letter to him, Marie had obviously told him she wished she had been born a man, so that she could enlist and fight for her country. Her brother suggested that if the desire was all that strong she should join the Red Cross and get paid for the work she did.

On Registration Day, June 5, William stood at a window looking down into the street and watched a parade of soldiers march by, flags waving and bands playing. When they had passed and the shouting and cheering had died away, he went to the nearest recruiting station and registered for service, as did nearly ten million of his fellow countrymen that day.

two

Service in the U.S. Marines

William Campbell enlisted in the Marine Corps on July 25, 1917, in New York. He was in excellent physical condition, just over five and a half feet tall, weighing 127 pounds and enjoying 20-20 vision. On the following day, he was transferred to the marine barracks at Parris Island, South Carolina. On July 31, after the preliminary induction procedures had been observed, he swore his oath of allegiance and declared his next of kin to be his mother, Mrs. John L. Campbell of 810 26th Avenue, Tuscaloosa, Alabama.[1]

By mid-August, he had been assigned to Company F and with his new buddies knuckled down to the rigors of the notorious Marine boot training and to a sequence of antityphoid injections. The life, he seemed to find, was not unduly unpleasant, although an outbreak of spinal meningitis in one of the other companies meant that the whole camp was obliged to go into quarantine. He received news that several of his old Phi Kappa Sigma fraternity brothers had obtained their commissions in the new army, but he professed not to feel in the least aggrieved about his own lowly status. There were ample opportunities for advancement through the ranks, and he dreamed, his ambition unabated, that he might even one day become "Captain Campbell."[2]

The first American troops had landed in France on June 13, 1917, just eight days after Registration Day, but William himself was not to reach French soil until late February the following year. He left Parris Island on January 7, 1918, joined the 133d Company in the marine barracks at Quantico, Virginia, on the eighth, and ten days later embarked on the USS *Von Steuben* at Philadelphia. The ship sailed the next day, January 21, joining a convoy to cross the Atlantic.

Life on the transports of those days was far from pleasant. Mostly, the accommodations were cramped and uncomfortable, hastily installed in ships which had never been designed for the mass transportation of men and equipment. One can imagine the emotions of these men, the majority of whom had probably never before been to sea, perhaps had never before even seen the sea, poised now on the brink of the greatest experience of their lives. Until a few months ago, they had been clerks, like William himself, or factory workers, or farmhands, or college students. Their mood was one of supreme optimism. They were buoyed up with a sense of patriotic duty. Few admitted to the possibility that they might be killed or even wounded, for they were convinced that God was on their side. They were sure that when they arrived in France they would be feted as the invincible warriors they felt themselves to be. If they sang with dreamy sentimentality during their more reflective moments "There's a Long, Long Trail A-winding," they put a deal of rambunctious fervor into the prophetically rousing "Over There."

In the meantime, they endured the winter Atlantic crossing, the misery of the confined spaces below or the cold wind- and spray-swept decks above, the boredom, and for some the unending seasickness. Weather permitting, they were kept as occupied as possible with shipboard drills, target practice, and inspections. Whatever the weather, they assumed duties as lookouts and gun-crew members, ever mindful of the constant threat of U-boat attacks.[3]

On February 24, 1918, the *Von Steuben* arrived in the landlocked harbor of Brest, by then the chief disembarkation port for the American Expeditionary Force. The likelihood is that it was raining as William and his buddies descended the gangway to the quayside and marched the six miles to temporary camp, for that year it rained every day except for seven in Brest and the surrounding area. Later, the company entrained for the pleasant French countryside, becoming part of Replacement Unit No. 2 far behind the front line, and there, instead of being thrown immediately into battle as they had anticipated, the marines commenced another course of intensive drilling and field exercises. Thus forced to curb their natural impatience for action, they perhaps consoled themselves in the knowledge that of the 325,000 doughboys then in France they were thought to be among the most advanced and efficient in training, thus fully satisfying the rigorous standards of smartness and discipline their commanding general, "Black Jack" Pershing, demanded.

On March 29, William was among those assigned to Forty-third Company (Company F), Fifth Regiment, U.S. Marines, forming part of the Fourth Infantry Brigade, Third Battalion of the Second U.S. Division. The Second Division was at the time occupying trenches near Les Esparges, twelve miles southeast of Verdun. Although the area had seen terrible fighting in 1916 and was still the front line, the positions in this particular sector had remained unchanged for more than two years. In consequence, living conditions were by no means unduly harsh. The trenches themselves were in excellent shape, the dugouts equipped with floorboards and electric lights. There were mattresses to sleep on. It was, in short, an admirable sector for providing raw and untried troops with their first taste of real war. Principally, however, boredom was the order of the day. The various regiments would take turns manning the trenches, relieving each other at specified intervals. When in reserve, the men occupied themselves in improving and repairing the existing fortifications, digging new trenches and renewing barbed-wire defenses. Nevertheless, the period did not pass entirely without excitement. One night in mid-April, the Fifth Regiment having just taken over occupation of the front line, the Germans made a spirited raid on the trenches but were driven back by the companies of the Third Battalion. Flushed with success from this first encounter with the enemy, the Fifth Regiment was even more eager for further action. Again, impatience had to be curbed.

Then, just over a month later, on May 27, the Germans attacked on a forty-kilometer front stretching from Soissons to Reims, approximately one hundred kilometers due west of the positions the Fifth Regiment had been occupying in the Toulons Sector, Verdun. By the time the German attack got under way, the Fifth Regiment had already departed from the front line and was exercising in picturesque surroundings and beautiful weather in the Gizors training area, almost forty miles to the northwest of Paris. Although the training was hard, the lifting of the constraints inevitably imposed by front-line existence was particularly welcome, and ample liberty was available to the men. This happy state of affairs was brought to an abrupt end after only ten days by the swiftness of the seemingly irresistible German onslaught, which was threatening the French capital itself. Having been assigned to the Twenty-first Corps, French Sixth Army, the Second Division was ordered eastward on May 30 to throw its weight against the enemy.

Seven days later, on June 6, William's company took part in the attack on Belleau Wood. On June 9, William was wounded in the head and left shoulder by shrapnel, presumably from a German trench mortar. The wounds, fortunately, were only slight, but they kept him in the hospital for nearly three weeks. On June 25, while he was still out of action, Belleau Wood was finally captured by the marines. The cost of success had been high. Of the 259 officers and men in William's own company, the Forty-third, 38 were killed, 112 were wounded or gassed, and 4 were reported missing in action: a casualty list of almost 60 percent. Even the 102 replacements drafted into the company during the month failed to bring it up to its full strength. The company muster at the end of June numbered 206 officers and men.

When he left the hospital on June 29, William was posted to a replacement battalion before returning to his own company on July 11. The whole of the Second Division had been moved in early July to a support area at La Ferté-sous-Jouarre, behind the Château-Thierry lines, and had spent a week and a half recuperating and making the most of the glorious weather. The men swam in the Marne and lazed along its banks, writing letters home or simply luxuriating in the sun. William was too late to see General Pershing, who arrived at La Ferté to award decorations the day before William reached the company. Legend has it that one marine gunner swam across the Marne to receive his medal. William did not have long to enjoy this idyllic existence, for on July 14 the Second Division, having now been assigned to the French Twentieth Corps, Tenth Army, received orders to participate in the assault on Soissons.

The attack was launched on the eighteenth. By the time the Second Division was relieved by a French division two days later and pulled back into reserve, the Americans were on the point of utter exhaustion. The division's two marine regiments alone had suffered two thousand casualties. William was one of the lucky ones. He came through the fighting unscathed and with the other survivors of his company moved back to the vicinity of Nancy, 170 miles east of Paris, where the Fifth Regiment and the other units comprising the Second Division rested, reorganized, and brought themselves up to strength.

On August 5, when they were at Vandouvre, the Fifth Regiment was inspected by the assistant secretary of the navy, Franklin D. Roosevelt. Three days later, the regiment was again at the front line in the Pont-à-Mousson area, approximately ten miles northeast of Nancy and sixteen miles to the east of the town of Saint-Mihiel, the apex of the German salient in that area. They remained in the Pont-à-Mousson area until August 17. It was a quiet sector of the front and opportunity was taken for further training, with particular emphasis upon target practice, advance under artillery fire, and the knocking out of machine-gun nests.

The day after they left the front line, while still in transit, William was made company clerk. The regiment spent a fortnight of further intensive training in the vicinity of Govilliers, eventually leaving there on foot on September 1 to take part in the offensive against the Saint-Mihiel salient. Ten days later, the marines began occupying trenches in the Limey Sector, ready to support the attack, spearheaded by army regiments, which was timed for five o'clock on the morning of the twelfth. The objective was to reduce the salient, thus setting up a strong defensive line that could subsequently be used as a jumping-off point for a final crushing attack to overwhelm the retreating enemy.

The marines did not take a major part in the Saint-Mihiel offensive. Although they took over the attacking role on the midnight of the second day, they met with little resistance, the single sustained enemy counterattack being beaten back by the marines' superb marksmanship. The marines remained in the area until September 16, pushing forward all the while, hunting out the enemy and maintaining contact. The Forty-third Company suffered three dead and forty-three wounded in the fighting, with another two men missing in action.

When relieved, the regiment and the rest of the Second Division moved south to the vicinity of Toul for yet more training. It was while the company was billeted in the village of Blenod-les-Tour that, on September 24, just six days after his twenty-fifth birthday, William was promoted to the rank of corporal. Shortly afterward, the division entrained for Châlons-sur-Marne and, moving only at night so as to escape the attention of the enemy, marched north the seventeen miles to Souain; from there the men marched another five miles to Somme-Py, recently taken from the Germans, in the French Meuse-Argonne offensive and now more than half a mile behind the front line. Somme-Py had been almost obliterated by four years of repeated shelling. When they arrived, shells were still falling on what remained of the town. There were no recognizable roads. Everything had been pulverized by high explosives. The marines had to scramble as best they could over the wreckage of houses, the shattered beams and powdered bricks. In the ruins of a church, the French had set up a dressing station. The stench that issued forth from it was not, to say the least, in any way encouraging to men knowing that within a few hours they themselves would be going into action.

This was the once-fertile Champagne area. Now Somme-Py was surrounded by a vast wasteland of mud and shell craters and blackened tree stumps. Complicated systems of trenches and rusted barbed-wire entanglements crisscrossed the tortured ground. Here, facing the ridges to the east of Reims and the two-hundred-foot-high Blanc Mont, the French Meuse-Argonne offensive, launched on September 26 with such high expectations, had ground to a halt. The Germans had been able to dominate the whole area by using Blanc Mont as a magnificent observation vantage point, inhibiting movement of any description and enabling them to shell at will Reims and its beloved cathedral, twenty miles or so to the east.

The task of capturing Blanc Mont was assigned to the marines. The Germans, during the four years they had occupied the sector, had been given ample time to convert the area into a seemingly impregnable fortress. Blanc Mont was an intricate maze of trenches and concrete emplacements, protected against infantry attack by masses of barbed wire. It was, in the words of one marine, "a place built for calamities."

On October 1, the day the marines moved into the front line and only a week after he had been made corporal, William was promoted to sergeant. He later wrote that the promotion was due to his "right living and clean thinking,"[4] but there is more than a touch of whimsical irony in that statement.

The assault on Blanc Mont began at 4:40 on the morning of October 3, the Sixth Marine Regiment leading the attack with the Fifth Regiment in support six hundred yards or so to the rear. The fighting was predictably bitter and bloody, but on the morning of the fifth, Blanc Mont finally fell to the Second Division. The price of success was again high. The marine brigade lost 494 killed and 1,864 wounded. In recognition of the gallantry displayed and the success achieved, the Fourth Marine Brigade was authorized to add the streamer of the Croix de Guerre to the regimental colors, and many marines in both the Fifth and Sixth regiments became entitled to wear the French Fourragère on their uniforms.

William was one of the men so honored, winning the Croix de Guerre as well as the Distinguished Service Cross and the Navy Cross, for "extraordinary heroism near Blanc Mont" during the period October 3–5. At the time, William was temporarily detached from the navy and serving with the army on statistical duties in conjunction with the French. His citation for the Croix de Guerre reads:

> During the operations in Blanc Mont region, October 3rd–4th, 1918, he left a shelter to rescue the wounded. On October 5th, during a counterattack, the enemy having advanced to within 300 meters of the first aid station, he immediately entered the engagement and though wounded refused to be evacuated until the Germans were thrown back.[5]

The Fifth Regiment was relieved on October 4, reverting to the brigade support role. The Second Division was subsequently allocated the task of spearheading the American First Army's Meuse-Argonne offensive, with the object of breaking through the German army and thrusting it back over the Meuse River.

By October 31, the Forty-third Company was in Exermont, poised to assume its central position in the front line. The attack commenced early on the morning of November 1. German resistance was light to begin with and the marine advance, behind the customary creeping barrage, set a speed and a distance record for the war. By the time they were relieved that night by one of the infantry brigades, the marines had captured something like 1,700 prisoners, whom they took back with them to the rear. On the second and the third, they remained in support, taking over the attack again on November 4. For the succeeding four days they maintained a steady advance along the Meuse. Plans to cross the river on the night of November 9–10 had to be temporarily abandoned because the necessary bridge-building equipment was unavailable. On the tenth, the marines attempted a crossing at Mouzon but were pinned down by intensive enemy shellfire. Here, on the west bank of the Meuse, on the following day, November 11, William and his comrades of the Forty-third Company received word of the armistice. The war was over.

Major James M. Yingling's official *Brief History of the 5th Marines* records:

> Accounts of the reactions of Marines and Germans to the news of the armistice differed. Some said that both sides celebrated, even together, while others stated that friend and foe alike received the report joyfully, but in silence. Regardless of sentiments, the 5th still had much work ahead of it; realizing that the cessation of hostilities might be temporary only, the men began organizing the ground for defense. Then, on 14 November, after being relieved, the regiment moved south to Pouilly, on the Meuse opposite Letanne, to re-fit and re-equip for the last phase of its European activities. . . . The March to the Rhine began before sun-up on 17 November, and the 5th had the honor of providing the advance guard for the division. The first phase of the movement—to the German border, approximately 60 miles away—was made in six marching days and one rest day. The route to the border took the regiment southeast through Montmedy, France, across Belgium, and into Luxembourg to its eastern border with Germany. Here, the regiment participated in a defensive alignment of the division until crossing into Germany the first day of December.[6]

The crossing of the Rhine at Remagen occurred on December 13 and by the sixteenth the regiment had arrived in Segendorf, in the Wied River Valley, which was to be its permanent winter quarters. The regiment assisted in the normal duties of an army of occupation, both in preserving law and order in the area and in supervising the conduct of local government. The men of the regiment attended school, maintained proficiency on the firing range, and participated in maneuvers and reviews. It was at one such review at Segendorf on January 14, 1919, that William was presented with his Croix de Guerre by Major General John A. Lejeune. Writing to his family, William told them that he had not physically changed much, although he had lost some weight, and that he had witnessed sights he knew he would never be able to forget.[7]

Taking advantage of the educational program arranged for the troops, William applied for a course of lectures at Oxford University on the subject of common law pleading. He was not, however, successful in his application, and instead, on March 3, left the Forty-third Company for detached duty at Toulouse University, where, for just over four months, he studied journalism. He was one of 122 men from New York State, who formed the largest contingent of the 1,135 students at the school department. Edmund Wilson, who visited Toulouse at this time, found that the town reminded him of Charlottesville, Virginia: "the hot summer climate, the leisurely tempo, the row of open hacks drawn up at the station in the heavy but dry southern night."[8]

The student body was an energetic and creative one. William soon became involved in some of the extracurricular activities which had sprung into existence. He was clearly in the sort of company which fostered expression of his as yet mainly untapped artistic qualities. Here, in Toulouse, he was able to luxuriate in the environment which, by dint of his own youthful efforts and determination, he had experienced so briefly on the campuses of Valparaiso and Tuscaloosa.

The students established and published their own newspaper, *Qu'est-ce que c'est?*, which sold at fifty centimes a copy. The issue for April 16, 1919, carried an announcement on its front page of the near-completion of a musical comedy to be staged by the students.

"Getting Toulouse," the musical comedy which has been in the course of preparation for the past two weeks by the American students of the University of Toulouse, is rapidly nearing completion. This play was written entirely by the men at the school, and is original throughout, both as to words and music.

The music, which was composed by Mus. C. W. Chylinski and Sgt. P. H. Bartley, is of the very highest type, and would not do discredit to the best Broadway productions. The book was written by Sgt. Clark E. Biggs, who has succeeded in making it different from the ordinary run of musical shows now touring the A.E.F. There is as little as possible of things military in either the book or the lyrics. The lyrics were written by Sgt. W. E. Campbell and Lt. G. H. Cole. . . .

According to present plans, four or five nights in Toulouse are contemplated for the show, as well as two nights in Paris and performances in the various large cities and leave areas near Toulouse. The Commandant has assured the promoters of his cooperation, and the show is being produced with his consent and approval.[9]

The show, William always maintained, was a huge success. Certainly it gave him his first real opportunity, outside the family circle, to indulge his fascination with the world of the theater, a fascination which was to stay with him throughout his life, although never dominate it. In later years, he was able to satisfy this interest to some degree through his oral storytelling and his awareness of the power he could pleasantly exercise over a willing captive and intimate audience at a party or in a bar.

While he was still in Toulouse, William received the Distinguished Service Cross in recognition of his heroism at Blanc Mont. It was presented to him by Major J. H. Wallace on June 28, 1919.

On July 11, William rejoined the Forty-third Company at Segendorf to journey back to America. The company arrived in Camp Pontanezon, Brest, on the twenty-first and four days later embarked on the USS *George Washington*. It disembarked at Hoboken, New Jersey, on August 3 and entrained for Camp Mills, Long Island. On August 8, the Second Division paraded along Fifth Avenue before a number of dignitaries and later, in Washington, was reviewed by President Wilson.

Returning to the marine barracks at Quantico, Virginia, a little more than eighteen months after the men had left it to go overseas, the Fifth Regiment was disbanded on August 13. William was "honorably discharged by reason of expiration of term of enlistment." His record sheet was noted by his commanding officer for both reenlistment and the Good Conduct Medal. A civilian once more, a mileage allowance of $261.68 in his pocket, William returned to Tuscaloosa and the bosom of his family.

three

Beginnings of
Two Careers

Almost from the moment he was discharged from the marines, William Campbell began fostering, whether intentionally or not, an aura of semimystique about his experiences in France. He clearly harbored an ambivalent attitude toward the war and his own participation in it. There can be little doubt that he had been deeply disturbed and affected by some of his war experiences, not all of which were necessarily related to battle. Although the fighting had been over for a matter of nine months or so, he was still obviously in a somewhat confused state of mind. In this, certainly, he was no different from thousands of other returning veterans. As time went on, he tended either to choose silence when the subject of his war exploits was raised or alternatively to regale his listeners with characteristically embroidered stories.

We do know from the official records that he participated, as he always claimed with pride, in all the major actions of the marines from the spring of 1918 to the armistice. We know that he was wounded at Belleau Wood. We know that whenever faced with a situation calling for courage, he was able to prove himself braver than most. Indeed, J. P. Case, one of William's Mobile friends and business associates, gained the very firm impression that William did not know the meaning of fear. Case has recalled an incident March related to him which ostensibly supports this view.

The story goes that on one occasion, when his company was in action, the Germans had managed to establish a small salient into the territory held by the Americans. William's company was occupying lines on one flank of the salient and, for some reason, it became imperative for information to be obtained from another company on the opposite flank. The only means of communication was by runner.

William volunteered for the mission. There were only two ways of getting to the other company: first, to skirt the edge of the salient, which, although less dangerous, was the longer route, thus sacrificing precious time; or, second, to chance the much shorter but infinitely more hazardous, if not suicidal, route straight through the enemy lines. March elected to take the latter course. He ran into the German lines, waving his arms like a madman and shouting gibberish at the top of his voice. The German soldiers, if his story is to be believed, simply stared at him open-mouthed, so taken aback that they had not the wits to fire even one shot at him. He reached the other company without a scratch, collected the required information, and returned to his own company by the longer route. It is an incredible story, but strange things do happen in war and this one is just strange enough to be true.[1]

The British novelist, short-story writer, and biographer Arthur Calder-Marshall, who met William in London in the mid-1930s, recalls a story which illustrates both March's penchant for the amusing off-beat situation and his ability to earn money in the most unlikely circumstances. March told Calder-Marshall that this particular incident occurred during the days when his company was in Camp Pontanezen at Brest, awaiting transportation back to America. In those days, any soldier who contracted venereal disease was liable to imprisonment. It was therefore essential for any infected soldiers to escape detection by the regimental medical officer. There were, of course, regular physical inspections, when the whole company, in alphabetical order, would line up in single file and, with trousers lowered, present themselves one by one to the close scrutiny of the doctor. The doctor was apparently so absorbed in his work that he never once looked up at the faces of the men who appeared before him. Knowing this, William devised an excellent scheme to save those of his buddies who were infected from inevitable military retribution. He would, in the normal order of things, present himself as Sergeant Campbell, then creep back along the line and in due course deputize for a man who had been infected. For this service, he claimed a small fee. For a while, it proved to be a fairly lucrative business for him, but he decided to abandon the service when, one day, deputizing for a man whose name began with "W," the doctor, still without raising his head, asked pointedly, "Haven't I seen *you* some place before?"[2] March subsequently used the incident as the basis for a short story, "Ballet of the Bowie Knives," which he wrote in 1945. One is again left in some doubt whether the incident did actually happen or if the anecdote was just another example of March trying out his narrative skill on a ready listener.

Although in later years March was generally noncommittal concerning his exploits in battle, one story crops up several times in the reminiscences of friends and acquaintances, a story which he clearly felt impelled to tell over and over again, almost as a form of expiation. The peripheral details may vary in the individual recollections of his friends, but the central traumatic incident is horrifyingly constant. Some accounts state that it occurred during a German attack on the American trenches, others that it occurred during confused fighting when William jumped into a shell hole to take temporary shelter from machine-gun fire, and in yet another version it all happened in a wooded area when William had become isolated from the rest of the company. Whatever the true circumstances, the crux of the story is that William came face to face with a young German soldier—a desperate boy with blond hair and blue eyes. William instinctively lunged at the German with his bayonet. The boy stumbled and the bayonet pierced his throat, killing him instantly, his eyes wide open and staring into William's face. The young German's death was to haunt William all his living days, even intruding into his dreams. Although he attempted to lay the ghost, as it were, in the Private Manuel Burt section of *Company K*, he evidently did not succeed and there is evidence that even up to a few years before his death he was still struggling to rid himself of the insistent, terrible memory of the boy's face and staring eyes. It is certainly not without significance that at various stages in his life March experienced hysterical conditions related to both his throat and eyes.[3]

These psychosomatic symptoms, which, when they manifested themselves in the throat condition, were serious enough to warrant sustained psychoanalytic treatment, possibly also had their origins in March's belief that his bronchial passages had been incurably damaged by the effects of poison gas. This was a conviction which drove him to the conclusion that not only had it destroyed the fine singing voice he had once possessed but also was the root cause of all the trouble he continually experienced with inflamed nasal passages and aching teeth. He even told many people when he first returned from France that he had been advised he did not have long to live and it had been recommended that he stay in the South, where the climate would be more beneficial to his condition, rather than returning to his position with the law firm in New York. While there is no doubt that, at some time or other during his service in France, March must have passed through gas, there is no indication in his marine records that he was on any occasion hospitalized as a result of gas contamination. The Germans did use gas in several of the actions in which March participated:

at Belleau Wood, for instance—although in that action the main gas bombardment, which was very intensive, occurred on June 13, four days after he had been wounded and evacuated to a hospital.

The principal gas used by the Germans against the Americans was mustard gas, universally regarded as the least deadly of all the weapons used in the war, requiring massive inhalation to inflict permanent damage to the lungs. Most mustard gas victims spent no more than two weeks in a hospital before being returned to their units. The issued gas masks afforded an effective protection, but there was no psychological protection for any man who had, as March undoubtedly had, a neurotic fear of gas. It was an insidious process which left those afflicted unable to accept either that they had never in the first place suffered the effects of gas, or, if they had, that they had been completely cured.

In *Company K*, March makes explicit his horror of gas warfare. The Corporal Lloyd Somerville section begins: "All the men in our ward were gas patients, and all of us were going to die" (*CK*, p. 71). This sense of resignation to the inevitable hangs like a pall over the whole episode, which includes a graphic description of one patient fighting for breath and life, like "a broken-down soprano practicing her scales" (*CK*, p. 71). In another section of the book, Private John Townsend, sheltering in a dugout after being gassed, hears the Germans attacking and tries to open his eyes, only to find that "they had festered and stuck together" (*CK*, p. 82). Blind and helpless, he is ruthlessly bayoneted by the Germans, the poignancy of his blindness making the manner of his death seem doubly terrible. In yet another section, Private Richard Starnes takes off his gas mask during a gas attack to save the life of a terrified German prisoner and, although immediately regretting what he has done, stoically accepts the inevitable. He is last seen in a hospital bed, with a doctor warning him, "Be quiet, or you'll start bleeding again" (*CK*, p. 170).

It is difficult to appreciate exactly what March's reasons were for wishing to instill in people's minds the fiction of his precarious physical condition. In later life, he admitted that the wounds he received at Belleau Wood had been superficial and did not amount to much. He was also, of course, wounded during the fighting at Blanc Mont, as his citations record, but the extent of his wounds on that occasion cannot be determined from marine records. He was not hospitalized afterward. It is reasonable to suppose that these wounds were even more superficial than those he had received in the earlier engagement. Another friend and business associate, J. Finley McRae, to whom March was to dedicate his third book, understood that he was wounded in the foot. Both McRae and March's sister Marie have declared that he had a silver plate inserted in his skull as a result of the wounds he received at Belleau Wood, but there is no evidence that this was so. In any case, one would expect that any soldier wounded seriously enough to require such treatment would have been invalided out of the service.[4] Although, even as late as 1937, in a letter to Fred B. Millett, March was still maintaining that at the time of his discharge he was "in pretty bad physical shape" due to the effects of gas, his marine records show that when he was demobilized his physical condition was rated excellent.

March seemed to adopt a particularly ambivalent attitude toward the medals he had won for his deeds in battle. For someone who was essentially a pacifist at heart and an abhorer of violence, it would perhaps have been a natural reaction on his part to repudiate the honors bestowed upon him. Indeed, according to McRae, March was nominated for the Congressional Medal of Honor but was professedly so disinterested that he refused to fill out the necessary papers for it, throwing them into the wastepaper basket.[5] His sister Marie told a different version of the story. She chose to believe that, although her brother was cited for the Congressional Medal of Honor, it was awarded instead to Sergeant Alvin York for his exploits at Blanc Mont. Whatever may be the true facts of the matter, the official records do not show that March was ever recommended for this particular award.[6] He was, however, awarded the Navy Cross on November 11, 1920, the second anniversary of the armistice. He certainly did not reject the congratulatory letter sent him by Josephus Daniels, secretary of the navy, which again referred to the heroism he had displayed at Blanc Mont.

In the short story "Not Very—Subtle," March describes the eyes of a prostitute as "fixed staringly forward in the unseeing vacuity of soldiers being decorated for bravery" (TB, p. 331). It is a telling analogy, comparing the prostitution of the human body for sexual gratification with the prostitution of the human body in the name of patriotism and military glory. One can speculate, nevertheless, that the analogy does not represent March's own personal view, even though the possibility exists that he may have wished to give the impression that it did. The evidence all points the other way, for he invariably mentioned his military honors in the routine biographies he supplied on request to editors. He liked to stress that although he did not consider himself a soldier, he had risen to the rank of sergeant in the marines and that, on discharge, he had been given an exemplary character marking of three fives, explaining, again with obvious pride, that this was something very rarely awarded.[7] The poet and editor Paul Engle recalls an evening he spent in March's London flat in the mid-1930s when he noticed

a cigar box sitting on a shelf. When he casually asked what it contained, his host opened it up and showed him his medals. It was typical
of the man, Engle concluded, that March had never mentioned his
medals before.[8] The incident is revealing in another, perhaps even
more important sense. Surely a man who is indifferent to his medals
does not take them with him on journeys all over the world.

There is little doubt that March, like many returning veterans, felt
an inescapable sense of guilt at having survived the war, when so many
of his comrades had been killed or horribly and incurably maimed.
There was also the terrible battle he knew he had to fight with himself—for nobody could help him in this—to come to terms with the
searing memories of the things he had seen and done, realizing that he
would have to live with these memories for the rest of his life. In the
Private Colin Urquhart section of *Company K*, Urquhart declares that
"in the name of humanity" there should be a mandatory execution "of
every soldier who had served on the front and managed to escape
death there" (*CK*, p. 254). This is an impossibly extreme view, of
course, but even if March himself did not hold it he recognized that for
some men the burden would eventually be too great: as it proved to be
for Harry Crosby, of whom Malcolm Cowley has written that the war
did not simply change the boy into a man but also produced a violent
metamorphosis from life into death. Crosby's suicide in 1929 was the
inevitable consequence of that metamorphosis.[9]

Although the trauma induced by the war was for March clearly as
profound as it was for Crosby, March was made of much sterner and
resilient stuff, his feet set more firmly on the ground. There is no
evidence at all that at any time during his life, even during his periods
of intense and almost unbearable mental stress, he contemplated his
self-destruction. He may have displayed no fear in the heat of battle,
but that is not to say that he did not fear death: certainly during the last
few weeks of his life he was manifestly terrified of dying. In *Company
K*, Private Theodore Irvine, dying slowly and painfully of his wounds,
chooses not to take the swift way out of his agony when the opportunity
presents itself, professing that it is preferable "to suffer the ultimate
pains of hell than to achieve freedom in nothingness" (*CK*, p. 240).
That quotation may provide some clue as to March's own feelings, but,
as always, it is dangerous to attribute an author's own beliefs to the
beliefs of his characters.

Writing to an aunt when he was in France, March told her that he
had looked death in the face and had seen the smiles of the dying when
they realize they are returning to God. There seems something a little
false about this—almost as if he was aware that this was the sort of

thing people back home wanted to be told—but it could be that at the time he was endeavoring to persuade himself, even against his better instincts, that this was indeed the great truth, that the war was essentially a religious struggle of good versus evil, with death as the reward rather than the ending. His better instincts, even if they had been placed temporarily in cold storage, were soon to be revived once the war was over, as is made abundantly clear in *Company K*, with its unequivocal criticism of the religious leaders of the war years who compared the conflict—the mass slaughter of men—to a modern crusade. The truth, as March saw it, was something totally divorced from glory, religious or otherwise. With typical dryness of humor, spliced with more than a grain of bitterness, he was, according to Alistair Cooke, to assert that the "experience of living as an acceptable member of a body of men whose lives were held cheap was . . . a cheering thing to him."[10]

His actual homecoming probably had not been as he imagined it would be. Ernest Hemingway, in his short story "Soldier's Home," has graphically described the difficulties the returning soldier could experience in trying to integrate himself back into civilian life. Like March, Hemingway's Krebs comes home to the United States when the Second Division returns from the Rhine in the summer of 1919. Like Krebs, March rarely, if ever, discussed his war experiences with his family. His brother Peter recalls that during those early days back home, March was still vulnerable enough to suffer from recurring nightmares, waking in the night with a "screaming need" and taking a drink from the bottle of whisky he always kept by his bedside.[11]

March did not remain with his family in Tuscaloosa for long, moving down to Mobile and obtaining a post as private secretary to Harry Hardy Smith, who ran a law business there. Smith obviously took a liking to the young veteran. March volunteered information about his war exploits, showing Smith his medals and citations.[12] Smith was apparently left with the impression that March had only six months to live because of the wounds he had received. It is not clear how this misunderstanding—if it was a misunderstanding—on Smith's part arose, but it was soon to have fortunate and far-reaching consequences for March.

At about this time, a local shipping man, John Barnett Waterman, founded the Waterman Steamship Corporation. Waterman, who was born in New Orleans during the 1860s and served as a private in the Spanish-American War of 1898, moved from New Orleans to Mobile shortly after the turn of the century, becoming an agent for several steamship companies. At the end of World War I, he obtained a federal subsidy and negotiated contracts to operate a fleet of government-owned ships which, having been built as part of the U.S. war effort, were now idle and moored in the Tensaw River in Alabama. An astute businessman, experienced in both railroading and shipping, Waterman realized the profits that were to be made in soliciting freight and then shipping it as accredited agent of the Emergency Fleet Corporation. Although the Waterman company did not become wholly independent until 1931, when the Merchants National Bank of Mobile loaned it the money to purchase outright fourteen of the ships from the government, the business, from its modest beginnings, expanded into one of the largest steamship companies in the world.

Back in August 1919, however, John B. Waterman was busily organizing and establishing the embryo company. He had become obligated to Smith for some legal favor or other and he asked the lawyer in what way he could show his appreciation. Smith suggested that Waterman might like to give his young employee, Bill Campbell, a job, and Waterman agreed, more out of a sense of pity for the returned veteran than anything else. Smith had apparently passed on to Waterman his understanding that March was doomed to an early grave, and Waterman, remembering his own involvement in the Spanish-American War, was sympathetic to the idea of employing wounded veterans.

March's first post in the company was as Waterman's personal secretary, at a monthly salary of $100. John B., according to stories March later related, was something of a pompous man who enjoyed the sound of his own voice. He was inclined to write in an extremely flowery style. On one occasion, while dictating to March, he used an impressive five-syllable word and, pausing in full verbal flight, asked his new secretary if he knew what the word meant. March said he did but pointed out that Waterman obviously did not, for it was meaningless in the context in which it had been used. Waterman was understandably much deflated at being so roundly corrected and, so the story goes, it was touch and go for a while whether or not he was going to sack the young upstart he had so generously employed. Perhaps it was only by reminding himself of March's ostensibly precarious state of health that John B. desisted from taking the drastic step.[13]

March became close friends with another young man who had started work with the company at about the same time as March. This young man, Edward Aubert Roberts, although not yet twenty-one, possessed a fine executive mind and, furthermore, was very much the industrious and ambitious type. He shared the same birthday as March (September 18), but there were five years between them, Roberts having been born in 1898. Roberts infected March with his enthusiasm. During those very early days, when it was still proving something of a struggle to get the business established, he persuaded March, after a short break at the end of the normal day's work, to return with him to the office in the evening and work half the night. During these night sessions, the two young men would liberally lace themselves with drink to keep going. John B., a confirmed teetotaler, thoroughly disapproved of any liquor on the company's premises. He would even resort to sneaking into his employees' offices when they were absent and look through their desks and cabinets in search of the forbidden liquor. He never found any, for the simple reason that the two young men were too clever for him. They hid the bottles in the one place they knew he would never look. John B. worked at an impressively large desk which boasted drawers both at the back and in the front. He never had cause to use the drawers in the front and it was in these that March and Roberts maintained a full stock of bottles for their overtime sessions.[14]

In the beginning, John B. was unable to pay his new employees an adequate salary for their considerable services, and March began the practice of taking some company stock each payday to compensate for the shortfall in remuneration. Finley McRae provided him with much good advice on the best way of investing his money. In such manner was the base for March's eventual fortune established. According to Harry Hardy Smith, March's holding of Waterman stock was finally worth $3 million.

As the years went by, John B., recognizing Ed Roberts's superior business acumen, became increasingly content to leave the running of the company to the younger man. Many have attested to the fact that Roberts was undoubtedly the presiding genius behind Waterman and almost solely responsible for the company's overwhelming success. March, too, was given further opportunity to demonstrate his own ability when he was transferred to Waterman's traffic department. He proved himself so proficient that in 1924 he was promoted to the position of traffic manager.

In 1926, the decision was taken to set up a branch office in Memphis, Tennessee, one of the world's largest hardwood and cotton centers. March was allotted the task. He arrived in Memphis on June 6, 1926, and, after interviewing and hiring people to work under him, very soon had the new office established. Once he had satisfied himself that the office was operating efficiently, he used it as a base and began traveling throughout the West and Middle West, making business contacts, negotiating contracts, and recommending the establishment of further offices wherever he saw the advantage of a permanent

Waterman interest. In a strange sort of way, he was doing in part the same job that his father had done as a timber cruiser. His trips took him to such places as Birmingham, Chicago, Cincinnati, Kansas City, Louisville, and St. Louis. At intervals, he returned to Mobile for consultations with John B. and Ed Roberts.

He was joined from time to time on these journeys by J. P. Case and Finley McRae. McRae presumably accompanied him in order to represent the bank's financial interests in whatever deals March may have been negotiating. Both men recall that even in those busy days March found the time to read a great deal and was absorbed by anything artistic. On one occasion in Missouri, McRae noticed a billboard advertising the play *King for a Day*, and March immediately said that they must, without fail, go and see it. Obviously surprised that his companion should wish to see such a show, McRae asked him why. March told him the story of François Villon. So vividly did he do so that he aroused McRae's interest, sending him in search of all he could discover about the French poet.[15]

Case often shared rooms and apartments with March during this period. Stacks of books, lodged on whatever shelves were available and piled on the floor and even on chairs, always littered their living quarters. Most of these books were on psychology, by Freud, Havelock Ellis, Jung, Adler, and others. March spent a considerable amount of time studying these texts. It was all grist to his mill, he informed Case, enabling him to deal satisfactorily with the various types of people with whom he had to conduct business. Case was suitably impressed by March's knowledgeable appreciation of human nature. March taught him that in the business world one simply had to adjust to the personality of the man or woman with whom one was negotiating. Case, for instance, intensely disliked one particular German grain dealer in Kansas City, but March persuaded him that if they were to get the German's business for Waterman, Case would have to ignore his distaste for the man's effeminacy and win him over with kind and gentle treatment. For other people, however, another approach might be appropriate. Most dealers, it is true, were rough, hard-talking, hard-drinking individuals. March could play up to them equally as well, giving them back as good as they gave, using their colorful language and, when necessary, adopting their own dubious bargaining tactics.[16]

March was based in Memphis from 1926 to 1928 and for a while was again able to indulge his fascination for the theater. He became an active member of the Little Theater Players, an amateur group which had been formed in 1921. After putting on several productions wherever they could find a suitable venue, in 1926 the Players merged with another amateur group, the Memphis Drama League. The Lee family (of Lee Steamship fame) offered the actors a stable of their mansion on the corner of Adams and Orleans, and the group converted it into a tiny theater, naming it the Stable Theater. Heated by a large pot-bellied stove, it could seat a hundred patrons on the benches borrowed from the nearby tabernacle where the revivalist Billy Sunday conducted his meetings. From all accounts, the productions were a great success, the hundred seats, as well as all the available standing room space, being entirely sold out for each performance. March himself played minor roles in two of the productions: *Dulcy* and *Outward Bound*. His involvement with the Little Theater Players not only provided him with a form of distraction and relaxation from the cares of business but gave him a certain identity and stability which the furnished rooms and apartments he was forced briefly to occupy could never give. More important, acting in front of an appreciative audience was something that had always pleased him, and was always to please him, allowing him, as it were, to act out some of his fantasies. Even working backstage, he could give his imagination full rein. It was for him a necessary means of escape from the realities of the everyday world.

When his stay in Memphis ended in 1928, he went to New York to arrange the opening of a Waterman office on Broadway. By then he had already started writing stories. March's social life had been sharply curtailed by a duodenal ulcer. His doctor had ordered him to take things easy for a while, and alcohol was forbidden. This was the era of Prohibition and drinking was almost de rigeur. During this period of enforced inactivity, he began casting around for something to do to stave off boredom. Eventually he decided that he would attempt to write a dozen short stories, purely for his own amusement and satisfaction. Although initially he had no intention of ever becoming a professional author, he began, shortly after his arrival in New York, to attend a course in creative writing conducted by Helen Hull at Columbia University. He soon realized, however, that her teaching was of little help to him, her ideas about writing not coinciding with his own. He knew what he wanted to achieve and he knew also that this did not conform to the usual commercial formula. Kafka once stated that for him writing was a form of prayer. For March, certainly to begin with, writing was a form of therapy. He once declared that he regarded commercial literary success with "slight distaste."[17] His views were to change later, but in those early days he was principally concerned in exorcising his own private demons. This escape into literary pursuits, ostensibly so casually undertaken, was, as were his activities with the Little Theater Players, yet another avenue to express the fantasies that crowded his mind.

There is some doubt about which of his extant mature work was the first to be written. His notebook, for instance, lists the short story "Flight into Confusion" (subsequently published under the title "The Shoe Drummer") as having been written in 1928, although the volume of his collected short stories, *Trial Balance*, gives the year of composition as 1930. In late years, March revealed that during that early period he wrote between twenty and twenty-five stories, very uneven in quality. Many of them he subsequently destroyed, but some were good enough for publication. "The Little Wife," also concerning a traveling salesman, was apparently the second story he wrote. It is one of his most famous short stories, certainly the most frequently anthologized of his works, and generally recognized as a minor masterpiece of the genre. March had set himself a very high standard from the start, a standard he was to emulate for the rest of his life.

"The Little Wife" grew out of March's perceptive observations of human life and his facility for creating character and situation from the most mundane and insignificant of incidents. One day, in a hotel lobby, he observed another guest being handed a telegram. The man opened it and read the message. The expression on his face changed. He ripped up the telegram, dropped the pieces into a waste basket, then rejoined the group he had been with, soon engaging once more in animated conversation. March was never to know the man nor to discover what message the telegram contained, but in his fertile mind the unknown man became Joe Hinckley, a hardware drummer, who, while staying at a hotel in Montgomery, Alabama, receives a telegram from his mother-in-law calling him home to Mobile and advising him that his wife, Bessie, desperately ill after a miscarriage, is not expected to live through the day. Joe immediately leaves the hotel to catch the first train to Mobile. Shortly after the train has pulled out from the station, a porter hands him another telegram. Joe, knowing in his heart the news it contains, is unable to bring himself to open it, feeling that as long as he does not read what it has to tell him Bessie will remain alive. He goes out on to the rear vestibule of the train and there, after some hesitation, tears up the unopened telegram, scattering the pieces to the four winds. He persuades himself that everything is all right and forces himself to preserve the illusion by laughing and joking with his fellow passengers, telling them about his happy marriage and the anticipated birth of the baby. But, of course, when at last the train reaches Mobile, he is met at the station by his mother-in-law, who confirms that the second telegram did inform him of the news he could not accept: Bessie is dead.

The story is essentially little more than a vignette, its whole plot, as with much of March's work, contained not in narrative sequences but in the exploration of the emotions and reactions of its characters. So persuasive is the manner in which March presents poor Joe Hinckley that the reader, knowing fully as well as Joe himself that the inevitable has happened, shares his fervent hope that the episode will have a happy ending, that there has been some ghastly misunderstanding and that husband and wife will eventually be reunited. One hesitates to use the word "professional," but the work displays an author who, as yet unpublished, is already a master of his craft, completely aware of what he is doing.

The story was published in the magazine *Midland* for January-February 1930 and was subsequently selected for inclusion in the annual short-story anthologies *The Best Short Stories of 1930* and *O. Henry Memorial Award Prize Stories of 1930*. The editor of the former collection, Edward J. O'Brien, awarded the story three asterisks, which placed it in the highest category in O'Brien's esteem. Blanche Colton Williams, the editor of the *O. Henry* anthology, called the story a "fine piece of realistic art." In the opinion of Harry Hansen, one of that year's judges, it was the best story of the year. The sixty-three-year-old author Margaret Deland, creator of the fictional Pennsylvania town of Old Chester, also thought so. She wrote to March from her home in Cambridge, Massachusetts, praising the story's remarkable precision and psychological understanding and opining that it was one of the few great short stories to have been written since the turn of the century.[18] This unsolicited and generous interest by an established writer in the work of a young unknown just embarking on his literary career was an act which impressed March greatly. He never forgot it. Margaret Deland's example was one which he was himself to follow in the years to come.

March had sent out several stories under different pseudonyms: William Randolph, William Hamilton, and William March. The first of these stories to be accepted and published was "The Holly Wreath," one of the works under the name of William March. In such fortuitous circumstances was the author "William March" born. "The Holly Wreath" appeared in the October 1929 issue of the magazine *Forum* on September 12, 1929, six days before March's thirty-sixth birthday.

The person responsible for "discovering" March was *Forum*'s perceptive fiction editor Edith Walton, who was, the following year, to be similarly responsible, again in the pages of *Forum*, for the publication of William Faulkner's short story "A Rose for Emily," probably the most well-known and most frequently anthologized of all Faulkner's short stories.[19] Edith Walton had graduated from Bryn Mawr and had worked on newspapers in Springfield, Massachusetts, and in New York, where her varied career, first as a literary critic, then later as a radio and television commentator, really began. Her first job in New York was in the publishing house of Alfred A. Knopf, which she left in 1928 to join the staff of *Forum*, at that time under the editorship of Henry Goddard Leach. After reading March's contribution, she marked it immediately for acceptance, and her recommendation was sustained by both the assistant editor, John Whedon, and the departmental editor and rewriter, Richard Sherman. Leach obviously agreed with them. It was not always to be so. The following year, writing to his sister Margaret, March complained that for the second time a story of his which he had submitted to *Forum*, although recommended by everyone, had been finally rejected by Leach, who considered March's work too "unhealthy and decadent." March recognized that the judgment was possibly a valid one but maintained that in the last analysis it was irrelevant. In his view, literature was not the product of contented, uncomplicated minds. He was certain that if his work was good enough he would assuredly find his literary niche. If, on the other hand, his work was bad, he still felt objective enough not to allow failure to concern him overmuch.

"The Holly Wreath" recounts the disaster that befalls a water detail, consisting of a corporal and two privates, and examines with painful clarity the reactions of the three men when faced with the reality of death. Corporal Reagan, the only experienced soldier of the three, feels a vague sense of almost fatherly concern for the two raw recruits in his charge, but he is an imaginative man and his assumed air of authority and his bantering attitude form merely a protective shell which, as it turns out, proves too vulnerable to prevent his death. Keeney is the sensitive one, the one who predictably is the first to crack. He panics and is killed, riddled by a hail of bullets. The third soldier, Bouton, is the eternal survivor, the practical man who neither says nor does anything without prior calculation. The disparate basic character traits of the three men are carefully established at the very opening of the story. Upon entering the devastated village, they see a dead soldier, one arm flung wide, lying by the well from which they will have to draw the water they seek. Reagan remarks that the dead man seems about to deliver a speech. Keeney makes no comment. Bouton notes that they will have to move the corpse before they can get to the well to fill their canteens. Reagan tells Keeney to drag the corpse behind a wall, "where he won't get hit again." Keeney carries out the order, but collapses white and trembling afterward. "I never had my hands on a dead man before," he tells the other two. After filling their canteens, the three make their way by detour across an unfamiliar field. They come under enemy machine-gun fire and are forced to take shelter behind a large boulder. They will be perfectly safe there until nightfall, when they will be able to make their escape under cover of darkness. Keeney's nerve, however, breaks after a while. He makes a run for it but is quickly shot down. He dies among the wheat and poppies, his head almost touching his feet, his green uniform stained with blood. To Reagan, Keeney's body is like "a huge, badly made holly wreath," and this image begins fermenting in his mind. As time goes by and he lapses into half-sleep, he relives an episode of his childhood when, standing precariously on a chair to hang such a holly wreath in the window of his grandfather's house, he lost his balance and fell. He sees again his mother bending over him, her eyes full of concern and fear. Absorbed now in the past event and oblivious of his present surroundings, he leaps to his feet to reassure his mother that he is all right and, in so doing, exposes himself to the enemy machine gunners, who shoot him down. Bouton, with calm deliberation, stays put until it is dark, then gathers up the filled canteens and finds his way back safely to his company (*TB*, pp. 16–25).

As the text which was used when the story was eventually reprinted sixteen years later in *Trial Balance* shows, March revised the story after its publication in *Forum*. As well as generally tightening up his prose and pruning the somewhat sprawling original text, he incorporated several additional short passages, among them a brilliant final touch which, as well as rounding off the story, typifies the practicality of Bouton's approach to any given situation. Arriving back at his company, he reports the facts objectively and tersely, like a military communique, telling all that is relevant, but omitting entirely any reference to human pain or suffering: "We lost our way coming back. Keeney got killed. So did Reagan" (*TB*, p. 25).

"The Holly Wreath" is an honest piece of realistic writing which pulls no punches. Death in battle, it makes clear, is by no means glorious. Keeney dies in a paroxysm of fear, screaming "Don't! Don't!" at the unseen Germans. Reagan dies smiling at the memory of happy childhood days, but, as he falls forward, the rock that has been his protection and now rises "to meet his smile" is the brutal fact of the present, breaking his teeth and bruising his mouth. It may all seem comparatively tame to the modern reader, but it should be borne in mind that at the time March was writing it was not permissible to portray man's bestiality to man in the sort of language and narrative that demonstrates unequivocally the full degradation of war. At about the time "The Holly Wreath" was published, Hemingway's *A Farewell to Arms* was appearing in serial form in *Scribner's Magazine*. Many of the magazine's regular readers were outraged by the outspokenness of Hemingway's prose, among them the general secretary of the Young Men's Christian Association in Mobile, who, canceling the association's subscription, wrote to the magazine's editors expressing his disgust in no uncertain terms.[20]

It is not known how all the Campbells reacted to having a published author in the family. John Leonard was no longer around to comment, either favorably or unfavorably, on his son's literary activities, for he had died in 1921. Margaret, who in 1918 had married an engineer, Homer Walter Jones, and was now living with her husband and their family in Williamsville, New Jersey, was, for one, clearly delighted with her brother's achievement in breaking into print. She made up her mind to do all she could to promote his initial success. She sat down and composed a short letter:

> May I venture to express my honest appreciation of the splendid story "The Holly Wreath" by William March which appeared in the October issue of your magazine? I think it shows great promise and is a story of unusual distinction. I congratulate you on its publication and hope to hear more from its author through your pages.[21]

Margaret signed the letter with her husband's name, "H. W. Jones, Williamsville, N.J.," and sent it off to the editors of *Forum*. It was printed in the December 1929 issue of the magazine and thus became the first published comment on March's work ever to appear.

four

The Two Worlds Established

In spite of Goddard Leach's coolness, March's relationship with the other members of the editorial staff of *Forum* went far beyond a mere author-editor footing. Lombard Jones has told of the friendly atmosphere that was engendered by March's contacts with Edith Walton and her colleagues:

> I never learned about Edith's first meeting with March, but I would guess he probably dropped in to meet the first person to give his writing substantial recognition and to deliver the biographical material she had requested of him, as she did of all about-to-be-published authors, for *Forum*'s biographical notes. Since the staff worked together in one large room, I am sure Bill met John Whedon and Richard Sherman at the same time. Certainly, great rapport sprang up among them, easily understood considering that all four of them were creative writers outside their regular jobs, and deeply interested in the new writers appearing in small magazines and literary reviews throughout this country and Europe.[1]

The mutual friendship was to deepen as the years went by.

During 1930, John B. Waterman suffered several bouts of ill health and there was talk of an impending operation. For some time, he had been handing over more and more responsibilities to Ed Roberts, not concerning himself with the minutiae of the day-to-day affairs of the business. In April, March was able to report to John B. that the Broadway Realty Company had executed in the company's favor a lease on Room 1155, 18 Broadway, and he assured his chief that, in his opinion, the premises were ideally suited for Waterman's needs.[2]

March was then occupying an apartment at 15 Abingdon Square, a large irregular square at the juncture of West 12th Street and 8th

Avenue, bounded by tall modern apartment buildings, older ware-houses, and business establishments. March's apartment, high up in the house, contained a big living room, comfortably furnished but with no particularly distinctive taste. March encouraged little contact with his neighbors. An apartment on a lower floor was occupied by a ménage of comely young ladies who clearly had their sights set on any eligible young bachelors around. March, however, would have nothing to do with them. On one occasion, when J. P. Case was staying with him, one of the girls called on the pretext of wanting to borrow an egg, and Case let her into the apartment. March steadfastly refused to acknowledge her presence, even to the extent of staring over her head when obliged to look in her direction.[3]

Why he should have wished to indulge in such extraordinary behavior must remain a matter for speculation. One possible explanation is that he always preferred to choose his relationships and not have them thrust upon him. He possessed an inherent shyness which he often attempted to disguise behind his more outrageous pronouncements, but once a friendship had been cemented then it was almost invariably for life. He had clearly decided, on the other hand, that marriage was not for him. He wanted the freedom to act as he pleased, and although in later life he may have regretted not having the stability of the enduring relationship a loving wife may have provided, it is extremely doubtful that he would have been entirely comfortable in the role of a husband. The domestic side of life was not one that greatly interested him and he had little patience with mundane day-to-day household chores. He never, for instance, washed his clothes during the time Case was staying with him at Abingdon Square. He simply discarded them when they became dirty, consigning them to the incinerator. Such irresponsible (some would say irrational) behavior is indicative not only of his rising affluence, but possibly also of his reaction against the memories of the poverty he had experienced as a child. He would surely have enjoyed a certain grim satisfaction in demonstrating to himself, as well as to others, that he could now afford to buy new clothes as fancy took him.

So far as his new career as a writer was concerned, 1930 began auspiciously with the publication in *Midland* on New Year's Day of his story "The Little Wife." During the course of the next twelve months, March was to develop a warm relationship with John Frederick, *Midland*'s editor, and although the two men were never to meet, their correspondence over the next few years reveals the deep respect they had for each other.

During the spring of 1930, March sent Frederick some "war sketches," each running only to between two hundred and four hundred words in length. These sketches, written in the first person and based on the war letter diaries he had sent from France to Margaret, related the experiences of the men in a marine company similar to the one in which he had served. He planned to write 150 sketches for a volume and had actually completed about a third of them. His aim was to compose each sketch as a separate viewpoint, all of them being bound together by "the common theme of the triumph of stupidity over everything." One publisher he had initially interested had already expressed the opinion that March had failed in his objective, advising him to abandon the project.[4]

Frederick's associate editor, Frank Luther Mott, liked only fifteen of the sketches March had submitted. Writing to the author in late May, Frederick asked him if he would agree to the separate publication of these fifteen. March replied swiftly and somewhat angrily that he could not agree to the proposal because the sketches Mott had selected could not be published in isolation without completely destroying the overall effect he had wanted to create. He pointed out that the sketches had not been written haphazardly but with an overall plan.[5] He suggested that instead of the selection the editors had proposed, assuming they still wished to restrict the number of sketches to fifteen, they should at least include the sketches of Mooney, Calhoun, Virtue, Somerville, Hart, and Terwilliger, and, so far as possible among the other nine, the sketches of Romano, Dresser, Frankel, Anderson, Howie, Dennison, and Citron. He stressed that he felt very strongly about the presentation of the sketches, making it abundantly clear that if the editors could not see their way to adopting his suggested alternative he would rather not have the sketches published at all.

Three months passed before Frederick was able to give March a firm decision by sending him a list of the sketches he wished to accept for *Midland* and to publish under the title "From Company K" or "Fifteen from Company K." The sketches selected were, in order of presentation: Lloyd Somerville, Frederick Terwilliger, Edward Frankel, Leslie Jourdan, William Anderson, Arthur Crenshaw, Edward Romano, Harold Dresser, Philip Calhoun, Sylvester Keith, Jack Howie, Marvin Mooney, Howard Virtue, Carroll Hart, and John Citron. As Frederick pointed out, he had not only included the six March had specifically chosen, but also, following a change of heart concerning some of the sketches he had not liked at first, all but two of the seven March had indicated he would place next in importance to these. Frederick added that he was not altogether sure if the order in which he had arranged the new selection was the best one and he asked March for his opinion.[6]

March let Frederick know immediately how delighted he was both with the choice and the proposed arrangements of the sketches, telling the editor he did not think anyone could have presented them in a more effective sequence. The new arrangement, March wrote, gave the sketches a unity which had been absent from his own arrangement.[7] So far as the suggested alternative titles were concerned, he did not care which Frederick used, although if he had to state a preference it would be for "Fifteen from Company K." He took the opportunity of slightly revising seven of the sketches,[8] asking Frederick to substitute the revised pages for the pages he already had but leaving the editor free to retain the original versions if he did not consider the changes an improvement. Frederick accepted all the revisions and advised March on September 16 that he proposed to publish the sketches in the November issue.

In such fashion, then, was the first collection of Company K sketches selected and presented to the world. The November-December 1930 issue of *Midland* was published on November 1, and by the beginning of December, Frederick was able to report to March that the magazine had received some very favorable comments on "Fifteen from Company K," one of the magazine's other contributors, for example, calling it "one of the most beautiful prose achievements I have read for a long time—genuinely great, not a single segment weakening!"[9] Frederick ventured to hope that some publisher could now be persuaded to consider the book March had originally planned. Indeed, urged on by those of his friends in New York whose advice and taste he trusted, March was already contemplating the composition of more Company K sketches, but he was still not altogether convinced it would be a worthwhile project. Writing to Frederick on December 26, he revealed his underlying sense of uncertainty by expressing ostensible surprise at and distrust of the unanimously favorable verdicts the sketches had received from *Midland* readers. Then, in almost the next sentence, he announced that he had, after all, decided to go ahead and complete the series, even though he had not been able to find the other twenty-five sketches he had written. He thought it possible that he might have destroyed them with a file of early manuscripts.[10]

In addition to the two stories published during 1930 in *Midland*, "The Dappled Fawn" had appeared earlier that same year in the winter issue of *Prairie Schooner*. Although written in the third person, this story was later changed into the first person and incorporated into *Company K*; not originally conceived as part of the *Company K* cycle, its integration into the book is not entirely successful. In his survey of the American short-story scene for the period from June 1, 1929, to April 30, 1930, in *The Best Short Stories of 1930*, Edward J. O'Brien awarded "The Dappled Fawn" one asterisk, "The Holly Wreath" two asterisks, and, as has already been noted, "The Little Wife" three asterisks. March could thus gain much satisfaction in the knowledge that the first three stories he had published had each received the kudos of recognition from one of the leading short-story anthologists of the day.

O'Brien's sponsorship, in fact, extended far beyond the inclusion and grading of March's three stories in his annual listing of distinctive work. He had written two letters to March early in 1930: one was a formal letter requesting permission to reprint "The Little Wife" in his 1930 anthology, the other a personal letter telling March that he regarded the story highly. There followed an exchange of correspondence between the two men, in which O'Brien made plain his intense interest in March's work and his willingness to do whatever he could to promote it. O'Brien was, March declared to Frederick, "a damned nice chap."[11] O'Brien wrote to several editors, recommending they give March their support by publishing his work. Such concern and kindness was typical of the man: March was not the first, nor the last, aspiring writer on the threshold of his career to benefit from O'Brien's sponsorship and encouragement.

O'Brien was not alone among anthologists in being impressed by March's stories. In May 1930, rumors came to March's ears that Blanche Colton Williams was also interested in including one of his stories in the 1930 volume of the *O. Henry Memorial Award Prize Stories*. At first, he thought that her most likely choice—if indeed one of his stories was selected—would be "The Dappled Fawn," the one he himself considered the least of the three. He did not know Miss Williams personally but was convinced that "The Little Wife" was not the sort of story she liked. On June 15, however, he received a letter from her, in her capacity as chairman of the O. Henry Memorial Committee, requesting formal permission to include "The Little Wife" in the 1930 volume. March agreed with alacrity, even though he professed not to be overly impressed with the general standard of the stories appearing in the O. Henry Memorial volumes.

When, in October of that year, he eventually met Miss Williams, he discovered to his surprise that she was a delightful, warmhearted, kindly, intelligent person. He concluded that while her literary judgments might not always be sound they were much better than one would imagine from the material published in her anthologies. Indeed, March gained the impression that she had such a poor opinion of the current literary output that she felt there was nothing to lose in selecting material which was entirely commercial, thus enhancing the sales of her volumes to the satisfaction of her publishers. She was able to advise March that Herschel Brickell, one of the judges of the prize contest and himself to assume editorship of the O. Henry volumes in 1941, had given "The Little Wife" first place, although in the final analysis, when the choices of the other three judges were taken into account, March's story did not rank high enough for a prize.

Despite O'Brien's sponsorship, the reaction of most editors to the stories March sent out during 1930 was disappointing. Apart from "Fifteen from Company K," he had only one other story accepted during the whole of that year. This was "Miss Daisy," which he had sent to Richard Johns, the young editor of the new quarterly *Pagany*, the first number of which had been published in Boston in early January 1930. Johns, Edith Walton, and Frederick gave March the maximum encouragement and support they could, as demonstrated by the fact that during the years 1929 to 1933, of the total of twenty stories March published, four appeared in *Pagany*, four in *Forum* and seven in *Midland*. Of the remaining five, two were published in *Story* and one each in *Prairie Schooner*, *Contempo*, and *Clay*. Apart from *Forum*, all were "little magazines" with limited circulations. Nevertheless, some of March's subject matter was regarded too strong, too daring, or too depressing for even the most sympathetic editors of these and other magazines.

One such piece was "Flight to Confusion." Even prior to 1930, March had submitted it to several editors, presumably including Goddard Leach, all of whom had thought it "silly or disgusting or decadent."[12] March believed deeply in the work. With startling vividness, employing the stream-of-consciousness technique, "Flight to Confusion" reveals disturbing insights into the disintegrating mind of a paranoid schizophrenic. The story climaxes with the man murdering, in circumstances replete with sexual overtones, the woman he has casually picked up and accompanied back to her apartment.

When sending it for Frederick's consideration on September 6, March noted that reaction to the story had taken two forms: that it was a convincing piece of work on its own terms and that the author should have his mouth washed out with soap and water. Informing Frederick that the story was based on the account of a murder he had read about some years previously, he stressed that he had taken the trouble to check that the development of the narrative was psychologically sound. Frederick did not reject the story outright, as had so many editors before him. Writing on September 16, he assured the author that he personally had not been disturbed or shocked by the story, nor did he consider it rot, as March had suggested he might well do. On the contrary, he thought March had succeeded in his attempt to bring off something of extreme difficulty. There were, nevertheless, one or two matters he was not sure about, and he wanted to ponder a little longer over the story before reaching a decision.

Frederick followed up these comments in a letter dated October 23, to which he attached not only an extensive commentary on "Flight to Confusion" but commentaries on two other stories March had sent him, "Diseur" and "Mist on the Meadow," setting out his reasons for deciding that none of the three stories was suitable material for *Midland*. His main objection to "Flight to Confusion" was, so he said, not on the grounds of the material itself but on its execution. He still professed that he would like to use the story, subject to March's making some changes which would rectify what he saw as psychological inconsistencies in the principal character. If March could see his way clear to adopting his suggestions, Frederick told him that he would like to see the story again.

March's artistic integrity was not to be undermined in this way. Replying five days later, he told Frederick that although he had some time ago determined never to question an editor's decision concerning his work, he could not on this occasion remain silent and subservient. He was convinced that Frederick was wrong and was seeing inconsistencies where no inconsistencies existed. At first, he admitted, he had been inclined to accept the editor's proposals, for he wanted this particular story published more than any other he had written, but when he sat down to incorporate Frederick's suggested revisions he found that he simply could not bring himself to do it. As evidence of the powerful impression the story had made on some people, he mentioned that a few weeks earlier he had casually met a reader from one of the magazines that had already rejected it and that this reader had immediately identified him as the author of "Flight to Confusion."

Frederick was honest enough to concede that he felt partially persuaded by these vehement arguments, and he left the matter open by suggesting that March should send him the manuscript again some time in the future if, in the meantime, he had still been unsuccessful in placing it elsewhere. Frederick repeated that he would like to publish the story, provided he could feel quite sure about it. He added that he was aware that was the only circumstance in which March would wish him to accept it for *Midland*. One gets the impression that Frederick was rather glad to have wriggled off the hook in this fashion, for he had a great deal of sympathy for March and what he was trying to do, and, like the reader March had referred to in his letter, he had been deeply impressed by the story. There is little doubt, however, that he was under some pressure from his associate editors to reject the story outright, and he was, as he always had to be, concerned about the possibility of offending and alienating a large section of the magazine's regular readers and subscribers. March had a similar reaction from Richard Johns, to whom he sent the story the following month. As a piece of literature, Johns found it worthy of *Pagany* but also thought the subject matter likely to cause offense.[13]

According to the dates March appended to the stories he collected in *Trial Balance*, six of the stories which have survived were written during the year 1930: "A Snowstorm in the Alps," "The Shoe Drummer" ("Flight to Confusion"), "Mist on the Meadow," "The Wood Nymph," "To the Rear," and "Miss Daisy." Five of these stories and the 1929 story "Diseur" had still not been placed by the year's end.

Lincoln Kirstein, editor of *Hound and Horn*, had rejected "Diseur," "A Snowstorm in the Alps," and "God and a Few Pigs" (an early title for "Mist on the Meadow"), as well as another story, titled "Nor Stone, Nor Earth," which had been originally planned by March as a work of 25,000 words and radically cut down by him when he realized it was too long for any magazine. March never had any success in getting his work published in *Hound and Horn*, although he and Kirstein, then a young man in his early twenties, met from time to time and remained good friends for many years. Kirstein's editorial colleagues at *Hound and Horn* had only contempt for March's work, and although Kirstein paid for the running of the magazine out of his own pocket, their combined approval was necessary for publication of any work.

Another magazine which never published March was the *Virginia Quarterly Review*. In August 1930, the magazine's editor, Lambert Davis, returned the story "God and a Few Pigs," ostensibly on the grounds that the magazine published very little fiction. Acknowledging the return of the story, March wrote that the fiction that was published in the *Virginia Quarterly Review* was so superior that he would "like to succeed in crashing [the magazine's] gates."[14] He announced his intention of continuing to submit stories in the hope that one of them might hit the editor's fancy sometime and he would want to make room for it. He sent only one other story to Davis during 1930, but this was returned in November with the comment that although the editor had been impressed by the unusual story and March's skill in handling it, he was regretfully unable to find a place for it in the magazine's pages. These two rejections, however, did not deter March, who persisted in submitting stories to Davis for the next year or so.

Toward the end of 1930, March was well on the way to developing his friendly working relationship with Richard Johns. Although Johns was not so immediately enthusiastic about March's work as Frederick had been and had felt unable to accept "Flight to Confusion" when March had sent it to him that fall, he did accept "Miss Daisy." In a letter to Johns early in December, March expressed his desire to write something especially for *Pagany* and asked Johns to advise him as to the maximum acceptable length of any such manuscript he might submit for the editor's consideration. He took the opportunity of enclosing with his letter another story, "A Goddess Bleeds," which, as he pointed out, was short and would not take up much space.[15] March had apparently forgotten he had already submitted the story to Johns on a previous occasion, and when the editor returned it again early in the new year March confessed that the error had occurred because he was the most unsystematic of people. He pronounced the story "lousy," and it would seem that he subsequently destroyed it, for it has not survived.

In addition to "Fifteen from Company K" and "Flight to Confusion," March submitted at least another six stories to Frederick during 1930: "The History of a Tic" in May, "Diseur" and "Mist on the Meadow" in September, "Starnes" in October, and "To the Rear" and "The Wood Nymph" in December.

"Starnes" came into being as the result of a discussion he had with a friend, during which March insisted that in writing stories the manner of presentation was infinitely more important than the plot. He theorized that any story could be made real or plausible if it was properly told. In an attempt to prove his point, he thought up the most artificial situation that came to his mind. He sent "Starnes" to Frederick on October 30, telling him that if he thought the story had no merit to return it immediately. The story is not mentioned in any of the surviving correspondence between the two men, so presumably Frederick did return it fairly promptly. Conceivably, this story was an earlier version of what was to become the Private Richard Starnes episode of *Company K*. March would unquestionably have described any situation in which a soldier voluntarily surrendered his gas mask to an enemy prisoner during a gas attack as being supremely "artificial" and "implausible."

"The History of a Tic" had a stormy career. In its original form, it was 14,000 words long, but March had shortened it at the request of an editor who was wavering between taking the story and rejecting it. After it had been drastically pruned, the editor decided after all to reject it because of its pathological nature. Several other editors found it interesting but not suitable material for their magazines, in each instance the old charge that the story was too decadent or unhealthy being invoked. March told Frederick that he thought the story had been more effective in its longer version, the revised text being too compressed, too full of incident, and thus far from perfect. It could, he speculated, if converted from first-person into third-person narrative, even be easily expanded into a novel. Frederick deliberated long over "The History of a Tic" and it was three months before he eventually returned the story to March. Mott, he reported, had thought the work unsuccessful, but he (Frederick) had found the story growing on him after two or three successive readings. He certainly found nothing offensive in it and intimated that he would have no hesitation in publishing the story if March could see his way clear to revising it further, tightening up its rather loose construction. March agreed on this occasion with all of Frederick's criticisms, reiterating his view that if the story were told in the third person and developed in the three distinct sections into which it naturally fell, it would make an effective novel. First of all, he announced, he proposed to test how it would work as a short story in the third person. He began work on this version immediately, but before he was aware of what was happening, it began stretching out into a novel. On September 6, he reported to Frederick that he had begun rewriting the story of "the tattooed man" again. He had completed the first third, amounting to approximately 15,000 words, and was pleased with the result. He foresaw difficulty, however, in making acceptable the continuous mysterious shadow hovering over the principal character, a boy, all his life.

All the other four stories he sent to Frederick during 1930 eventually appeared in print, although only two of them, "Mist on the Meadow" and "To the Rear," were published in *Midland*. After being rejected by Lincoln Kirstein for *Hound and Horn*, "Diseur" had been accepted by Grant Overton and Hugh Leamy for publication in the series "The Most Distinguished Story of the Month" in their magazine *The Mentor*. Unfortunately, before March had even received payment for the story, *The Mentor* changed hands and all the stories that had been accepted but not yet published, including March's, were returned to their authors. March, who rated "Diseur" a good, average story and decided that it was probably too good to be destroyed, sent it to Frederick. Frederick thought it a first-rate tale with a lot of good work in it but felt that there was some subtle weakness in the last third of the story which he was unable to put his finger on. In sending the story back, he offered, as he so often did, to take another look at it if March failed to place it elsewhere. "The Wood Nymph" was also returned by Frederick, apparently after Mott had turned thumbs down. March had to wait nine years before he finally saw "The Wood Nymph" in print.

When sending "Mist on the Meadow" to Frederick on September 25, March warned the editor against reading unintended meanings into the story. The story, he asserted, was basically nothing more than a retelling of the miracle of the swine. The main objection that had been leveled against it by other editors was that the story was out of focus. That, however, wrote March, was the way he wanted it to be.

Frederick was considerably impressed by the story and expressed his desire to publish it, but, as usual, he suggested that March make a few changes to the manuscript. In particular, he felt that the reader's acceptance of the central "miracle" was crucial to the success of the work. For his part, he was not wholly convinced that the problem of overcoming possible skepticism on the part of the reader had been adequately solved, and he asked to see the story again after March had considered his suggestions. Within five days, March had completely rewritten the story, not without some regret, although he felt that its new form was an improvement. On the other hand, he was adamant that he should not attempt to rationalize the miracle, as this would, in his opinion, completely ruin the story. He did not think it was of any consequence whether or not his readers accepted the reality of the miracle. In fact, his own view was that if they did not accept it their reaction to the story would be intensified.[16] Frederick, nevertheless, still remained unhappy about the story and subsequently sent it back to March.

Although, one way and another, he had encountered many setbacks during the years, March could afford to look back over 1930 and feel pleased at the progress of his literary career. Three of his stories had been published, one having been selected for reprinting in the two leading short-story anthologies of the day, and one further story had been accepted for publication. Two more stories were in Frederick's sympathetic hands, awaiting his final decision. A novel, in which he had the house of Simon and Schuster interested, was in progress, and four other stories were in the works at the year's end.[17]

The furtherance of his new literary career was slowly preoccupying him at the expense of his business activities, which he seemed to find were becoming more and more onerous and time-consuming. Writing to Frederick on October 18, he deplored the fact that he had no free time, even in the evenings, to devote to literary matters, because of an almost continuous procession of business acquaintances who had to be entertained after the day's work at the office was completed. He was also delegated, in his ambassadorial role for the company, to take under his wing "all sorts of nice old ladies," ensuring that they were safely conducted into their berths on outgoing steamers or taken on outings to sample the atmosphere of some of the less salubrious night spots around town. Then there were various business trips to be made down South, including a visit to Alabama for two to three weeks in late September and early October to make a series of calls on the cotton exporters. He complained of the effect on his stomach of all the bad corn whisky and local food he was obliged to consume in the cause of good business relations. As if that were not enough, he caught a severe cold on the train returning to New York and was laid up miserably in his apartment for several days, suffering with an aching head and watering eyes. On the sixth day of the new year, he again moaned to Frederick that he had been prevented from doing any writing for a month because of the many customers who wanted to be escorted around town to observe "the vicious night-life." He expressed the hope that things would revert to normal in the near future, if only so that he could catch up on his lost sleep.[18]

The year 1931 was to prove to be a successful one for March, particularly in his role as business executive. On October 8, he received a Western Union telegram from John B. Waterman: "It gives me pleasure to announce that the board of directors of Waterman Steamship Corporation in the exercise of excellent judgment yesterday elected you a vice-president of the corporation. You have my congratulations and best wishes."[19] March wrote back immediately, acknowledging his elevation to "featured roles" and telling John B. that the promotion had brought "no end of pleasure to my sentimental heart."[20] Twelve days later, in reply to a routine communication he had received from John B., he noted that his chief was obviously back in harness and expressed the hope that he had been fully restored to health. He offered his own congratulations to John B. for wearing his ailments "so sportingly."[21]

On the literary scene, his success, though by no means so spectacular in monetary terms, was no less satisfying and certainly more meaningful for March. For the second year in succession, one of his stories was selected for inclusion in the 1931 editions of Edward J. O'Brien's and Blanche Colton Williams's annual anthologies. This was "Fifteen from Company K." Frederick told March that selection of the story for the O. Henry anthology was an immense triumph, as no other work as unconventional in form as "Fifteen from Company K" had ever appeared in the volumes.[22]

Shortly after the story had appeared in *Midland* the previous year,

March had received what he described as a "damned nice" letter from O'Brien, who told him how much he liked the story and mentioned that he had advised Jonathan Cape, who published the British editions of O'Brien's annual anthologies, to get in touch with March regarding a possible collection of stories. March revealed to Frederick on January 6, 1931, that he had about two hundred Company K sketches planned and that even though some of them might not work out finally he should eventually have enough to make a volume. He added that some of the new sketches had "a little more blood in them" than the ones published in *Midland*. He expressed the hope that O'Brien would bring out the sketches in his anthology but thought this unlikely. In his opinion, "Miss Daisy," which was still awaiting publication in *Pagany*, stood the better chance of selection by O'Brien. Knowing that the anthologist would be choosing from stories published during the twelve months to the end of April, March wrote to Johns on February 23, urging him, if possible, to bring out the story in the spring number of the magazine. Johns obliged. The story was published on April 1. All these efforts on the part of both March and Johns proved unnecessary when O'Brien wrote to the author and to Frederick in June, requesting permission to reprint "Fifteen from Company K." O'Brien's sponsorship of the war sketches encouraged March to resume work in earnest on a book of the sketches, as he had always planned. He reported to Frederick on July 6 that he had never found the sketches he had lost the previous year but that he had done twenty-five or so new ones and now had about fifty completed. He admitted they were uneven in quality but felt he had succeeded here and there. He added that it seemed to him he could go on producing them indefinitely.

In addition to the work he did on the Company K sketches, March completed at least seven stories during 1931: "A Shop in St. Louis, Missouri," "George and Charlie," "Woolen Drawers," "Happy Jack," "He Sits There All Day Long," "This Heavy Load," and "The Unploughed Patch." Six stories were published during the year: three ("To the Rear," "A Snowstorm in the Alps," and "Mist on the Meadow") in *Midland*; two ("He Sits There All Day Long" and "Nine Prisoners") in *Forum*; and the sixth ("Miss Daisy") in *Pagany*. Each of these stories was eventually to be awarded a three-asterisk rating by O'Brien in his annual listings.

Although Frederick had rejected "Mist on the Meadow" the previous year, he wrote to March on May 27, to tell him that he recalled "with regret" having turned down the story and to ask if he had yet succeeded in placing it. He suggested that if no one else had taken it March should resubmit it for consideration by the *Midland* editors.

March sat down and revised the story yet again, sending it to Frederick on June 19 under its original title "God and a Few Pigs" but leaving it to the editor's discretion to use whatever title he preferred should he decide to publish the new version. March had eliminated all the fire symbolism which had puzzled so many people and which he now realized was not essential to the story at all. But he doggedly retained the "miracle." He could not believe that American readers were so unimaginative that they could not occasionally accept something which was different from the realistic, literal stories they had become conditioned to reading. Whatever symbolism the story might contain was still, in his view, of small consequence, feeling as he did that it was up to each reader to read what he wanted into the story. He admitted that he was not sure in his own mind if the story was of the first class, but he sensed that the violently opposing reactions it had already aroused—and would assuredly arouse in the future—made it the sort of story on which any editor would be prepared to take a chance.

This time, Frederick was won over. The story was published in the October issue of *Midland*. Whatever doubts March may have expressed concerning his own work, O'Brien clearly thought the story was first class, for he selected "Mist on the Meadow" for inclusion in his 1932 anthology.

In addition to "Mist on the Meadow" and "A Snowstorm in the Alps," March sent several other stories to Frederick during the course of the year, but the editor regretted he could not find a place for any of them in *Midland*. Among these stories was "Flight to Confusion," the work March was so anxious to see published that he was willing to take up Frederick's rather ambiguous conciliatory offer of the previous year to have another look at the story if a home could not be found for it elsewhere. March submitted the story again to Frederick on February 23 but obviously with little hope that the editor would change his mind. March still refused to revise the story in any way, preferring, so he said, to destroy it or to file it away for his literary executors.

Frederick returned the story on April 1. He again seemed loath to close the final door on it, but he did not think the time yet ripe for the story to appear in its present form in the pages of his magazine. He told March that he would keep the story in mind and promised that as soon as he saw a chance of publishing it he would ask March for it.

During the first six months of 1931, Frederick rejected four other stories March sent him, including "The Monument" and "Happy Jack." March submitted "The Monument" on February 12, in the hope that it would make the April issue of *Midland*. He apologized to Frederick for being so near the magazine's deadline for that issue, explaining that the visit of three out-of-town business colleagues had prevented his working on it. In addition, he had lost three pages of the original and it had taken him almost the same length of time to write new pages to fill the gaps as it had taken him to write the entire story. Having obtained the reaction of two friends, to whom he had read the story that same evening, he decided to rewrite the last page, sending this to Frederick the following day, February 13. Frederick, however, was not sure that the story had come off and, replying to March five days later, said he would prefer to publish "To the Rear" in the April issue and leave the new story in abeyance for the time being. He sent the manuscript back to March with a few suggestions for strengthening the story. March decided instead to submit the story to *Scribner's Magazine* and, if necessary, to one or two others, before revising the story along the lines Frederick had indicated and resubmitting it to *Midland*. The story was not accepted by *Scribner's Magazine*, nor did Johns find it suitable for *Pagany*. Somewhere along the line, March changed the title of the story to "A Shop in St. Louis, Missouri." He must also have changed his mind about revising it and resubmitting it to *Midland*, for it was not published until 1935, when it appeared as the one previously unpublished story in the collection *The Little Wife and Other Stories*.

He sent "Happy Jack" to Frederick at the beginning of July, but within a few days was regretting that he had released the story before he was really satisfied with it. He realized that in its present form it was far too concentrated and needed to be expanded to approximately twice its length. Frederick returned the story on July 11, agreeing with March that more work would have to be done on it but noting that it contained some excellent material.

March's lack of success in being published in the *Virginia Quarterly Review* continued during 1931. On March 30, Lambert Davis returned "A Snowstorm in the Alps," regretting that he could not use it. Another story, "The Mail Order Dress," which was never to appear in print and was apparently destroyed by March, was returned by Davis a fortnight later. "Woolen Drawers" was rejected on June 30. A fourth story, "George and Charlie," already rejected by *Forum* and several other magazines, was returned on July 23. Davis's most consistent explanation for these rejections was that the magazine did not publish much fiction and that the editors were currently overstocked with stories. Even an author as tenacious as March could not fail to be discouraged by this constant rejection of his work. He did not submit any further stories to the *Virginia Quarterly Review* for another nine months or more.

If some editors, like Lambert Davis, were solidly unenthusiastic about March's work, others were anxious to be given the opportunity of publishing it. A seventeen-year-old Filipino student at the University of New Mexico, José Garcia Villa, later to become the best known of Philippine writers in English, had been reading with great interest the annual O'Brien anthologies:

> In one of O'Brien's introductions, he mentioned the founding of *Story Magazine* by Whit Burnett in Vienna. It was only a mimeographed magazine and yet he considered those stories for his anthology. So I did the same thing. I founded *Clay* in New Mexico. It was only mimeographed and we got our good stories listed on O'Brien's Roll of Honor. I was the only editor. I typed and ran off the mimeographed sheets and took them to the printers to be bound. I selected all the various stories to be published. I don't believe in coediting.[23]

However, when one is starting up such an undertaking and before one can even begin to think about bringing out the first issue, one has to announce one's existence and persuade writers that they should contribute, even though there is no question of any fee being paid for work published. Villa accordingly wrote to several authors, introducing himself and *Clay*. On August 5, he wrote to March, inviting him to submit material and to publicize the new magazine:

> The magazine is not a commercial venture, but is for the expression of worthy talent. It will be after the manner of *The Gyroscope*, and will maintain a very strict standard. The magazine will, I am sure, fall in Mr. Edward J. O'Brien's list of distinctive magazines. Mr. O'Brien, by the way, has a high opinion of my work, and in my magazine I assure you the best company.[24]

Although in his reply March promised his support for the venture, he did not immediately send any of his work to Villa. Writing to him again on October 23, Villa expressed the hope that March would shortly be able to contribute something to *Clay*, announcing that support for the magazine had been most encouraging and that the first number had almost sold out. He proudly added that Blanche Colton Williams was listing all the five stories that appeared in the first number in the O. Henry volume for 1932.

One possible reason for March's not having sent Villa any of his work was that he virtually stopped sending out any work during the late summer and fall of 1931. On November 2, he told Frederick he had written no new stories at all during the preceding three months or so, other than two, which had been accepted by *Forum*.[25] He had concentrated his literary effort almost entirely on completing the book of war sketches. By the end of October, he had finished the book. It consisted of 125 sketches, arranged chronologically, each standing alone, but cumulatively giving the effect, as March himself described it, of "something near an uninterrupted narrative." Although several publishers professed themselves interested in the book, he had not yet submitted it, wanting to have Frederick's permission to use the "Fifteen from Company K" sketches in the book before doing so. By mid-November, however, the book had already been rejected by one publisher. Writing to Granville Hicks on November 17, March revealed that the book was at present in the hands of another publisher but that he expected it back any day. "They are," he wrote ruefully, "far from being on the rafters, gawping, over its merits."[26] Hicks had urged him to send the book to the publishing house of Macmillan. March assured him that he would do this, just as soon as the expected rejection came from the publisher who now had the manuscript.

Another, more unified, collection of Company K sketches appeared under the title "Nine Prisoners" in the November 1931 issue of *Forum*. This collection of sketches was eventually to form the central incident of the book: the arbitrary shooting of a group of unarmed German prisoners by the marines and the emotional effect on the men who had carried out their captain's orders. When the story was published in *Forum*, it created an immediate furor among many of the magazine's readers. While many letters that arrived in the magazine's office praised March's work—one letter proclaimed that he had written "the mightiest of mighty expositions of the inhumanity of war"—many other letters abused him, for example, for "having murdered the good name and good sense of millions of American soldiers."[27] In the February 1932 issue of *Forum*, the editors published extracts from three of these fiercely critical letters, the last of which accused March of being "one of these peace-at-any-price people, who, having either never been a soldier at all or having been stationed at some camp during the war, believes himself an expert on the horrors of fighting." The letter concluded: "That such a person should be accepted as a qualified observer of war is ridiculous, and that his story should be paid for and printed by any editor is to me incomprehensible."

This particular accusation must have stuck in March's throat. For the first and last time, he felt it necessary to defend and justify his work in public. In the same "Our Rostrum" section of *Forum*, the editors printed his reply to his critics. It is worth quoting his letter in full, revealing as it does March's public, if not private, attitudes:

To the Editor:

My story, "Nine Prisoners," is, so far as I am aware, strictly fiction. I had hoped to make the men and their reactions universal in their implications, beyond military boundary lines, and there is, I think, nothing in the story to indicate that its characters are drawn from the Marines or the American Army at all.

I resent bitterly any inference that because I have written such a story I lack either patriotism or physical courage. To those who do imply such things, let me say that I enlisted, voluntarily, when war was declared; that I participated in all action that my regiment saw; that I was discharged honorably with the highest possible rating for a Marine—a perfect 5, given, I understand, rarely. I was awarded for personal bravery under fire every decoration except the Congressional Medal of Honor, and as a result of wounds I received in action, I shall never be entirely well again so long as I live. I dislike mentioning these things: I do it now merely to defend myself.

My present attitude toward war is this. If there were a war impending, my conscience and my special knowledge would impel me to do what I could to prevent it. Failing that, I would make the best of a bad situation and reënlist immediately in any combat unit which would accept in its ranks such a battered, half-blinded old hulk.

I am unaware, except in a general way, of the temper of the letters you have received regarding the story, or the reaction of your readers, but from the tone of those that have been addressed to me personally, I have learned one thing: it is futile and it is hopeless for any man who has actually served on the line to attempt to make well-meaning, romantic folk share his knowledge; there is, simply, no common denominator.

William March

New York, N.Y.

March was becoming gradually more and more integrated into New York literary circles. In August, he moved from Abingdon Square and rented a large apartment at 302 West 12th Street. The youthful Villa was somewhat overawed when, the following year, he came to New York and called on March:

The building was rather swanky, with a doorman downstairs. You couldn't go into the elevator without being announced by the doorman. So unless you were confirmed as a guest, you couldn't go up at all. It was a rather large apartment with a step-down living room, a large dining area, kitchen and a bedroom—maybe two bedrooms, I don't know. It was spacious and certainly expensive. I think he had paintings on the walls. They were random paintings, mostly by friends, something like that, but by unknowns.[28]

In this apartment, March gave occasional parties for his ever-increasing circle of friends. Among these was Lombard Jones, who had joined the *Forum* editorial staff in March 1931 as an advertising-production assistant. He met March at the *Forum* offices not long afterward. Jones has recalled:

> He had come there on some errand to do with one of his manuscripts. I was introduced to him and was surprised to discover how well his appearance concealed any evidence of his avocation. About five feet ten inches tall, slender, blond, smooth-shaven, bespectacled, immaculately dressed in a dark suit, I would have taken him exclusively for the shrewd, alert businessman he was, had I not learned about him from my associates. His blue-gray eyes looked at me rather searchingly, and he acknowledged our introduction with a completely disarming and contagious smile and a softly spoken acknowledgment in the best tradition of southern courtesy. I noticed that, in repose, Bill had a sort of a tic, slightly evidenced at intervals by quick, spasmodic swallowing. This seemed to be a chronic affliction.[29]

When he came to know March better and learn something of his background, Jones assumed that the tic and the involuntary swallowing were probably connected with March's deep-seated feelings of guilt over the bayoneting of the young German soldier.

Granville Hicks was another who, through Edith Walton, met March at about this time, although their friendship was never to progress beyond a fairly superficial level. Hicks was then writing reviews for *Forum*.

> I was at March's apartment only once that I remember, but I saw him several times at parties Edith gave. . . . He was pleasant, easygoing, and not at all argumentative. At this time I was strongly leftist in my political views, but I can't remember his taking much part in the discussions that went on. I do remember something he said about the race problem that interested me at the time—that he would just as soon sleep with a black woman but he wouldn't dance with one.[30]

Edith Walton's parties, as March's own in later years, were almost legendary. She lived with her mother in an apartment at 26 East 10th Street and it was here that the parties were held. Lombard Jones has described what they were like:

> The entrance hall opened into a large living room. For the party, the chairs, sofa, and tables were lined up tightly against the wall. The rugs

were rolled up and removed to one of the bedrooms, also assigned to receiving the hats and coats of the guests. The bootleg so-called gin had been purchased days before and carefully tested by a reliable chemist. To mitigate its astringent taste a generous supply of mollifying mixers had been brought in—ginger ale, fruit juices, and the like. And, of course, there were appropriate hors d'oeuvres and small sandwiches to help hold down the beverages. In one corner of the living room stood a Victrola with an attachment designed to hold a collection of twenty-five records and play them through one at a time. . . . Along about 8:30 or 9:00 P.M., the guests would arrive, the men in business suits, the women in gaily printed evening dresses. After introductions, the ice was broken on the streams of conversation. Everything was discussed: news, scandals, and the arts. Here and there, small controversies might spring up over technocracy, communism (Lenin's or Trotsky's), humanism (Irving Babbitt's), Marxism, New Deal socialism, and proletarian novels. The decline of fundamentalism was never mentioned, to my knowledge. Sometimes we would interrupt the dancing for a go at charades. It was all great fun.[31]

March was frequently invited to these parties and, according to Jones, seemed always to enjoy himself. He was a good mixer, having a marvelous sense of humor and a tremendous interest in what motivated people. Unfortunately, as Jones further recalls, he would on occasion take this interest in people too far:

He was an avid student of the works of Sigmund Freud and an analyzer, in Freudian frames of reference, of people he had met and observed. When he revealed intimate details of the lives of some of his friends and associates, I felt a bit squeamish, wondering what, if anything, he might have deduced about me. Edith shared my feeling. Dick Sherman, I heard from someone I cannot bring to mind, reacted rather angrily to this preoccupation of Bill's and told Bill off in no uncertain terms. I wasn't present at the scene of this flare-up. Nor do I know how it affected their relationship afterward.[32]

What understandably annoyed most of those involved was that while being so absorbed in other people's sex lives, March himself was particularly reticent, if not completely elusive, about his own. Case has also remarked on this aspect of March, commenting that he had a wonderful gift for conversation but did not often use it, preferring to be quiet. Once, visiting Case's house with several other of Case's male friends, March sat hardly opening his mouth while the conversation was being entirely given over to cars, baseball, fishing, and other sports, activities about which March cared nothing. He became increasingly bored as time went on, then suddenly, out of the blue, asked several startling, pertinent questions concerning the sex lives of the company in general. This ploy halted all talk of sport, and March assumed full command of the conversation, probing into the subject of sex in a manner which provoked from the others thoughts and statements and confessions of the most personal and secret matters imaginable. [33]

Everything had to be analyzed in psychological terms. Lombard Jones recalls how March shared with Edith Walton a great interest in the theater: "I shall never forget Bill's analytical discourse with her after he had gone to see Eugene O'Neill's *Mourning Becomes Electra*. To a casual, uninformed listener it would have been hard to determine afterward who had written the play—Sigmund Freud or Eugene O'Neill." [34]

Lois Cole, who, after running the Atlanta trade department of the Macmillan publishing house, came to New York in mid-June 1932 to join the editorial department of the company's head office, recalls another absorbing interest March had cultivated, giving him further opportunity, albeit on a more superficial level, to burrow into the minds of the people he met at parties and literary gatherings. This was his faculty for analyzing handwriting. He was, from all accounts, rather good at it and he was frequently invited by his host or hostess to amuse the other guests with his "powers." He was never slow in obliging. He would ask any strangers present who wished to participate to write three lines on a sheet of paper and sign their names. Although he maintained that had he more time or a more generous sample of the individual's handwriting he could have done much better, he apparently seldom failed to impress his audience, astounding them with his ability to interpret their qualities and their weaknesses. [35]

To many people, both those who knew him intimately and those who knew him only casually, this slight, composed, cool, soft-spoken businessman, whose words were certain and measured and who gave the impression of knowing exactly what he was going to say before he opened his mouth, was something of an enigma. So far as Granville Hicks was concerned, for example, March's family background was always a mystery, as it was to most people, and March never related any of his war experiences to him. Although one of Hicks's most vivid recollections is of March talking at great length about Freud, he cannot remember any remark March may have made on literary matters.

Lincoln Kirstein recalls that although March could put away liquor he was not a really heavy drinker:

We drank at his place or mine, and at a small restaurant speakeasy called Luigi's, near where he lived. He was only thirteen years older than myself, but this seemed much more to me, at the time. Besides, he had been in the war, and that was magic. . . . He called me "Kiddo," which was rather a Southern nickname—of his, not my, generation. I called him "Cap" (Captain). . . . I remember he said all Southern writers were bent, one way or another; as are most other writers. He was a provincial and did not feel at home in New York, really. . . . He was shy of my literary friends; he always dressed conventionally and avoided any trace of Bohemianism like the plague.[36]

Albert Halper, who also met March during this period and whose novel, *Union Square*, was to appear in 1934, remembers, however, that he and March "indulged in a lot of shop talk." Halper sensed that March was somewhat envious of the breaks he was getting at the time, particularly as he was ten years March's junior, but he is sure there was nothing deep-rooted in the envy.[37] In any event, it did nothing to diminish a friendship which was to last well into the 1940s. If indeed there was any envy at all, it was uncharacteristic of March, who, like Edward J. O'Brien, was generous to a fault in promoting the interests of any unknown writer struggling for recognition, provided, of course, he was convinced of the positive worth of the unknown's work.

In a similar way, he was unstinting in his efforts to promote José Garcia Villa's brave venture in publishing *Clay*, and he gained Villa's lifelong loyalty as a consequence. He put Villa in touch with Granville Hicks and with Miss Sylvia Chatfield Bates. Miss Bates conducted a course in creative writing at Columbia University and very much had her finger on the pulse of the current literary scene, with emphasis on the short-story genre. When, at the beginning of February 1932, Villa arrived in New York, intending to set up residence there, he felt lonely and bewildered in the big city. From his room in John Jay Hall, Columbia University, he wrote to March, asking if he could visit him at his apartment some night. March obviously took the younger man under his wing. As Villa wrote to him sometime afterward: "But for you I would have had a most lonely time."[38] When circumstances prompted Villa to return to New Mexico a few weeks later, an animated correspondence passed between them. This was, in part, the result of March's agreeing to allow Villa to use his apartment on West 12th Street as a mailing address for *Clay*. March and Villa each admired the other's work, and so far as Villa is concerned, his admiration of March has not decreased one iota over the years—if anything, it has probably grown.

There is a great deal of innate poetry in March's stories. Not poetic feeling, but poetic insight. That's why I think he is a very great writer. Most short-story writers haven't got that poetic insight at all. Their works are really trivial. Whereas he had that. Not only the feeling, but the impact. There was a punch at the end of the story, but not in the O. Henry sense. He knew the economy of the form. He knew how to develop a story. He never had too much and he never had too little. He had the right fleshing out and the right spirit behind him.[39]

As it happened, only one of March's stories appeared in *Clay*. This was "Sixteen and the Unknown Soldier," another group of Company K sketches. It appeared in issue number 3, which was published on April 4, 1932, and was destined to be the last number of the short-lived magazine. Another story, "Comfort Me with Apples," was accepted by Villa for the projected issue number 4. On June 20, he wrote March enthusiastically about this particular story, which had already been rejected by *Story, Midland* and inevitably, *Virginia Quarterly Review*. Villa predicted that it would be recognized as one of the finest stories to have appeared in *Clay* and rated it "ecstatically beautiful."[40]

Villa, nevertheless, was not always so enthusiastic and certainly did not assume the role of a slavish admirer. At his insistence, March sent him copies of almost all his new stories as he wrote them. In a letter dated July 26, Villa discussed the latest batch but was lukewarm in his response to all of them.[41] Perhaps it was not a good batch, for only one of the stories, "The Eager Mechanic," has survived in its original form and under its original title. Possibly Villa's enthusiasm was temporarily dampened by his own physical condition. That month he had fallen ill with a severe cold and hay fever. In addition, he was having trouble with his eyes, necessitating the prescription of glasses. His letter sounded the first death knell for *Clay*. He informed March that although a quarter of the contents of *Clay 4* had been typed, his typist was leaving the campus that week with the ending of the summer term. Villa complained that he just did not have the time or the energy to complete the job himself. Six days later, he confirmed that *Clay 4* would not be published.[42]

By mid-August, however, other plans were afoot. Villa had gone to Los Angeles for a short vacation and made a promising contact with Stanley Rose, the publisher of *Experimental Cinema*, a high-class art magazine with a revolutionary and leftist trend. Rose professed a great interest in *Clay* and hinted that he would like to take over responsibility for its publication, leaving Villa with a completely free hand to continue as editor.[43]

Villa was still optimistic when he wrote again to March on August 22, predicting that *Clay* would be published and that he would have to recall all the manuscripts he had returned.[44] Two days later, he wrote that he would be using "Comfort Me with Apples" and that arrangements had been made to have the magazine printed in Los Angeles.[45] On August 27, he reiterated that he had received further assurance that Rose would publish *Clay*.[46] According to a letter March wrote to Frederick on September 19, Villa was intending to include three of March's stories in the new *Clay*: "Comfort Me with Apples," "Time Has Taken Her," and "Darkness Is over Me." But somehow the arrangement with Rose broke down and *Clay 4* never materialized.

None of the three stories Villa had accepted was ever published. "Comfort Me with Apples," which March described as going back to the Songs of Solomon and "thus establishing me as a modern,"[47] was presumably incorporated into March's third published novel, *The Tallons*. "Time Has Taken Her" was an earlier version of the extant but still unpublished story "The Red Jacket," extensively revised by the author in 1946. "Darkness Is over Me" became the Private Manuel Burt episode of *Company K* and was probably not integrated into the book until the late summer of 1932, after March had failed to place it as a short story.

Another war story March had difficulty in placing during the previous year, "Diseur," originally had some *Company K* connotations, which, after the story was accepted by Johns for *Pagany* in December 1931, March decided to eliminate. He wrote to Johns, asking him to change the title of the piece from "Diseur" to "The American Diseur" and to change the name of the company's captain from "Magee" to "Boyce," adding that if Johns did not like the name "Boyce" to change it to whatever he liked, just so long as it was not "Magee."

Johns accepted another story for *Pagany* the following month. This was "George and Charlie," which March judged the best thing he had done to date, although he conceded that the weight of opinion was against him. Several editors had already rejected it on the grounds that it suggested that the American social structure was "somewhat less than perfect."[48] Both "George and Charlie" and "The American Diseur" (with "Captain Boyce") were published in *Pagany* during 1932.

Although editors may have flinched at March's criticisms of the domestic social structure, many of them, not buttressed by corporate financial support, were unable to escape the stark reality of the current economic situation insofar as it threatened the very existence of their particular publications. When March heard that *Midland* was in financial straits, its future hanging in the balance, he immediately wrote to

Frederick pledging a contribution of up to one hundred dollars to help tide the magazine over its difficulties. He sent the first installment of fifty dollars on January 25, telling Frederick he could have the balance whenever he said the word. He was able to pass on the news that he had just finished the 25,000-word novelette "The Unploughed Patch," which he was intending to submit for a story contest organized by *Scribner's Magazine*, and that he was working on a new story called "I've Baked My Bread," which he thought was a grand title, irrespective of how bad the story itself might be. He was hoping to begin work on another novel in the near future.

By the beginning of May, he had completed four chapters of the new novel, which he had provisionally titled *The Man with a Mark on His Heart*. He thought the temporary title "a little arty" but liked it nevertheless. He planned to write a chapter a week and anticipated that if he maintained that rate of progress he would complete the book in sixteen weeks. His literary output in those first two months of 1932 was truly impressive, for, in addition to the four chapters of the new novel and the completion and revision of the novelette "The Unploughed Patch," he had also written three stories, "The Arrogant Shoat," "Upon the Dull Earth Dwelling" and "Comfort Me with Apples"—and all this had been achieved in spite of the fact, as he continued to complain, that most of his time had been taken up by Waterman customers eager to sample the New York nightlife.

Company K had still not found a home. With Edith Walton's and Granville Hicks's support and recommendation, March had submitted the manuscript to Macmillan. He was still awaiting a decision on March 7, when, in a letter to Hicks, he uncharacteristically revealed his impatience and irritation with the publishing hierarchy. "The poor publishers," he declared, "don't seem to realize that I'm not a refined, thin-skinned arthur who can be rebuffed with a word or reduced to tears with a sentence. After all I'm a freight solicitor: one whose daily bread is earned by being scorned. So let them beware! . . . The bastards!"[49] It may be that he was hoping the message, possibly in less explicit form, might get back to Macmillan via Hicks. It is unlikely that it did, but if it did, it certainly did not have the desired effect. By the time Lois Cole joined the New York editorial staff in mid-June, Macmillan had already rejected the work. It is possible that Macmillan, like the other publishers to whom the book had been submitted, feared that too many war novels had been published in recent years. There was some evidence, to be sure, that the reading public was becoming rather weary of the subject. Coping with the depression was enough without life being further dampened by the revival of old,

painful memories. Moreover, the war book to end all war books, Erich
Maria Remarque's *All Quiet on the Western Front*, had been published
only three years earlier, in 1929, and had seemed at the time a definitive statement, leaving nothing further to be written on the subject, at
least not in the immediate future. In March's view, however, Remarque had not entirely succeeded, for the German author had confined himself mainly to the experiences of one man, the book's first-
person narrator, and had thus presented a far too one-sided, ostensibly
autobiographical picture. March's concept had been to write a book in
which the background of the war, so vividly described in the narratives
of previous writers, could be simply taken for granted, thus allowing
him to concentrate almost exclusively on the *reactions* of men to war.
During the time of his service in the marines, he had been particularly
struck by the diversity of men's reactions under fire and to the general
abnormal conditions under which they lived in the trenches, camps,
and billets. Whereas his own experiences had had a traumatic and
everlasting effect on him, many men, he had been astonished to
observe, regarded their time in the marines merely as another job of
work. He was further shocked to realize that some of them had even
enjoyed it. His aim, therefore, in *Company K* had been to assume the
purely objective role and present all sides of the picture.

In addition to the collection "Sixteen and the Unknown Soldier,"
published that April in *Clay*, March was hoping that other selections
from the *Company K* manuscript would appear in print and help to
persuade some publishing house that the book was a viable commercial proposition. At one time, it seemed that the magazine *Contempo*
was going to take approximately twenty-five of the sketches, but eventually it published only two sketches, in May 1932, under the title
"Two Soldiers." Other groups of sketches were rejected by *Hound and
Horn*, *Midland*, and *Pagany*. Kirstein thought the sketches too accidental and felt that "their general effect, to be cumulative, should either
be placed in a very careful arrangement, or have a thread running
through the whole business."[50] Frederick did not consider the new
group of sketches as good as the one *Midland* had published in 1930.
Johns, also, seemed to think that the sketches could not be presented
as a cohesive whole.

There were to be other disappointments that year, including further
fruitless correspondence with Lambert Davis of *Virginia Quarterly
Review*. Davis returned four stories during the year: "This Heavy
Load," "Comfort Me with Apples" (which he called "a very moving
story"), "Time Has Taken Her," and "The First Sunset." When he
returned "The First Sunset," on December 6, Davis explained to

March that although he liked all the work he had seen, he did not see a place for it in the pages of *Virginia Quarterly Review*. March took the hint, finally admitted defeat, and never again submitted anything to Davis.

Two other stories, "Mrs. Joe Cotton" ("Woolen Drawers") and "A Shop in St. Louis, Missouri" ("The Monument"), suffered the same fate as had the three stories which had been scheduled to appear in *Clay 4*. The two stories had been accepted by William Carlos Williams, editor of the recently revived magazine *Contact*, but were returned when the magazine folded, like *Clay*, after only three issues, its last number coming out in September 1932.

Pagany, too, was nearing the end of its life. In 1932, Johns printed "George and Charlie" and "The American Diseur," and in the fall of that year had three more of March's stories—"The Unploughed Patch," "This Heavy Load," and "Happy Jack"—waiting for future issues. When, however, it became apparent that the magazine was going to have to cease publication and that possibly only one further issue was feasible, John returned two of the stories. He decided he would be doing March the greater service by printing the novelette "The Unploughed Patch"; its length, he felt, would make the work more difficult to place elsewhere than either of the two other stories. Johns showed excellent prescience, for both "Happy Jack" and "This Heavy Load" were fairly quickly accepted, the first appearing in the December 1932 issue of *Story* and the second appearing almost exactly a year later in the December 1933 issue of *Forum*. "The Unploughed Patch," unsuccessful in the *Scribner's Magazine* story contest because of its pathological theme, appeared in the spring of 1933 in the very last issue of *Pagany*.

The fate of *Midland* was also still in the balance. March sent another twenty-five dollars to Frederick on June 2 and on September 19 the final twenty-five of the hundred he had promised. He told Frederick he was willing to send another hundred dollars next year, if it was decided to keep *Midland* going. Frederick, as it happened, had not been particularly sympathetic toward March's more recent work, having rejected during the year not only the new collection of *Company K* sketches March had sent him but also "This Heavy Load," "Time Has Taken Her," "Comfort Me with Apples," and a revised version of "The Monument" ("A Shop in St. Louis, Missouri"), which March had cut by almost one-half. March was especially aggrieved when Frederick did not take "Comfort Me with Apples." In fact, *Midland* took only two of the stories March submitted during 1932: "The Arrogant Shoat," with which Frederick found himself "very much pleased," and "The

Eager Mechanic," which he considered one of the best things March had ever done.

By mid-1932, March was receiving invitations to submit his work to the national magazines, such as *Saturday Evening Post, Collier's* and *Cosmopolitan*, but he turned these offers down, flattering and potentially lucrative though they may have been, for he was determined not to write simply to the commercial formula. He knew what he wanted to write and how he wanted to write, and money was not of prime importance to him in this respect. Integrity was.

There were, accordingly, other compensations. All six stories he published during 1932 were subsequently given three asterisks by Edward J. O'Brien.[51] One of these stories, "Happy Jack," which was considered revolutionary in its treatment of the race problem when it was first published, became in March's eyes a piece of work of which he was inordinately proud. Another story, "Come in at the Door," was accepted by *Story* in September but for some reason was never published in that magazine. It was eventually incorporated into March's second novel, bearing the same title.

For the third year running, March had stories reprinted in the two leading short-story anthologies. Earlier in the year, O'Brien had written to request permission to reprint "Mist on the Meadow," and in June, March was advised that Blanche Colton Williams wanted "Nine Prisoners" for the 1932 O. Henry collection. "Nine Prisoners" received third ranking from the five members of the selection committee, being placed first by one member, second by another, fourth by another, and ninth by the remaining two. The committee member who gave the story first place was Mrs. Frederica Field, editor of *Golden Book*, who maintained that it was "the only one story which attempts to do anything with the short story as a means of expression." The committee member who gave the story fourth place noted perceptibly that "one gets a cumulative effect of horror which the experience of no one man could give."[52]

During the summer of 1932, March spent a short vacation at Martha's Vineyard and made several business trips to Mobile and Tampa. Returning from one such trip in mid-September, he expressed his pleasure at being back in New York after three disagreeable weeks in the South with the temperature consistently about 95 degrees.[53] During this last trip to Mobile, March, John B. Waterman, and Ed Roberts, now executive vice-president of the company, had completed plans for developing the European markets and for opening up offices on the Continent and in London. March, being the company's senior traffic manager, was elected to organize these operations on the spot, initially by setting up offices in the German capital and in Hamburg. He was to project a top-flight image of Waterman, meet all the "right" people, and hire efficient staff who could be relied upon to safeguard the company's interests in his absence: in other words, to establish on an international scale exactly the same sort of network he had created so successfully in the United States during the 1920s. When the offices were working to his satisfaction on the Continent, he was to carry out similar operations in London, where, for the time being, the Waterman European business was being capably handled by Runciman (London) Ltd.

The proposal that March should go to Germany was originally discussed as early as May of that year, and it is clear that he never viewed the prospect of the assignment with overt enthusiasm. He had by now become very much part of the New York literary scene and he was understandably loath to bid farewell to the close circle of friends he had made. He nevertheless began taking French and German lessons but found the learning of foreign languages "pretty tough sailing." He was, however, looking forward to at last meeting Edward J. O'Brien, who had lived in England since 1922 and was now residing in Oxford.

During those summer months, with the impending European trip hanging over him, he made some final revisions to the *Company K* manuscript. It was probably at this stage that he introduced the Private Manuel Burt episode. He also deleted eleven of the original sketches, reducing the total number from 125 to 115. He sent the revised manuscript to Simon and Schuster, apparently for the second time, in mid-August, but the editor, Clifton Fadiman, turned it down again. Although he was himself impressed by the work, Fadiman did not rate it a safe publishing venture at that time. March was by now almost desperate to place *Company K* before he had to go abroad, as planned, in October or November. He sent the manuscript to Harrison Smith and Robert Haas, and on September 19 was able to report some rather more encouraging news about the book to Frederick, intimating that Smith was on the verge of signing a contract. March, however, had experienced too many disappointments in the past to allow himself the luxury of being completely confident about the outcome, and he reminded Frederick that "several [publishers] have been that close before and got away."[54] March's fears on this occasion were not realized. On October 12, he wrote to Frederick to tell him that Harrison Smith had taken *Company K*, subject to confirmation that all the material in the book was free to be used. Frederick immediately provided the required written permission for the material published in *Midland*, as, presumably, did the other editors concerned, and the contract for the book was signed on October 16. It was something of an act of faith on Smith's part. He had no great confidence that the book would sell, an opinion that the author himself was beginning to share. March hoped that the first printing of 1,000 copies would sell out and urged Frederick, if he could do so, to mention the book's forthcoming publication in the pages of *Midland*.

A little more than five weeks after the contract for *Company K* had been signed, March sailed for Hamburg on the SS *President Harding*. He had delayed leaving America as long as he possibly could, and his unhappy frame of mind on the eve of his departure is evident in the letter he wrote to Granville Hicks on November 22: "I bitterly regret to advise you that I am sailing tomorrow. . . . I got your letter Saturday and meant to answer it immediately but got drunk instead."[55]

When he embarked the following day, he carried with him several letters of introduction, including one from Lincoln Kirstein to the American consul in Hamburg, Alan Steyne, Kirstein's first cousin. Despite all his misgivings, March seems to have settled down fairly quickly in "furrin climes," as he often referred to them in his correspondence. He met Steyne and found him very pleasant and intelligent. After staying for a short time at the Atlantic Hotel in Hamburg, he obtained living accommodations at Mundsburgerdamm 24 and established a Waterman office at Alsterthor 21, overlooking the Alster.

His publishers wrote to him on January 5, 1933, wishing him a happy new year and informing him that copies of *Company K* were now in from the bindery and that two of the six free copies he was entitled to under the terms of the contract were being sent to him. They expressed continuing enthusiasm for the book and assured him that in spite of the current "slow days" in the publishing trade they were doing everything in their power to see that *Company K* received as good a chance as possible. The dust jacket was to bear a glowing testimonial from the author and critic Christopher Morley, who regarded it as one of "the few great cries of protest."

One can imagine March's growing excitement now that the publication of his book was so imminent and his feelings of frustration at being so far away in Germany. He asked that the remaining four of his six free copies be sent to his mother, his sister Margaret, Edward J. O'Brien, and Margaret Deland.

On January 13, he reported to Smith and Haas that he was already one-third of the way through a new novel, tentatively titled *Come in at the Door*, which he had begun the previous October. The book was a reworking of material contained in "The History of a Tic," "The Man with a Mark on His Heart," and "Come in at the Door," all of which he had several times before attempted to meld into a full-length work. His preoccupation with business matters, which at this stage were requiring his immediate attention at all levels, had, he told his publishers, prevented him from doing any work on the new book in recent weeks, but he hoped soon to be in a position to return to it in earnest. He estimated that he needed another three or four months to finish it.[56]

Company K was published in New York six days later, on January 19, 1933. It contained the simple dedication: "To Ed Roberts An Unchanging Friend."

five

Company K and
Hitler's Germany

The published version of *Company K* contains only 113 of the 115 sketches in the manuscript March submitted to his publishers. According to Lincoln Kirstein, several episodes were not included because of their sexual content, and it seems safe to speculate that this was the reason for the omission of two of the original sketches.[1]

A skeleton history of the fictional Company K's war exploits, indicating how similar they were to those of the company March actually served with, is provided in the novel by Corporal Stephen Waller, the company clerk, the same post, indeed, that March himself held in the Forty-third Company, Fifth Regiment, U.S. Marines:

> Company K went into action at 10:15 P.M. December 12th, 1917, at Verdun, France, and ceased fighting on the morning of November 11th, 1918, near Bourmont, having crossed the Meuse River the night before under shell fire; participating, during the period set out above, in the following major operations: Aisne, Aisne-Marne, St. Mihiel and Meuse-Argonne. . . . The percentage of casualties in killed, wounded in action, missing or evacuated to hospital suffering from disease, was considerably higher than average (332.8) percent. [*CK*, p. 184]

While this sparse, official, communique-like statement traces the factual combat history of the company, the other 112 sections, varying in length from a mere nine lines[2] to ten pages,[3] provide an emotional history of the men of the company, extending beyond the boundaries of the war itself.

At the time of publication, most critics and reviewers accepted the book's episodic structure as a valid and potent literary techique. But some reviewers, the British novelist L. P. Hartley among them, were

68

disturbed by it. Hartley declared: "Looked at from the aesthetic standpoint *Company K* has this defect: the individual pieces are so short, and often have so little relation to those that precede and follow them, that they give no impression of continuity. The book is a collection of fragments."[4] It was, of course, a criticism March had already encountered several times before in his endeavors to get various groups of the sketches published in magazines.

In fact, considering the manner of its rather piecemeal composition, *Company K* is in many respects a superbly ordered book. Despite the apparent looseness of its construction, it possesses an underlying density and unity. Interrelating thematic threads weave their courses in and out of the individual narratives, linking them and knitting the whole into a structure of remarkable tensile strength. The deliberately pithy style succeeds in saying more in 250 or so pages than is normally said in a volume three or four times that length. A considerable achievement for a first novel, its power surely could have been attained, in the final analysis, only by the most selective and persevering distillation.

Of all the episodes, the one which gives the most eloquent thematic shape to the book is that which tells of the inhuman execution of the German prisoners. Although the specific thesis at the root of this episode, uttered by Private Walter Drury, "We're prisoners too: We're all prisoners" (*CK*, p. 129), made explicit in the original *Forum* "Nine Prisoners" text, has inevitably been dissipated by scattering the nine first-person narratives throughout the length of the book, the impact of the concept is so powerful that it is not entirely lost. The men who are involved in the killing of the unarmed prisoners become, through an irredeemable sense of guilt arising from the remembered horror of the crime they had committed, prisoners of the deed itself.

As March horrifyingly illustrates in the Sergeant Marvin Mooney section, many of the men in the company are so susceptible to and have become so conditioned by the accomplished art of the war propagandists that they have been persuaded to cast logic and reason aside, enabling them to find, temporarily at least, justification for their actions. Even counter-accusations can be summarily and angrily dismissed, for, as everyone knows, atrocities are committed only by the enemy. The "fat little German boy" captured by Glass, Brauer, and Mumford tells them he would "rather be killed outright than taken prisoner, because the Americans chopped off the hands and feet of all their prisoners." Bernie Glass is incensed by this: "Well, the dirty little louse, . . . to say a thing like that when everybody knows it's the *Germans*, and not ourselves who do those things. Christ Almighty, that's what I call crust!" But the domination of propaganda over men's minds *does* work both ways, *does* know no logical or reasonable boundaries. When, in jest, the Americans tell the terrified boy that they are intending to carve their initials on his belly, the German is convinced they are in deadly earnest. As Jakie Brauer reaches forward to unbuckle the prisoner's *Gott Mitt Uns* belt he covets as a souvenir, the uncomprehending German, in a gesture of final panicking desperation, slashes Jakie's throat with a trench knife (*CK*, pp. 78–79).

The ultimate evil of war propaganda on the receptive minds of the opposing combatants is perhaps most fully epitomized in the section narrated by Private Manuel Burt, which, as has already been noted, was originally conceived as a separate short story, "Darkness Is over Me," and becomes the second longest section in the book. There is a certain air of the theater about Burt's story, which, in a strange sort of way, serves to heighten the poignancy of it all. The reader is left in no doubt whatsoever that here March the humanitarian is writing truly from the heart, and—with some changes of detail—from personal experience, in endeavoring to express unequivocally all his bitter thoughts and raging emotions on the subject.

The war is within weeks of its ending. March pinpoints the date: October 2, 1918. The company is occupying a reserve line and Burt is ordered by Lieutenant Fairbrother to carry some reports back to regimental headquarters. The detail is not without its obvious hazards. The route back to regimental headquarters lies through a wood frequently patrolled by the enemy. Before he sets out, Burt is instructed by the near-hysterical Fairbrother to fix his bayonet. As he proceeds through the wood, he encounters a young German soldier, sitting against a tree, eating bread. The German sees Burt also, and for a moment they stare at each other, neither quite knowing what to do. Burt observes: "He had brown eyes, . . . and golden brown skin, almost the color of an orange. His lips were full, and very red, and he was trying to grow a mustache. It was dark brown, as fine as corn-silk, but it hadn't come out evenly on his lip" (*CK*, p. 247). It is very nearly a lover's description. "Then," says Burt, "I remembered what they had told us in training camp about Germans, and I began to get sore at him. I could see that he was getting sore, too" (*CK*, pp. 247–48).

There is an exchange of fire, and the German is hit. As he tries to raise himself from the ground and defend himself with his trench knife, Burt bayonets him under the chin, through his mouth and into his brain. Burt finds himself unable to withdraw the bayonet from the transfixed body, even though he resorts to the expediency of putting his foot on the dead German's face to give himself better leverage. He is eventually obliged to unsnap the bayonet from the rifle. He reaches regimental headquarters, and, later, returning through the wood, endeavors once more to extricate the bayonet from the body. He is again unsuccessful. On an impulse, he removes a ring from the dead German's finger to keep as a souvenir of the first man he has ever killed, but before he arrives back at the company lines he experiences a twinge of atavistic fear and throws the ring away into the undergrowth.

Back home after the war, Burt finds himself haunted by the memory of the man he killed. He imagines that the ring is still on his finger and that he cannot remove it. The German invades his dreams, pleading with him to take the bayonet out of his brain. He discovers that no matter what he does, no matter where he goes or tries to hide, the spirit of the dead man is not to be shaken off. "Why did you kill me? . . . Why did you want to do that?" the German asks. Burt replies: "I wouldn't do it again! . . . Before God, I wouldn't!" The German continues: "All we know is that life is sweet and that it does not last long. Why should people be envious of each other? Why do we hate each other? Why can't we live at peace in a world that is so beautiful and so wide?" Burt in the agony of his remorse and the remembered horror of what he had done, like all sensitive and thinking men freed from the immediate mental conditioning of war propaganda and thus bereft of the spurious justification for their deeds, gives the only response it is possible to give: "I don't know . . . I can't answer your questions..." (*CK*, pp. 252–53). Burt's obsession finally, inevitably, spills over into madness.

The question must be posed: To what extent is *Company K* as a whole based on fact? March maintained that the book was not autobiographical, but there is no denying that there are many real-life parallels between the fictional company and the company in which March served with distinction during the year 1918. When Clint Bolton asked March if any of his old marine buddies contacted him after the book's publication, March told him: "A couple wrote me in care of the publisher, wanting to know if this or that person was So-and-so. . . . I never answered their letters. What good would it do? I would only get involved in needless correspondence."[5]

There is no doubt that for March the gradual composition of *Company K* was in some part an exercise in self-therapy. The writing of the book did not, however, result in the complete eradication of the scars the war had ingrained in his mind. Dr. Edward Glover has recalled that during his analysis March

would occasionally give you a *Company K* reminiscence, but it wasn't a dominating feature. . . . His reaction to the war was, "What do you expect of life?" It wasn't cynical exactly. It was as if he said, "I know the worst. It's unprintable, but there it is." He filtered these disillusioned convictions through the osmotic filter of literary activity, combining it, however, with creative and reparative impulse.[6]

Although March was already thirty-nine at the time of the publication of *Company K* and despite the almost unanimous acclaim with which the book was greeted on its appearance, it is in many ways an apprentice work. A certain stiltedness about some of the dialogue and passages of too-perfect syntax give the prose a degree of lifelessness. The style is, indeed, for the most part unremarkable. Individually, some of the episodes are difficult to accept, and in the aggregate March tends to overstate his case, producing—despite his avowed intentions—a somewhat one-sided and oversimplified view of the soldier's existence and his reactions to the exceptional circumstances of war. Just over one-third of the 132 named characters in the book are either wounded, killed, commit suicide, or suffer mental breakdowns of varying severity. Truly, as the anonymous soldier in the London Independent Television program "Warrior," broadcast on November 11, 1975, declared: "War is a study of extreme situations." For all that, the war could not have been—indeed, surely was not—so consistently intense and dark an experience for the overwhelming majority of the marines in France as it is shown to be in this book. It is to this extent that March does not accomplish his plan of being the authorial disinterested bystander, presenting all sides of the picture. The book does not adopt the objective viewpoint at all but very much imposes, as it was bound to do, the subjective one.

Nevertheless, the book's virtues far outweigh its faults. *Company K* is a minor masterpiece. It is certainly one of the most considerable works of art to have emerged from the holocaust of World War I: one writer's lasting and virulent indictment of "men, and their unending cruelty to each other" (*CK*, p. 16). Not without justification, March was able to say more than once to friends during the last years of his life: "*Company K* has become a classic in my lifetime."[7]

A week to the day after *Company K* was published, Robert Haas wrote to March, reporting that the book had received a "remarkable press" and, by way of confirmation, enclosed copies of the reviews that had come out to date. Haas added that although the advance sale had been very small, every effort was being made to stimulate sales. All the indications were that the book was catching on, and preparations were well under way to bring out a second printing.[8]

Several reviewers referred to the book as "the *Spoon River Anthology* of the trenches." The *University of Alabama Alumni News* hailed it as the "Book of the Year." Other reviewers pointed out that, compared with *Company K*, Remarque's *All Quiet on the Western Front* seemed "comparatively gentle" or "almost idyllic." Arthur Ruhl in the *Saturday Review of Literature* obviously thought so, too, and consequently had certain misgivings:

> The author's freedom . . . to pile horror on horror, cynicism on cynicism, ends by leaving one with a sense of that "too much" which defeats itself. Of routine romanticism there is, indeed, no trace; but the continuous heaping up of bitterness and irony without any of the compensatory elements which were there, also, in life results in a sort of reverse-romanticism, so to say, in an overemphasis which is also false.[9]

At the end of the month, Harrison Smith wrote to express his delight at the extremely favorable reviews the book had elicited. He informed March that sales were bigger than anyone had dared to hope "in these tough days."[10] The publishers had surely taken a calculated gamble, for, as everyone concerned had known all too well, the war novel had virtually exhausted its readership potential by the time March's book came out. One weary critic had even gone so far as to pronounce that it would be preferable to fight another war than to have to read another war book. Ironically enough, this despairing expression of war-fiction weariness almost exactly coincided with the advent of Hitler's accession to power in Germany, which, as the world was to discover, was ultimately and inevitably to lead the isolationist-inclined American nation of the 1920s and 1930s into sending her young men again to be killed and maimed in a European war.

For most of America in 1933, however, war was essentially part of history, albeit recent history, and not part of a threatening future. There were domestic problems enough to cope with: the aftermath of the stock market crash, the depression and widespread unemployment, Prohibition, the cancer of gangsterism in the big cities, the Red menace in the labor unions, corruption in public office. Everything considered, the success of *Company K* seems all the more remarkable.

There were, of course, the usual dissenters. *The Catholic World* found five or six pages "so gratuitously coarse as to unfit the book for general circulation."[11] In his letter of January 31, Harrison Smith mentioned that Robert Haas had sent copies of the book to several friends and had received some "interesting" letters concerning it. Other letters had been received from a pacifist society and from readers raising again the old objection to the episode of the execution of the German prisoners, that it could not have happened. Smith asked March if he could quote chapter and verse in relation to an actual incident where such a thing did happen. March refused to be drawn, referring Smith to the conversation between Joseph Delaney and his wife in the very first section of the book, which leaves the question of whether or not the prisoners were actually shot as a matter of little importance. March felt it was better that there be no attempt by him or his publishers to prove or justify any of the material in the book, as this might involve living persons and be more than a little embarrassing, in more ways than one, to all concerned.

One further matter was troubling Harrison Smith. Several reviewers had pointed out that although March had undoubtedly killed Captain Matlock on page 157, when he is hit between the eyes by a machine-gun bullet during an advance through a wheatfield, Matlock makes another appearance after the war on page 257 when Yeomans meets him and invites him and Mrs. Matlock over to dinner one evening. Harrison agreed that to have Yeomans invite someone other than Matlock to dinner would destroy the whole ironic point of that particular section and suggested that it be implied that Rickey (who is the one who records having seen Matlock fall in battle) had been mistaken in thinking that the officer who had been hit was Matlock.

March confirmed that he had no intention at all of killing Matlock, and wrote Smith telling him that he knew of a man who had suffered the same wound Matlock had received and was still alive, well and happy. He was not, however, greatly concerned if Smith's proposed amendments were made to the Rickey section, and he left it open to the publishers to decide finally whether or not to revise the text for the next printing. Smith did, in fact, incorporate the changes in the third and last printing of the first edition, issued that February, but all subsequent editions of the book, including all British editions, reverted to March's original text.[12]

By February 28, the publishers were able to report that sales had reached 3,000 and that by further advertising it was hoped that an eventual sales figure of at least 5,000 would be attained. March, naturally, was impressed and extremely pleased by the praise *Company K* had received and despite his heavy business commitments in Germany was encouraged to press on as swiftly as possible with work on the new book. At the beginning of February, he reported to Robert Haas that he had completed approximately 170 pages, or about one-half of the book. With the prospect of more time becoming available to him in the weeks ahead, he anticipated finishing the book toward the end of April or May.[13] By the end of the month, however, when he wrote to Harrison Smith, it seemed that very little further progress had been achieved during the intervening weeks. He still referred to the book as being only half-completed, and he indicated that he would need to rework all the material considerably before he would be satisfied with it.[14]

In the meantime, Smith had been able to pass on the welcome news that *Company K* had been accepted by the London publishing house of Victor Gollancz, Ltd. Gollancz, socialist, humanitarian, and founder (in 1936) of the influential Left Book Club, found the novel the only completely truthful war book he had ever read.[15] Although he assured March's British literary agents, Hughes Massie, Ltd., that he would promote the book as energetically as possible, he expressed his fear that it was so horrible and so devoid of the saving grace of false idealism that the public would recoil from it.[16] The contract for the book was signed on February 14, and *Company K*, in one of Gollancz's distinctive yellow dust jackets, was published in London on March 20, 1933.

The British reviews were, on the whole, equally as enthusiastic as the American ones. Phyllis Bentley, writing in the *Evening Chronicle*, called the book "one of the most poignant and significant war novels yet written."[17] Miss E. M. Delafield noted: "*Company K* contains some almost unbearable things, and the author has recorded them with iron courage and sincerity."[18] Gerald Gould was another of those reviewers who admitted to being a sufferer from a surfeit of war literature: "There have been many moving war-books: so many, that anybody who has read a large proportion of them may be excused if they sometimes get tangled in his memory. The questions to ask about a new one are: 'Does it stand out? Will it remain?' In this case, for my own part, I should answer strongly in the affirmative."[19] H. L. Morrow wrote: "*Company K* is a masterpiece about which I can safely say that no critic who lavishes praise on it today will be ashamed of his ecstasies when he comes to re-read them in cold print three or four years hence. . . . There are pages that ought never to have been published for the sheer cruelty they contain."[20] Eric Gillett in *Time and Tide* was one of the very few who were completely hostile toward the book: "As a work of literary art, the book is negligible. Some of the incidents are really well told, graphic, and gratifying in themselves, but, as a whole, the book is of little consequence, and is both sensational and morbid."[21]

On April 4, Gollancz sent March some extracts from the British reviews and, while reporting that the book had not commanded a great sale so far, noted that it had scored an undoubted *succes d'estime*.

Gollancz repeated his conviction that to ensure the sale of a war book, the work had to contain a generous amount of false idealism. He assured March that in his opinion *Company K* was the best war book yet written and pointed out that most reviewers were clearly in complete agreement with his view. He promised the author a full set of review clippings, and these he was able to send over to Germany on May 15.

March's business activities continued to occupy most of his time during this period, preventing him from doing any substantial work on the new book. Despite his desire to pursue with all his energies his increasingly successful literary career and to consolidate his position as a contemporary author of note, he did not allow himself to overlook his first loyalties. With his proven application and drive, he was establishing a solid foundation on which an expanding Waterman interest in Europe could be based.

A few weeks after arriving in Hamburg, March sent John B. Waterman a picture postcard of the Hamburg waterfront, indicating the location of the Waterman office at Alsterthor 21. He hoped that John B. was maintaining progress so far as his health was concerned, and he referred to the "exciting times" they were all living through at the present.

This euphemism "exciting times" was March's cautious way of describing the situation of explosive political unrest and accumulating uncertainty he had discovered on his arrival in Germany. The U.S. presidential election had been decided on November 8, only a fortnight before he sailed for Europe, with Franklin D. Roosevelt, the former assistant secretary of the navy who had inspected the Fifth Marine Regiment at Vandouvre fourteen years before, achieving a Democratic landslide victory of 472 electoral votes against the Republican Herbert Hoover's 59 votes. In the four months between November 8 and March 4 the following year, when Roosevelt delivered his famous inauguration speech, warning the American nation that "the only thing we have to fear is fear itself," Germany had seen three separate governments: those of Franz von Papen, General K. von Schleicher, and (on January 30) Adolf Hitler. On February 27, the Reichstag went up in flames, and Hitler, as chancellor of Germany, denounced the fire as a Communist plot and suspended civil liberties and the freedom of the press.

In a letter to John B. on February 18, March confined himself to expressing the pleasure he felt at the news he had received recently via one of the Waterman captains of his chief's apparent restoration to full health, and he commented again on John B.'s fortitude in bearing his ills of the past several months so bravely. He mentioned the new secretary he had hired, a Miss Blumenfeld, who fortunately was not only intelligent but beautiful as well, and reported on his increasing prowess in mastering the convoluted syntax of German grammar.[23] The letter made no reference to the disturbing political situation in Germany, although March was too perceptive a being not to have appreciated the extremely dangerous, and predictable, turn that events were so rapidly and inexorably taking.

The situation back home in America seemed almost as precarious. Harrison Smith wrote to March the following month: "As you've heard the banks are closed and after they open we will have to live on scrip issued by the clearing house. Just now everyone is hanging onto their nickels and dimes. We've been the prodigal son among nations and I don't suppose we'll get much sympathy abroad."[24]

On March 5, in the last democratic election to be held in Germany during Hitler's lifetime, the Nazis won 288 of the 615 seats in the Reichstag, not enough to provide them with an overall majority but sufficient apparently to engineer the passing of the Enabling Act on March 23, granting Hitler dictatorial powers for a period of four years.

On the very day that the Enabling Act was passed, March wrote Ed Roberts an extended letter, in which he reported in depth on the current political and economic scene in Germany. He compared the Nazi party to the Ku Klux Klan in America, in that they both advocated extreme policies of nationalism. Hitler, he considered, was "probably one of the greatest orators of our days," and he credited Hitler's persuasive speeches as being the mainspring of the Nazis' success. He noted the beginnings of the persecution of the Jews, the banning of all Russian and American music, the establishment of the first concentration camps. While, of course, condemning by implication these manifestations of newly acquired total power—the letter is, in a way, a model of guarded objectivity—March rather naively suggested that in time these extreme measures would adjust themselves to a more acceptable norm. The business world, which was naturally his main consideration, had been disrupted to a certain degree but no more than one would expect on the coming to power of a new administration. He predicted that within a few months the situation would improve.[25]

Reading the letter, one is especially conscious of the fact that here and there March is taking the greatest possible care in his choice of words. Possibly he was not altogether sure of the ultimate loyalties of his new secretary, the beautiful Miss Blumenfeld, and he may have suspected that because of his status as a nonnational in this suddenly most nationalistic of countries, there was the constant danger of his mail being opened and examined by the government censor. He obviously saw little point in making unnecessarily rash statements regarding the new regime and the present trend of events.

If there had been any doubt in some people's minds at the time of the resolved intent of the Nazis, the countrywide boycott of all Jewish businesses and professions on April 1, the suppression of the trade unions on May 2, the infamous "burning of the books" on May 10, and the suppression of all other German political parties on May 28 soon made it crystal clear to one and all that the Nazis meant business and that democracy in the Fatherland was a thing of the past. The burning of the books, in particular, must have given March much pause for thought. Among the books flung on the flaming pyre in the Unter den Linden opposite the University of Berlin were Remarque's *All Quiet on the Western Front* and Arnold Zweig's *The Case of Sergeant Grischa*, two World War masterpieces to which his own *Company K* had been most frequently compared. He must have felt himself in an unenviable position, knowing that the Nazis were almost certainly aware of who he was. Copies of the book had been sent to him by both his New York and London publishers. The official censors would have been left in no doubt whatsoever that he was the author of the recently published and widely acclaimed pacifist war novel.

In a further letter to Ed Roberts at the end of May, March again conveyed, without making any explicit statement, the general atmosphere of unease and, in the case of many people, justified fear, which was already spreading under the Nazi regime, together with the growing sense of distrust which was being generated between one person and another, even between the individual members of the same family.[26]

If, however, the businessman William Campbell was careful to "express an opinion to no one" and to "discuss politics with no one," excusing himself by maintaining that what was happening was none of his business, the author William March felt no such constraint. In the short story he wrote about this time, he put down on paper some of his true feelings about the events he was witnessing and in which, inevitably, he found himself from time to time so closely involved. This story, "Personal Letter" (originally titled "Letter from Germany"), was not published until 1945, when March included it in the collection *Trial Balance*. One of the few really political pieces he ever wrote, it is loosely based on his March 23 letter to Ed Roberts and, as its title suggests, itself takes the form of a letter, datelined "Hamburg, Germany/December 17th, 1932," from a Robert B. McIntosh to the president of his company, Mr. Tyler. The letter, supplementing the "long, official letter" which McIntosh had mailed the previous week, is in response to Mr. Tyler's request for a private report of McIntosh's personal impressions of the country. McIntosh writes that he considers the most effective way of achieving this is by simply recounting an incident that had happened to him a few days earlier. He had been the guest for dinner and at the opera of a certain Herr Voelker, "an intelligent and highly educated man" according to McIntosh, who is the director of an agency Tyler is hoping will represent the company's business in Germany. After the opera, the two men visit a beer cellar. The place is crowded with storm troopers, several of whom apparently take exception to the fact that the two businessmen are discussing their affairs in English. The leader of the storm troopers informs McIntosh in no uncertain terms that when in Germany he should speak German or not speak at all. McIntosh takes offense at what he naturally enough regards as the man's impudence, but the storm trooper angrily repeats his demands, telling him that the German people will take no more insults from foreigners. McIntosh is so taken aback by this outrageous and ludicrous outburst that he begins to suspect that it is all part of an elaborate joke devised, for some obscure reason, by his host, Herr Voelker. He decides to play along with it and, assuming a mock-seriousness, berates the storm troopers for not being true Germans, in that they had failed to appreciate that, being an American, he is intellectually inferior to them, and that rather than humiliating him in front of his friends, they should make it their duty to instruct him, not only in their language but also in their superior way of life. Feeling smugly contented that, in the context of the joke situation, he has given as good as he has received, McIntosh accepts the apologies of the leader of the storm troopers, and they all end up buying each other drinks. Expecting that at any moment the whole charade will be brought to an end amid laughter and congenial back-slapping, McIntosh becomes gradually more and more uneasy as he begins to realize that they have all taken his words to heart and that the storm trooper had indeed been in deadly earnest when he delivered his initial tirade. McIntosh is even more astonished and frightened when he realizes that Herr Voelker, that "intelligent, educated man," has also taken his words extremely seriously, even to the degree of telling McIntosh: "Every point you made was logical and entirely true." It is then that McIntosh experiences an icy hand clutching at his heart, instinctively aware, perhaps without being able to put it into so many words, of the threat that the nationalistic consciousness of these people poses not only for the unfortunate, less-favored of German nationals themselves but also for the rest of the world.[27]

March's purpose in keeping the story under wraps until 1945 surely could not have stemmed from any fear he may have entertained of reprisals at the hands of the storm troopers he had so effectively satirized. As a foreign national temporarily resident in Germany, there should have been little chance of his personal safety being threatened, yet the thought conceivably hovered at the back of his mind, and understandably so. He would have had no illusions about the ruthlessness of the new regime in arresting and deporting anyone who sought to oppose or ridicule it. As the author of *Company K*, he was perhaps already a marked man, listed in some bulky bureaucratic file as a potentially undesirable alien, and he could be by no means certain how secure his position would be if it came to the crunch. He was not frightened of the Nazi bullies: he simply did not trust them and saw no virtue in antagonizing them after being in their country for so short a time, the job he had come to do barely off the ground.

It is far more likely that he feared that the story might cause embarrassment, or worse, to the many friends, acquaintances, and business associates he had in Germany. Also, and possibly above everything else, he would have had the interests of the Waterman Steamship Corporation very much in mind. He was not only an employee and representative of the company, he was also one of its principal officers and stockholders, and he would have been well aware that the Nazis could make things difficult for Waterman if they felt so inclined. March would have made loyalty to the company a matter of prime consideration in a situation such as this.

Even while notching up some fair amount of success in avoiding the personal complications that could arise following an inadvertent lapse in diplomacy or the uttering of an ill-advised comment against the state, he was continuing to find business life in Germany difficult enough. It was a period of worldwide uncertainty in shipping, mainly brought about by the fluctuating dollar. He was obliged to attend many freight conferences designed to stabilize freight rates. In addition to these international problems, new rules and regulations were issued in Germany as, during the course of the year, Hitler gradually acquired more and more power. Most of these new regulations had the intended effect of diverting cargoes from foreign bottoms to the bottoms of the reviving German marine. Such developments resulted in the sudden cancellations of contracts and charters entered into weeks, or even months, earlier. The international shipping community was obliged to exist on a shifting day-to-day basis, and the utmost care was necessary in all dealings.

During all these uncertain and confusing times, however, and despite all the business pressures that must have been upon him, March was proceeding with work on the new novel. He was also contemplating the possibility of preparing a volume of short stories. He wrote to his publishers on April 29, asking them if they would be interested in bringing out such a book, say, that coming fall, followed by the new novel in the spring of 1934. He reminded them that they had published two volumes of short stories by Kay Boyle (*Wedding Day and Other Stories* in 1930 and *The First Lover and Other Stories* in 1933) and so assumed that short stories were not the complete loss publishers always tried to make them out to be.[28]

March had by now produced sufficient short stories to form an extremely impressive collection. Four more stories were published in 1933.[29] Each of the four stories he had published during the previous year in the eight months from May 1 to December 31, 1932, received a three-asterisk rating in O'Brien's listing in *The Best Short Stories of 1933*.[30] None of his stories was actually reprinted in the O'Brien or O. Henry anthologies for 1933, but "Happy Jack" was selected by Whit Burnett and Martha Foley for inclusion in *A Story Anthology 1931–1933*, which collected the cream of the work appearing in *Story* during those years.

By the end of June, the Nazis had consolidated their position in Germany to such a degree that they had attained virtually absolute power. Nothing now could overthrow them, but to make completely sure of their inviolability they finally banned all other political parties on July 14.

March enjoyed a brief respite from the oppressive atmosphere of Hitler's Germany when he made a trip home to America in August to consult with his Waterman colleagues in Mobile. He took the opportunity to spend a few days in New York, visiting his old friends, and he was saddened to hear confirmatory news of the demise of both *Pagany* and *Midland* earlier that year. He returned to the turmoil of Germany with considerable regret. The letters he wrote in the fall of 1933 express again and again the hope that within a few more months he might be back in America for good.

On October 14, Hitler announced Germany's intention to withdraw from the Disarmament Conference and the League of Nations. A plebiscite would be held in Germany the following month to obtain popular support for this action, combined with a single-party election of the Nazis. The plebiscite and election were held on November 12. Of the 96 percent of voters who registered their vote, 95 percent agreed with the decision to withdraw from the league, and 92 percent supported the Nazi party. The writing was plainly on the wall for all to see.

Seven days after the announcement of Germany's proposed withdrawal from the league, March wrote to his publishers, telling them that he had at last completed the new novel and would be mailing it aboard the SS *Manhattan*, due to sail from Hamburg on October 27. He asked them if they would check whether or not the Negro song from which he had taken his title, *Come in at the Door*, was copyrighted. If it was, then the four lines he had quoted on page 119 of his manuscript should be deleted. He admitted to being, in any case, not altogether sure he had quoted the lines correctly, relying on his memory from childhood days. He expressed the wish not to see any proofs if it was decided to accept the book for publication. The book was now written exactly as he wanted it and he felt he could not improve upon it. He admitted that it had turned out a somewhat longer book than the 80,000-word novel he had planned.[31] Smith and Haas notified him on November 8 of the manuscript's safe arrival in New York. The publishers made a quick decision, for on December 2 March wrote to them saying he had been pleased to receive that day a note from his agents, Curtis Brown, advising him that the book had been accepted. Encouraged once again by the response his work had received, he added that he was already at work on a third novel.[32]

Two days before Christmas, Smith and Haas assured March by letter that the quotation posed no copyright difficulties: it was, in fact, from an old Negro spiritual, which as such could not be properly ascribed to anybody. They suggested that the quotation be simply identified as "Negro Spiritual" and that rather than breaking up the text of the book itself with an attribution, the quotation be reproduced again, with its attribution, on a separate page of its own, either facing the title page or following the dedication page. The publishers expressed their immense enthusiasm for the book and said that they were looking forward to being able to promote it through their own recently established sales department.[33]

March escaped again for a few days from Germany to spend Christmas that year in Paris, where, as he put it, he learned more of the "abstruse" facts of life. He was back in Hamburg before New Year's Day.

The contract for *Come in at the Door* was signed on January 8, and the following day Smith and Haas advised March that the book was being scheduled for publication on the nineteenth of the next month. Louise Bonino, champing at the bit to justify the existence of the company's newly formed sales department, requested the names of any towns or cities in the South, especially in Alabama, where the author was well known or had friends or relatives who could be counted on to help along initial sales of the book. She also asked for a list of special reviewers to whom advance copies should be sent to enable them to "set the town talking."[34]

Come in at the Door was published, as planned, on February 19, 1934. It was dedicated to the author's mother, Susy March Campbell, "with much affection."

six

Come in at the Door
and Escape to London

In his Pearl County stories and novels, March created an apocryphal world comparable to Faulkner's Yoknapatawpha County, and he peopled it with a cast of characters who, because of their basic ordinariness, are in the final analysis more believable than Faulkner's rather larger-than-life Sartorises, Compsons, Snopeses, and McCaslins. In the same way that Faulkner's fictive county seat of Jefferson was modeled on the actual county seat of Oxford, Mississippi, in March's country of the imagination Lockhart becomes Hodgetown and Mobile becomes Baycity, while his memories of small county seats in southern Alabama, such as Andalusia, Evergreen, and Monroeville, form the basis of the fictitious Reedyville.

Like Faulkner, March also intended originally to write an ambitious series of books in which minor characters in one book would reappear as principal characters in another, so that the whole project would become not so much a chronicle of a family but the chronicle of an entire community, with Chester Hurry, the "hero" of *Come in at the Door*, being the overall unifying factor and becoming again the principal character in the final volume of the series. March eventually abandoned the idea as being somewhat pretentious, but probably his overriding reason was his preference for working on a small scale. Vestiges of the grand design can be clearly traced in the work he did complete and publish. The same characters appear again and again in the Pearl County short stories, sometimes in subordinate, sometimes in leading roles. The same applies to the Pearl County novels. For instance, the two Tallon boys, Andrew and Jim, who appear as minor characters in *Come in at the Door*, become the principal protagonists in March's next novel, *The Tallons*, while certain members of Reedyville society, mentioned almost in passing in *Come in at the Door*, play

84

leading parts in his most accomplished full-length work, the 1943 novel
The Looking-Glass.

While *Come in at the Door* is a complete work, perfectly capable of
standing on its own, it must also be regarded as no more than a
component part of an unrealized project. Any judgment of it must be
tempered by such consideration. The "Whisperer" sections which
appear in *Come in at the Door* were originally intended by March to be
part of the unifying structure of the series of novels he had planned,
each Whisperer story illustrating the specific theme of each individual
book.[1] The Whisperer stories were conceived as Chester Hurry's fantasies at various times during the course of his life, several of them, by
definition, being related by Chester or conjured up in his imagination
some time after that period of his life covered by the narrative in *Come
in at the Door*. Not altogether surprisingly, at the time of the book's
publication, most critics and reviewers, unaware of the grand design of
March's original concept, misunderstood the relevance of the Whisperer stories. Indeed, it would have been remarkable if they had
understood. One must suppose that March retained the Whisperer
stories in *Come in at the Door* because at the time the book was
published he still entertained the idea of completing the series of
books. Had the project been completed, the purpose and significance
of the Whisperer episodes would have become clear. As it is, they
serve merely to confuse a close reading of the novel, for there are
obvious dangers in attempting to relate in any definitive manner the
specific theme of each episode to the events described in *Come in at
the Door* alone. On the other hand, the themes of the Whisperer
stories are, in themselves, so universal that such attempted pairing off
can be shown, sometimes vaguely, sometimes too obviously, to buttress or emphasize some of the novel's secondary themes. If nothing
more, they reflect in a very revealing way the author's own bitter,
cynical, ironic, and frequently whimsical view of the human condition,
consequently clarifying the underlying subtleties of the work as a
whole.

The Whisperer sections are, in their own right, impressive little
fables, precursors of that particular literary form which was to occupy
so much of March's creative energies in later life. There are ten
Whisperer stories, all told: nine in separate sections dotted throughout
the book, the tenth forming part of chapter 16, when Chester, during a
flight of fancy, meets the Whisperer himself in Bushrod's wood. Indeed, the clue to the identity of the Whisperer—simply a figment of
Chester's imagination—is contained in this chapter.

These little stories tell of the arrogance of the young in their conviction that nothing can ever destroy the love they have for each other, and of the arrogance of the old who endeavor to deny the ageing process; of the loss of innocence; of parental love which shields a child from fear and pain but cannot save it from death; of unquestioning love which, rejecting the evidence before its eyes, chooses to see only the beauty and the purity it wishes to behold; of the absurdity of ingrained conflicting religious doctrines which ignore the basic religious truths on which they are founded; of the salvation that can be gained by man only through the love of his fellow men and not through the agency of an unforgiving and disinterested God; of the inevitability of death and the discovery that the promised heaven of afterlife does not exist; of the realization that nothing which has any importance can be expressed in words. These are powerful and controversial themes, as one would expect from a writer of March's uncompromising honesty. One can only regret they were not fully worked out in the series of novels he planned but did not write.

The first Whisperer story, however, does state the principal theme of *Come in at the Door*. It tells of a sick man who fancies he has discovered the secret of mankind's misery. As he sees it, God has woven a thread for every man born into the world and instilled in him the desire to find and follow his thread, which is the course of his true destiny. Even so, few men find their thread, or, if they do, they discover that it is tangled with the threads belonging to other men, that it is full of knots which have to be unraveled, that it is broken by other men's feet and scattered to the four winds. As a consequence, only a very few men are allowed to live out their destinies. The mother of the sick man comforts him, assuring him that when he is better he will forget these "terrifying things." The mother's words reveal her own desire to live in a world of uncomplicated unreality, for she senses that the truth of the reality her son recognizes is too dreadful to be faced. This seems to be yet another expression of March's fundamental philosophical maxim, which predates the Laingian theory that the only really sane man is the so-called madman (and, presumably in this context, the truly innocent). In the Whisperer story, the sick man's cry of despair and his inability to find and follow the thread of his destiny is echoed at the novel's end, when, during a violent storm, Chester runs along a country road, fleeing from the house of his childhood and all the memories it contains, shouting at the top of his voice: "I'm very amusing. . . . I'm essentially a comic character!" Even this gesture is pointless, for there is no one to hear him, his words being "lost in the larger sound of the world's fury" (*CIATD*, p. 348).

Almost all the characters in *Come in at the Door* can be seen, in one way or another, to have lost the threads of their true destinies. Robert Hurry loses the thread of his destiny when his wife Ellen dies shortly after the birth of their son Chester. He lapses into a state of self-pity and of hatred toward the child he blames for his wife's death, going steadily and inexorably downhill, forming a progressively developing liaison with the black servant Mitty, fathering six mulatto children by her, and being denied a Christian burial by the outraged local church leaders when he dies. Chester loses his thread when, at the age of eight, he becomes the not altogether unwilling, if basically innocent, collaborator in the destruction of the mulatto Baptiste, and, twenty years later, after rediscovering his thread in a moment of appalled revelation, deliberately chooses not to follow it but hurls himself into the chaotic night and the dark uncertainty of the uncharted future, rejecting the salvation he might have been able to achieve, preserving the guilt he might have been able to expiate, maintaining the lie of his ostensibly happy marriage. Baptiste, by denying his origins and pretending to be what he is not, probably never does find the thread of his true destiny and in his failure sows the seeds of his own destruction. Mitty loses her thread by plotting Baptiste's downfall and subsequent terrible death, losing the love of her "baby," Chester, never to regain it, and so discovers that all she has ever worked and schemed for over the years, biding her time, has ultimately become meaningless without his love. Bushrod Tarleton loses his thread when he meets and marries Ruby, the worthless but curiously pathetic woman who time and time again abuses his forgiveness and his love and eventually destroys him. Bushrod's younger sister Bessie loses her thread when, in a fit of pique, she breaks off her engagement to Bradford Tallon and, when he is killed in France during World War I, unable to bear the thought of her lover's beautiful body rotting away in its grave, finds herself consumed with remorse and full of unforgiving animosity toward her own family for helping to bring about the separation. Chester's wife, Abbie, loses her thread when she allows vanity to insist that Chester have her likeness tattooed over his heart, and by so doing, and without Chester knowing precisely why, alienates him forever.

In addition to the Whisperer stories, the main narrative of the book is further interrupted by extracts from the diary of Chester's great-aunt, Sarah Tarleton. These diary extracts have three important functions. First, they provide a very effective shorthand method of disseminating essential facts, which would otherwise encumber and slow down the main narrative. Second, they provide historic perspective, the reader being kept fully informed of the passage of time, which proceeds in proper chronological order but with several marked

changes of pace. Third, they act as a counterpoint to the main narrative, giving the work an almost three-dimensional quality, providing a
small, quiet voice which interrupts every now and then the narrative
of the terrible happenings, both manifest and psychological, of which
for the most part, for all intents and purposes, Sarah Tarleton remains
in blissful ignorance. She presents herself in her diary as an essentially
somewhat shallow person, mainly concerned with the social graces and
worried only by the trivia of life. She does not choose to explore the
darker side of human nature nor does she wish to understand the deep
emotional and psychological forces which arouse violent reactions from
the people around her, thrusting them irresistibly into extreme
courses of action. She approves or condemns without analyzing reasons. Ironically, she poses on the very last page of the book what is
possibly the sole really interesting thought she has entered in her
diary. She suggests that, despite her supposed stupidity (which, of
course, she does not for one moment accept), she leads a happier
existence than all her nephews and nieces who, unlike her, have
received the benefit of a fine education. The truth of her proposition is
undeniable.

It will be evident from this brief summary that structurally *Come in
at the Door* is not only complex but somewhat diffuse, betraying its
obvious haphazard genesis and its isolated existence as part of an
abandoned grand design. For example, too many narrative lines are
abruptly ended and never resolved. Bushrod and Ruby disappear from
the scene five-sevenths of the way through the book and we never
know what eventually happens to them. Bessie's life history weaves in
and out of the main narrative, but after her disastrous visit to Chester
and Abbie, when it is made clear that she has not been able—and
probably never will be able—to reconcile herself to the cruel blows life
has dealt her, she is not mentioned again and we never know whether
she has returned to her left-wing political activities in New York or has
found some other media in which to direct her considerable talents.
We do not find out what becomes of Mitty and her six bastard children,
although that particular situation contains the kernel of a fascinating
and, what would have been in those days, pioneering sociological
study of the relationship between black and white, a study which,
remembering how proud March was of his short story "Happy Jack,"
would, if nothing else, have been unequivocal in expressing the
truths, as March saw them, about human rights and the psychology of
racial prejudice and intolerance. Finally, we are left completely in the
air regarding the state of Chester's marriage. Although, when he
leaves home to attend his father's funeral, he determines to be good to

Abbie on his return, he nevertheless, when showing his tattoo to his father's Negro servants, Jim and Hattie, distorts the likeness of his wife's face by manipulating the skin on his chest with his hand, so that its intrinsic prettiness is made grotesque and becomes the object of laughter. This action is a sort of betrayal of his good intentions, revealing his true deep-seated feelings toward Abbie and restating the total superficiality of his regard for her. When, at the very end of the book, he is made to realize the source of the subconscious guilt that has troubled him for almost twenty years, he presumably at the same time appreciates to the full what earlier he felt only subconsciously: that as a result of his wife's overweening vanity he will never be able to expiate his guilt and will have to live with it for the remainder of his days. The auguries for a mended marriage certainly do not appear propitious. Clearly, many vicissitudes lie ahead.

The conflict between male and female is indeed explicit in practically every relationship explored in the book, and it is significant that in every one of these relationships the female takes the dominant role. March goes even further by offering the proposition that the female of the species is not only deadlier than the male, but, like the praying mantis, is the devourer of the male. All the principal male characters in *Come in at the Door* are crushed by women—and in some cases destroyed by them. Robert Hurry is initially neutered by his domineering mother, deserted (albeit in death) by his wife at a time when he is beginning to find a place for himself in life and needs her most, and finally destroyed by Mitty, who acts as the instrument of his ultimate downfall and excommunication by his own kind. Baptiste is, of course, deliberately destroyed by Mitty. Chester is abandoned by his mother, whose death exposes him to the hatred of his father, deeply psychologically wounded by Mitty, who forces upon him the burden of a guilt he cannot bear, and is nudged toward destruction by Abbie, who denies him the means of expiating that guilt. Bushrod, whose innate kindness and forgiving nature make him completely vulnerable to all life's infinite cruelties, is eventually destroyed both psychologically and physically by the worthless Ruby he adores. Even Bradford Tallon is, by implication, destroyed by Bessie's rejection shortly before he goes off to war and to his death. Ironically, March does not allow these women to escape scot free, for by acting as the agents of male destruction they find neither happiness nor contentment, however brief. They are themselves destroyed.

Many of these male-female relationships entail a surrogate element. Mitty acts not only as surrogate mother to Chester but also as surrogate mother and wife to Robert Hurry. Chester, in fact, is the object of a series of surrogate mother figures. After he has left the Hurry place and the influence of Mitty, Sarah Tarleton possessively assumes the mother role. She is supplanted in due course by Aunt Lillian Chapman, who loves Chester as her own son, principally, one suspects, on account of his academic and business successes. Lastly, there is Abbie, who attempts to play the dual role of wife and mother, only to lose Chester's love completely.

The one happy parent-child relationship in the book is also a surrogate relationship. When Chester first arrives in Pearl County, Bushrod assumes the protective role of father toward the boy. This initial relationship gradually changes over the years as Chester grows into early manhood. Indeed, at one stage, just as in the relationship between Chester and Baptiste, homosexual undertones seem to intrude. Although there is a measure of physical intimacy, it is apparently at arm's length, and there is no reason for suspecting that any possible sexual feeling on one side or the other is manifested in overt physical activity. March's treatment of the Bushrod-Chester relationship is skillfully handled, subtly evolving with the passage of time, so that at the last the roles become completely reversed, and it is Chester who regards himself as the father figure and his uncle Bushrod as the child.

We can sympathize with Chester for the impatience and irritation, even anger, he feels toward his uncle for the manner in which Bushrod allows himself to be used by Ruby. Bushrod's overriding infatuation for his wife is one of the book's most troubling mysteries. On the face of it, Ruby has no redeeming quality to justify Bushrod's slavelike acceptance of her every whim. His is the behavior of the archetypal masochist. The more Ruby hurts and humiliates him, the more he abases himself before her. His stoicism is extraordinary. He can command admiration, he can attract ridicule, he can find his love reciprocated, he can have it flung back in his face accompanied by shouted obscenities. He considers himself a practical man and the attitude he adopts toward Ruby he sees as a demonstration of his avowed practicality. She is his wife and he is responsible for her, whatever hurt she may do him.

This claim of Bushrod's that he is a practical man does not, of course, bear close scrutiny. He declares he has no belief in religion, because he does not believe in anything he cannot see and touch. Believing deeply in the sanctity of art as one way to salvation, translated in part into the exorcising tattoos that cover his body, he tells Chester: "Art is a great thing . . . made by unhappy people for other people who are unhappy. . . . That's practical. . . . That's being practical about things" (*CIATD*, p. 171). The basic flaw in Bushrod's belief that he is a practical man is wryly pinpointed during a family discussion, when his father expresses regret that Bushrod did not finish college. Bushrod explains that he had learned all he wished to know, that he had learned that "art alone endures." Frank Tarleton quickly reminds him, "Education is the greatest thing in the world" (*CIATD*, p. 153), an opinion Bushrod does not bother to dispute.

Sarah Tarleton, on the other hand, does dispute what both her brother and her nephew have said. She strongly declares, "Honor is greater than everything else combined" (*CIATD*, p. 153). As representative of the old South, Sarah Tarleton occupies very much the same place in *Come in at the Door* as Mrs. Jenny Du Pre in Faulkner's *Sartoris*. She is the still center around whom the other characters revolve in their endless tortured permutations. She observes, she comments, she clings to the old customs, resisting change, outraged by contemporary mores. She typifies a way of life which is inevitably passing, unable to prevent or accept the evolution March so brilliantly, but almost unobtrusively, traces in the book: the decline and eventual breakup of many of the large plantations, the growth of the towns and cities, the deliberate destruction of the pristine forests, the gradual industrialization of the area, the flow of population from agrarianism to urbanism.

Shortly after Chester's arrival in Pearl County, the Hodge brothers announce their intention to secure options on timber in the vicinity, to build a sawmill and create a town, to be called Hodgetown, for their employees. Bushrod refuses to sell his timber. Probably one of the first conservationists of the twentieth century, he maintains that before long, if everybody sells out to the Hodge brothers, there will not be a tree left standing in the county. His is a lone voice calling in the wilderness of an increasingly materialistic society. Hodgetown, with its sawmill, commissary, and workers' homes, is duly erected. Bradford Tallon works on its construction, and Bessie and Chester often go to watch the work in progress. Only when Bushrod desperately requires funds to take Ruby away on a long recuperative sea voyage does he eventually agree to sell his timber. For reasons of expediency, big business triumphs again.

March is ruthless in his depiction of the various strata of southern urban life during the first quarter of the century. His commentary on the uppercrust Reedyville social scene reveals a community obsessed by distinctions of class, wealth, and breed, dominated by a clique of superficial, scheming women who fill their days with empty chatter in elegant drawing rooms, sipping tea and listening to poetry readings. These basically well-intentioned ladies are anathema to March. He pokes sometimes gentle, but more often malicious, fun at the expense of such worthies as Mrs. Lillian Chapman, Mrs. Wentworth, and Mrs. Porterfield, many of whom are to appear again and again in future stories and novels. He did, it is clear, incur much resentment in some quarters, even within the Campbell and March families themselves, by these uncompromising portraits, for several people, rightly or wrongly, identified themselves with some of his characters and took exception to the way in which he had ridiculed them.

On the other hand, his treatment of his Negro characters—even the diabolically misguided Mitty—is uniformly sympathetic. They are not presented, as they had been so often in the past, as mere caricatures— amiable, backward children dependent upon the guidance and protection of a liberal-minded master, or creatures existing on a level only slightly higher than that of the animals they tended in the fields. March's Negroes are flesh-and-blood people, simple perhaps in their basic outlook on life, certainly painfully superstitious, but having exactly the same desires, the same aspirations, the same needs, the same feelings as their white counterparts. They proclaim the dignity of their race, even when, like Baptiste, they attempt to deny it. The outrage that is committed on Baptiste by those who condemn him to death elevates this rather insignificant mulatto into a tragic figure of near classic, if not religious, proportions. His passion on the end of the rope is no less appalling than Christ's passion on the Cross. The dreadful manner of his death is emphasized by March in two unforgettable sentences at the end of the description of the hanging: "His hands were like the splayed claws of a dead hawk. They were rigid and curved with pain" (*CIATD*, p. 109). As the dead body swings gently to and fro under the peach tree, the blossoms fall around it "in flurries like pink, intermittent snow" (*CIATD*, p. 109), and the watching Negroes begin singing the spiritual which gives the book its title:

> *My lord is so high, you can't go over him,*
> *My lord is so wide, you can't go 'round him,*
> *My lord is so deep, you can't go under him,*
>   *You must come in at the door.*

March himself considered *Come in at the Door* a failure as a novel. He felt that he had succeeded in the first 115 pages and that the last part of the book was also satisfactory but that the middle sagged, as he put it, "like a bride's cake."[2] It is difficult to disagree with the author's assessment. The principal structural fault of the book lies in the fact that its horrifying emotional and narrative climax (Baptiste's execution) occurs on pages 108–109. Everything that subsequently happens is in the nature of an anticlimax. March's dilemma was similar to F. Scott Fitzgerald's when he wrote *Tender Is the Night*: whether to maintain strict chronological sequence in the narrative or to fracture and manipulate that chronological sequence to create mystery by withholding essential information until an extended flashback reveals all. Had March restructured his narrative in this latter fashion, the reader would have been both excited and intrigued by those various aspects of Chester's unexplained behavior patterns flowing from the trauma he had experienced as a child of eight, but it is doubtful that a better book would have resulted. As it stands, it is an impressively rich work, the more so when one reminds oneself of the circumstances under which it was written. That March could have produced such a book, flawed though it may be, despite all the business pressures to which he was concurrently being subjected and the oppressive atmosphere and fear in which he was living in Hitler's Germany, is a measure of his growing stature as a writer and of his dedication to his chosen art.[3]

In a letter he wrote in 1943 to Richard Crowder, March gave as one of his reasons for abandoning the ambitious series of novels he had originally planned the fact that *Come in at the Door* was not very well received at the time of its publication.[4] While the reader response and consequent sales of the book were disappointing, many contemporary reviewers, accepting its various faults, regarded it as a logical step forward from *Company K* and as evidence that here was developing what one critic was unabashed to describe as "the unmistakable imprint of greatness, if not of genius."[5] Another critic, Charles Clayton, expressed what was possibly the general view: "One cannot help but feel that Mr. March is still experimenting with his undeniable talents, and that he will ultimately fulfill the promise suggested in this novel."[6]

Fred T. Marsh, writing in the *New York Times Book Review*, was severe in his judgment, but the very severity of the review proclaimed unequivocally his deep respect for March, who, he adjudged, "cannot write badly" and whose mind was "keenly intelligent, speculative and originally imaginative." Marsh ended his review with the observation that the author would, after the failure of this second book following the brilliance of *Company K*, have "to start again almost from the bottom," for he had "stepped off too quickly into unfamiliar depths to swim with graceful strokes in various directions toward a shore which neither his readers nor he can discover."[7]

Marsh had, of course, put his finger precisely on the principal fault of *Come in at the Door*: its seeming diffuseness when viewed in isolation and its intrinsic ultimate dependence on the books which should have followed it. Had its place and its purpose in the proposed overall design been made explicit on the dust jacket, it is conceivable that the tone of the reviews would have been somewhat different and the doubts expressed by some critics regarding March's ability to provide an adequate and rational structure for his narrative to some extent modified.

The Whisperer stories worried many reviewers. Very few liked them, or indeed saw the point of them: "pretentious," "confusing," "extraneous," were some of the words used. One reviewer regarded the use of the Whisperer sequences as betraying March's technical inexperience.

Clearly, it was not a book with which the critics, as a whole, felt at ease. They recognized its undoubted power and the almost invariable excellence of its prose, but they could not fully appreciate what March was driving at. *Company K* had delivered a simple message with a capital M, but the message of *Come in at the Door* tended to elude them. The book's symbolism irritated them. Perhaps, more correctly, most of them were endeavoring to read into the book things that were not in fact there. Part of the blame for this, indeed most of it, must be laid at the author's door. Even so, the consensus seems to have been that in surmounting the notorious hurdle of a second book, March had done a more commendable job than most writers of distinguished first novels. Certainly, he had demonstrated he was not a one-book author.

Come in at the Door, having been rejected by Gollancz and Jonathan Cape, was published in England by the London publishing house of Rich and Cowan in August 1934. The British reviewers were, generally speaking, as enthusiastic about the book, and as puzzled by it, as their American counterparts had been. Francis Iles considered the new novel "a remarkable advance" over the "rather hysterical *Company K*," and noted: "Here we have life in the round, and not a monotonous harping on one side of it only." Iles, too, had little patience with the Whisperer sections and commented that "they only detract from an otherwise unusually good novel."[8] Graham Greene felt that the novel from Baptiste's death onward was "a little less satisfying" than the earlier pages, but he thought that as a whole it was a work of "exceptional interest." To Greene, March seemed "to write with all his senses when most novelists write with one." He saw March's "economy and freshness of phrase" as "the results of clear sight and clear hearing." In Greene's opinion, had the first hundred pages of the book been published separately as a long short story they "could have ranked with the best stories of childhood in English. Placed alongside *The Turn of the Screw* the opening section retains its significance, it is not overshadowed."[9]

By the time *Come in at the Door* was published in England, March had left Germany for good. Indeed, he had left Hamburg shortly after the book had come out in America in February. In 1943, he told Richard Crowder that his reason for leaving Germany was that he was not quite able to stomach the Nazis,[10] but patently the truth goes deeper than this. There is some evidence that during the later months of 1933, or very early in 1934, he suffered a "mild" nervous breakdown. The prime cause of this may have been the overwork resulting from pursuing concurrently his considerable business and literary activities. Undoubtedly he expended a prodigious amount of physical and mental energy during this period. Whatever the truth of the matter, the external political factions, including those which did not directly encroach upon his business life, quite definitely played their part. It would appear that he became almost paranoid where the Nazis were concerned. Some accounts suggest that he first consulted an analyst at this time. According to his sister Marie, he explained to the analyst that he was being followed everywhere by a man, presumably a Nazi agent. The analyst advised him to talk with his mother and to ask her to tell him about all the things that had happened to him in his childhood. March astonished the analyst by maintaining that he was already able to remember everything from the time he was born.[11] Whether or not this course of analysis was ever completed before he left Germany is unclear.

March's conviction that he was being followed is not so farfetched a story as might at first appear. Christopher Isherwood has recalled in his published memoirs how the atmosphere of terror in the Germany of those days created fantasies and hallucinations: how, in the middle of the night, he imagined hearing heavy wagons drawing up outside the house, how he began seeing swastika patterns in the wallpaper, and how everything in his room seemed to change to the same basic color of Nazi brown.[12] Whatever his fears, March had his small moments of defiance, on one occasion sending a note to the Nazi censorship department, saying that, while he did not particularly mind his private letters being opened and read, he wished that the son of a bitch who read them would stop dripping sausage fat on them.[13]

Finley McRae's version of the reason for March's sudden departure from Germany is somewhat more explicit and contains the ring of truth. Whether or not it provides the full explanation, one cannot say, but given March's obviously agitated state of mind at the time, the events which McRae has related must have seemed to March to have put him into an impossibly dangerous situation. It appears that when he first became one of the original stockholders of the Waterman Steamship Corporation he borrowed money from the Merchants National Bank of Mobile for this purpose, entering into an arrangement for the bank to take payments from his monthly checks on his notes, with Ed Roberts, as his power of attorney, signing them. In this way, he would pay off the loan and leave it to the bank to acquire more and more stock on his behalf as the years went by. None of this business was sent to him while he was in Germany, as he would have been obliged under the new laws to declare all his holdings to the Nazi government. McRae engaged a new secretary at the bank, who, unfortunately, was not briefed on these procedures. Unaware of the ramifications of her action, she unwittingly sent March all the notes and other papers. He cabled by return that he was leaving Germany forthwith and that a letter would be following. He later explained to his puzzled colleagues that the letter McRae's secretary had sent him had been opened by the censors and that when it eventually reached him he had immediately realized the potential danger he was in, not only of being heavily fined but even perhaps of being jailed by the Nazis. A friend of his, so he said, had been in a similar situation and had received a five-year jail sentence. In his opinion, therefore, it had been expedient to get out of the country without delay. Almost overnight, he booked passage on a steamer to England and never returned to Germany again.[14]

Just to what extent the bank's letter had actually constituted a threat to March's position as a foreign national is not known. It is, of course, possible that in his extremely nervous state of mind he persuaded himself to see the issue in absolutely clear-cut terms. The pressures of life in Germany had already taken their toll, both physically and mentally, and to have remained in the country with this cloud of brooding uncertainty hanging over him, even had nothing further transpired, would surely have been a recipe for disaster. On the other hand, he may simply have seized upon the incident as an excellent and opportune excuse to make his escape from the hateful atmosphere of nazism. Whatever the truth of the matter, the work he did in Germany in organizing the Waterman interests on the Continent probably represents the peak of his achievements for the company. From then onward, although he still had some good work to do in the business world, that side of his life slipped into fairly rapid decline.

Transferring his business activities to London, he established an office in Leadenhall Street, the center of London's shipping world, and began working in conjunction with Runciman, Waterman's general European agents. After the strain he had endured in recent months, he found life in the British capital particularly congenial. Initially, he seems to have found the notorious reserve of the English character something of a barrier, but he soon adapted to the new rhythm of life and it was not long before he had established a circle of friends.

He visited Edward J. O'Brien in Oxford and through O'Brien was introduced to several British writers, including H. E. Bates, Elizabeth Bowen, John Davenport, Margiad Evans, and Arthur Calder-Marshall. Calder-Marshall is the only surviving member of this group of writers. Now a distinguished novelist, biographer, essayist, and critic, he was, in those days, a young man on the threshold of his literary career. He has recalled his early impressions of March:

> I found him a warm, sympathetic man with a Rabelaisian strain of humour and a preference for bourbon or rye to Scotch whiskey. He was lonely in London, as indeed I was, until I married. Physically he was an insignificant man, of average height, but slightly built, with pince-nez spectacles. [His appearance] never made much impression on me, but I found it did to friends I introduced him to, especially women. . . . He kept his business and literary lives quite separate; and appeared to dislike the need to have to earn his living by business. He also professed a strong dislike of Mobile, Alabama.[15]

By March 1934, March was able to inform Margaret that his writing was not progressing as well as it might because he was enjoying himself too much in England. Nevertheless, he reported that he was in the process of turning the long short story "The Unploughed Patch" into a full-length novel.[16]

Another literary project of 1934 arose from his friendship with Kay Boyle, who was then living with her husband in Kitzbühel in the Tirol. He had long admired Kay Boyle's work. They had commenced corresponding during the previous year. Kay Boyle recalls:

> It must have been because of his book, *Company K*, that we first corresponded, a book I found deeply moving; and it must have been because of *Company K* that my husband, Laurence Vail, became obsessed with the idea of bringing out a collection of one-page stories. The example of Bill's stories, some of them little more than a printed page in length, yet complete in characterization, and in some instances complete in plot, brought Laurence to the envisaging of a collection which would be entitled *365 Days*. Each would be allotted one page, and each page would be a day of the same year. The year was 1934. . . . Because

Bill's stories were clearly based on actual experience of actual incidents, Laurence felt that every story in 365 *Days* should be based on an actual newspaper clipping, which the short story writer would submit with his contribution, and which would also be published in the book. In the case of Henry Miller (who sent us a number of short stories for the collection), and in the case of William Saroyan, and the experimental French writers we knew (Raymond Queneau and others), little heed was paid to the request for newspaper items on which their stories were based, and thus the editors had to invent newspaper paragraphs to serve as impetus for the stories. This delighted Laurence Vail and he gave his imagination full rein. In the case of Bill March, no kind of game-playing was necessary. The newspaper item he selected for one story reads: "Broadcasting from Capitol, Senator Predicts Happy and Prosperous New Year for All." Another reads: "Unemployed Crowd Benches of New York Parks as New Year Begins."[17]

These two stories appeared in 365 *Days*, which was eventually published in 1936, under the headings "January 2, New York," and "January 6, United States." When March reprinted the stories in the 1939 collection *Some Like Them Short*, he titled them "Senator Upjohn" and "The First Dime," respectively.

By mid-1934, March was back in America, primarily for consultation with the other Waterman executives. He spent two months altogether in the States, most of the time in Mobile, which he found unbearably hot after England's more gentle climate.

In June, his satirical story "Mrs. Joe Cotton" appeared in the July 1934 issue of the recently established man's magazine *Esquire*, the first issue of which had made its debut on the newsstands the previous October. The story was awarded two asterisks in O'Brien's 1935 anthology. After being reprinted in the June 1935 issue of *Golden Book Magazine* under the title "The Woolen Drawers," it obviously rose in O'Brien's estimation, for he awarded it three asterisks in his 1936 anthology. Although this was the only new story of his to be published in 1934, March's work continued to receive recognition in the 1934 O'Brien anthology, which reprinted "This Heavy Load" and awarded three asterisks to each of the four stories he had published during 1933.[18]

While he was in Mobile, his publishers, Smith and Haas, corresponded with him regarding the proposed volume of short stories, tentatively titled *The Bread of Affliction*, scheduled to appear early in the new year. There was clearly some difference of opinion concerning the selection and the number of stories to be included. In August, Harrison Smith wrote to March and suggested that for economic reasons, if for nothing else, five of the proposed twenty-one stories be dropped. He felt that sixteen was about the right number for the book. He did not want March to feel that he was being uncompromising over the issue. He was simply offering his advice as publisher. The stories Smith wished to omit were "The Little Wife," "Flight to Confusion," "The Wood Nymph," and two shorter pieces, "The First Sunset" and "The Pattern That Gulls Weave." His selection of these stories for exclusion was, he admittd, purely personal preference. He thought "The Pattern That Gulls Weave" a rather pointless story, and he felt that both "The Wood Nymph" and "Flight to Confusion" should be dropped because the main character of several other stories in the collection was either insane or became insane. He did not explain why he wanted to exclude "The Little Wife" but mentioned that "The First Sunset" did not, in his opinion, fit in with the other stories.[19]

In the final arrangement, the book contained only fourteen stories. "The Little Wife" and "The Pattern That Gulls Weave" were, however, retained. March's first published story, "The Holly Wreath," was also discarded, on the grounds that enough war stories were being included in the book as it was. Whether or not another of the stories omitted was the one March had intended to use as the title story for the collection, "The Bread of Affliction," is not at all clear from the available correspondence. If there was such a story, it has never been published and is no longer extant, at least not under that title.

March left America on September 7, sailing from New York on the liner *Majestic*. Back in London, he rented a basement flat in Nottingham Place, near Marylebone High Street, a stone's throw from Madame Tussaud's famous waxworks exhibition and Baker Street Station, and began work once more on the novel he had started earlier that year. He wrote Robert Haas in October that he intended to work solidly on the new book until it was completed and wished only that he had more time to pursue his literary activities, the world of business and the permutations of his love life encroaching far too much into the time he should be devoting to his writing. He suggested that the solution for him lay in acquiring a sympathetic wife, who was both physically and financially well endowed. Possibly Haas could put him in touch with a reliable marriage broker?[20]

In actual fact, although March was to reiterate on several occasions his desire to marry and settle down to a placid and ordered way of life, he inevitably fled from any relationship that tended to become too possessively intimate, feeling that such a relationship, while giving him the essential atmosphere of contentment for which he craved, would shackle him in an unbearable sort of way. Edward Glover, indeed, has told how March lived for a time in the Nottingham Place flat with a girl who, as it turned out, was rather frigid. March succeeded after about a year in releasing her entirely from her inhibitions. It was a challenge he accepted and won. Presumably, once he had proved his point, he terminated the relationship, fearing that now that the girl had been thawed out it could develop out of his control. Glover felt that

> the traumatic nature of his upbringing had led to his developing a kind of skepticism as to the value of love, of love as a whole. It was difficult for him to believe in it, even if it came along. It was as if he had always sort of stood on the sidewalk, watching sympathetically. If he let himself go in a sentimental way, elaborating it in any way you like—verses and whatever—he was never satisfied. He was caught between just saying, as it were, "All right, call it a day! Let's live and just do the usual thing and make a success of it, having one's own recreations," and a very strong, sentimental, idealistic longing which he was nevertheless not inclined to look down his nose at. He didn't despise it in any way. But he didn't believe in it. That was the problem that was never quite settled in his life, and the one I would have thought would have always given him difficulty.[21]

Another literary project March worked on at this time was a series of twelve sonnets, which he composed from October 5 to November 18, 1934. Glover has said that March was half-ashamed of the sonnets, but Glover thought that they were very good. March gave them to him as a souvenir. One of the sonnets was, in fact, published. The eighth in the series, it appeared in the February 1936 issue of *Harper's Bazaar*. After March's death, Margaret wrote to Glover, asking him if he would allow her to borrow the sonnets. He sent them to her. She typed out copies and returned the originals to Glover.[22]

While March was away in America, Arthur Calder-Marshall had married. He and his wife were "very broke" at that time and, with typical generosity, March allowed them full use of his flat when, on one occasion, they were engaged in a desperate search for somewhere to live.

Albert Halper, the thirty-year-old Chicago-born novelist, whose *Union Square* had been published the year before and who was in England on a Guggenheim Fellowship, saw March frequently in London. March told him that his flat had once belonged to Sir Arthur Conan Doyle, creator of Sherlock Holmes. He also told Halper that he used to go to school with William Faulkner. Halper was not so naive as to believe these stories, recognizing them for what they undoubtedly were: examples of March's whimsical sense of humor and nothing more.[23] On the other hand, Halper had no reason to doubt the accounts March related of his experiences with the Nazi shipping officials:

> He was shrewd and clever in his dealings with them, and nothing gave him more pleasure than to best Hitler's minions on a freight contract. When he wasn't giving an account of his transactions, he spoke of the depravity of the Germans. Some of the Nazi officials had taken him to parties which he described to me; and in his soft, well-modulated voice, March detailed the perversions he had witnessed. The details of so-called abnormal behavior are always fascinating for a while; but soon, if these details are repeated enough, one feels the narrator is perhaps obtaining too much pleasure from telling them, and this is what I felt about March.[24]

According to Halper, it was during this London period that March and Alistair Cooke first met; and it was through Cooke that March met the young American poet Paul Engle. Then in his mid-twenties, Engle was a Rhodes scholar at Merton College, Oxford. March often traveled to Oxford to stay with either O'Brien or Engle. For a while, Engle looked upon March as his closest friend in England. On March's weekend visits to Oxford, they would go for long walks together in the countryside on Sunday mornings, catching a bus out to Wood Eaton and hiking over the gentle hills to the sound of church bells and bird song. Whenever Engle went over to the Continent, or returned from it, he would drop off in London and visit March in his flat. In a letter he wrote March some years later, Engle recalled those days:

> Now and then I see a picture of London and the whole emotion, with which I remember your place and your kindness and the red-brick houses and the evening light, comes back almost with violence. Sometimes it seems the urgent present is lived through only so that it can become the urgent and intimate past. There must be something in this which corrupts.[25]

Sometimes when Engle was visiting, March entertained business associates from Germany. Engle was fascinated to hear March conversing with them, "his Alabama voice pouring out the umlauts."[26] Engle remembers March as a very modest and a very shy man. One evening, as he and March stood in line at a London underground ticket office, a man standing directly behind them, hearing their voices and identifying them as Americans, said bitterly, "Why did you Americans wait to come to France until most of us were killed? Scared?" Engle remained silent, feeling that it was neither his right nor duty to make any riposte. Then, after a moment's pause, March turned to the man and said, very gently, "I'm sorry about that."[27]

Although life appeared pleasant enough on the surface, not all was well, and the emotional and psychological stresses which March had partially succeeded in repressing for so many years were soon to manifest themselves. More and more, he delegated the work of re-organizing Waterman's London office and interests to the young German assistant, Heinz Ahrens, he had brought with him from Hamburg,[28] leaving him with further time to work on the new book and to complete arrangements for the publication of the volume of stories.

The Little Wife and Other Stories was published in New York by Smith and Haas on February 4, 1935, bearing the dedication "To Finley McRae, whose ancestor remarked: 'I have slain ten Campbells to-day. Do you think I have earned my supper?'"

seven

The Little Wife
and Other Stories
and Analysis with Glover

In a year that also saw the publication of F. Scott Fitzgerald's *Taps at Reveille*, Thomas Wolfe's *From Death to Morning*, Erskine Caldwell's *Kneel to the Rising Sun*, and James T. Farrell's *Guillotine Party*, March's first short-story collection was in fiercely competitive company. If March's book may have seemed at the time somewhat overshadowed, it does not seem so in retrospect. Indeed, the claim can be made that *The Little Wife and Other Stories* was the most distinguished volume of short stories by any American writer to be published in 1935. It fails as a masterwork by reason only of its one-sided, consistently bleak vision of the human condition, whatever humor there is being purely incidental and invariably bitter and double edged. The stories, written between 1928 and 1933, are permeated, on the one hand, with March's uncompromising philosophy of life, a philosophy which was hardly to change to the day he died, and, on the other hand, with his overriding compassion for those who are obliged to bear all the pain and humiliation that fortuitous or intended circumstance forces upon them. Collectively, the stories present a world in which man's indifference to the suffering of his fellow beings seems to predominate, a world, moreover, which is presided over by a God who, when not uncaring, is cruel, demanding, and unforgiving.

The collection contains at least four short stories which are close to being masterpieces in the genre: the title story itself, "To the Rear," "The Pattern That Gulls Weave," and "Happy Jack." Of the other ten stories, only one, "The Eager Mechanic," is something less than first class.

With the exception of two war stories ("To the Rear" and "The American Diseur"), a story of postwar Germany ("The Pattern That Gulls Weave"), and one story set in New York ("He Sits There All Day

Long"), all the stories are set in the Deep South, many of them in Reedyville. We meet again many of the characters who appeared in *Come in at the Door*. In "The Arrogant Shoat," for example, Miss Sarah Tarleton comes to visit Rancey on her deathbed, and—among others— old Mrs. Porterfield and Mrs. Kenworthy, members of the Browning Club of which Aunt Lillian Chapman is president, make short appearances in "Miss Daisy" and "A Shop in St. Louis, Missouri." The same characters appear or are mentioned in several of the stories: the Porterfields, the Palmillers, Mrs. Joe Cotton. The widow Findley's rooming house is home for Daisy Burton in "Miss Daisy" and temporary home for Jack Sutton in "Happy Jack," as well as being next door to the Tatums in "A Shop in St. Louis, Missouri." As they go about their day-to-day business, we grow to know these people in the same way we grow to know our neighbors. The sense of shock we experience when, from time to time and with unrelenting surgical precision, March peels away the public images these upright Reedyville citizens have assumed, so exposing their true natures, is the same sense of shock we would most likely experience were the fronts to be ripped from the houses of some of our neighbors, enabling us to witness what was taking place in the rooms within. March, aware that no man is completely devoid of sin, does not set himself up as judge and jury vis-à-vis his characters. He goes out of his way to condemn only when the private vice is masked by the hypocrisy of assumed public virtue.

Only three of the stories are written in the first person: "He Sits There All Day Long," "Miss Daisy," and "This Heavy Load." The first and second deal with the theme of betrayal—the former with the betrayal of a father by his son, and the latter with the betrayal of a young boy's faith in mankind by the discovery that the person he worships has feet of clay.

"He Sits There All Day Long" is written in the semivernacular, reminiscent of many of Sherwood Anderson's stories and of Hemingway's derivative "My Old Man." As in the Hemingway story, March's tale is concerned with the relationship between a son and his father. In the Hemingway story, however, it is the son, Joe Butler, who is the one betrayed and ultimately left abandoned and desolate by reason of his jockey father's involvement in crooked deals on the race course, whereas in the March story it is the father who is betrayed and condemned to an institution by his son's lack of determination in following the dictates of his conscience. Just as Joe Butler recalls the good times he spent as a child with his father in the countryside around Maisons-Lafitte in France, so Danny recalls the good times he had as a child with his father on trips to Coney Island. There, any close comparison between the two stories ends, for "He Sits There All Day Long" is essentially a study of guilt, the guilt of a son who fails in his filial duties when faced with the first moral dilemma of his life.

In "Miss Daisy," the betrayal perpetuated is, if anything, even more traumatic, for the victim is still in the early formative years of his life and totally unable to cope, either emotionally or rationally, with the truth that has been revealed to him. Miss Daisy Burton, teacher in charge of the intermediate section of the Presbyterian Sunday School, is regarded by the townspeople of Reedyville as "the best practicing Christian" many of them had ever met. For nine-year-old Harry Piggott, who has come to Reedyville to live with his aunt, Miss Daisy becomes a symbol of love and gentleness, a surrogate in many ways for his dead mother. A tiny, gray, dried-up woman of fifty, Miss Daisy walks with the aid of crutches, having suffered from tuberculosis of the hip since she was a little girl. She had undergone twelve painful operations at various intervals throughout her life, all of which she had borne with great fortitude and without complaint. Then, during a Sunday school picnic, she falls and hurts her hip. A fever sets in and she is confined to bed. When Harry visits her, he finds her in a delirium, unable to face the pain of yet another operation, all the bottled-up hatred and violence she has suppressed over the years surfacing at last. She tells Harry she hates the sight of him, that she hates everyone in the town and only believes in God because He had tortured His son on the Cross. Harry's belief, fostered by Miss Daisy's ostensible saintliness and love, that all is sweetness and light in the world is shattered. He has achieved his traumatic moment of maturation. He runs from the sickroom and hides himself away. "Nobody will ever fool me again!" he avows (*LW*, p. 250).

Young Harry Piggott's words are, in substance, echoed by Private Ernest Lunham in his own moment of appalled revelation toward the end of the story "To the Rear." Abandoned by his comrades, he reflects on all the idealism that surrounded his enlistment and his time in France, when he entertained only romantic thoughts of valiant deeds and heroic death on the glorious fields of battle. Now, because of what has happened to him, all that idealism has been swept away and for the first time he is able to see his company and the war for what they are. He thinks: "By God, they sold me out! . . . The things they said were all lies!" (*LW*, p. 142).

"To the Rear," "The Holly Wreath," and "The American Diseur" form a related trio of stories concerning an infantry company, similar to the one in *Company K*, in France during World War I. "To the Rear" is the best of the three. Without introducing any scenes of actual combat, it seems to encapsulate the whole ethos of life in a fighting unit, vividly illustrating the way in which war brings out the best and the worst in man. March's ultimate message, however, is that there is no escaping the all-pervading corruption war brings in its wake. No matter how noble a man's purpose may be at the outset, that corruption finally triumphs, destroying all the accepted mores by which men live their normal lives, substituting the law of the jungle. No one, victim or survivor, remains untainted. The old French woman's "Je ne comprends pas!" echoes Lunham's own state of mind and the theme of the story, ironically harking back to the string of circumstances which have brought him to his final parlous state. "To the Rear" is a story that remains long in the mind, mainly because it succeeds so admirably in putting across its message, without resorting to descriptive or stylistic pyrotechnics, building up the tension slowly to its inevitable, appalling climax.

Eddie La Bella, who appears briefly in "To the Rear" and who is seen by Lunham as "cheap and flashy, his theatrical prettiness caked with dirt and streaked with sweat" (*LW*, p. 139), is the principal protagonist in "The American Diseur." It is impossible to avoid a sneaking sense of sympathy for La Bella. Thrust by wayward circumstance into a situation over which he has no control, he is a victim of cruel fate. In endeavoring to become what he never can be, he maps out his own destruction, driven by the undisguised contempt of the men he is supposed to be commanding. He completely loses his identity and consequently, as many other of March's characters, escapes from the world of reality into his own private world of fantasy and insanity. He deserts and is arrested two months later in Paris.

Another soldier seemingly irreparably damaged by the war is Downey in "This Heavy Load." Downey is the archetypal March man. Before he goes off to the war, he is "an idealistic, highly emotional man with little actual knowledge of the world," believing "the nonsense of the war speeches and the war posters" (*LW*, p. 208). As a result of his experiences, he suffers deep psychological wounds. When, after his discharge, he returns to his wife and children, he feels that it is only by accident he is still alive and that he can no longer give any meaning to the concepts of good and evil.

The story of Downey's spiritual odyssey is related by an anonymous seafaring man who lives in the room across the hall from Downey in a dilapidated boardinghouse near the river front. This unnamed narrator occupies the same sort of role as does Joseph Conrad's Marlow in such works as "Youth," "Heart of Darkness," and *Lord Jim*. It was a brilliant decision by March to employ this literary device, filtering and interpreting Downey's own narrative through the narrative of the "Marlow" figure. To have used the impersonal authorial approach would have been to have lost all the nuances which, arising from the relationship between the two men, give the reader a sense of personal involvement. To have had Downey tell his own story directly to the reader would have seemed embarrassingly self-pitying, possibly artificial. At one remove, Downey's history takes on a greater depth and significance. It would also, without the "Marlow" device, have been impossible to close the story with the statement which Downey, safe and sure now in his new-found faith, would no longer be able to appreciate but which the unnamed narrator himself, still being burdened with his own "heavy load," can recognize as an all-embracing truth: "I knew then for the first time that man is not a completed thing: that he is only part of other things which he cannot name, and which he but dimly understands. He talks a great deal about freedom, but he can never be free: for he is a frail, lost creature, too weak to walk unaided" (*LW*, p. 223). So saying, the unnamed narrator ties up his symbolic heavy sea bag, preparatory to picking it up and setting off to resume his own briefly interrupted wanderings.

"This Heavy Load" is a seminal work in the March canon. Written in 1931, before *Come in at the Door*, it contains literary, philosophical, and psychological elements which were to appear again and again in subsequent stories and novels. Although the story did not attract a great amount of interest at the time it was first published in the December 1933 issue of *Forum*, its underlying importance as a statement in crystalized form of March's view of life has become increasingly appreciated over the years. The analogies between Downey and March himself are almost too self-evident to require spelling out here: the innocent idealist who is psychologically shattered by his experiences in war, his inability to relate to family and environment on his return home, his restlessness, his feelings of extreme guilt at having survived the war, his wanderings over the United States, his utter rejection of organized religion. Unlike Downey, March found his way to salvation through his writing and, to a degree, though not altogether successfully, by immersing himself in the frenetic day-to-day dealings of the business world. The harking back in the story to pagan gods is somehow almost Lawrentian in spirit, an uncarved block of wood picked up on the beach evoking in Downey's mind a vision of a South Seas paradise. This longing for a return to nature is touched upon in *Come in at the Door*, when Baptiste regales Chester with his fantasies in which he imagines himself made king of an island tribe and worshiped like a god. Such form of escapism was seen by March as little more than a temporary dreamworld with no basis in reality and not to be taken too seriously, although he did use it most effectively as a basis for his penultimate novel, *October Island*.

Just as Miss Daisy rejects the cruel God who has done nothing to alleviate the pain to which she has been a martyr all her life and who has denied her sexual fulfillment, so Downey rejects the cruel God he sees as being overly responsible for all the evil and suffering in the world. In "Mist on the Meadow," this same conceptual cruel God is again represented as a deity entirely without benevolence, demanding the infliction of pain in return for salvation. Christ, too, is represented in this story as achieving purity in the bodies and minds of worldly sinners, not by any demonstration of overwhelming love for mankind but by inflicting flagellation and inducing self-abasement. In its implications, "Mist on the Meadow" is one of the darkest stories March ever wrote, providing absolutely no glimmer of hope for the ultimate spiritual salvation of mankind via the path of Christianity. God's agent leaves the simple countryfolk with their way of life destroyed, the pigs, the principal source of their livelihood, lying scattered dead in the river, the placid twenty-year-old idiot of a son now a gibbering lunatic, fit only for the asylum his parents have saved him from for most of his life. Whereas many of March's characters escape from the insanity of the world into their own private insanity, Tolly is paradoxically driven out of his private insanity into what is ostensibly a state of sanity, but is, in reality, a much more terrifying state of insanity.

The two shortest stories in the book are also the two latest in date of composition: "The Eager Mechanic" and "The Pattern That Gulls Weave." While "The Eager Mechanic" is the weakest story in the collection, "The Pattern That Gulls Weave," only marginally longer, is one of the most hauntingly beautiful stories March ever wrote. Written during his sojourn in Hamburg, it concerns a well-bred lady, Fraulein Giesecke, who, in the parlous economic atmosphere of postwar Germany, has been reduced to eking out an existence by giving German lessons to English girls. She despises her pupils, who make fun of her when they think she is not listening and who react to the discipline of her instruction with barely muted hostility, intent always on having the last word and in undermining her briefly assumed authority.

One winter afternoon, leaving the home of three of her pupils, she walks along by the Alster in the misty rain. Ice is forming on the surface of the lake. Swans are gliding between the fragile pieces of ice and gulls wheel and swoop overhead in the gray sky. A boy beggar, standing forlornly under a tree, begins to sing, repeating the same song over and over, holding out his cap for money. None of the passers-by takes any notice of him. Eventually Fraulein Giesecke experiences a sudden feeling of anger that the boy should be abasing himself so. She goes across to him and gives him some money, upbraiding him for his lack of pride, telling him that he is obviously ill and should be home in bed. The boy pays no heed to her words, simply continuing his plaintive singing. She realizes that, of course, she has no right to upbraid him, that the boy is doing what he is forced to do out of dire necessity and that the pittance she has contributed and her words of angry advice will not help him one iota.

In a final brief but unforgettable tapestry of words, the graceful and helpless swans become a metaphor for Fraulein Giesecke herself and for the elegance and serenity of her past opulent way of life, while the constantly searching gulls are a metaphor for the harsh reality of life in contemporary Germany, their whole purpose, like that of the boy singer, centered on the need to find sufficient food to keep body and soul together. Such bald summary cannot begin to do justice to this beautiful story. "The Pattern That Gulls Weave" is a mood poem, blending atmosphere and narrative into a perfect work of art.

Irony, as with much of March's work, predominates in most of the stories in this first collection. Rancey, for instance, in "The Arrogant Shoat," dies a painful and lingering death from stomach cancer, bemoaning the fact that her life has been wasted, that she should never have married but should have followed her original intention, as a girl of eighteen, of running off to join a circus with her pet shoat. Her broken-hearted and unsuspecting husband consoles himself with the thought: "We had a sweet, full life together" (*LW*, p. 77). His remark, which forms the final sentence of the story, is exceeded in its frightening irony only by Mrs. Forsythe's remark to the bereaved Mr. Penmark, "You still have Rhoda to be thankful for," which forms the final sentence of March's last novel, *The Bad Seed*. Rancey's is the epitome of the humdrum life. Indeed, in many ways, the pig she trained accomplished more in performing its parody of dance than she ever did in her lifetime. She, too, was arrogant after a fashion, like the pig, not learning much from life or contributing to it other than to produce eight children, her body becoming grossly overweight and assuming an almost porcine appearance. The wedding dress she purchases from the proceeds of the sale of the pig becomes ultimately as worthless as her marriage.

Another Reedyville story, "A Shop in St. Louis, Missouri," explores the similar theme of a wasted life. Mattie Tatum scrimps and works all hours to save the three thousand dollars she requires to set up her own dress shop in St. Louis. When confronted with the choice of using her hard-earned savings to pay for the expensive operation which will prolong the life of her cancer-stricken mother, she resolves she will not be denied her shop, that she will be hard and practical and not throw her money away on an operation that, at best, will only postpone the inevitable. Upon her mother's death, Mattie is overcome with remorse and collapses at the graveside, crying out to her mother to forgive her. In her acute distress and guilt, she determines she will never leave Reedyville and that she will not spend a penny of her savings upon herself. Instead, she uses all the money to erect a grandiose marble monument over her mother's grave. It becomes a symbol of expiation and retribution before which she abases herself regularly every Sunday, a monument to her callousness, its pristine whiteness soon to be befouled by soot and bird droppings, while she herself, her life completely without direction, becomes a shriveled, joyless woman, old before her time. The story is a devastating study of the effect that guilt may have on the individual who does not keep in touch with reality.

Irony is heavily present too in "George and Charlie," in which March tells the story of two men who, when they first meet at the beginning of the story, are both in their early twenties. George is a quiet, methodical fellow, whereas Charlie is a crusading socialist, forever upholding the rights of the underdog. George's pragmatism is repelled by Charlie's idealism. George feels that Charlie, like all idealists, has his head in the clouds and should be treated with amused tolerance. But by the end of the story, their roles have become completely reversed. George even despises Charlie a little for having discarded so completely the burning beliefs he once held, in order to obtain a job and begin over again. The supreme irony of the story is, of course, that, with them both approaching middle age, George, whose life has been eminently successful, can *afford* to demonstrate his liberalism, whereas Charlie, who has suffered all the knocks that life could bestow, is now *obliged* to conform.

Like Charlie, Mrs. Joe Cotton in "Woolen Drawers" is, through expediency, obliged to assume standards of conduct which are basically alien to her nature, subsequently and quickly learning of the advantages that can flow from such changed life-style, a life-style which she embraces with unalloyed and bigoted enthusiasm. She becomes secretary of Mr. Palmiller's Reedyville vice and temperance society and, in a position to use her past personal knowledge about such matters to good effect, is able to advise the other members of the society of the things that take place at Mattress May's sporting house and of the services that are made available to the transient male guests at the Magnolia Hotel. The other members of the society, unaware of her past life, are amazed at the extent of her insight, believing her to be guided in her crusading activities by the sure hand of God. Virtue and vice are changeable things, March seems to be saying, dependent upon one's point of view and the vagaries of circumstance. "Woolen Drawers" is the only story in the whole collection which can be described as humorous, and then the humor is bitterly satirical.

Just how bitter that satire actually is can be best judged from Sister Joe Cotton's small but vital role in "Happy Jack," the last story in the book, when her crusading busybodiness encourages, in the name of God, all that is worst in human nature, triggering off in this instance the violence which results in physical mutilation and in far-reaching misery for a number of people. According to Robert Clark, "Happy Jack" was one of the stories March regarded with "a keen sense of pride."[1] In a letter written late in his life to Dudley Nichols, March stated that so far as he was aware, "Happy Jack" was the first story ever written with such a theme and that it was thought revolutionary when it was first published.[2] Certainly, in this story, March does not pull any punches in his condemnation of his own race—and, incidentally, of humanity in general—for its cruelty, its intolerance, and its utter lack of understanding. In a nonmilitary environment, it restates all the themes of *Company K*.

The world, as March has noted before, is full of do-gooders and moral crusaders, who believe they, and they alone, have the true answer, forever wanting to put the world to rights, at every opportunity rooting out the evil they see around them. In this, as we have observed in "Woolen Drawers," Sister Joe Cotton is powerfully proficient. It is she who lights the fuse to the powder keg which, when it explodes, brings out into the open all the terrifying manifestations of ordinary people's fears and prejudices. When incensed and frightened, people frequently react with violence. Thus when Sister Cotton discovers by chance that a white widow and her Negro farmhand are living together as man and wife on the widow's farm three miles out of town, she publicly denounces them. Eight masked men go at night to the homestead, seize the Negro, and castrate him.

When Jack Sutton, the town printer, who ironically chose to settle in Reedyville because he was impressed by the beauty and tranquility of the town the first time he set eyes on it, learns what has happened, he is perplexed that people should do such a terrible thing to a fellow human being who has not harmed them in any way and who has asked only to be left in peace to provide companionship and solace for a woman and to receive companionship and solace from her in return.

The fact that the woman is white and the man black has, in his view, no bearing at all on the matter. What has passed between the couple is nobody's business but their own. He becomes obsessed with the need to convince the townspeople of the error of their thinking. But his one-man crusade is doomed to failure from the start. In the same way that the Negro had been physically castrated by Reedyville's ignorance, prejudice, and basic immorality hiding itself under the cloak of "civilized" respectability, so Jack, the only man with a true sense of morality and Christian ethics in the community, is himself psychologically and spiritually castrated by the evil which exists in human nature. The final tableau of the old, crazed, weeping man kneeling in the mud, surrounded by the taunting townspeople, is a true vision of the reversal of the sane and the insane.

It is a powerful theme and as shocking a story as Faulkner ever wrote. Yet it does not encroach into the realms of Grand Guignol as do so frequently the chronicles of Yoknapatawpha County. In Pearl County, reality is always there on the page, discomfiting the reader by the very ordinariness of the people to whom things are done and, perhaps more disturbingly, the people who do things to others. The absence in March's work of the "cordon sanitaire" to which Alistair Cooke has referred[3] is nowhere more frighteningly apparent than in this unforgettable tale of one man's futile stand against a town's acceptance and approval of an act of unnecessary and unforgivable violence which has been perpetrated in its name and in the name of God.

Collections of short stories are notoriously anathema to publishers, and it probably says a great deal for the faith that Harrison Smith and Robert Haas had in their author that they should have agreed so readily to the publication of *The Little Wife and Other Stories*, for they would have been aware that the book would never be a best-seller and make money for them. The dust jacket blurb refers to March as occupying "a prominent place among contemporary writers" in "the field of the short story." The book triumphantly confirmed that such a claim was undeniable.

The reviewers of the day, however, were generally more cautious in their judgment, one of the more consistently favorable reviews being that of Fred T. Marsh, who had been so disappointed with *Come in at the Door*. In his enthusiastic piece, Marsh declared:

> His special gift as a storyteller is his faculty of catching on the wing some bit of penetration into human life, and creating about it a slight tale, a short narrative, an episode, a piece of realistic description, by way of elucidation. . . . These are . . . superior stories. They are slight on

surface compared to the best American short stories being written (and they may be compared with the best), but they have intelligence, depth and quality. And the prose is irreproachable. Mr. March is on the right track.[4]

Understandably, many critics deplored the relentlessly monotonous theme of futility that pervades the stories and the almost total absence of "comic relief." For all that, March was compared, not always unfavorably, with Faulkner, A. E. Coppard, James Stephens, and, perhaps inevitably, Sherwood Anderson. In the *New York Herald Tribune Book Review*, Elizabeth Hart was careful to place the matter into proper perspective: "Yes," she admitted, "this book is disquieting and painful. It is also a necessity for anyone who makes the slightest pretense to believing in the short story as an art."[5]

The Little Wife and Other Stories was published in England by Rich and Cowan two months later, in April 1935. Cyril Connolly was circumspectly hostile, observing that the stories were "competent and graphic descriptions of the extremes of human pettiness, unhappiness and degradation," and summing up with uncompromising finality: "Misery is not enough."[6] On the other hand, in a fairly long and favorable review, the anonymous critic of the *Times Literary Supplement* considered the stories to be "both in form and expression admirable specimens of their *genre.*" He ended the review with the thought that if perhaps "Mr. March were less anxious to make a political case in a considerable proportion of these stories he would be even more effective, but it cannot be said that he ever allows a plot or character to take second place to propaganda."[7]

The critical response to the book, even though by no means uniformly enthusiastic or wholly sympathetic with the content of the stories, must have been pleasing enough to March, particularly with so many reviewers comparing his work favorably with the acknowledged short-story masters of the day. He had now published three books, all of which had, in general, been critically well received. His future as a writer seemed assured.

For some time, he had been experiencing trouble with his throat. At certain periods, he found difficulty in speaking and in swallowing. Several years later, recalling this phase of his life, he told Clay Shaw that he had known of a woman who had been similarly afflicted. She might be walking along the street with her husband during a time when the condition was manifesting itself and would suddenly feel her throat muscles loosening. She would urgently tell her husband that she thought she could at last take some food. They would rush to the nearest restaurant, but by the time they were seated and the waiter had come to take their order, it would be too late. Her throat would have tightened up again.[8]

Expressing his old phobia once more, March suspected that the condition in his case may have something to do with the fact that he had been "gassed" in France during the war. He consulted several doctors in Harley Street, which was conveniently but a stone's throw away from his Nottingham Place flat. The specialists who examined him, however, pronounced that they could find nothing organically wrong, that his throat muscles were operating perfectly. Eventually, he was advised—or decided himself—to consult an analyst. The name of Dr. Edward Glover was suggested and March made an appointment to see him.[9]

Glover was soon able to demonstrate that the intermittent paralysis of the throat muscles was nothing other than a hysterical condition. He explained that a man can have psychological reasons for paralyzing himself, so that, as in March's case, he cannot talk and cannot converse with other people. The throat condition was soon cured. Glover himself has confirmed: "The hysterical side of his makeup was quite small. His emotional makeup was very sensitive. It was the emotional reactions he had which was the most important thing with him."[10] Although Glover maintained that the hysterical condition "wasn't a very dramatic affair," March continued to play it up to maximum effect whenever he was recounting his experiences under analysis. He told Harry T. Moore that his treatment continued for a long time without achieving any real results, "until one day, as he was indulging in free association chatter on the analyst's couch, a wartime memory came to him, something he had 'forgotten' years before; from the Freudian standpoint, he had buried it in his unconscious (apparently to such a depth that it didn't even turn up, disguised, in dreams)." March then related to Moore a version of the incident when he had bayoneted the young German soldier in the throat: "He went through agonies as he told [Glover] about it—but he never had his throat close up on him again. He then told me that mere remembrance of something that might have created a complex is not enough; the patient has to re-live the experience in all its agony, and then he is purged of it. . . . He was really a quiet, very gentle man, but he had been in hell."[11]

The truth of the matter is possibly somewhat more mundane than the graphic version March gave Moore. As Glover has noted: "Whatever his unconscious conflicts may have been, there is no doubt that consciously he was torn between the idea of a successful economic career as a lesser tycoon (perhaps an off-set to the stringent economic situation of his childhood) and a feminine vocation as a writer and poet. The result was, as is so often the case, a *compromise*: he did both."[12] It could be that the hysterical throat condition was merely the manifestation of his desire at that particular time to escape from the business world and to devote himself full time to writing. Certainly, without the power of speech, his ability to conduct face-to-face business negotiations and to take part in the inevitable socializing which formed part and parcel of his duties for Waterman would have been seriously prejudiced, if not made impossible. On the other hand, such disability would in no way have presented any bar to his literary activities. Indeed, as already noted, March tended to leave most of Waterman's London business matters in the capable hands of the young German assistant who had accompanied him from Hamburg, while he concentrated on his writing.

Whatever the truth may have been (and the specific details of his analysis will, of course, never be known), it is clear that even apart from the hysterical condition, March did feel the need for help, that he had for some years been in a somewhat confused psychological state and required the comforting and understanding presence of an analyst in whom he could confide all the doubts and fears he had regarding himself. As much as anything else, he was obsessed with curiosity to discover as much about himself as he possibly could by peeling away, one after another, the layers of his psyche, until ultimately everything was revealed to him.

Two or three years earlier, when he was in Hamburg, he had written to Margaret in this vein, informing her of his intention to consult the best psychiatrists in Berlin whenever the opportunity arose for him to travel to the German capital on Waterman business. His avowed hope, as expressed to Margaret, was that an analyst would help to disperse his overriding fears and suspicions of involvement in enduring personal relationships. He told her that it was his wish one day to marry and have a family of his own.[13] He impressed on her that there was nothing radically wrong with him, and this Glover has confirmed:

> There was no question of a psychosis in his mind. In a funny way, he wasn't even neurotic. You would have thought, Well, at least he can be privately neurotic if he likes. But I'm not very keen on just converting professional labels—like neurosis and psychosis—into personality labels. We are all to some extent schizophrenic and neurotic. The great question is if it is important enough to govern an individual's life in a way that is detrimental to himself or to others. It was in some respects detrimental to March, and this was the justification for his analysis.[14]

In a letter to Richard Crowder in 1944, March explained that although he had found it necessary to undergo analysis, it had been nevertheless "a rather painful ordeal," even though he understood that for some people the experience could be enjoyable. His analysis had been important to him, he averred, in that he had discovered, as he had always wished, much about himself. Additionally, many things he had known or suspected about himself had been confirmed. It appears to be beyond dispute that the matters which had been troubling him stemmed not from his war experiences but from his childhood. He indicated to Crowder that, as a child, he had been puzzled by the motives of adults and that many of the ideas he had held and the emotions he had felt in those far-off days had been laughed at whenever he had attempted to give expression to them, with the result that, with no comparative standards to refer to, he had begun to imagine that he was somehow "stupid or depraved."[15]

Just how painful an ordeal the analysis must have been for him is illustrated by an incident recalled by Paul Engle. Engle still regarded March's flat as "a haven and a home" whenever he was in London, a drink always available when he needed one, and bed and breakfast always there. But on arriving late one afternoon during this period, the warmth of welcome with which Engle was usually greeted was absent:

> It was winter gray outside. I was just back from watching the Nazis stamp up and down the Unter den Linden in Berlin, and I had a lot to talk about. . . . No answer to my knock. Bill often left his door unlocked when he went out briefly, so I turned the knob. The door swung in and I walked into the room, which was exceptionally dark even for a winter's day. Silence. Then I sensed a breathing presence, and I called out, "Bill?" Silence. I started to close the door, when his voice came from the far corner of the room, as if muffled in a scarf, "Don't turn on the light. I've just gone farther back into my childhood with my analyst. I can't stand light for a while. The pain in my head is too much. Go away. Come back tonight. I'm sorry. I can't bear any more life, not just now."[16]

At least two of March's friends are on record as considering that he was never the same after his analysis with Glover and, moreover, that the change was not for the better. Paul Strickland, whom March first met in Mobile shortly after his New York breakdown in 1947, felt that all the author's troubles could be traced to the time he underwent analysis in London.[17] Arthur Calder-Marshall is more explicit: "I think that whatever psychoanalysis did to his mental health, it may have drained off the reservoir of literary inspiration. Conflict is a writer's

head of steam and to have the safety valve kept open on the psychoanalyst's couch may mean you stay static. . . . I think Glover got hold
of the wrong end of the stick."[18]

The reminiscences of the New Orleans artist Joseph Dickinson provide an interesting footnote on the subject of March's analysis. Dickinson became a close friend of the author during the final year of March's
life and he has recalled how March, during one of their many conversations, put his analysis with Glover into perspective, as he saw it, in the
following terms:

> He said . . . he had always thought his success was due to his not
> being afraid of anything, nothing in the first world war, nothing in the
> business world, nothing in the world of art and literature. But after his
> analysis, he learned that his success was due to his being afraid of
> everything. He had captured the enemy because he was afraid not to; his
> writing was a hedge against failure in business; his art collection was
> insurance [against the possible time] when his stock and other invest-
> ments might be valueless. . . . He made no venture without hedging
> against loss.[19]

Whether or not the process of analysis can be said to have damaged
March's creativity in any way is something which is impossible to
assess. Certainly, during the years 1928 to 1935, prior to his analysis,
he wrote not only most of his best short stories but also his first three
novels, *Company K, Come in at the Door,* and *The Tallons*. On the other
hand, afterward he was still to produce forty or so short stories, more
than one hundred fables, and three more novels, including his finest
full-length work, *The Looking-Glass*. If it is argued that there was any
marginal decline in March's literary powers during the final phase of
his life, then no accusation can be specifically leveled against Glover,
for it cannot be gainsaid that Glover did play a significant and life-
saving role in March's life at a time when the author was desperately in
need of a father-confessor to help him, among other things, to expunge
the residual but deep-rooted childhood fears of being "stupid or depraved." Had some of Glover's understanding been available to March
in 1947, his disastrous New York breakdown might well have been
averted.

In the spring of 1936, March's recently completed novel, which he
had titled *The Tallon Boys*, was accepted by Rich and Cowan in London
and in New York by Random House, which, since the publication of
The Little Wife and Other Stories, had acquired the publishing interests
of Smith and Haas. Neither the British nor the American publishers

were happy with the proposed title. Random House sent him a telegram on May 20, observing that *The Tallon Boys* sounded like a juvenile
yarn and suggesting the alternative title *The Tallons*, to which March
agreed. The British edition eventually came out under the title *A Song
for Harps*.

Probably because he concentrated all his creative energies on com-
pleting the new novel, March wrote no new stories during 1935, but in
1936 he produced four: "The Last Meeting," "Bill's Eyes,"
"Geraldette," and "Sweet, Who Was the Armourer's Maid." Three
stories were published in magazines during 1936. "Upon the Dull
Earth Dwelling," written in 1932, appeared in the January issue of
Literary America. One of March's most subtle stories, "A Sum in
Addition," also dating from 1932, appeared in the *New Republic* in
March and was subsequently selected for inclusion in the *O. Henry
Memorial Award Prize Stories of 1936*, being awarded the $100 special
prize for the best short short-story by the judges for that year, Nancy
Hale, Ernest Brennecke, Jr., and Frank Luther Mott. The third story,
the recently written "Bill's Eyes," appeared in the November
Scribner's Magazine under the title the editors of the magazine had
given it, "Maybe the Sun Will Shine." It was picked by Edward J.
O'Brien for *The Best Short Stories of 1937* and was to become one of the
more frequently anthologized of March's short stories. Each of the
three stories published in 1936 received a three-asterisk rating from
O'Brien.

It was during one of March's visits to Oxford to stay with O'Brien and
his wife that the scholar J. L. N. O'Loughlin, who was to become
O'Brien's executor, first met the author. O'Brien had told O'Loughlin
beforehand that he had a great respect for the way March had "overcome various psychological problems by sheer will-power." From what
Paul Engle told him later, however, O'Loughlin gained the impression
that March had solved his problems "by the Wildean solution of
overcoming temptation by giving way to it." O'Loughlin's own recollections of March are unfortunately somewhat vague, but he does
recall one discussion at O'Brien's during which March advanced the
thesis that all great writers have some sexual deviation in their
makeup, a thesis which O'Loughlin countered by pointing out that
that did not apply to Keats.[20]

In the summer of 1936, March and Kay Boyle at last met. Kay Boyle
and her husband had moved with their children from Austria to England, renting a house near Seaton, Devon, where they lived for
approximately a year, making occasional trips to London. When on
these visits to the capital, Kay Boyle's publisher, Jonathan Cape,

generously gave them unrestricted use of his flat over the publishing
house in Bedford Square, Bloomsbury. It was here, at Jonathan Cape's
flat, that the meeting with March took place. Kay Boyle has recalled:

> We had invited him to drop in before the children went to bed, and
> then we would go on to dinner at the *Etoile*. When Bill arrived, he
> seemed almost aggressive in his shyness and uncertainty. Laurence and I
> and the children were playing cards. It was a game we had invented,
> called "Family." Each member of our rather large family was depicted in
> a cartoon-like, colored drawing on his or her leading card, and five other
> cards must be drawn either from the cards other players held, or from
> the kitty, to complete each family's suit. . . . The cards were mostly
> drawn and painted by Laurence, although the older children did some of
> them, and they were all small works of art. Laurence gave Bill a drink,
> and the children dealt out cards to him, and he sat down in great
> distress. Although all the lead cards had printed on them the names of
> the other cards needed to complete the suit, Bill was totally helpless,
> bewildered, and almost irritable in his distress. It was not until we had
> put the children to bed and the three of us went out for dinner that the
> strain lessened. He had thought that Laurence was Jonathan Cape, and
> he couldn't make any sense of what was going on. (I don't remember
> thinking of it then, but I thought about it many times in the years that
> came after: that the cause of his intense uneasiness was his mistrust of
> children. He was somehow infuriated by their innocence. It was as if he
> suspected children of having access to some kind of knowledge that he
> had no inkling of. Perhaps *The Bad Seed* is a partial confirmation of this.)
> What we talked about at dinner, I don't recall. I know we talked a
> great deal, probably at some point about Paul Engle, whom Bill had sent
> to visit us in Kitzbühel. . . . I have a vague memory of Bill describing the
> functions of his job in an alien world, but speaking of it without any
> particular distaste. It seemed to me then (or after) that he was gratified
> by his success in being able to handle the job and at the same time be a
> good writer. I don't remember how much was said about this on that first
> evening, but I know that through the years I learned how alien were all
> worlds to Bill.
> We invited Bill to visit us in Devon, but he was not able to come, and I
> don't remember meeting with him again in England.[21]

The book, *365 Days*, which Kay Boyle had been editing with Laurence Vail and Nina Conarain, and which contained March's two contributions, was published in New York on November 11, 1936, three
weeks after the appearance in the bookshops of *The Tallons* on October
21. The British edition of the new novel preceded the American
edition by seven weeks, being published in London on September 3.

The British and U.S. editions carried the same dedication: "To ED-
WARD GLOVER as a slight recompense for the gray hairs I have put in
his head,"[22] to which, in Glover's personal advance copy of the U.S.
edition, March had wryly added: "or, possibly, as a horrid revenge for
the thirty pounds melted from my frame. Campbell. October 5th.
1936."

eight

The Tallons and
Resignation from Waterman

The Tallons was the first of March's novels to be written in the form of a continuous narrative. The book opens in late February 1929, when Andrew Tallon is introduced to Myrtle Bickerstaff shortly after she and her family arrive from Georgia to live in Pearl County, and it concludes in October of the following year, when Andrew is executed for the murder of his brother Jim. The tale is unfolded with an unrelenting grim inevitability, relieved but very occasionally by a brief humorous passage, and explores in the minutest psychological detail the triangular relationship which exists between the two brothers and Myrtle. The book is, as March himself described it, "a study in paranoia."[1] According to Robert Clark, March still thought kindly of *The Tallons* to the very end of his life, "because it had permitted him to talk at 'arm's length' of his peers, his family and of the insipid quality of living a casually stupid life."[2] He did not hide his disappointment at the reaction of the critics when the book appeared, considering it in his own mind "head and shoulders over everything I've done."[3]

The book is a reworking and expansion of the novelette "The Unploughed Patch," which had appeared in *Pagany* in 1933, and possibly also contains elements from the discarded short story "Comfort Me with Apples." Of "The Unploughed Patch," William T. Going has written:

> For uncompromising realistic tragedy it stands among March's most memorable tales, and among his many unattractive women Hallie Barrows, as she is called in this version, is a true Southern mill-town Emma Bovary. . . . Though it is a rather long story in its original form (about 24,500 words), it is compressed into "one Saturday afternoon in June" when Andrew Tallon pays his regular weekly visit to Gramlings store. On

the way he rehearses the longings and defeats of his life, thwarted as he is by his disfiguring harelip. He tries vainly to forget the body of his brother Jim buried in the "unploughed patch." He now finds his life not simpler, as he had hoped, but more complicated. All he is sure of is that the sky is "deeply blue—all one color." The neat compressed frame is sacrificed in the novel, and the apprehension of Andrew in the end weakens the novel's main idea of fraternal love and hate.[4]

There are in *The Tallons* many links with the previous novel, *Come in at the Door*. In the earlier novel, it is from the ten-year-old Andrew Tallon and his nine-year-old brother Jim that Chester Hurry first learns that his uncle Bushrod has had the whole of his body covered with "smutty" tattoos. In *The Tallons* we renew acquaintance with Miss Sarah Tarleton and her niece Bessie, whose life was so radically changed when her lover, Andrew's and Jim's elder brother Bradford, was killed in France during World War I. The sawmill town, Hodgetown, the creation of which was described in the earlier novel, is now a thriving community. In the later novel, Carl Graffenreid, with whom Chester shared a desk at Professor Drewery's school in 1913, marries Susan Tallon, sister of Andrew and Jim, and takes her away to set up home in Oklahoma. Other of Chester's school companions, such as Rafe Hall and Herb Outerbridge, play peripheral but important roles in *The Tallons*. Holm Barrascale, who calls at the Tarleton store in *Come in at the Door* for some peanut candy for his pregnant wife, is the person, together with his wife, to whom Andrew publicly confesses his crime.

The basic story line is the very essence of simplicity: indeed, it is nothing more nor less than the age-old legend of the eternal triangle. The good, simple man (Andrew) courts and is brutally rejected by the shallow, flighty girl (Myrtle) who desires the feckless, conceited brother (Jim). To add somewhat heavy-handed symbolic weight to the contrast between "good" and "evil," the light-haired Andrew bears the burden of an unsightly harelip and a grunting, sometimes almost incomprehensible, way of speaking, whereas the dark-haired Jim is irresistibly handsome and graced, when he chooses to turn on the charm, with a silver, persuasive tongue. Jim seduces Myrtle, by no means without her connivance. They run off together one night to Reedyville, unbeknown to anyone, to be married by a justice of the peace. Shortly afterward, they take up residence at the Tallon farm with Andrew in uneasy trinity. Jim, of course, soon becomes bored with married life, which restricts his former free and easy ways, carousing with the boys and making up to the girls. He becomes convinced that Andrew and Myrtle, left on their own all day at the farm while he goes to work at the sawmill, are having an affair behind his back and that his wife is carrying his brother's child. The conviction hardens into an obsession. In anger, he hits Myrtle, cursing both her and Andrew for making a fool of him. He incites monumental quarrels, which are the talk of the neighborhood. Periodically, he experiences bouts of shame for the way he has been acting but nevertheless remains constantly on the lookout for any excuse to accuse his wife of infidelity. He decides to go away. He calls on his old sweetheart, May MacLean, explaining to her that he has to leave because he is sure Andrew is determined to kill him. The tension at the Tallon farm intensifies. When at last Jim packs his new suitcase, Myrtle pleads with him to stay, but he knocks her to the floor when she tries to prevent his leaving. He begins kicking her. Andrew attacks him and breaks his neck. Myrtle takes charge of the situation. She helps Andrew bury Jim's body in the field. She tells her family and the neighbors that Jim has deserted her. At first her story is accepted without question, for Jim had made no secret of the fact that this was what he was threatening to do. Bound together in their shared guilt, Andrew and Myrtle can find no contentment. Indeed, when, inevitably, they sleep together one night some months after the murder, Myrtle's old feeling of physical revulsion for Andrew returns. Finally, unable to bear the weight of his guilt any longer, Andrew confesses, half-believing that because of the extenuating circumstances surrounding Jim's death, he will not suffer the supreme penalty. The district attorney finds no case against Myrtle and, after testifying at Andrew's trial, she leaves Pearl County for good. Andrew, however, is found guilty of first-degree murder and is executed.

Apart from the fact that "The Unploughed Patch" ends at the point when Andrew makes his public confession, so that his eventual fate is left to the reader's imagination, all the above basic elements of the plot of *The Tallons* are contained in the shorter work. William T. Going suggests that the *Pagany* novelette "seems better" than the full-length novel March created from it and observes that although *The Tallons* "expands the time structure and the atmosphere of the mill town," March not only abandoned the compact, single viewpoint of Andrew but additionally became "inordinately obsessed with applying T. S. Eliot's theory of the objective correlative."[5]

T. S. Eliot propounded his thesis in his essay "Hamlet" (1919), when he wrote that "the only way of expressing emotion in art is by finding an 'objective correlative'; in other words, a set of objects; a situation, a chain of events which shall be the formula of that *particular*; such that when the general facts which must terminate in sensory experience, are given, the emotion is immediately evoked."[6]

In a long statement written in 1937, March set out in some detail what he had attempted to achieve in *The Tallons*. As it is the most revealing and certainly the most sustained statement March was ever to make about his work, it is worth quoting at length:

> In that particular book, I wanted to write an objective novel, preserving, if I could the shadings of character and situation which must be elided in the Hemingway, James Cain school. The only thing I dislike about the hard, fast moving modern novel is the fact that the people all seem to be cut out of the same piece of wrapping paper, and that they must be over-simplified. The old timey, subjective book is too damned long and too omniscient, and too tiresome. So I wanted to solve the problem, if I could, by writing an objective book on the surface and by projecting the emotions of the people onto animals, scenery or inanimate objects, give them an added depth of character and subtlety and variation.
>
> In other words, here's an example of what I mean: I haven't a copy of the book before me, but somewhere toward the end Andrew takes his sister-in-law to the doctor to determine whether or not she's pregnant. It has already been established with care that he's a thrifty man. On the way back from the doctor, Andrew stops, and looks up at the sky. Instead of saying what he's thinking, I show a circle of buzzards high against the sky who appear moored to an invisible mast and who are drifting outward in wide circles until they are pulled up suddenly. At that moment Andrew turns to Myrtle and suggests that they go back to the town, draw out his savings and spend them while they have time. Before that, they have both declared that they didn't know how the situation at the farm, the triangular situation between the woman and the two brothers was to end, but with the picture of the buzzards, I was projecting, or endeavoring to do so, at any rate, their hidden thoughts. They did know how it was going to end, both of them, and this is shown by what happened.
>
> Buzzards, obviously, indicate nothing so completely as they do death. Ropes and poles equate hanging. So Andrew, possibly only unconsciously, knew and accepted the fact that he must kill his brother. He knew that he must hang for it, and this projected statement of his character makes much of the latter part of the book more deeply comprehensible.
>
> Myrtle, when pressed, stated that she wanted a black velvet opera coat, the most inappropriate thing she could select. I let her rationalized reason appear in the book, but underneath she knew what she wanted the cloak for. She selected her present appropriately. Later, when her husband had been killed, and she had got her revenge on both the brothers, she stated that she had kept the cloak a secret from the county.

She took it out and used it for the purpose she had intended: she buried her husband in it. She first clipped the lock of hair over his forehead—or maybe she did that later, I don't remember precisely. At any rate she made him a woman and buried him that way. She rationalized her conduct again by saying that she wanted to bury Jim in something soft and since the county didn't know of the cloak, it was an ideal shroud, or words to that effect.[7]

It is, of course, hardly surprising that this highly individual and frequently obscure exposition of the objective correlative theory was simply not appreciated by the greater mass of his readers. Some critics would doubtless argue that there is little point in creating a literary work of art if readers are unable to recognize the ideas the author is attempting to convey. While there is an undeniable validity in such argument, it is not, on the other hand, totally necessary that the deeper significance of certain passages be wholly understood by un-initiated readers, provided their emotional response to those passages are the ones the author has carefully set out to evoke. Indeed, the extent of March's success can surely be measured by the manner in which he has applied his psychological skills so expertly and so co-vertly that readers remain for the most part blissfully unaware of the way in which their minds are being manipulated. It is only when readers take the trouble to subject the text to a close scrutiny that they will begin to realize just how cunningly March has achieved his effects.

For example, the seasons and the weather seem to reflect the moods and the changing natures of the principal characters. The springtime mirrors Andrew's sensual awakening, his sudden decision to plow the field preparatory to the planting of the seed occurring on the day after he first meets Myrtle, the rising of the sap and the budding of the leaves complementing the swelling of his passion, the passion he can adequately express only in his strange, forceful, biblical poems, so reminiscent of the Songs of Solomon. The heat of summer coincides with Myrtle's frantic pursuit of Jim and their eventual marriage in August. The fall charts the progressive barrenness of life on the Tallon farm. By December, Jim is dead. The winter months reflect the bleakness of Myrtle's attitude toward Andrew. The advancing spring corresponds with Andrew's slow coming to terms with himself, his inability to plow over the top of Jim's unmarked grave, and his even-tual confession which enables him to feel whole again.

On the day Jim brings his bride to live on the Tallon farm, Andrew takes his niece Edna Cleaver, who has been housekeeping for the two brothers after their sister's marriage and departure for Oklahoma, back to her parents' home. Andrew's emotional state is beautifully suggested in March's description of the countryside through which he drives his car:

> The land lay burning under the heat of August, with light trembling upward in spirals from fields. Occasionally a stray wind blew for an instant and stopped, as if its force had been expended in bending once the spearheads of the pine saplings, or in dipping once to swirl the dust languidly upward from the red clay of the roadbed, and to powder it finally upon the parched grass that grew by the roadside. [*TT*, p. 164]

Similarly, the precise moment when Jim's short-lived passion for Myrtle finally dies is symbolized by the collapse of the slab-pit. Jim has been out roistering with his friends. It is late at night, and Jim separates himself for a moment from his noisy drinking companions:

> The slab-pit lighted the sky with a salmon-colored glare, as if some false and terrifying dawn perpetually impended. He stared at the sky for a time, but not conscious of it, and then the weight of the pyramided wood, under which the fires burned eternally, shifted and sank downward with a low, booming noise, and showers of sparks were thrown upward into the sky like burnished insects frightened to flight. . . . The burning sparks had separated themselves from the thrown mass in which they had risen above the horizon, and were drifting outward now, but dimmer, and dying together in falling curves. He rubbed his cupped palm over his face, bringing himself back to the world of reality. [*TT*, p. 208]

In such a mood, he willingly falls in with the suggestion made by one of his companions that they should all spend the rest of the night at Violet May's sporting house in Reedyville.

The objective correlative is employed by March with equal effectiveness through the agency of animals and nature. On his way to call on Myrtle for the first time, Andrew walks along a road edged with sweet-myrtles and plumed second-growth young pines, which are clearly meant to represent Myrtle and Andrew as well as the way in which Andrew was already anticipating their coming relationship: the fragile, perfumed flower and the phallic pine.

Later in the book, when Jim's jealousy of his brother is at its height, he leaves the house after quarreling with Myrtle and Andrew and, sitting by the roadside, hears in the distance a penned stallion kicking at the walls of its corral. This sound and the stallion's shrill whinnying echoes Jim's own feelings of being hemmed in by his ill-conceived marriage, as well as his own sexual frustration. A few nights later, after yet another quarrel, it is Andrew who, this time, leaves the house and hears the beating hooves and the cries of the stallion. This scene immediately follows the scene of the circling buzzards, which has established Andrew's acceptance of the final outcome of the doomed triangular relationship. The savage restlessness of the unseen stallion demonstrates that his actions are not going to be motivated solely on account of Jim's thoughtlessness and cruelty toward Myrtle but are in fact to be dominated by his unabated carnal desire for his sister-in-law. He falls to his knees, praying to God to wipe out the evil within him and to show him the true way.

Birds, too, become a metaphor for sexual desire. When, prior to their marriage, Jim, filled with remorse for having betrayed his brother, avoids all contact with Myrtle, she finds a way to be near him by taking him lunch each day at the sawmill. The night song of birds echo her own happiness at having discovered such a simple and ostensibly satisfactory method of solving her problem. To Andrew, however, the same bird song is an expression of his love for the worthless Myrtle. He sits at his open window, listening to the birds and smelling the pungent aroma of the spiced pinks in the flowerbeds below.

If, on this occasion, the smell of flowers or vegetation represents for Andrew a conscious association with Myrtle, it was not always so. At the very beginning of the book, Andrew sits on the kitchen steps of the Tallon farmhouse, happily thinking of Myrtle: "He felt against his cheeks the wind that blew from the creek, a wind that lifted his hair and brought to his senses a delicate odor of spiced decay" (*TT*, p. 22). It is unfortunate that he does not recognize the omen. From that moment on, like the opening chorus in some Greek tragedy, a sense of brooding inevitable disaster hangs like a pall over the whole book.

That same evening, Andrew calls for Myrtle and takes her to the drugstore, where she sees Jim for the first time. Jim, who is with his sweetheart, May MacLean, and a number of his cronies, tells a "true" ghost story about a murdered girl whose dismembered body is buried in a field. Her murderer is apprehended and lynched. Having led his audience on, Jim eventually admits he has made up the whole yarn. He has, however, in his imagination preordained his own fate and his brother's fate.

Jim, indeed, appears to go out of his way to create the circumstances which will culminate in the final tragedy. Shortly after he has seduced Myrtle, at a time when his brother still regards her as his sweetheart, Jim vows: "I swear to God I'll never see her again! I swear it! If I touch her again may I rot forever in hell!" (*TT*, p. 76). Unable to help himself, he breaks his oath and thus symbolically condemns himself to death. From the moment he marries Myrtle, he strives subconsciously toward his own destruction. He allows suspicion insidiously to take over his mind. He provokes quarrels, for no other reason it sometimes seems than to make his wife and his brother hate him. Toward the end, possibly by then consciously aware that he is engineering his own execution, he asks himself: "What's to become of me? What's going to happen?" (*TT*, p. 249). When he tells May MacLean that Andrew is determined to kill him, he feels a sense of release: "Maybe I really believed it when I told her . . . but I don't any more . . . I don't have to think of such things any more. I'm free now" (*TT*, p. 270). But the freedom is merely the freedom from uncertainty that a man on trial experiences when at last the sentence of death is passed on him. The overwhelming sense of inevitability that Jim himself has played such a major part in fostering becomes so strong that, just before the murder, Andrew finds himself thinking of Jim in the past tense, as if "already he was someone like Bradford, who existed only as a part of a remembered past" (*TT*, p. 280); and when Myrtle, wilting under the blows from Jim's fists, calls to him for help, Andrew responds calmly and unhurriedly, "as if he had been awaiting this all the time" (*TT*, p. 280).

The supreme irony of the story is that Myrtle, the superficial creature who acts like a malignant catalyst on the brothers, turning their love for each other into hatred, and who is directly responsible for both their deaths, escapes scot-free. She feels no remorse whatsoever for the role she has played, even if, which is unlikely, she accepts the extent of her responsibility for what has happened. After Andrew has confessed to his brother's murder and she knows that she is at last done with their guilt-ridden and impossible relationship, her feelings are precisely conveyed as she stares into the night sky:

> To the east, behind the trees that marked the limits of the Cornell's land, a moon colored like an orange was rising. The moon seemed caught in the web of the trees and unable to escape them, until, imperceptibly, it lifted clear of the entangling branches and swung upward, washing the woodland and the quiet fields evenly with a yellow light. [*TT*, p. 341]

It is Myrtle's inability to choose between the two brothers and her playing off one against the other which provokes the final tragedy. She is repelled by Andrew's physical appearance and infatuated by Jim's good looks, eager to capture the affections of the most desirable young buck in the county. When she has at last got her way, however, and Jim is snared in matrimony, she becomes disgusted by his drinking and his infidelities, as if she had imagined that marriage would somehow miraculously change his character and settle him down into a life of quiet domesticity. She realizes that she needs the tender consideration that only Andrew is able to give her. She secretly and pleasurably suspects that the passion her brother-in-law had once so gladly revealed to her in his poems still smolders on beneath the surface of his stiffly correct behavior. In an extraordinary exchange, on the day following that on which Jim and Myrtle move into the Tallon farm, Myrtle discusses with Andrew her need for them both:

> "I was just thinking about you and Jim," she explained. "I was wishing you and him could be one man instead of two."
> "And that the composite man was *Jim.*"
> "I guess so. I guess that's what I really mean." [*TT*, pp. 181– 82]

While Jim lives, Andrew knows that his case is hopeless. If only he had his brother's good looks, his brother's body, he is sure that Myrtle would have chosen him and not Jim. But Andrew is not his brother. Before his first date with Myrtle, he uses some of Jim's toilet water and tries unsuccessfully to get into a pair of Jim's drawers. It is no more possible for him to wear his brother's clothes than it is possible for him to assume his brother's character and charm. Following Jim's death, Andrew, endeavoring both to give comfort to Myrtle and to assuage his own overpowering sexual desire for her, takes over his brother's place in the conjugal bed and forces his will upon Myrtle, making violent love to her. This demonstration of his pent-up passion merely serves to revive Myrtle's old physical abhorrence of him.

Andrew's only crime is this terrible love he has for this worthless chit of a girl. The poems he writes for her, declaring that love, are redolent with sexual images:

> In the sight of my beloved, I am like iron that the smith has heated at his furnace: iron whose surface gives heat.
> I am a bar that is rigid and will not bend. [*TT*, p. 55]

When, at the beginning of their relationship, Myrtle shows one of Andrew's earlier and less explicit poems to her mother, Mrs. Bickerstaff comments: "I for one think it's real sweet, and besides that, poems ain't supposed to make real sense" (*TT*, p. 49). Myrtle also does not really understand these written outpourings of Andrew's adoration and, more important perhaps, she does not truly begin to understand just how deeply he feels the emotions he reveals to her. His passion is honest in its extreme sexuality. He does not attempt to hide his feelings, for he does not regard his desire as in the least shameful. There is a purity about Andrew, for all his male lusts, that is lacking from almost every other character in the book. He is the archetypal innocent to whom things are done. He passively accepts Myrtle's spiteful heartlessness when, for the amusement of whatever audience she can command, she mocks him by reading aloud the poems he had written for her eyes only, compounding the cruelty by imitating his garbled way of talking. Despite all the slings and arrows of outrageous fortune he has to endure, he speaks ill of nobody, until his brother, with his suspicions and insinuations, eventually drives him beyond endurance.

Andrew's basic purity of nature, of spirit, is emphasized by his concern for personal cleanliness. The book includes several descriptions of him bathing. These ablutions seem to acquire an almost symbolic significance, as if, on each occasion described, he is engaged in performing a ritualistic act of physical purification. Before his first date with Myrtle, he goes up to his bedroom and carefully washes himself all over, "as if his flesh, with love, had taken on a new importance for him" (*TT*, p. 24). Before going to the Bickerstaffs' for Sunday dinner, he goes to the pool to bathe, the water making a "kissing noise . . . as it touched and withdrew from his wallowing flesh" (*TT*, p. 57). After Jim has revealed to him that he and Myrtle have made love behind his back, Andrew visits a Negro whore in order to slake the frustrated demands of his flesh and, on returning to his own bedroom, undresses and washes his body all over. This particular act of purification does not, however, succeed in expunging from his mind the envy and hatred he feels toward his brother. He tells himself:

> "People are born in sorrow and move about the earth in patterns of sorrow without sense and without plan. Why should I take myself so seriously? I am no more important to the Creator than the trees or the vegetation which live with me on His earth. There is no eye to watch over me nor a hand to direct me, and there will be no preferred fate for me at the end, no matter what I am, or what I do with my life." [*TT*, p. 107]

He is shocked by the sacrilegious drift of his thoughts and in church the following Sunday he steps out in front of the whole congregation and renounces the Devil. Thus publicly accepting Christ, he experiences "the slow impact of God" (*TT*, p. 113). His public renunciation of the Devil, of the sinful pleasures of the flesh, is seen by Myrtle, who is in the congregation, as Andrew's public renunciation of her. And, indeed, Andrew suggests to his brother that Jim should go ahead and marry Myrtle. Andrew buttresses this spiritual purification by undergoing baptism, but as he emerges from the Pearl River he is disappointed to discover he feels "no vast and shattering changes" in himself (*TT*, p. 134). He "had expected his despair to cease with his sins" (*TT*, p. 135), but his frustrated love for Myrtle, though sublimated, is by no means abated. When Jim and Myrtle marry, Andrew is unable to bring himself to go to them voluntarily and congratulate them. For Andrew, there was to be no easily found and enduring comfort from his desperate embracing of religion. He joins the ranks of so many other of March's characters whom God has failed.

One final act of purification remains to be carried out. When he believes that the murder can be hidden no longer, Andrew goes to the pool to bathe. Standing naked in the shallow water, he looks up to heaven, "questioning it as if he wanted to find guidance there, but all he could tell surely was that the sky was blue, all one color" (*TT*, p. 336). The water chills him and even after he has put his clothes back on he still feels cold. He tries to bring warmth to his blood again but does not succeed. He knows what he must do and he knows, in his heart of hearts, that he is already a dead man, just as he knew before he killed his brother that Jim was already a dead man. Almost immediately afterward, Andrew goes out and confesses to the murder.

Andrew's inherent goodness inexorably brings about his downfall. He foolishly believes that outward purity of conduct will overcome the desires that trouble his mind and body. He fights vainly to preserve his brother's love and the love he has for his brother. Even after he has killed Jim, he turns the body face upward in the grave he has dug for it, remembering how, as a child, his brother had a great fear of sleeping on his face. Even this act of thoughtfulness proves to be another nail in Andrew's coffin, for, later, when the time comes for the field to be plowed, Andrew cannot bring himself to plow over Jim's upturned face, presumably for fear of mutilating it, in the same way his own face is mutilated. Ironically enough, it has been revealed earlier in the book that Jim had long thought that his brother's mutilated mouth had, in fact, been meant for him and that he had only escaped it by an accident of nature, resulting in Andrew's being "condemned to carry the burden of his, Jim's own, unforgivable sins" (*TT*, p. 233).

Probably the most damning testimony, hearsay though it is, which is heard at Andrew's trial is that of May MacLean, who recounts to the court the story of Jim's late-night visit, when he told her he was sure his brother was determined to kill him. Myrtle's tale is dismissed by the prosecuting attorney as the worthless testimony of a self-confessed adulterous woman, and Andrew's poems are presented to the jury as evidence of his innate depravity of character. The prosecuting attorney, in his extremely persuasive summing up, tells the jury that this is essentially a straightforward case of a brother who "wanted his brother's wife and . . . was not content until he had planned his deed and murdered that affectionate brother in cold blood" (*TT*, pp. 349–50). He assures the jury that after years of practice and study, he has come to understand absolutely the workings of the criminal mind. In his view, there is not the shadow of a doubt that Andrew is a depraved and insensitive murderer.

His words are an echo of words uttered earlier by both Myrtle and Jim. When Jim and Myrtle first move into the Tallon farm after their marriage, Edna Cleaver warns Myrtle that she will have her work cut out keeping Jim in place. Myrtle replies: "I guess I know Jim inside and out by this time" (*TT*, p. 162), a patently foolish statement to make after having known him for little more than six months and lived with him as his wife for no more than a few days. That same evening, Jim wins a bet that Andrew will act in a particular way and triumphantly proclaims: "I know him like a book! . . . I know old Andy inside and out by this time!" (*TT*, p. 175). The tragedy is, of course, that Myrtle does not understand Jim, and Jim does not, at root, understand Andrew, despite having grown up with him and been closer to him than anyone else. March is once again repeating his insistent theme that each human being lives in isolation, deriving no enduring comfort from external contact.

In later years, March commented (rather unfairly as far as some American critics were concerned) that only a handful of British critics seemed to have appreciated the book. Most reviewers, he thought, had entirely failed to see what he was trying to do. "I can't assume that all critics are nitwits," he wrote in 1937, "that would be silly, so I should logically take for granted that I didn't accomplish what I set out to do. But somehow I feel that I did."[8]

The anonymous *Times Literary Supplement* critic may have been partly on the right track at least when, in an extensive review, he wrote: "Whatever one makes of his new novel as a whole, the sensation of life, rendered in its fine particularity of detail, is undeniable. Whether he describes a person or a scene, a movement or a thought, the thing is instantly clear before one."[9] Most British reviews, all published in early September, were indeed encouraging, so that the eagerly awaited first reviews from America must have been particularly discouraging and painful for March. Many of these early reviews were almost wholly unsympathetic, beginning with Charles Hanson Towne's piece in the *New York American* on October 21:

> Perhaps we have had enough of this dark realism, which leaves a sorry memory in the mind. Such a novel, for all its masculine strain and stress, is not to my taste; and the bleak ending leaves me with a sense of the futility of these disordered and agonized lives. "What is going to happen to us all?" the characters keep asking one another. "The worst," one feels like answering. And it does.[10]

Possibly the most hurtful of all was the first of the major reviews of the book to appear in America—that of Harold Strauss in the *New York Times Book Review*. Strauss's review was almost uncompromising in its dismissal of any consideration of March as a writer of stature and condemned the new novel as "a pedestrian and undistinguished story."[11] Mark Schorer, writing in the *New Republic*, expressed a similar opinion: "Mr. March wrote meaningfully in *Company K*, his first novel, and at least interestingly in his second, *Come in at the Door*. This time he just writes."[12]

One of the most thoughtful and objective critiques of *The Tallons* appeared in the *Nation*. In it Helen Neville put her finger squarely on what she saw as the central reason for the book's overall aesthetic failure: "what is chiefly lacking in this tragedy is the tragic sense—that element of power which can take us beyond the act into the significance of the act: we feel at all times in the presence of craftsmanship rather than of power."[13]

March had to wait until the January 1937 issue of *Forum* for what was possibly the most sympathetic and enthusiastic of the American reviews. Under the title "Tragedy of Inadequacy," Mary Colum was not troubled by what other reviewers had seen as the failure to establish an acceptable connection between psychological cause and effect. Indeed, she held quite the opposite view:

> Most remarkably and without effort does March show us the disintegration of a man who, though strong and vigorous, has always had (and this becomes clear when we reach the end of him) something mad in his make-up. This is as it happens in life; when people show themselves insane we always remember the things in their lives that pointed to this consummation.
>
> I have had occasion to note before in this department William March's remarkable power in drawing psychopathic characters, characters driven beyond themselves by frustration, by feelings of inadequacy, by the complexity of life. The realists who copy life or caricature it can never

give the illusion of a living world as can a writer of this kind, who has so few of the tricks of realism but who can take human passions, human longings for happiness and love and beauty and make a world for them.[14]

Shortly after the publication of *The Tallons*, March had occasion to write to Random House, troubled by the fact that one of his friends had been in touch with him to say that instead of receiving from the publishers the expected complimentary copy of *The Tallons*, she had been sent a copy of Gertrude Stein's latest opus, *The Geographical History of America*. March wondered if this was an isolated error or whether all those who were to receive a complimentary copy of his book had been sent the Gertrude Stein book. Strangely enough, he pointed out, none of his other friends listed on the invoice had written him acknowledging receipt of *The Tallons*. A hurried check in the shipping room at Random House revealed that March's worst fears were realized, that the Gertrude Stein book had indeed been sent to all the listed recipients. The matter was rectified forthwith, with appropriate apologies to all concerned. March treated the matter good-humoredly, but there is little doubt that he was annoyed, and the incident may have had some influence on the decision he was to make two years later to part company with Random House when little enthusiasm was shown for his proposed second collection of short stories.

In May 1937, the business manager of *American Mercury* approached Random House to propose that the magazine reprint *Company K* in its new twenty-five-cent edition, subject to permission being granted to cut the work to conform with the normal 128-page format used for the series, most of the editing being confined to the postwar sections of the book. To achieve this, it would be necessary to omit whole sections here and there, or to rearrange some sections to achieve suitable continuity, but there would be no question of emasculating the work as a whole or of any rewriting. March was content to leave all the details of the negotiations in the hands of his publishers and his recently appointed literary agent, Max Lieber, who gave his approval to the project, subject, on March's directive, to his being happy with the final edited text. The contract for the book was signed on August 26, 1937.[15]

March had not yet embarked on the writing of a new novel, although he had one planned and hoped to start it in the coming fall. He was, however, working on a book, possibly a collection of related stories about Reedyville. He was also toying with the idea, so he said, of producing a compulsively readable treatise on "Rate Structures or Procedure before the Interstate Commerce Commission." He regarded this as one of his "little boy phantasies."[16]

He continued to produce short stories of high quality. The year 1937, in fact, was an exceptionally good one. The dates appended to the stories in *Trial Balance* indicate that during that year he wrote thirteen stories, including some that rank among his finest.[17] In the previous year he had produced only four stories,[18] and in 1935 he had produced none at all. As well as being the all-time vintage year of March's short-story output, 1937 can also be viewed as a watershed in March's career as a short-story writer, for, of the fifty-five stories published in *Trial Balance* in 1945, forty-two were written during the ten years 1928 to 1937 and only thirteen during the seven-year period 1938 to 1944, nine of these being written during the final two years. The years 1940 to 1942 were completely unproductive so far as the short story was concerned, March being otherwise engaged on his novel *The Looking-Glass* and on another literary form which was absorbing his interest during that period: the fable.

Four stories were published during 1937: "The Last Meeting" in the February issue of the *Atlantic Monthly;* "Geraldette" in the August issue of *Harper's Bazaar;* "The Listening Post" in the autumn issue of the *Yale Review;* and "The Toy Bank" in *Redbook Magazine* for December. "The Last Meeting" was selected for inclusion in the *O. Henry Memorial Award Prize Stories of 1937* and in *The Best Short Stories of 1938,* receiving a three-asterisk rating from O'Brien. "The Listening Post" also received a three-asterisk rating, but the two other stories each received only two asterisks.

For some time, March had become increasingly enamored with the idea of devoting himself full time to his literary career. His work for Waterman in London was virtually at an end. The organization had been established to his satisfaction and could be safely left in the hands of his subordinates. He was now a rich man and, so he told his brother Peter, he had determined that as soon as he held sufficient investment in Waterman stock to provide him with an annual income of not less than $15,000 he would resign from the company. He apparently achieved this income goal in 1937, while he was in London, and he wrote to Ed Roberts and his other colleagues in Mobile, notifying them of the decision he had reached.[19]

After tidying up his business and personal affairs in London, he returned to the company's New York office and began completing plans for his retirement. He took a relatively small apartment in Manhattan at 124 West 55th Street, near the theater district and not far from Central Park. His sister Margaret brought him a supply of homemade preserves and the books he had left in her care when he had gone abroad. By December 29, he was able to report to her that all the curtains were up at the windows and that he was ready to receive visitors. He also told her that he was working on a novelette, "Bonny May's Dolls," but that he was unfortunately not progressing with it as well as he might have wished. He was also tinkering with the idea of writing some sketches for the *New Yorker*, feeling (perhaps incorrectly, as he admitted) that they would be comparatively simple to do and would, moreover, provide him with a steady market. He may have changed his mind, or possibly was to discover—and this seems more likely—that his contributions did not conform with the rigid *New Yorker* formula. At any rate, nothing was ever published in the magazine under his name.[20]

In addition to enjoying his reunion with his older sister and her husband and family, he also saw something of his younger brother Peter, who was then living in New York and was engaged to, or shortly to be engaged to, Thomas Wolfe's secretary, Gwen Jassinoff. He renewed contact with many of his old friends, including Edith Walton and Lombard Jones, who had married in 1933. Edith was now pregnant. In 1938, she and her husband became the proud parents of twin boys and their days of literary party-throwing and party-going declined. They had earlier moved from East 9th Street to Lexington Avenue and 96th Street, which was "a long, long trek" for most of their friends who still lived downtown. Edith continued reviewing books for the *New York Times Book Review* and the *Sun*, as well as acting as a reader for Macmillan. Jones, by this time, was involved in art directing and production for *House Beautiful* and *Architectural Review*. March still saw them from time to time during this period, inviting them to the small literary parties he had begun to hold occasionally at his 55th Street apartment and over which Margaret sometimes presided as hostess. It was at one such gathering that Jones recalls meeting Carson McCullers.

March had been introduced to the work of Carson McCullers by Sylvia Chatfield Bates, who had been McCullers's writing teacher. Sylvia Bates and her former pupil had continued to keep in touch and when Bates learned that McCullers was writing a novel she suggested that the manuscript should be sent to March for his opinion, further suggesting that if March's opinion was favorable she (Bates) would ask him to sponsor it for the Houghton Mifflin Fiction Fellowship Award, a recently instituted contest founded by the Boston publishing house and open only to unpublished writers. McCullers followed her former teacher's advice, sending March a detailed outline of her book and the first six chapters, which was all she had completed to date. March thought *The Mute*, as the book was then titled, the work of a young writer of genius and, so the story goes, was unable to accept that it was indeed a first novel. He had no hesitation in joining Sylvia Bates in sponsoring the book. When McCullers wrote thanking him for his support and belief in her work, she revealed that she had long been an admirer of his own work and that she had been so surprised and delighted by the enthusiasm he had shown for *The Mute* that she had lapsed into a state of near transport for several days.[21] Carson McCullers was awarded a Fiction Fellowship of $1,500, which enabled her to finish the book. It was published two years later by Houghton Mifflin under the title *The Heart Is a Lonely Hunter.* March's judgment and enthusiasm for the first six chapters proved not to be misplaced, for the book is now regarded by many as one of the key works of American literature of the 1940s.

It was also in 1938 that March first met Clay Shaw, then in his mid-twenties, at a dinner party given by a mutual acquaintance who had been told how greatly Shaw wanted to meet the author.[22] Shaw was struck by what he saw as March's rather birdlike quality: "He had a sort of prehensile nose, fine bones: the kind of thing you associate with birds. I always thought of Bill as some sort of bird-type creature."[23] During the course of the dinner party, the conversation turned to the subject of the ethical progress of mankind, opinions varying as to the level to which man had succeeded in climbing up from the slime of prehistory. March, speaking in his mild, soft voice, declared that in his view the last real ethical advance had been when mankind had given up voluntary cannibalism. His comment created something of a stir, particularly when he went on to point out that it would be foolish to doubt that mankind would not revert involuntarily to cannibalism again should the necessity arise. Shaw was immediately intrigued by the manner in which March produced this philosophical bombshell, sitting there quietly, almost apologetically, at the table.

Because he felt they needed it, March loved shocking people, and he often accomplished this very successfully, as he had done on the occasion of his first meeting with Shaw, by making arbitrary and quite outrageous remarks or statements in their presence. At another social gathering, after silently enduring the superficial chatter of those around him for several minutes, he turned to the woman sitting beside him, who was, incidentally, a complete stranger to him, and asked her in his quiet southern voice: "Have you ever had intercourse with a corpse?"[24] In the year before his death, he shocked his youngest sister, Patty, by telling her that he had become convinced that all the major crimes perpetrated by mankind are committed in the name of love.[25]

The freedom he had at last gained from business affairs, which enabled him for the first time to concentrate undisturbed on his literary work, did not produce the dramatic results March had anticipated, for, although he had settled down to a steady program of writing, his output did not appreciably increase, if, indeed, it increased at all. He followed a strict regime, allocating a certain number of hours each day, both in the morning and early afternoon, for writing. He would take an afternoon stroll in Central Park, or perhaps go to a movie, but he was by no means an avid film-goer. In the evenings, he would dine quietly with friends, go to the theater, or occasionally throw his own party. At times, preserving his intermittent need for absolute privacy, he would exist as a virtual recluse, shutting himself away from life, as if he found he could no longer bear to be part of it. It was a pattern of behavior which was to persist during the years he lived in New York and was to culminate, when he became almost paranoid in his need for privacy, in the serious breakdown he was to experience in 1947.

March and Clay Shaw became good friends. They met each other once, sometimes twice, a week and had dinner together. One incident Shaw has recounted illustrates perfectly March's painfully ambivalent attitude toward personal relationships, his yearning for human warmth and security, his natural need for sexual stimulation, his overwhelming fear of becoming too involved. Shaw had gone to his apartment one evening for drinks and dinner. His host began complaining bitterly about the woman who lived on the other side of the courtyard. "That woman drives me utterly crazy," he told Shaw. "She's not pretty. In fact, she's ugly. If she was in this room and took off all her clothes, I wouldn't even bother to look round. I'd stay glued to my typewriter. But because she's over there, across the court, I have to stop what I'm doing and watch while she strips. I'm sure there's some sort of moral there. If she was in the room, I'd take no notice, but because she's across the court, I have to watch."[26]

Ira Graley, one of the characters in *The Looking-Glass*, makes the observation that "everyone must seem crazy if you see deep enough into their minds" (*LG*, p. 196), and it was evident to Shaw that March possessed such capability of X-ray perception:

> I was enchanted by his mind, that really tremendous mind he had. He was one of the brightest and most perceptive human beings I have ever known. As I got to know him, it became clearer and clearer to me that for Bill March most people had glass heads. He could look inside and see the machinations and the things that were going on in their minds.[27]

March's explorations in his work into the murkiest depths of the human psyche prompted one reviewer, at the time of the publication of *The Looking-Glass*, to comment that "even the sanest of William March's characters seem a little crazy."[28] Another reviewer reached the conclusion that the novel remained "a loosely knit collection of case histories, nothing more," and went on to point out that the book's failure, as he saw it, typified "the fate of writers who go to the clinic for their inspiration, and not to life."[29]

Shaw, observing how people, particularly hostesses, tended to become annoyed at the habit March had of pointing out the Freudian implications of people's most common actions, was by no means the first, and would certainly not be the last, occasionally to have cause to be embarrassed by his friend's behavior. March became even more intensely interested in "perverted" relationships, claiming to recognize them between all sorts of people. This kind of obsession, as Albert Halper had earlier found, became increasingly wearisome to those who had to listen to his expositions on the subject. For all that, few would deny that March, when he was at his usual best, was an extremely entertaining companion, his conversation, even accepting its almost inevitable drift, being at its most amusing when he was with one or two or three others. Another friend has recalled:

> He was one of the few I have ever known to whom I could listen for a long time without a tinge of boredom. I have found that many novelists, endowed with a real talent, are abysmally dull talkers, but this was emphatically not true of him. His remarks were often hilarious, spoken in his soft gentle voice. His sharp eyes and ears missed little. He was always observing others' speech and mannerisms, especially seeking the outré or bizarre. He did not talk much in groups, but looked and listened, and later could and would make devastating comments about certain persons, tinged with malice, both sly and light. Almost always his comments were all too accurate.[30]

More and more, it was becoming his practice, while a story was germinating in his mind, to try out the story on anyone ready to listen to him. In this way, he was able to judge the reactions of his audience. If he did not achieve the desired effect, he would try again and again with different audiences until he got it right, and only then would he apply himself to the real task of getting it down on paper. If he could not get it right with his audiences he would scrap the whole thing as yet another failure.

It was about this time that he first told Shaw the plot of *The Bad Seed,* the novel March did not actually begin writing until 1953. March maintained that it was to be his "really great book," but Shaw became convinced finally that he had talked the book away and would never write it.

Most writers prefer not to talk about their work in progress and prefer even less to reveal any detailed exposition of plot or character, finding such discussion almost inevitably destructive to the fundamental creative process. That March found such discussion beneficial to his own creative processes is a matter which unfortunately places the earnest biographer in search of factual data at a distinct disadvantage, especially as March was so superb a raconteur. The borderline separating truth and fantasy becomes hair-thin, frequently blurred, and just as frequently indistinguishable. One can never be absolutely certain that stories March told ostensibly as the truth, including reminiscences of incidents he himself supposedly had experienced,[31] were not, after all, merely further examples of his testing out on an enthralled and unsuspecting audience the validity of his art as a storyteller.

As an example of this, March told several friends of the following extraordinary events, which he presented as fact and which his listeners unquestionably accepted as such. According to March, in the early 1920s, shortly after he had commenced employment with the Waterman Steamship Corporation, he was living with some other unmarried employees of the company in a Mobile boardinghouse. This was during the days of Prohibition. One evening he went to a drinking party in someone's room in the Battle House Hotel, then one of the leading hotels in Mobile. When eventually the party broke up, the revelers became aware that one of their number, who was in a state of extreme inebriation, was a complete stranger to everyone else present. How he had come to the party, nobody seemed to know. Possibly he had just wandered in uninvited. It was obvious to all that the stranger could not be left to fend for himself in the condition he was in, so March volunteered to take him back to his boardinghouse for the night. He got the man home, undressed him, and put him to bed, getting in beside him and sleeping soundly through the night. When he awoke next morning, he was horrified to discover that the stranger was gray and lifeless. He summoned the old black servant, the mainstay of the boardinghouse proprietress, whose loyalty to her mistress and concern for the reputation of the establishment knew no bounds. She instructed March to go to work as usual, as if nothing had happened, to say nothing to anyone, and to leave her to cope with the situation. He did as she suggested and when he returned to his room that evening there was no trace of the stranger's body or clothes.

When he saw the black retainer again, she made no mention of the incident, nor did she ever refer to it during the remainder of his stay at the boardinghouse. Many years later, long after he had left and long after the proprietress and her retainer had died, the boardinghouse was demolished to make way for the construction of a new building. During preliminary excavations, a skeleton was found buried under what had probably been an outbuilding, possibly used as a storage shed, at the back of the house. The identity of the skeleton was, according to March, never established.[32]

Whether the story was fact or pure fantasy will probably never be satisfactorily determined, but it seems more than likely that it was simply another example of the gestation of a projected short story. Certainly, in a list March left at his death of some of the stories he still wanted to write was the title "Man Who Died in My Bed."[33] It is not unreasonable to speculate that the genesis of the story did have some basis in fact—most possibly in the marrying of two quite unrelated incidents: namely, the personal experience of providing a drunken companion with a bed for the night and a newspaper report of the discovery of a skeleton in the foundations of some demolished building. March's vivid imagination would have done the rest. As Clay Shaw has put it: "I think he did tend to a little dramatizing himself, but I don't think that's so unusual. I think we all do it. It's all a matter of degree. After all, a storyteller wants to make a good story about anything. So he will correct a few details to make the story more interesting, even if they don't accord with facts."[34]

Glover told Alistair Cooke that March taught him "more about schizophrenia, by his idle fantasies on his lazy days, than all the books and thirty years of analytic practice."[35] When asked to expand on this statement, Glover explained:

> By that somewhat loose generalization I did not mean to suggest that March was schizophrenic. On the contrary, his reality sense was unusually acute. In a sense, of course, it can be said that every individual during his early development passes through a phase which, if assessed by adult standards, could be described as schizophrenic. The question turns on the relation of fantasy activity to reality control. The schizophrenic suffers in varying degree from a persistent defect in reality sense. The artist, on the other hand, gives rein to his archaic fantasy, but in the ordinary affairs of life preserves to a greater or lesser extent his sense of reality. It follows that the fantasies to which he gives expression in his creative work are less archaic and accordingly consonant with normal mental functioning. . . . March was particularly gifted in this way. . . . He was a man who impressed me very much by the facility of

the operation of his fantasy systems. For example—he liked doing it, actually—he would come in some day, having come up in a bus or tram, and we would be talking about spinning ideas off other people under observation. He'd say, "I'll tell you——" and he would start up and give me a fairly coherent and collected fantasy of everyone he had observed in that bus. It just came absolutely freely from him. . . . He was a very human person. I was never in anything but a professional relationship with him, but I'm quite sure he would have been the most entertaining companion.[36]

Five of the stories March had written during the good harvest year 1937 were published during 1938: "This Little World" ("A Short History of England") in *Alabama Rammer Jammer* for April; "Runagate Niggers" in the May issue of *Coronet*; "Time and Leigh Brothers" in the December issue of *Tanager*; "A Haircut in Toulouse" in the winter issue of *Prairie Schooner*; and "Tune the Old Cow Died To" in the December issue of *American Prefaces*. Of these stories, Edward J. O'Brien awarded only the last a three-asterisk rating in *The Best Short Stories of 1939*. "This Little World" was not even listed among the distinctive stories of the year, possibly because a copy of the small college magazine in which it appeared was not sent to O'Brien. The other three stories were given only one-asterisk ratings.

March completed three stories during 1938.[38] This did not represent his total output for the year, for as well as working on his new novel, titled *Kneel to the Prettiest*, he was planning and composing a volume of fables. In addition to all this, he was busy revising a further selection of short stories for a new collection he hoped to bring out in the fall. Due to a number of unforeseen difficulties, however, the book was not published until the following March.

March wished to include all five stories which had been accepted for publication in magazines during 1938 in the new collection, and in order to accomplish this, while preserving his magazine readership, he had come to an arrangement with the editors of *Tanager* and *Prairie Schooner* that if they were unable to publish the stories "Time and Leigh Brothers" and "A Haircut in Toulouse" in their magazines prior to the book's publication, they could publish them for nothing, on the understanding that March could go ahead and include them in the collection. The editor of the *Yale Review*, who had accepted "Tune the Old Cow Died To," was not, however, willing or able to agree to such an arrangement. March wrote to the editor, Helen McAfee, on July 19, explaining his problem and intimating that while he wanted to include the story in the collection he also wanted to ensure that it appeared in the *Yale Review*. Would it be possible, he wondered, for the story to be printed in the fall issue of the magazine at the latest and permission granted for both it and "The Listening Post" (which had appeared in the magazine's autumn 1937 issue) to be reprinted in the new collection? He enclosed a revised ending for the later story, asking the editor to use it if she preferred it to the old one, otherwise to throw it in the wastepaper basket. The changes he had made to the last three pages of the story were few, his main purpose being to change the hymn sung by the old woman Ella to "Safe in the Arms of Jesus," as he thought this more appropriate than the one he had originally used.[38] Miss McAfee replied by return post, giving the necessary permission regarding "The Listening Post" but explaining that unfortunately it would not be possible, as March had suggested, to publish the new story in the forthcoming fall issue. In the circumstances, subject to his confirmation, the best solution would be for her to return the story to him so that he could use it in the collection he was planning.[39] March, however, was unhappy about relinquishing the kudos to be gained from publication in the *Yale Review*, sensing furthermore that the story was an anthologist's item and could well be selected for O'Brien's 1939 anthology. He accordingly decided to leave well enough alone by omitting it from the collection and allowing Miss McAfee to print it when she was able.

As it happened, there was a further development two months later. Random House, much to March's disgust, declined the book of stories. He informed Lieber that he wanted to break with Random House and find a new publisher. By September, the Boston publishing house of Little, Brown and Company, which was to publish three of March's remaining five books, had accepted the book and had fixed publication tentatively for March 1939. Little, Brown was anxious, however, that "Tune the Old Cow Died To" should be included in the collection. March wrote again to Miss McAfee on September 13, explaining the changed situation and asking, in view of the delayed publication of the book, if she could now say if there was any likelihood of the story coming out in the *Yale Review* before March.

By October, the new collection had been given the title *Some Like Them Short* by the new publisher. It was not March's choice and he never liked the title, maintaining that he flinched whenever he saw it.[40] Subject to the final outcome of the continuing negotiations in respect of "Tune the Old Cow Died To," he had decided on the list of contents for the book. On October 28, he sent Ray Everitt, his editor at Little, Brown, a copy of his first published story "The Holly Wreath," explaining that he had left it out of the new book because he thought there were perhaps enough war stories in the collection as it was. He told Everitt that although he did not consider "The Holly Wreath" in his best grade of work, he had revised it somewhat, mainly by cutting it, and that he was certainly not ashamed of it. He suggested that it should be kept in reserve, in the event that "Tune the Old Cow Died To" did not become available.[41] Everitt, however, was adamant. He agreed there were too many war stories in the book. He sent "The Holly Wreath" back almost by return mail, making it plain to the author that he was counting on using "Tune the Old Cow Died To."

As Miss McAfee had not replied to his letter of September 13, March wrote to her again on November 2, advising her of the firm publication date for the book: March 6, 1939. He requested a definite reply regarding the story, reiterating that Little, Brown liked it very much, wanted to include it in the book, and was pressing him for an answer because it wanted to start setting the book in type. He reluctantly suggested that if it were more convenient, he would appreciate her considering the story withdrawn and sending it back to him.[43] Miss McAfee replied two days later, telling him that there was no possibility whatsoever of the story coming out in the *Yale Review* before the spring number, due on March 20.[44] There was no question of Little, Brown's delaying publication of the book until after that date, so March was left with no alternative but to ask Miss McAfee to return the story. It was sent to him on November 12 and almost immediately accepted by the editor of *American Prefaces,* who was able to fit it into the December issue of that magazine. The matter was accordingly resolved fairly satisfactorily so far as March was concerned, in that he had achieved magazine publication as well as having the story in the new collection. On the debit side, he had lost the desired publication in the *Yale Review* and his ultimate hopes for the story were not realized when O'Brien failed to select it for reprinting in his 1939 anthology.

Some Like Them Short was published on March 18, twelve days later than had originally been planned, but still preceding the *Yale Review* spring issue by two days. The book, dedicated to a fellow Mobilian and a longtime friend, bore the simple legend: "To Marion Davenport."

nine

Some Like Them Short and Life as a Full-Time Author

Of the twenty stories in *Some Like Them Short*, eight were written in 1937, four in 1936, three in 1934, two in 1932, and three in 1930. Thus, at the date of its publication, the book effectively spanned March's literary career until that time. Only two of the stories had not previously appeared in magazines: "A Memorial to the Slain," written in 1936, and "Flight to Confusion," now printed under its new title "The Shoe Drummer," the story he had written in 1930 which so many shocked or frightened magazine editors had regarded as unacceptable because of its morbid and outspoken sexual content.

Another of the stories dating from 1930 was "Nine Prisoners," published in *Forum* in 1931, now rearranged and slightly revised for inclusion in the book. On January 16, 1939, two months before the new story collection was published, a radio version of "Nine Prisoners," adapted by Brian J. Bryne, was broadcast on Columbia's "American School of the Air" for the benefit of juvenile audiences. In response to listener demand, the play was repeated on February 20, 1939, in the Columbia Workshop series.[1]

According to March, the play was well received on both occasions, but Marion Davenport, who was also living in New York at the time, recalled that many listeners to the February 20 broadcast were apparently upset and incensed, as some of *Forum*'s readers had been eight years before, by the implication that American soldiers could ever be capable of perpetrating such atrocities as the shooting of defenseless prisoners.[2]

With the publication of *Some Like Them Short*, March confirmed his position as one of the leading practitioners of his generation in the exacting art of the short story. Although the perceptive reader may now and then be conscious of a certain artistic unevenness in the collection as a whole—not perhaps to be altogether unexpected, considering the time span of composition—most of the stories are memorable. Inevitably, March examines the mores of small-town life, exposing the bigotry, cruelty, and smugness that so readily rises from the town's collective psyche. He explores unceasingly the manner in which reality and dream can become interchangeable, sometimes even seeming inseparable. He weaves yet again for us a unique tapestry of life, unremitting in its honesty, forcing us to look when we would prefer to avert our eyes. Indeed, if any criticism can be leveled at the book, it is simply that March's oppressive philosophy is even more dominant than it was in *The Little Wife and Other Stories*, so that many readers are left with the overriding impression of unrelieved gloom.

In this respect, "Geraldette," the first story in the book, set in the fictional sawmill town of Williston, is somewhat unrepresentative of the collection in that its portrait of the community is virtually without malice and almost affectionate, its irony not bitter but verging upon the slyly humorous. The events of the story are seen through the eyes of an unnamed ten-year-old boy, who discovers, as did Harry in "Miss Daisy," both the failings and the hypocrisy of adults. The revelation, however, is not for this narrator the traumatic experience it was for Harry, for one gains the impression that the boy is already versed to some extent in the ways of the world. He is, moreover, merely an observer of the drama that is enacted and not one of the principal players. Drama it most certainly is, and March deliberately resists playing down the atmosphere of theatricality that pervades the whole story. Indeed, the theatricality almost becomes the raison d'être of the piece, all three main characters playing their parts like the actors in a semifarcical, semitragic charade. Arguably, he carries the atmosphere of theatricality just a little too far and, in so doing, oversteps the bounds of credulity. Several loose ends are left trailing at the end of the story. While these are troublesome, it can be maintained that March is artistically correct in setting out to create this vague sense of unsatisfaction in his readers, for by this means he succeeds in introducing an intriguing element into what is otherwise a fairly commonplace plot.

The second story in the book, "A Haircut in Toulouse," is a more subtle, more serious study than "Geraldette," although March's touch is again ostensibly light. As in "Geraldette," he explores the correlation between reality and fantasy as it particularly applies to the question of human identity. We are all given to fantasizing at one time or another about our dream selves, which few of us ever have the courage to parade in front of the world and which are truly just as much our selves as the selves we allow other people to see. It cannot be questioned that the flamboyantly attired Decker in this story is the real Decker, the man he would like to be, his usual conforming self merely a sad charade.

These first two stories have as their theme the question of human identity and the ambiguity surrounding an individual's outward personality, but the next two stories concern themselves with the tragedy of human disillusionment. "The Listening Post" contains, as does "Nine Prisoners," close connections with March's first novel, for it is essentially a restatement, in a much elaborated form, of the theme of the Private Edward Romano sketch in *Company K*: that in the context of war Christianity is meaningless and ineffective. March demonstrates his bitter thesis with a neat interweaving, once again, of realism and fantasy, exemplified in the contrast between the conversation carried on by the two soldiers, Johnnie and Alan, as they stand guard in the listening post and the working of Alan's imagination when he sees "a column of mist moving detached and ghostlike across the field. . . . like a man gliding about in a long, white robe" (*SLTS*, p. 37) among the men lying dead in no-man's land, "their bodies outlined in the light of the thin, late risen moon" (*SLTS*, p. 36). With his description of the early morning sky, March establishes the whole tone of the story in the opening paragraph: "Morning was not far away, but there was no sign of light breaking against the sky: there was, as yet, only a dimming of stars already diminished, and the moon that lay close to the horizon gave, now, an unpolished and an ashen glow" (*SLTS*, p. 35). Just as the vast canopy of the heavens becomes a metaphor for the sense of utter hopelessness experienced by the two soldiers, so Johnnie's recollection of the Alabama countryside in springtime becomes a metaphor for their lost innocence. Indeed, at the end of the story, Johnnie tells how at home the boys and girls would meet on Sunday afternoons at Eden's Drug Store. The symbolism of the name is fundamental. "God, I wish I was there again!" Johnnie says, as they prepare to hand over to their reliefs (*SLTS*, p. 48).

In "The Listening Post," the disillusionment stems from the failure of Christianity to provide a solution to the human predicament. "The Toy Bank," as does "Miss Daisy," presents the disillusionment of a child when his implicit faith in an adult is rudely shattered. The trauma that the six-year-old Arthur Kent undergoes in "The Toy Bank" is, however, more subtle, more heartbreaking, and, one suspects, even more enduring than that suffered by Harry in the earlier story. Harry's disillusionment is the result of the pain-crazed ravings of his adored Sunday school teacher. Arthur's disillusionment follows his discovery that his mother has been stealing money from the toy bank his paternal grandfather had sent him as a birthday present. Having given the key to the bank to his mother for safekeeping, he cannot believe she has betrayed his trust. He is unwilling to listen to her tearful explanation that she has been forced to take the money, being at the end of her tether and not knowing which way to turn. Later, when he begins to understand the extremes of her desperation which had given her no alternative but to act as she had, Arthur forgives her, but he senses that the incident "would lie between them like a barrier as long as they both lived" (*SLTS*, p. 59). Poverty, March demonstrates, tarnishes and even sometimes destroys human relationships.

The various manifestations of poverty is a theme explored in many of the stories in the book. Indeed, every one of the next six stories examines the influence of poverty on human behavior and relationships and the attendant misery and suffering it brings in its wake.

"A Sum in Addition" has been frequently and deservedly anthologized, for in little more than a thousand words March manages to convey, in the most poignant and explicit terms imaginable, not only the awful despair and desperation of an indigent husband and father when faced with his wife's hospital bill while mourning the death of his newborn child, but also the superficial or totally uncomprehending reaction of his more fortunate fellow beings to his dilemma.

"The First Dime," one of the two pieces originally contributed to *365 Days*, is little more than the briefest of sketches, recounting how an unemployed man feels cheated and cheapened when he is obliged to resort to begging for the first time and thus betray his self-respect.

"Runagate Niggers" is a searing comment on the circular situation that existed on some plantations: the white master advancing food to the Negro sharecropper and his wife to enable them to farm their crop, taking part of the harvested crop as repayment, and then advancing more food against the following year's crop. When the two Negroes are sent money by a relative and endeavor to escape from the vicious economic circle by attempting to run off to the city, they are chased, captured, and whipped by the white landlord. A white woman from the North reports the matter to the government as a case of peonage, and the landlord is arrested and sent to jail, his wife protesting that her husband's fate only goes to prove that it is the whites, not the Negroes, who are denied their freedom.

"Senator Upjohn," the second of the *365 Days* sketches, is even more loaded with irony than "Runagate Niggers," comparing the fantasy of a radio political broadcast with the reality of a man searching for a job. The senator extols the richness of the nation, uttering his platitudes with an air of smug complacency, revealing his ignorance (or his hypocrisy), while the unemployed man is rejected by the manager of the employment agency as being too old at fifty-five.

The next story, "A Short History of England," one of the direct fruits of March's sojourn in London, develops the theme of "Senator Upjohn." Written in 1937, the year of King George VI's coronation, it is couched in the unconventional format of extracts taken from the agony column of a London newspaper. Accepting the artificiality of some of the entries, the "story" provides a succinct comment on the class-ridden British society of those days, as March obviously saw it, and of the gulf existing between the well-to-do and the poor sections of the community. March achieves this by contrasting the advertisements for expensive seats along the route of the forthcoming coronation procession and for fine-sounding palliatives designed to ease the minor complaints, real and imagined, of the rich with the continuing saga of the unemployed Alf and his wife and family.

The character and the plight of the old woman Ella in "Tune the Old Cow Died To" is far more convincing. Crippled with rheumatism and almost blind, Ella is totally dependent on her cousin Dermott for a roof over her head. Knowing that she will soon have outlived her usefulness as housekeeper and general factotum, she appreciates "more and more each day the uncertainty of her position, the slender thread that bound her to this household" (*SLTS*, p. 82). Cousin Dermott and his two unfeeling sons are nothing if not pragmatic. In Cousin Dermott's eyes, Ella is of no more account than the old cow in the barn who has also become a drag on the farm economy. Ella's almost pathological fear of the "po' farm" forces her into employing various subterfuges to disguise her increasing disability, but in her heart she knows she is fooling nobody. Ella is surely one of the most pathetic creatures in the roll call of March's characters. Under the burden of her ill health, her bad eyesight, and her confusion of mind, her indomitable spirit is at last beginning to crumble. Yet the shame of being sent to the "po' farm" keeps her going. Despite her own desperate predicament, she can still feel compassion for the old cow, visting the barn and going through the unproductive motions of milking the animal, as if trying to give it some sense of self-respect. Significantly, Ella is unable to obtain any comfort from the Bible when she tries to read it in her bedroom, shortly before the cow is led away by the slaughterhouse man. She does not attempt to kneel and pray for her own deliverance from the fate she is aware awaits her. Just after she begins singing the hymn "Safe in the Arms of Jesus," Cousin Dermott asks the slaughterhouse man to let him know if he runs across "a strong woman that appreciates

a nice home and ain't a-feared to work for her keep" (*SLTS*, p. 95).
Once again, March's message is loud and clear: there is no salvation
through the agency of God.

This didacticism is repeated in the next story, "Bill's Eyes" ("Maybe
the Sun Will Shine"). On the surface, it appears to be simply a tale of
psychological suspense: will Bill, who has undergone eye surgery, be
able to see when the swathing bandages are unwound from around his
head? On closer examination, the allegoric implications of the story
become clear. Bill has a pathetic belief in the doctor's infallibility.
When the doctor prepares him for the unveiling, warning him of the
procedure so that he will not be afraid, Bill tells him: "Christ! . . . did
you think I didn't trust you? Christ! I've got too much faith in you to be
afraid" (*SLTS*, p. 101). In Bill's mind, the doctor is equated with Our
Lord, the worker of miracles. He pledges himself to the doctor, in the
same terms that converts pledge themselves to Christ: "If you ever
want me for anything, all you got to do is to say the word and I'll drop
everything and come running, no matter where I am. And when I say
anything, I mean *anything*, including my life" (*SLTS*, p. 102). He
"sees" the doctor as an idealized God figure: "You're a dignified man
with snow-white hair, and I see you about a head taller than any man I
ever met. Then you've got deep brown eyes that are kind most of the
time but can blaze up and look all the way through a man if you think
he's got any meanness in him, because meanness is the one thing you
can't stand, not having any of it in you" (*SLTS*, pp. 100–101). When the
bandages are eventually removed from his eyes and it becomes obvious to the doctor and the nurse who are with him in the sunlit room
that the operation has been unsuccessful and that he is blind, Bill asks
the doctor to turn on the lights, so that he can check if his description
of the doctor was accurate. The doctor tells him in a slow, compassionate voice: "I'm about five feet, eight inches tall. . . . I weigh around a
hundred and seventy-five pounds, so you can imagine how paunchy
I'm getting to be. I'll be fifty-two years old next spring, and I'm getting
bald" (*SLTS*, p. 107). Yet again, Christ does not live up to man's beliefs
and expectations.

"The Last Meeting" is another product of March's stay in England.
In one respect, it is a tour de force. One has continually to remind
oneself that this brilliantly realized story was written by an American,
so steeped is it in the English tradition. In fact, March even playfully
takes a gentle knock at his own countrymen, as seen by the English,
referring to one character as being "a man with no more dignity than
those Americans who call noisily to acquaintances across dining-room
floors" (*SLTS*, p. 129). In this story, March has captured exactly the

atmosphere of an English seaside resort in April and yet has done so in artfully oblique fashion, scorning all the usual detailed descriptions of deserted stalls, forlorn unpainted bandstands, and the "vacancies" signs in boardinghouse windows. He relies almost entirely upon the setting of a rather seedy restaurant to mirror the general out-of-season tattiness of the town. The uneasy father-and-son relationship of the two main characters, their relationships with the waitresses, and the father's physical state seem to encapsulate the sad, unlovely atmosphere of the place.

Roy and Jeanette Newberry in "Upon the Dull Earth Dwelling" are, in some ways, the American counterparts of Alf and Florrie in "A Short History of England." Roy and Jeanette are similarly trapped in poverty, and although Roy does at least hold down a job with a New York freight brokerage firm, his salary is barely enough to provide for the support of his wife and their three young children. Just as Florrie accuses Alf of not being man enough to find a job, so Jeanette upbraids her husband for not having the courage to ask for a raise. Roy is another of March's inherently decent but weak men who are bedeviled by sharp-tongued and somewhat domineering women, although in this instance one cannot but feel real sympathy for Jeanette, struggling to make ends meet with three small children on her hands. Roy is the eternal dreamer, escaping from the sordidness of his surroundings into a world of make-believe peopled with princesses and handsome swains. It is implicit in the story that he will never make anything of his life, that his wife will become more and more embittered and old before her time, and that his flights into fantasy will never provide him with the enduring happiness and security he desires.

The stream-of-consciousness fantasies of Johnnie Holliday in "The Shoe Drummer" are also a means of escape from the unhappiness of everyday existence. As an escape, however, they have acquired a deeply sinister significance, for it is clear from almost the very beginning of the story that Johnnie is emotionally and psychologically unbalanced, that tragedy is imminent: "Sometimes I think that nothing around me is real; that the people walking on the sidewalks aren't real people at all; they are tailors' dummies worked by machinery. They frighten me and I want to spring into the air and fly away" (*SLTS*, p. 174). Johnnie indeed bears all the hallmarks of the classic paranoid schizophrenic. By the end of the story, he has completely lost his hold on reality, believing he has destroyed the universe and calling to his mother to save him from the crucifixion he is sure awaits him. One can appreciate the reasons why so many editors fought shy of publishing the story in their magazines. Some of its sexual content was very explicit for its day. And, of course, as a powerful and convincing study, immensely concentrated both in its imagery and in its psychological insight, of a mind disintegrating into madness, it would have made disturbing fare for a great many magazine subscribers.

Reality and fantasy yet again provide the theme for "Sweet, Who Was the Armourer's Maid." Another of March's "English" stories, it is more believable than "A Short History of England," though lacking the perfection of atmosphere and characterization of "The Last Meeting." The story concerns three old charladies, Lilian, who was once a celebrated beauty, Ella, a former American burlesque queen, and Hennie, a German. Like the customers of the public house they frequent, who annually, in a traditional ceremony, search for the queen's silver coin, Lilian and Ella search for the glory of their younger days by reliving their past conquests in their memories. Hennie is the only one of the three who does not experience a sense of loss in acting out her particular fantasy, for in her mind her dead lover still exists, still faithfully accompanying her wherever she goes.

In some ways, it is possible to identify Joe, the hick boy in "A Snowstorm in the Alps," with March himself. For Joe, who comes up from Reedyville, arrives in New York armed with the dream of working his way to the top of some large corporation. Whereas for March the dream of business and financial success became a reality, for Joe, who comes to the big city at the time of the depression, it becomes a nightmare. He eventually obtains a job as a busboy in a lunchroom run by the avaricious Mrs. Glab and in time is promoted to counterman. One evening, he goes out on a party with one of the other countermen, Fred, and two girls. Joe's girl is annoyed when he proves to be so shy, and Fred's girl, Gloria, likens him to the St. Bernard dog pictured in the painting called *A Snowstorm in the Alps* she has hanging in her room. Joe's sense of loyalty to his undeserving employer is rewarded by his being shot and killed when the lunchroom is raided by two stickup men. Ironically, he recognizes the man who shoots him as a boy from Indiana whom he met shortly after his arrival in the city. He dies with a look of almost doglike devotion on his face. The crux of the story's meaning becomes clear. The St. Bernard dog in the painting in Gloria's room has the traditional little barrel of life-giving brandy slung around its neck, but its mission of mercy has been abortive. The little fair-haired girl the dog has been seeking is already dead, lying across the dog's paws in the snow. Like the St. Bernard, Joe brings his wholesome sustenance to the city, but the violence and the greed typified by the metropolis overwhelm him: he cannot help those who are already "dead" and unable to appreciate the goodness he brings in his "barrel."

"A Memorial to the Slain" introduces a welcome change of mood from the majority of the stories preceding it. One of the more recently written works in the collection, it is an example of March at his comically ironic and bitingly satirical best, his target—which he hits fairly and squarely, with no holds barred—being the self-styled "respectable" citizens of Reedyville and, in particular, the members of Mr. Palmiller's vice society. The target is, as already indicated in the stories "Woolen Drawers" and "Happy Jack" in the earlier collection, a favorite one of March's. The mood of the story is, however, more in the astringent humorous vein of "Woolen Drawers" than in the starkly tragic vein of "Happy Jack."

The history of the town's war memorial is related by the ubiquitous Mrs. Kent (who, as did the unnamed narrator in "This Heavy Load," frequently assumes the role of the March counterpart to Conrad's Marlow) to her guest, Clark McBride. Her story is intermittently interrupted by her husband, Dr. Kent, and their colored housemaid, Mamie, who is experiencing difficulty in cooking the fresh-water turtle eggs the doctor has brought home for supper. Mrs. Kent explains to her guest, who has remarked on the fact that the town does not appear to have a war memorial, that there was indeed a memorial once. In 1920, the local newspaper had urged the formation of a committee to raise funds for the erection of such a memorial. The necessary committee was formed, comprising all the leading citizens of Reedyville, including Mr. Palmiller. Ironically, Reedyville's one and only war hero and its only citizen to have been killed in the war was Breck Boutwell, the town Lothario, who, before his enlistment, had enjoyed a herculean love life, sired several bastards, and spent most of his remaining hours playing pool and gambling on horses. An engaging rascal, he had never once been betrayed by any of the factory girls he got into trouble. But for the fact that they could obtain no proof of his sexual profligacy, the members of Mr. Palmiller's vice society would have made it their business to run him out of town, just as, several years previously, they had been instrumental in exiling his equally promiscuous sister, Honey. Honey Boutwell provides the second ironic twist to the story, for it is she who has become the only internationally celebrated person Reedyville has ever produced, taking up residence in Paris, becoming a professional singer, and being feted by the French as a very great artist indeed. When Honey learns of the plans to erect the war memorial, she instructs her French lawyers to write to

the memorial committee advising its members that, in memory of her
brother, she is willing to finance the entire project herself and that,
moreover, she has commissioned a very famous French sculptor to
create the memorial. The committee accepts her offer with alacrity,
her past misdemeanors excused and forgotten. Even Mr. Palmiller and
his society conveniently find it possible to adopt the view that Honey
must have repented her sins, so that the only Christian attitude to take
is to forgive her and obtain the memorial for free. The statue duly
arrives, but when the members of the committee view it they decide
that it would perhaps be unwise to erect it, as was intended, in the
courthouse square. They announce that it will be sited instead in a
nearby park, where, so it is declared, it will show up to better advantage among the surrounding greenery. When the day for the official
unveiling arrives, the reason for the change of venue becomes apparent. The main figure on the white marble memorial is that of a
completely naked man, whose facial features and the characteristics of
one thumb undeniably identify it as a represenation of Breck Boutwell
himself. The likeness to Honey's brother is immediately acknowledged
by a group of giggling factory girls. The town is split into three factions
over the statue. Mr. Palmiller and his society think it should be
removed, another group feels that its undisputed value as a work of art
cancels out any local inferences it may have, while the third sector of
the community sees the whole thing as a huge joke. Mr. Palmiller and
Sister Cotton begin a campaign to rid the town of this ever-present
reminder of Honey's subtle revenge, but popular feeling is against
them. Eventually, they are constrained to take matters into their own
hands. One Sunday morning, the vice society gathers at the foot of the
statue. After a moment of prayer, Sister Cotton and Mr. Palmiller
climb upon the pedestal and, with cold chisel and hammer, emasculate
the marble figure, making "Reedyville safe for both maidens and ladies
already married" (*SLTS*, p. 259). The statue thus vandalized, the town
has no option but to dismantle it for repairs. The repairs, however, are
never carried out. The detached genitals disappear, some less charita-
ble members of the community avowing that the missing piece of
marble is used by Sister Cotton as a paperweight. The statue remains
in storage in a shed back of the livery stable.

The satire is truly merciless and March is absolutely unrelenting in
the manner in which he holds up to ridicule the posturings of the
Palmillers and Cottons of this world. The humor ranges from gentle
comedy to almost broad farce, March's observations are devastatingly
accurate, and the complicated structure of the work allows the story to
be gradually unfolded in the context of interrupted conversation dur-

ing the course of a minor household crisis. The manner of the telling is, indeed, reminiscent of Quentin Compson's narration to his roommate Shreve in Faulkner's *Absalom, Absalom!* The story remained one of March's personal favorites to the end of his life. Writing to Dudley Nichols in 1952, he mentioned how he had been glancing through some of his old work and "was surprised to see how some of the humorous stories held up: I still like 'The Borax Bottle' and 'A Memorial to the Slain.'"[3]

The last story in the book, "Time and Leigh Brothers," tells of a man who has built a wall against the passage of time by living his life according to strict schedules, ensuring that not a minute is wasted. Once the idea of death begins to dominate his mind, however, this notion that he can preserve time by using it in its fullest degree is shattered. Leigh Brothers realizes that time is inexorable. His life ceases to be an exercise in drawing time out by measuring it meticulously day by day and becomes instead a race against death, an attempt to see how much he can cram into the time left to him. Either way, time is both the enemy and the inevitable victor. March appends the moral at the end of the story: "the days pass so imperceptibly that a man can be tricked into thinking that they will never end, that by his thriftiness he can make them last forever" (*SLTS*, p. 277). The already defeated Leigh Brothers will not accept this truism, telling himself: "No! No! . . . I don't agree! I am not resigned!" (*SLTS*, p. 277). On this note of abortive defiance the last story in the collection ends.

When the reviews began appearing, Little, Brown and Company must have been delighted with the reception given to this book by their new author. With few exceptions, the critics welcomed *Some Like Them Short* as being one of the best short-story collections of recent years. Although most reviewers added the rider that there were some indifferent stories in the bunch, they were nevertheless quick to point out that this could not be regarded other than as an acceptable percentage of failure or near-failure in considering the book's overall excellence.

There were, of course, the inevitable comparisons with other writers of the day: particularly William Faulkner, William Saroyan, and Ernest Hemingway. N. L. Rothman in the *Saturday Review* unequivocally suggested that March had learned something from Hemingway, then went on to admit: "But he is far from being a derivative writer. He has something to teach as well, a highly personal quality of emotion, and affirmation."[4]

In his "The First Reader" column of the *New York World-Telegram*, Harry Hansen, at the time the editor of the *O. Henry Memorial Award*

Prize Stories, tended to be somewhat less enthusiastic, possibly even damning with faint praise: "The March stories are . . . apt to be episodic; some of them are short, crisp bits. Never at any time does he overwrite."[5]

There were the out-and-out dissenters. James Gray in his piece headed "Brevity Carried To Inane Degree by William March" wrote what was overall the most unfavorable review the book was to receive. Gray could see no virtue in the compression March achieved in so many of the stories, maintaining that they "would have been a great deal better had he taken the trouble really to develop them" and had not employed the "gossip's technique" of suggesting "over and over again that there is something very interesting and amusing that he might tell if he would." The fault, Gray implied, lay not in the contrived brevity but in the "insufficiency of Mr. March's imagination."[6]

Although work on the new novel *Kneel to the Prettiest*, as it was then titled, was progressing, March also had another project under way. By November 1939 he was putting the finishing touches on a book of 120 fables, which he had collated to achieve a unity of emotion. The book was as yet untitled. The fabular form had engaged March's interest for some years, but it had not been until his return to New York and his resignation from Waterman that he had found the time to plan a whole book of fables.

The dates in *Trial Balance* indicate that March completed only one short story during the year 1939, "The Slate," which was not published until 1944, when it appeared in *Esquire* under the title "The Slate and the Sorrow." Four stories were published in magazines during 1939, two of which—"The Funeral" and "Sweet, Who Was the Armourer's Maid"—appeared shortly afterward in *Some Like Them Short*. The other two stories were "The Wood Nymph" and "Not Very—Subtle." The former, an early story dating from 1930, appeared in the May issue of the *New Mexico Quarterly Review*, and the latter, dating from 1937, appeared in the December issue of the *University of Kansas City Law Review*. "Sweet, Who Was the Armourer's Maid" and "Not Very—Subtle" were each awarded three asterisks by O'Brien in his anthologies for 1940 and 1941 respectively.

Early in 1939, March renewed contact with José Garcia Villa. Villa had read March's story "A Haircut in Toulouse" in *Prairie Schooner* and from that magazine had learned that March was back in New York. Villa wrote to March care of Random House, unaware, of course, that since the publication of *The Tallons* March had changed publishers. March, nevertheless, duly received the letter and a meeting was arranged. Villa had much to tell. Life had not been easy for him.

Apparently he had been existing more or less at poverty level, but his indomitable spirit and his glowing belief in his work had carried him through the depression years. There is little doubt that March had no hesitation in lending a helping hand, for in a letter dated May 24 Villa thanked him for his "kind favor," telling him that he appreciated it "very greatly and will remember it."[7]

It was at this time, too, that March's brother Peter married Gwen Jassinoff. Peter wanted to take his bride to Tuscaloosa to meet his mother and his family but was unable to buy Pullman reservations simply because neither he nor Gwen had the money for such luxuries. When March heard about this, he immediately sent them a check for a hundred dollars, saying he would not have them sitting up throughout the journey.[8] One can well imagine that the newlyweds were closely questioned by the rest of the family, who were undoubtedly anxious to know what their errant relative was doing up there in New York, throwing away the well-paid security of his position with Waterman in order to satisfy his whim to be a full-time writer. The news of his resignation from the company must have been received by the family with dismay and disbelief. What they possibly did not know at the time was the extent of his holding in Waterman stock and the income he was deriving therefrom. It seems that these investments, initially considerable in themselves, were rapidly appreciating. According to Clay Shaw, March admitted to an annual income about this time of approximately $80,000.

Peter and Gwen saw March frequently during this period, after their return from the South:

> He was a strange man. He was garrulous when he was in a good mood, but he could also be very withdrawn. . . . He was up and down. He got depressed—two times unfortunately very depressed. He was always angry. He had a lot of rebellion in him. It was possibly a reaction to life in general, life in the South—not specifically his war experiences. He was a complicated man. He was complicated because of his personal relationships with the mother, with the father.[9]

Peter's reminiscences reveal the same curious, ambivalent, even cryptic, attitude toward his brother that one can sense colored all the relationships between William and the rest of the Campbell family. There was undoubtedly brotherly and sisterly love. Yet even those of his siblings who were closest to him—Margaret and Peter—probably never really understood him. With the exception of Margaret and Peter (although his relationship with Margaret soured during the later years of his life), March carried on a strange love-hate relationship with his family, never forgetting his duty and loyalty toward them as eldest son and senior brother but, for all that, continuing to keep them carefully at arm's length. This last was an attitude he apparently felt compelled to adopt, all the while regretting it should be so. Had he been able to embrace the family, or, more importantly perhaps, had the family been able to embrace him and accept him for what he was, how different, one wonders, would his whole outlook on life have been?

Three more stories appeared in magazines during the year 1940: "Cinderella's Slipper" in the *Kansas Magazine 1940*; "The First Sunset" in the January issue of *American Prefaces*; and "The Marriage of the Bishops" in the autumn issue of *Accent*. The first two stories date from 1937 and 1938 respectively, "The First Sunset" being a reworking of a story he had written seven or eight years before. The third story, written in 1940, as well as being the most recent in composition, was, as William T. Going has observed, probably one of the 120 fables March had been writing over the past several months. He had found a title for the proposed book: *The Wittins and the Bretts*.[10] According to Going, "The Marriage of the Bishops" did not fit happily into the book, being appreciably longer than any of the other fables, and March decided to exclude it.[11] Of the three stories published in 1940, O'Brien included only one, "The First Sunset," in the list of distinctive stories in his 1941 anthology, awarding it three asterisks.

Little, Brown was not at all enthusiastic about the volume of fables March offered as his next book. The publishers wanted a new novel from him, understandably feeling that it would not be a wise publishing move to bring out a book of fables immediately following a volume of short stories, which, however critically well received, had not proved to be by any means a money-spinner either for them or their author. Novels, not short stories, and certainly not fables with their classic connotations redolent of the schoolroom and children's first readers, were what the public wanted.

March therefore began seeking other avenues of publication for the fables. The first to get into print was "The Wild Horses," which appeared in the *New York Post* on January 22, 1940. The following day, the same newspaper printed "The Crow and the Parrot" and on April 2, "The Pigs and the Dirty Doves." Another New York newspaper, the *Sun*, printed a fourth fable, "The Gull and the Earthquake," on May 3, exactly one week before the German invasion of Holland, Luxembourg, and Belgium. The editors of the magazines *Rocky Mountain Review* and *Tanager* accepted another ten fables. A further eight were published in December 1940 in the *Kansas Magazine 1941*, bringing the total number of fables published during the year to twenty-two.

Among the various publications to which March subscribed was the *Little Man*, a literary magazine edited and published by Robert Lowry from the basement of his home in Cincinnati.[12] March wrote to Lowry, commissioning him to produce a limited edition of the story "The First Sunset," which he proposed sending out that year to family and friends as elaborate Christmas cards. Lowry accepted the commission, designed the book and printed it on an eight-by-twelve Chandler and Price platen press. There was, Lowry has recalled, no haggling over price or design. March accepted Lowry's quotation without question and approved the design Lowry suggested, even down to the cut-out Christmas trees Lowry pasted on the front cover of each book to produce a three-dimensional effect. The only concession made to commercialism was that the type was machine-set by a professional typesetter in downtown Cincinnati.[13]

Another four fables appeared in the February 1941 issue of *Tanager* under the collective title "More Fables." In England, later that same month, Edward J. O'Brien died of a heart attack at the early age of fifty-one. His passing deprived the literary scene of the man who possibly had done more than any other single person in promoting the short-story genre to its current high-ranking status. Those whose cause he had so consistently, enthusiastically, and tirelessly championed over the years were left with a deep sense of irreplaceable loss.

Many felt that it was essential for O'Brien's work to be perpetuated so far as possible and that there should be no break in the continuity of the annual anthologies. On March 17, Villa wrote to March, suggesting that the two of them collaborate as editors of *The Best Short Stories* series where O'Brien had left off, beginning with the 1941 edition. Villa had carefully considered their possible working relationship on the project:

> If you have not got the time to read the stories (i.e. if you have too much personal work) I can shoulder most of it, and I shall do all the technical work. We will pick only from American magazines and from magazines that fall under the American rule, as for instance those published in the Philippines. I have been doing a Best Short Story series for the Philippines for years now, and I can tell you there are fine stories now being written there and which could be brought to the attention of the American public.
>
> I hope you will join me in this venture, because you and I have similar tastes, and I respect your critical judgment very much. A collaboration

between us should also facilitate securing a publisher—it would be really harder if I were alone, I must confess, for I am practically unknown now to American publishers. But I should like you to understand that it is not for this reason alone that I want you with me: I really should like us to work together: I am sure we can put out marvellous collections.

Please let me hear from you immediately about this. As for a publisher, I was thinking of our writing first to Houghton Mifflin, the present O'Brien publishers. If that fails, I naturally suggest your publisher. But we should act soon. If we start right away, we'll only have a few months of back periodicals to read. But naturally we should get a publisher first.[14]

No record is available of March's reaction to Villa's proposals, but it is doubtful that he would have been overly enthusiastic. Assuredly, he would not have viewed the prospect of any sort of collaboration, however loosely established, as a workable arrangement, recognizing that both he and Villa, for all their possible "similar tastes," were strong-minded people who would be unwilling to compromise on any issue of disagreement. There would conceivably be too many clashes of professional personality, no matter how deep their friendship. Above all, of course, such an arrangement would be for March a commitment to a quasi-binding relationship with another person, a situation he had always eventually eschewed, no matter how much he may initially have desired it. The 1941 anthology was, in fact, published under O'Brien's editorship, and the following year Martha Foley assumed the editorship of the series, a position she continued to hold with great distinction until her death in 1977.

Fourteen more fables were published during 1941, six in *Prairie Schooner*, four in *Rocky Mountain Review*, and four in *Accent*, making a grand total of eighteen published that year. Since the beginning of 1940, therefore, a third of the fables March had written had found their way into print. The readership they reached was not large, except for the four which had appeared in the New York newspapers, but March had demonstrated to his publishers, who nevertheless remained apathetic toward them, that the fables were certainly publishable.

March continued to give whatever assistance he could to any young writer who approached him and in whose work he believed. Just as three years before he had sponsored Carson McCullers's novel for the Houghton Mifflin competition, so in 1942 he sponsored the novel of another young unknown, Elizabeth Hardwick. She wrote to him on August 19, 1941, thanking him for his letter discussing her book and for his offer to write a letter of recommendation to Houghton Mifflin. "I was very interested in your comments upon the material," she wrote. "And I must say that I agree with the substance and implication of your remarks. You very wisely hit the core of the difficulties I am having and will have with the book. These remarks will be very helpful to me when I start rewriting and I appreciate them equally as much as your willingness to write a recommendation." Of March's own work, she said: "In one of Malraux's books the question is asked: What can a man best do with his life? The answer given, as I remember it, is: He can transform into consciousness the broadest possible experience. You have done that in your books. The only way I can express the very deep feeling of respect I have for you and my gratitude to you is by saying that I hope you will always be well and happy enough to do this work which must be done."[15]

The year 1942 proved to be a lean one for March so far as publication was concerned. As in 1941, none of his short stories appeared in any magazine. Indeed, the sum total of the work he did publish amounted to the seven fables which appeared collectively in the spring issue of *Prairie Schooner*.

By this time, March had other matters on his mind. He was immersed in his new novel *Kneel to the Prettiest*, and in April 1942 he was able to report to Raymond Everitt at Little, Brown that he had completed and typed, in what he hoped was final form, the first 70,000 words of the book. Having more time now at his disposal, he was planning to complete the work within the next two months, most of the remainder being already completed in one form or another and only the final two chapters still unwritten. He estimated that the novel would run to approximately 125,000 words in its finished state. It was, he admitted, the most difficult book he had yet attempted, so that he had been forced to write ten or twelve drafts of some parts of it before he had been satisfied that it was as good as he could do. He did not think, however, that this somewhat painful gestation was evident in the finished product and he offered to send Everitt the finished section of the typescript so that he could judge for himself.[16]

The letter also notified Everitt of March's new address. For some time, March had had it in mind that he would like to move to more elegant surroundings, now that his enhanced income enabled him to indulge himself in such fashion. In addition, he was still very much in contact with his former colleagues at Waterman, and they were desirous of having a suitable address in New York where they could come from time to time and entertain their customers. For this facility, they were willing to pay part of the rent. A proposed working arrangement was amicably arrived at. March eventually decided to take a rather large apartment on the thirty-second floor of the Century Towers, a fashionable apartment block erected in 1931 between 62d and 63d Streets on Central Park West. One end of the apartment overlooked the East River and the other end overlooked the Heckscher Playground in Central Park, with its carousel and wading pool, and the pond and menagerie beyond. Paul Engle has recalled the superb view of the park from the apartment window and how, on visits there, he would "watch the multiple light move across the trees, the grass, the granite, the people."[17]

It was here, in Apartment 30-K, 25 Central Park West, that March gave the more flamboyant of his legendary cocktail parties. Finley McRae, on one occasion arriving early for a party, found in the refrigerator jugs of cocktails which had been mixed the previous day for the large influx of guests. McRae would not touch the stuff, asking March for some good rye whisky instead.[18] Clay Shaw has also recalled those parties in the "tremendous living room" with its "marvelous view out over the Park," and the seemingly inexhaustible jugs of prepared cocktails:

> He would invite, oh, maybe fifty or sixty people. He had a couple of Filipino houseboys in for the occasion. He would serve only martinis and Manhattans, which he would make in the morning in gallon jugs and put in the deep freeze. They were ice cold, but they had no ice *in* them, so there was no dilution at all. There was also no way of knowing exactly how much you had had to drink, because you . . . would be standing talking to someone, and all the while the houseboys would be circulating with these pitchers of drinks. They would keep filling your glass. You drank maybe half—they filled it up. You drank three-quarters—again, they filled it up. So you really had no way of knowing. Bill would go around, looking very curiously at everyone. You see, as we got drunker and drunker, he got more and more interested in seeing what inhibitions were dropping where, who was doing what, who was insulting whom, who was propositioning whom, and so on and so forth.[19]

It was not an uncommon occurrence for these somewhat bemused guests suddenly to discover that their host was missing. He would become bored with them all and, rather than suggest that it was time for the party to break up, he would simply leave them to their own devices, letting himself unobtrusively out of the apartment to go for a stroll in the park or even to a movie. It could be that he never really enjoyed the parties he gave, merely regarding them as a means of providing grist to his writer's mill. This frequent practice of so arbitrarily abandoning his guests without a word of apology or explanation was accepted as a sort of norm by those who knew him well. According to Albert Halper, who attended several of the parties, March's manners on these occasions were always "impeccable," and in keeping with his southern origins, he was unswervingly "gallant to women." Halper, nevertheless, detected at times while the parties were in full swing the "skillful facade" March was forced to assume, the eventual uncontrollable crumbling of which facade prompted his escape from all the chattering and posturing in the crowded room.[20]

Essentially, March's life-style had not changed. The parties were, of course, held during his gregarious periods. At other times, following what had been for so long an established pattern, the need for solitude was overwhelming and he became an absolute recluse. As with his behavior at the parties, his friends accepted such complete withdrawal from society as the norm. They knew that when he was ready, and not a moment before, he would emerge from his self-imposed isolation and carry on as if nothing untoward had occurred.

Throughout the summer months of 1942, March worked systematically on the new novel. By July 17, he had received Everitt's approval of the section he had submitted and was promising his publishers that he would finish the book as soon as possible, setting himself a target of the middle of the following month. He had virtually completed the last section of the book, and one of the two remaining sections was well under way. On July 25, he sent Everitt three rewritten pages to be substituted for ones already in the editor's possession, deleting some material he now thought belonged more appropriately at the end of the book. He reported that the manuscript was going along fairly well and again expressed the hope that it would be in its finished state by August 15.

On August 9, however, he was obliged to revise his timetable. He had approximately forty pages to write and over the past several weeks he had been averaging three pages a day. It was clear that at this rate of progress he could not possibly finish the book by the fifteenth. He sent Everitt a new page he had rewritten at Everitt's suggestion and said that he wished to change the title of the book. He knew that Little, Brown was not very happy with the title anyway. He had also apparently discovered that the title he had proposed to use, *Kneel to the Prettiest*, or one very similar to it, was also being used for a play to be produced in New York that coming fall. March suggested as an alternative one of the first titles he had considered for the book: *The Looking-Glass*. He told Everitt he thought the book's title should be simple, pointing out that Little, Brown had done quite well in the past with that sort of title. He cited, as examples, John P. Marquand's *Wickford Point* and *H. M. Pulham, Esq.*[21]

The book was still not completed by September 1, when March sent revised drafts of two further pages from which he had again transposed material to the end of the book. He reported that he was sending all the remaining portions of the book, except the last fifteen or sixteen pages, to Harold Ober, who had recently become his literary agent. These final pages still needed a little more work and he did not want to release them until he was absolutely satisfied. He assured Everitt that everything would be completed within the next week.[22]

Two days later, Everitt wrote, telling March that in his opinion the book was the first major novel to have emerged from the previous generation's learning of Freudian doctrine.[23] It was a comment which was bound to please the author greatly and in his reply on September 10 he thanked Everitt, expressing the hope that the book's eventual sales would not prove to be too humiliating for his publishers. He was also able to report that to his professed astonishment he had finally finished the book and had sent Ober all the remaining pages. "No matter what else may be said about it," he wrote, "nobody can say it is carelessly done. Every word, every comma is calculated. The quality which I hoped to get into it was that of the deep, unconscious phantasy set in a background of the real world. Whether I've succeeded or not is something else. I can only say I hope so."[24]

Three more revised pages were sent to Everitt on September 22 to replace three of the existing pages in the typescript. On one, March had described a one-armed man cleaning his fingernails with a toothpick, which, as he admitted, was a somewhat difficult thing for such a man to do. Another page contained a phrase "about Nature taking charge of Mrs. Palmiller's unwilling interior"—and this, on reflection, March thought sounded unnecessarily cute. On the third page, a young man was said to be gathering material on Honey Boutwell for a doctorate. On Alistair Cooke's suggestion, March had changed his text, making the young man a researcher from the Library of Congress. The library, according to Cooke, who was an authority on such things, had been engaged in precisely such activities over the past few years.[25] By making the change Cooke suggested, the legendary figure of Honey Boutwell was effectively endowed with a patina of additional importance and cultural recognition.

Further minor amendments were sent to Everitt on October 2, among them a request to delete the "Kneel to the prettiest" quotation from the title page. The quotation, taken from an old children's game, read:

Bow to the wittiest,
Kneel to the prettiest,
And kiss the one you love the best.

With the change of title, the quotation was now ostensibly inappropriate, although in the context of the novel as a whole, its narcissistic implications would still have been relevant.

March admitted that there were undoubtedly some incorrect spellings in the typescript which he hoped the publishers' reader would pick up. He also gave Everitt virtual carte blanche to instruct the copy editor to make any changes in punctuation he deemed necessary. He made only one stipulation—that the editor first read each sentence aloud before making any changes. If, after having done that, the editor still felt that the punctuation was wrong, then March was prepared to accept the decision.[26]

The letter of October 2 also informed Everitt that March was hoping to commence work almost immediately on a new novel. He was, he indicated, feeling creatively very energetic. The novel, unlike *The Looking-Glass*, would be a short one of approximately forty thousand words and would be a "honey" if it turned out the way he wanted. This short novel was a reworking of the novelette "Bonny May's Dolls," which March had been writing at the time of his return to New York from England in 1937.

Work on this new novel had to be interrupted because of a family crisis. About Thanksgiving time, Susy March Campbell suffered a stroke. By November 20, her condition had begun giving such cause for concern that March felt impelled to leave New York for Tuscaloosa almost at a moment's notice to be with her. The crisis, fortunately, passed, and March was back in New York for Christmas, the new year, and the publication of his book.

The Looking-Glass was published on January 6, 1943. It contained the dedication: *To My Sister* / MARGARET CAMPBELL JONES."

ten

The Looking-Glass and
Wartime New York

The Looking-Glass, his longest and most ambitious novel, is March's finest literary achievement. Despite its complex structure, it is the most perfectly integrated, both narratively and thematically, of all his full-length works.

Company K, to be sure, attained a high level of narrative and thematic unity through the brief first-person sketches of the various men in the marine company. This unity, however, was already implicit in the fact that all the men shared the same experience of war, even though they may individually have reacted in different ways to that experience. Each sketch, with perhaps one or two exceptions, can stand completely on its own as a satisfactorily self-contained unit, and indeed, of course, both the sketches of Private Leo Brogan and Private Manuel Burt were originally conceived as short stories in their own right. The structural unity of *Come in at the Door* is somewhat suspect, for it represents only part of an unrealized whole. What unity the book possesses—and it has a great deal—has been skillfully but artificially imposed upon the disparate material of which it is composed. *The Tallons* achieves its structural unity from a simple, straightforward time sequence and from the underlying and, for most general readers, obscure linking of psychological analogies between environment and human behavior patterns. Although masterfully accomplished, these designs are not always sufficiently self-evident to generate the interest and excitement of the ordinary reader and raise the somewhat mundane tale of love, lust, and murder in a small sawmill town to the level of classical tragedy.

On the other hand, *The Looking-Glass* cannot, to begin with, be divided up easily and satisfactorily into its component parts, as can *Company K*. When Robert Loomis selected the material for the collec-

166

tion *A William March Omnibus* in 1956, he "searched through *The Looking-Glass* twice to see if there was some fine episode that might stand alone." But, as Alistair Cooke points out in his introduction to the volume, the book "is too well-knit to unravel into fragments, its several tragedies overlap like the leaves of an artichoke, and you must strip them away one by one to reveal the core."[1] Unlike *Come in at the Door, The Looking-Glass* was planned as a cohesive whole and there is no part of the book that could have been excerpted without destroying its unity. Conversely, there is nothing that could have been added to it without upsetting its delicate but impeccable balance. Its psychological explanations and analogies, although not unduly simplified, are not particularly shrouded in obscurity, so that, for example, the recurring symbols of both the "Sweethearts' Looking-Glass" and mirrors give depth to the narrative, explaining the influences which motivate the behavior of the tormented inhabitants of Reedyville and playing a significant part in bringing them so vividly to life.

The book's narrator and undoubtedly March's alter ego, Richard Mellen, a former resident of Reedyville, employs what he calls "the basting thread technique" in telling his story. The term possibly suggests a somewhat haphazard tacking together of material. Nothing could be further from the truth. Complex the narrative structure certainly is, as complex as anything Faulkner ever wrote, but March never once loses control over his material. The "present" is April 1942, when, after revisiting Reedyville that January to gather material for a book, Mellen joins a small gathering of Reedyville citizens, all now fairly advanced in age, at the New York apartment of Minnie McInnis McMinn, Reedyville's successful novelist, screenwriter, creator of popular radio soap operas, and unofficial town historian. Within this 1942 "present" is contained another "present": the evening of a hot September day in 1916, when the fourteen-year-old Dover Boutwell is sent by his mother Ada to obtain the three dollars demanded by Dr. Snowfield before he will consent to attend Dover's drunken father Wesley, who has injured himself by stumbling into a ditch on his way home from Mattress May's sporting house. The main time scale of the book covers the years 1898 to 1916 and Dover's frantic journeying from house to house supplies the "basting thread" which stitches together the individual histories of the principal protagonists. These histories interweave in the most subtle fashion, each being totally dependent upon the other, so that the reader, initially embarking on what appears to be a haphazard and confusing narrative, finds by the time he reaches the end of chapter 9 that March has in fact created a perfect narrative and thematic structure. Chapter 10 rounds off the book by describing

Mellen's visit to Reedyville in 1942 and the gathering in Minnie McInnis McMinn's apartment three months later and, by means of the general conversation, completes the histories of the various characters over the twenty-six years that have passed since the fateful evening in September 1916. In no way can this final chapter be regarded as a self-indulgent appendage to the story proper. It is an integral part of the book. Without it, many of March's thematic threads would have been left dangling ineffectively in mid-air.

In 1943, March wrote Richard Crowder that he thought Stanley Edgar Hyman's review of the book in the *New Republic* the most penetrating review ever written concerning his work. "It is," March observed, "most heartening to a writer to have anyone make an effort to understand him on his own, not their, terms."[2] In this context, therefore, it is useful to examine precisely what Hyman had to say. Hyman's review appeared under the heading "Alabama Faulkner." He compared March favorably to the Mississippi author, declaring that March had "come up with material fully as striking" as Faulkner's but not handled with "Faulkner's somewhat excessive symbolism of horror." After referring very briefly to some of the book's characters and tracing the theme of guilt and expiation in *The Looking-Glass* as a constant motif running through March's three previous novels, Hyman compared the book's "inchoate" form to Faulkner "at his worst." He went on, however, to note:

> What gives this seemingly formless book its high degree of organization is the imagery, which is as tight and carefully woven as a good symphony, and is impossible to do justice to within the brief space of a review. The central image of the book, the looking-glass itself, translates as "sacrificial death by immolation in ice" (as, for example, the twelve-year-old prodigy's suicide in a frozen pond), but it also partakes of such diverse characteristics as sex, blood, deformity, incest and the ultimate end of the world (a more terrible and final destruction, March says, than that by water, drought, fire or decay) and thus serves as a bridging device to unite all the scattered imagery of the book.
>
> . . . March seems to believe that all men must live in loneliness and isolation, their only possible communication "lies," but that the threads of their lives are nevertheless inseparably bound together. He tends to see all people as either mentally or psychologically deformed, and all the relationships between them, particularly close family relationships, as only endless variants of sadism, masochism, hatred and answering love, murder and expiation.[3]

While accepting that the theme of guilt and expiation was one that had greatly preoccupied him, March pointed out to Crowder that there were other themes of equal importance:

> The theme of *The Looking-Glass* was man's inability to love an object other than his own image. . . . The Looking Glass, or the World, which reflects our own precious image is consistently used all through the book. . . . Since man is so inescapably narcissistic, his loneliness is inescapable.
>   . . . I think the theme of narcissism is perhaps one of the oldest in the history of man. Aside from the classical one of the pool, the Joseph story in the Bible is the oldest I know. Or perhaps the story of Adam and the Garden of Eden has its roots in that same source.[4]

This theme of man's destruction by his own narcissism and the isolation it engenders is powerfully demonstrated toward the end of the sixth chapter of the book, after Ira Graley, Mattress May's illegitimate son, has exacted his "revenge" on his unsuspecting mother, who abandoned him when he was a mere babe in arms. He visits her establishment as a paying guest on his twenty-first birthday, arriving at the door at the precise time of his birth. His revenge, however, does not turn out as he had anticipated, for he realizes as he says goodbye to his mother and she invites him to call again that "none of the things which he had thought or imagined about her were of the slightest importance" (*LG*, p. 214). He ponders over the reality of the transience of life:

> For a time, . . . he was aware, in the deep, hidden parts of his mind, of the unnumbered ones who had lived before him: those who, like himself, had believed their unique identities the precise core of the universe, who had desired so greatly to imprint their own images against the surface of the world on which they moved and breathed. They had longed greatly and they had struggled with desperation; and yet the sum of all their lives together was now of less importance than a dinosaur's foot on a river bottom, or a fern leaf embedded in coal. . . . if man could only feel the immensity of time, could accept the unimportance of his own small part in it, he might plan his life with less arrogance and shape it more intelligently. . . . man had drowned himself in a looking-glass which had neither softness nor depth; . . . he valued, in reality, only that image of himself which he projected so earnestly onto others: the image which, when he needed it, he rediscovered with ingenuous cries of pleasure. This ability to value himself alone had been at once the symbol of his power, and the measuring stick of his defeat, for he had tripped at last and had broken his neck in a senseless effort to embrace his shadow.
> [*LG*, pp. 216–17]

This concept of the inexorable passage of time and of man's ultimate unimportance in the overall scheme of things is forcibly counterpointed in the book's final ironic image of the gathering of elderly Reedyville citizens at Minnie McInnis McMinn's apartment being invaded by the younger guests she had also invited:

> Then the butler opened the door, and all those young, successful people, the ones with so much blood and energy in them, came into the room with a rush, filling it completely with movement and bulk and sound. [*LG*, p. 346]

Ira Graley, then, is saved from self-destruction by the realization of his own intrinsic unimportance and of the unimportance of the image he had always had of himself as a bastard child, an image which had intimidated him and held him back for so long, drowning him in a sea of bitterness. After the debacle of his visit to Mattress May's, he implores Joseph St. Joseph, the principal of Reedyville High School, to teach him everything he can, so that he might better himself. He marries Fodie Boutwell but is again almost destroyed by her overwhelming desire for the high-class respectability he cannot achieve for her. When their ten-year marriage finally breaks up in 1916, on the very night Dover calls in the hope of borrowing the three dollars to pay Dr. Snowfield, Ira goes to New York to pursue the studies for what he intends will be his future life's work. He becomes a famous psychiatrist, who, according to Joseph St. Joseph, is "one of the truly great people of our day" (*LG*, p. 319). When Mellen meets him, he immediately recognizes Ira's simple humility. Ira's goodness stems from his unflinching understanding of man's fallibility and, perhaps more important, of his own shortcomings. As a boy of nineteen, he had astonished St. Joseph with his perception, declaring that "it's not how deep you see into another person's mind that determines what you really know about him: the important thing is what level of your own mind you are able to see him with" (*LG*, p. 196).

Whereas, by shattering the symbolic mirror that for so long had reflected the bitter image he saw of himself, Ira Graley manages to rise above the knowledge of his despised origins and the memory of his appalling childhood at the hands of his brutal grandparents, Manny Neholla nourishes his own bitter image, tortured by the conviction that Negro blood flows in his veins. Manny's narcissism mirrors itself upon the ideal of Clarry Palmiller, whose skin is of an unbelievably pure milky whiteness. His repressed childhod love of Hubert Palmiller's daughter intensifies into an all-consuming obsession based on the idea that "as long as she remained immaculately white, it was impossible for him to be black" (*LG*, pp. 46–47). He is too ashamed of his hand-me-down clothes to attend the New Century Party held by the Palmillers to celebrate Clarry's tenth birthday in January 1900 and shortly afterward he and his nondescript parents leave Reedyville. Sixteen years are to pass before he returns, unrecognized, a medical practitioner using the assumed and symbolic name Dr. Albert Snowfield. He wants to be near Clarry once more. Without realizing his identity, Clarry, who has been seduced by Dover Boutwell's elder brother Breck and is carrying his child, consults him, for she is too ashamed to discuss her dilemma with Dr. Kent, the family physician. She asks Snowfield to perform an abortion. He agrees, stipulating his usual fee of three dollars. He feels that by her fall from grace and the defiling of her purity, she has betrayed him, leaving him no longer with any ideal to cling to. "I must leave things to chance," he reasons. "I'll do what I can to help her, but I won't sterilize the instruments I use" (*LG*, p. 284). Inevitably, Clarry dies as a result of his ministrations, but rather than feeling guilt and despair over what he has done and what he has lost, Manny experiences "an unexpected sense of well-being, of contentment: a deep feeling of happiness such as he had never before known" (*LG*, p. 314). He comprehends that he has at last escaped from the destruction which had been implicit in his now-abated obsession and joyfully tells himself: "I'm free of her now! I'm free of her and her whiteness forever!" (*LG*, p. 314). He leaves Reedyville again, this time for good, abandons medical practice, and dedicates his life to the radical labor movement. Eventually, denouncing the capitalist land of his birth, he goes to Russia and there, as Minnie McInnis McMinn tells the guests at her party, "They shot him" (*LG*, p. 335).

Clarry is destroyed not only because of what she represents for Dr. Snowfield in the confusion of his mind but also because of who she is: the daughter of Hubert Palmiller, the rich banker and chairman of the Society for the Fostering of Temperance and the Eradication of Vice. It is her fate to become the instrument of Breck Boutwell's campaign of revenge against Mr. Palmiller for his treatment, many years before, of Breck's sister Honey. Honey, a girl of easy virtue, is hounded by Mr. Palmiller's vice society and is forced to flee from Reedyville, accompanied by Mr. Paul Kenworthy, her infatuated former employer. Breck overhears the proceedings of the vice society committee meeting during which Honey is denounced by her own sister Fodie and at which it is voted that Mr. Palmiller should swear out a warrant for Honey's arrest on a morals charge. "We must make an example of her!"

Mr. Palmiller declares. "A depraved girl of that sort isn't fit to breathe in the same air that a pure girl like my own daughter breathes!" (*LG*, p. 179). Twelve years or so later, Breck, now manager of the pool parlor and the town's Lothario, himself attracts the full attention of the vice society, infuriating its members by the series of cruel practical jokes he plays on them, collectively and individually, making them appear fools in the eyes of the community. Try as they may, Mr. Palmiller and his committee are totally unable to get the better of the wily and irrepressible Breck. Mr. Palmiller, goaded finally into a frenzy of impotent rage, shouts at Breck: "Your whole family is an eyesore, and the sooner Reedyville is rid of the lot of you, the better off the town will be! . . . There's no decency in any of you! I thought we'd taught you a lesson when we ran your filthy sister out of town" (*LG*, p. 267). With these words, Mr. Palmiller effectively signs his daughter's death warrant, for as he speaks them Breck recalls how, on that night long ago, Mr. Palmiller had declared that Honey was not fit to breathe the same air as Clarry. It is through Clarry that Breck decides to exact his revenge, knowing that Mr. Palmiller has no more vulnerable spot than the daughter he so blindly adores and regards as the most precious thing in his life, mirroring as she does his own image of himself. Breck's plan, however, backfires on him, for after he has seduced Clarry he realizes the she has fallen in love with him. Smitten with conscience, reminding himself that no matter what her father may have done, she herself was innocent, he confesses to her, and she tells him she never wants to see him again. He is so ashamed of what he has done that he decides to leave Reedyville. He boards the train to New Orleans, determined to join the marines, unaware of the fact that he has made Clarry pregnant and that she is even now lying on her deathbed. He is killed the following year in the fighting at Saint-Mihiel. Mr. Palmiller, crazed by Clarry's death, keeps asking: "Why couldn't it have been me instead?" (*LG*, p. 312). He cannot begin to understand why this terrible tragedy should have happened to him. In his own eyes, he has never done a mean or unkind thing in his life, has never harmed anyone, and has led an upright and honorable existence. Clearly, he can overlook the pain he has caused those whom he considers beneath his contempt. He never really recovers from the trauma of his daughter's death. He is ruined in the 1929 economic crash and shortly afterward he and his wife, Cindy, are divorced. He moves to New York and the last news we have of him, through Mrs. McMinn, is that he is leading a life of near destitution, dependent upon the allowance provided by his surrogate son Ralph and spending much of his days in Central Park, feeding the birds. As Mrs. McMinn reports:

I've often seen him at the lake bending over the water, his hand stretched out to the swans. But he never looks at the birds he feeds: he looks at his own reflection in the water instead; and as he kneels there, you can see his lips moving. I think that it isn't really himself he sees, but Clarry, who looked so much like him. I think the words he repeats over and over are the ones he kept saying the night she died: "My God! Oh, my God! Why wasn't it me, instead!" [*LG*, p. 334]

March demonstrates here the same feeling of compassion for Hubert Palmiller as he has for Mr. Palmiller's past victims. It is inevitable that Mr. Palmiller should live out the last years of his life lonely and unloved, for he had placed himself high on a pedestal, reserving his love only for his daughter at the exclusion of even his wife and his son, Rance. Strangely enough, this man who calls upon God in his hour of grief and need, had always professed to believe neither in God nor in the existence of the soul. "I believe," he declares pompously, "that men are not the children of God, but are the test tubes of nature" (*LG*, p. 107). At university, he experiences a four-year-long "marriage of spirit" with a fellow student, Clarence Lankester, Cindy's brother. He feels betrayed when Clarence becomes a missionary, goes to Africa, and dies of fever. Hubert marries Cindy, principally because he feels that she is "healthy, attractive and could, no doubt, be trained easily enough to become the sort of wife he wanted" (*LG*, p. 112). In other words, she would be eminently suitable for breeding offspring in his own handsome and Grecian athletic image. There is, to be sure, more than a trace of the Nazi master race theory in Hubert's philosophy.

Clarry is their first child and does not disappoint him, but the son, born two years after his sister, reminds Hubert of Clarence. He feels a sense of animosity toward the boy, considering him "stubborn, timid and unnatural" (*LG*, p. 114) and subjecting him to a harsh regime of athletic discipline. He almost drowns Rance when he tries to teach the child to swim, at the age of three, by throwing him bodily into a lake. Rance has no interest in any of the athletic pursuits in which his father strives to involve him and increasingly incurs his father's irritation and contempt. As he grows older, however, it becomes apparent that the boy has the mind of a genius. As soon as he is able to read, he devours all the books in his parents' library and by the age of six, when it is time for him to enter school, he is in fact ready for the eighth grade. He uses his mental superiority in a deliberate fashion to isolate himself from others. He becomes universally disliked by both his contemporaries and his elders, all of whom feel somewhat intimidated in his presence. He no longer fears Hubert, able now to take pleasure in deriding his father's high-flown theories and in countering his jibes, harsh words, and pomposities with well-timed ridicule.

For all that, deep within himself, Rance has an urgent need for his father's love. When the New Century Party is arranged, in an attempt to please his father and effect a reconciliation between them, he determines to go dressed as Willie Keeler, the baseball player he knows his father admires more than any other. He takes great pains to ensure that Ada Boutwell makes the costume for him exact in every detail. The plan goes wrong, for at the party he is unable to disguise his condescending attitude when he presents himself before his father. Mr. Palmiller reacts predictably by extolling Clarry's beauty and stressing her virtues in the hearing of the gathered children. Rance flees upstairs to his sister's room, dresses up in her clothes, and rejoins the party, burlesquing his sister's voice and gestures. Hubert is furious and embarrassed. To teach his son a lesson, he immediately takes him out, dressed as he is, to the main square of the town and parades him in front of the astonished shoppers. Rance even turns this apparent setback to his own advantage, encouraging the laughter of the townspeople by informing them: "Did it ever occur to you yokels that you look even sillier to me than I do to you?" (*LG*, p. 135). He silences their jeers with questions they cannot answer, deriding them in French they cannot understand. He regards the whole exercise as "the perfect example of the persecution of genius by the stupid" (*LG*, p. 136). One person, however, does not join in the general laughter and pleasure in seeing Rance getting what is ostensibly his comeuppance. Wesley Boutwell's heart goes out to the eight-year-old boy and he berates Mr. Palmiller for the way he is treating the child, pointing out that Rance is obviously not right in the head, for he cannot "even talk plain enough for folks to figure out what he's saying" (*LG*, p. 139). Wesley's words, well-meaning and compassionate, forge the instrument of Rance's destruction.

> There was a long, waiting silence. In it, it seemed to the child that the last shred of his old protection was taken from him. If the stupid hated him because they recognized his superiority to themselves, that was one thing. It was a situation he was familiar with, and one that he could handle well. . . . But if the stupid pitied him because he was not as slow-witted as they were, then he was lost indeed, and there was no security left him anywhere. [*LG*, p. 139]

From that moment of appalled revelation, Rance's personality changes completely. At school, he becomes subdued and withdrawn.

The other children, instantly detecting his newly acquired vulnerability, bully him unceasingly. At home, he sits for hours staring out of the window of his room. Four years later, at the age of twelve, he drowns himself in the shallow pond on the outskirts of Reedyville, known locally as the Sweethearts' Looking-Glass. When he is pulled from the water, his face is seen to have lost in death the cringing sickly look it had possessed for the past several years: "His lips curled downward now with their old insolence, and his eyes stared back at the world once more with amused, haughty contempt" (*LG*, p. 143). Mr. Palmiller hides his true feelings over his son's death by explaining that Rance was "plainly one of those unsuccessful experiments which Nature sometimes makes" (*LG*, p. 143), but fearing his son's early death might in the future cause those who did not know the true circumstances to speculate that it was the result of some genetic fault passed on by the father, he orders that the boy's gravestone shall make it crystal clear that Rance died by his own hand. Ironically enough, when Cindy has a third child, named Ralph Porterfield Palmiller after her lover Robert Porterfield, the child's father and eventually Cindy's second husband, Hubert Palmiller, preserving the outward integrity of his marriage, accepts the boy as his own, seeing in Ralph the desired qualities he had found so completely lacking in Rance.

Wesley's farcical accident and Clarry's sordid death, the two central events of the climactic evening in September 1916, linked again and again by Dover's desperate journeyings around Reedyville, themselves typify the contrasting ways in which the Boutwells and the Palmillers, two families occupying opposite extremes of the social scale, react to adversity. Whereas the Palmiller family slowly disintegrates and is destroyed by the misfortunes which not only are imposed upon it by exterior forces but which it brings upon itself, the Boutwells, although very much the underdogs, who enjoy none of the financial and social privileges of the Palmillers, are nevertheless the more resilient and are ultimately victorious in the battle of life. Breck may be killed in his early twenties leading an assault on a German machine-gun post, but he gains posthumous honor as Reedyville's one and only war hero. Honey, run out of town by Mr. Palmiller and his vice society, gains fame as a "Negro" singer in Paris, where she is known as *Madame Honey, la Negresse d'Alabama*, and respectability and wealth through her art and by her marriage to a prince. Even the discontented Fodie achieves, by way of a second marriage, the social standing which she has always craved.

It would seem that whenever the parallel lives of the two families touch, unhappy and frequently tragic consequences follow for the

Palmillers. Ada Boutwell makes the baseball uniform with which
Rance vainly attempts to capture his father's affections. Her husband,
Wesley, voices the thoughts which prick the bubble of Rance's armor
and nudge him along the road to suicide. Ira Graley, who lives with
and has been adopted by the Boutwells, is the one who wades into the
pond to recover Rance's lifeless body. Fodie betrays her sister Honey
to Mr. Palmiller and his vice society and thus sets in motion the whole
sequence of events which are to culminate in her brother's planned
seduction of Clarry and Clarry's subsequent death. Even long after the
Palmiller family has been destroyed, the Boutwells' unconscious triumph still remains to be completely realized. The final screw is
twisted by Dover Boutwell himself, for in adulthood he acquires the
old Wentworth house on Reedy Avenue, the house which Mr. Palmiller had purchased as the ultimate status symbol when he was at the
zenith of his banking and social careers at the beginning of the century,
demolishes it, and builds a successful garage business on the site. The
full circle of fortune is thus completed.

In picking out the principal narrative threads from the book's
layered and fractured structure, little or no mention has yet been
made of the many other unforgettable characters March introduces
into the pages of this immensely rich and complex work. There is, for
example, Miss Virginia Dunwoody Owen, whose presence hangs like a
pall over the whole book. Known locally as the Goodwife of Death, she
is convinced that she has "married" Death and devotes her life to
serving him, in the forlorn hope that he will exempt her from his
dominion. It is she, and she alone, who really understands the reasons
for Rance's insufferable arrogance, telling him: "You and I aren't like
other people at all, and we've always known it. It's the reason we're
afraid of things which others don't concern themselves about. . . .
arrogance is as necessary for you as what I do is for *me*. . . . But it
seems to me that as long as you say over and over that you are strong
and clever, and others aren't, then you needn't be so afraid of the
people you despise. . . . You must never lose your protection! Never!"
(*LG*, pp. 102–103). She is herself condemned by fate to live to the age
of ninety-six, completely bedridden, her body racked with continual
pain, watching "the decay of her own body, feeling all the terrible
pangs of dissolution without first knowing the mercifulness of death"
(*LG*, p. 343). But continuing life made unbearable by extreme physical
pain is not the ultimate irony of her existence, for

> when her suffering became greater than her dread of death, she came
> back from the mad, individual world where she had dwelt so long, to the

everyday world of reality which others knew. Thus, when it was too late to retrieve what she had lost, she was given the final bitterness, the knowledge that she had wasted her breath and her days on an illusion; that she had sacrificed herself needlessly, and had escaped nothing at the end. [*LG,* pp. 343– 44]

She loses her protection, just as Rance had lost his nearly forty years before, for the first time seeing herself for what she is. When Richard Mellen visits her, she tells him: "I was never the Bride of Death. I was never a great queen. I was nothing. Nothing at all. Only a frightened, insane old woman. No more. . . . Let me die! Be merciful to me! I am old and sick and I've suffered too long! Be merciful! Merciful!" (*LG,* p. 344).

The poignancy of the Goodwife's terrible fate is counterpointed by the farcical circumstances attendant upon the funeral of Mrs. Paul Kenworthy. At the time of her death, Mrs. Kenworthy has become so immensely stout that she is unable to walk and there is no coffin in Reedyville large enough to accommodate her cadaver. After the undertaker's men have spent more than an hour in a futile attempt to cram her into the largest casket available, she is eventually buried temporarily in the wooden crate the casket was delivered in, until a made-to-measure casket can be specially constructed for her. Before her marriage, Mrs. Kenworthy had been Miss Millicent Wentworth Reedy, the town's heiress and blue blood. Her surprising marriage at the age of twenty-one to the rather insignificant photographer Paul Kenworthy, twenty years her senior, to her relief soon breaks down, for she "always found her husband's warm, incessant advances repugnant, even on their honeymoon; for no matter how unromantic his exterior might be, inside, he was a small volcano of passion" (*LG,* p. 149). In seeking an outlet for his frustrated sensuality, Mr. Kenworthy becomes besotted with Honey Boutwell, but he is able to worship only from afar, as it were, for fear of being arrested as a child molester. When Honey is run out of Reedyville by Mr. Palmiller and his vice society, Mr. Kenworthy accompanies her and becomes her manager, sharing her fame in Paris. In contrast with those of his wife, his own funeral arrangements are magnificent. He is buried in Paris, mourned by hundreds, his funeral service attended by cabinet ministers.

Joseph St. Joseph, the town's acknowledged wit, imagines Mrs. Kenworthy, divested of her clothes, her body released from the molding confinement of her corsets, as looking like "a big saucerful of melting peach ice cream" (*LG,* p. 146). He is fond of making such epigrammatic remarks about his fellow citizens. Of old Miss May-banks, he notes that she "believes it's sinful to teach physiology, since man's body is the province of God" (*LG*, p. 98). When Minnie McInnis marries Morgan McMinn and becomes Minnie McInnis McMinn, he refers to the union as "merely alliteration claiming another of its small victories" (*LG*, p. 220). His persistent wooing of Minnie after her divorce is doomed to failure. She steadfastly refuses to marry him, being just as revolted by the physical side of marriage as Mrs. Kenworthy.

The foregoing somewhat incomplete summary of the principal narrative and thematic structures of *The Looking-Glass* by no means does full justice to March's accomplishment. As has already been noted, and as Richard Crowder pointed out in his pioneering 1948 essay on the four novels March had so far published at that date, the development of the dominating looking-glass motif "is accomplished in at least four ways: by literal mirrors, by metaphorical mirrors, by pools of water, and by narcissism in the characters."[5] This mirror symbolism has been threaded by March throughout the narrative in a subtle and intriguing fashion, never unduly stressed, but insistently repeated again and again. Manny Neholla, for instance, is, as a child, obsessed by mirrors, striving to find in them some reassurance that he is not, as he suspects, negroid. Searching among the secondhand clothes in his father's shop for a suitable costume which will gain him entry to Clarry's New Century Party, he sees himself in a mirror transformed into the doctor he is eventually to become. Honey Boutwell, too, as a child, gazes at herself in a mirror, seeing in her image what the future holds for her. Rance, after dressing up in his sister's clothes, studies himself in her mirror, aping her gestures and mannerisms, uncertain if by so doing he wishes to please or annoy his father. The child Ira Graley adopts the name of the kindly drummer he meets one day in the local store, the man being a reflection of all that seems good to the boy, so long starved has he been of love and understanding. After Breck has made his first physical advances, Clarry, almost panic-stricken, inspects her thigh in her mirror to satisfy herself that the still-burning imprint of his hand has not left a mark on her white skin, defiling the purity which is her hallmark. When Clarry is small, Mr. Palmiller gazes "with fascination into her face, as if it were a reducing mirror in which his own image was reflected, tender, precise and softened with babyhood" (*LG*, p. 114). As father and daughter stand together to receive their guests at the New Century Party, Mr. Palmiller gazes frequently into the long mirror opposite, telling himself how greatly he and Clarry resemble each other (*LG*, p. 234). In old age, he still endeavors to recapture the beautiful and ageless image of his dead daughter in the worn face he sees reflected in the Central Park lake.

The pool, which is equated with the mythical story of Narcissus, is a very real feature of the landscape of the novel. The small, circular pond lying directly in front of the Boutwell house was known as the Sweethearts' Looking-Glass because before the surrounding trees had been cut down it had been a favorite meeting place for lovers, who

> could be seen at twilight, after their work for the day was done, walking the path together, with arms intertwined, while their long, inverted images followed them faithfully in the water. . . . The shining pond, because of its shallowness, was the perfect looking-glass for depths greater than its own. [*LG*, p. 25]

It is precisely these depths, of course, not the superficial mirror surface, that March explores so relentlessly with his surgeon's scalpel. The calm, untroubled water of the pond becomes the element in which Rance chooses to take his own life, as if, by physically breaking through the mirroring surface and thereby shattering for once and for all his own image, he will be able to end the agony of his long-exposed vulnerability and find peace at last.

At the end of the book, when Richard Mellen visits Reedyville, he discovers that the area around the Sweethearts' Looking-Glass has become a municipal park, that the pond itself has been filled in and grassed over, so that no tangible evidence of its previous existence remains. No longer does the pond's symbolism have any significance. Its irradication complements the demise of so many of the book's characters. Those who have survived at the time of Minnie McInnis McMinn's party have found with the passing of the years a new contentment that has eroded away whatever latent narcissism they may have possessed. Other than for the demented Hubert Palmiller, mirrors and water no longer reflect the beauty and promise of youth and so have no attraction.

On the penultimate page of the book, Ira Graley observes: "A world is ending before our eyes. . . . What will life be like afterwards? Will the change be a small one, so reasonable that we will hardly notice the difference? Will it be something overpowering and dramatic? . . . But it is ending. A whole world is ending as we sit here talking together. I wouldn't try to hold it back, even if I had the power to do so" (*LG*, p. 345).

Throughout the narrative, there are references to fire and ice, the

two elements most generally assumed to herald the world's ultimate
destruction. The fire metaphors are mainly contained in the various
descriptions of the sunset on that eventful September night in 1916.
The ending of the day becomes a symbol for the ending of the world:

> at the center of the pond, where there was still water above the springs,
> the color cast by the rays of the sun was the dark red of clotted blood.
> The color of the stagnant water in the ditches beside the road was the
> color of blood as well, and the lantana and ironweed grew from it red and
> unreal and withered, as if rooted in carnage too rich, too strong for their
> lacy roots to digest. [*LG*, p. 31]

As if to make the point explicit, the Negroes in the nearby church
begin singing an old slave song, proclaiming that the world "gwiner
end with a burnin' in the sky" (*LG*, p. 32). The song is repeated on the
very last page of the book, when Honey sings another verse for Minnie
McInnis McMinn's guests: "The world gwiner end with cold ice upon
the land" (*LG*, p. 346). The ice theme is, of course, linked with the
mirror motif, the aridity of the snow metaphor, especially in connection with Manny Neholla and the fatal whiteness of Clarry's skin.
There is a certain poetic justice in the fact that Dr. Snowfield meets his
death among the snows of Russia.

A world may be ending, but the septuagenarian Minnie is determined not to end with it but to associate herself with whatever new
world may be beginning. She will not be left behind. She tells Richard
Mellen: "Don't you simply *hate* old people, Mr. Mellen? Heaven
knows, I do. They seem so helpless and apologetic and pitiful to me!
Why, old people actually *smell* old! That's the reason I surround myself
with the young. People with life and energy and blood still in them.
People who accomplish things!" (*LG*, p. 332).

An awareness of smells, indeed, pervades the whole book. In an
astonishing passage in the ninth chapter, March describes Reedyville
by its smells alone:

> In the unmoving air, the enduring smell of Reedyville, dissipated,
> unremarked, when wind blew, came perceptibly to the senses. Now,
> there were the rich odors of eaten food still living, but as dim as ghosts,
> in the quiet world above the town; there was the moldy, gunpowder
> scent of decaying flesh which died relentlessly while its host still talked,
> spat, and regarded with neither amazement nor concern the world in
> which he was imprisoned. There was the smell of the town's massed bed
> linen, saturated with the odors of those who had slept so intimately upon
> it; the tang of liniments rubbed on a thousand aching backs; the sad

smell of mown grass dying on yellowing lawns; of wet, rotting woodwork, and of old dresses put away forever. Then, too, there was the smell of horse dung from the town's stables, and of scented, late-blooming flowers: petunias, phlox and larkspur, which, blending first with themselves, blended again with wood smoke, and with the seasoned ammoniac odor of urine. [*LG*, p. 292]

Later that same evening, when Dover Boutwell is finally on his way home after all his journeyings, the long-awaited rain begins to fall:

It moved slowly down the streets of the town like a gray unwavering wall—calm and unhurried, as if knowing that all things are accomplished in time. . . . All at once he had a wild desire to outrun the rain, and . . . he leaped forward, lowered his head and sprinted furiously. . . .

It was almost as if Time itself pursued him, and that it would catch up with him inevitably, and pass him on the road when it chose to do so. . . . But Dover was too young as yet to be concerned with such possibilities. He did not even believe in them, for the testimony of his strong, slowly beating heart, of his vigorous racing legs, was too overpowering to disregard; then, at that instant, the rain struck the road and moved down it, closer and closer to his flying heels. It was almost as if somebody beat a carpet behind him with a keen, swishing stick, and when he heard the sound he laughed and leaped forward, shouting excitedly: "Not me! Not me! . . . You're not fast enough to catch me!"

He summoned the last ounce of his energy, running faster and faster, but try as he would, he could not outdistance the rain, and a moment later he felt the drops against his tough, back-flung heels. Then the rain came up to him and held a course evenly with his moving body, as if it gathered momentum for a greater effort; and slowly, imperceptibly it pulled away from him easily, swishing and sighing and rushing down the road ahead. He stood there in the middle of the roadbed, wet to his skin and laughing with delight, hearing the rain as it struck Sweethearts' Looking-Glass with a spread, shallow sound, as if it were only an old, outworn drum which could summon nothing. He was exhausted from his long run and he sat down at the roadside, hugging himself with delight, laughing with a senseless, animal pleasure. "We needed rain," he said to the vacant air. "We needed rain bad. Everybody will be glad it came." [*LG*, pp. 315–16]

The metaphorical implications of this passage, one of the most beautiful and powerful March ever wrote, are obvious. Nothing, not even the assumed invulnerability of youth, can outdistance the inexorable march of time. No one would be more aware of this than the author himself, as he sat writing the passage in the fiftieth year of his life. Like

Minnie, he too, as he grew older, frequently sought the company of young and vital people. The onward rush of rain, cleansing Reedyville of its smells and its corruption, can be seen to be exactly complemented by the concluding passage of the book, describing the incoming rush of young guests at Minnie's party. If the novel does not end altogether on a note of unequivocal affirmation, it does perhaps indicate that March, albeit uncharacteristically, was on this occasion suggesting that there was, after all, some sort of promise for the future of the world.

The immediate critical reaction to *The Looking-Glass* was, predictably, similar to that aroused by the earlier books. Approximately 55 percent of the reviews were unabashedly enthusiastic, several of them going so far as to suggest that it would prove to be the most distinguished novel to be published in the whole of 1943. Of the remaining 45 percent or so of the reviewers, approximately 15 percent wrote unfavorable pieces, while 30 percent were more or less indifferent to the book, ostensibly baffled by what was for them the obscurity of March's intent.

There were, naturally, the inevitable comparisons with William Faulkner, Erskine Caldwell, Carson McCullers, Thomas Wolfe, and Sherwood Anderson, as well as the less familiar comparisons with such British writers as Thomas Hardy, T. F. Powys, and Norman Douglas. Inevitably, too, the book was linked, both from the aspect of its generic origins and its psychological overtones, with Henry Bellamann's recently published best-seller *Kings Row* and (like *Company K* ten years earlier) with Edgar Lee Masters's *Spoon River Anthology*, one reviewer in the *Los Angeles Times* noting that March "is a skillful short-story writer, so that it is not surprising that his novel is essentially a series of tales, deftly interwoven with what one of his characters calls 'the basting-thread technique.'"[6]

Several critics felt that the book's heavy psychological overtones were nothing short of detrimental. William Du Bois ended his review in the *New York Times Book Review* with the observation that "the symphony that this gifted author has composed with such careful workmanship ends only in dissonance; his novel remains a loosely knit collection of case histories, nothing more. Such is the fate of writers who go to the clinic for their inspiration, and not to life."[7]

Writing in the *Nation* what was possibly the most damning of all the more intellectual critiques of the book, Diana Trilling found *The Looking-Glass* "scarcely interesting at all," noting that "in his Reedyville, not a family but has its lunatic or other horror, and although this may be accurate reporting—after all, *all* Southern novelists can't be themselves crazy, much as a reader unacquainted with their territory may sometimes like to think they are—Mr. March is rather too coy with his psychopathology to hold even our morbid interest."[8]

In another antagonistic review, Helen B. Cole saw the mirror which March tried to hold up to the life of his small Alabama town as "a Coney Island distorting glass, which reflects only the grotesque, in swelled, squashed, twisted versions of humanity."[9] On the other hand, Iris Barry in the *New York Herald Tribune* referred to *The Looking-Glass* as "a remarkable book" because of the manner in which "though it is a mirror to the imagination which William March holds up to life . . . the reflection presented is sharply credible and inordinately alive."[10] Only a small handful of critics, like the *New Republic*'s Stanley Edgar Hyman, were apparently able to see beyond the fundamental symbol of the pond to the book's central theme of narcissism. For one such reviewer, writing in the *Wilson Library Bulletin, The Looking-Glass,* "written around 'the inherent narcissism of man,' is premised on the assumption that the world, for most of us, is something that throws back to us our image."[11]

Alistair Cooke, then special correspondent on American affairs to the *London Times* and the British Broadcasting Corporation, wrote to Little, Brown on February 19. After acknowledging the copy of the book that had been sent to him and revealing that the BBC had asked him to do a broadcast on the novel, Cooke continued:

> *The Looking-Glass* seems to me to be the masterpiece of the most underrated of American writers, living or dead. An exquisite work.
>
> The current best-seller lists inexplicably don't mention *The Looking-Glass* and are enough to make one despair of the taste and vitality of the American reading public. Of course, it is a sad and ancient story. Mark Twain was a boor to the literature fanciers of Boston, Melville a crackpot, Whitman to most of his contemporaries an obscene bum, Emily Dickinson an anonymous neurotic.
>
> These are the eminent dead whom we now, with careful hypocrisy, most delight to honor and whose works would, in their times, have sent us retching to the more palatable fare of writers long since lost to any fame but memorials in genteel marble.
>
> Today we brood with Faulkner, or become misunderstood little boys again with Hemingway, while all the while William March goes on writing his incomparable mature fiction. By 1990, however, he will be thoroughly dead and Congressmen, bishops, college boys taking English-A, and Ambassador-designates to Australia will be fumbling hastily through his unread volumes to prove the soundness of their cultural training.
>
> I hope somebody somewhere will sit up and take notice.[12]

Ray Everitt sent a copy of Cooke's letter to March, who replied in typically whimsical fashion, thanking Everitt for letting him see Cooke's "profound tract" and expressing the hope that even though the book had proved to be a late starter it would eventually begin to sell.

A month later, he wrote to Everitt asking for six additional copies of the book, as friends had walked off with all the spare copies he had. The manifested enthusiasm of these friends for free copies was apparently in sharp contrast to the continuing lack of enthusiasm on the part of the paying reading public, for March again expressed the hope that the book was selling better than it had been. Sales, however, were failing to live up to expectations. Little, Brown reproduced Cooke's letter in a full-page advertisement on the back of the *Saturday Review* for May 1 and sent copies of the letter to a thousand leading bookshops in the hope that "it might stir up something."[13] It was obviously going to be a repeat of the same old story: a majority of glowing reviews but disappointing sales.

March published only two other new works in 1943: the short story "The Female of the Fruit Fly" in the May issue of *Mademoiselle* and the fable "The Escaped Elephant" in the spring issue of *The Old Line*. "The Female of the Fruit Fly" was selected the following year by Martha Foley for inclusion in *The Best Short Stories of 1944*. This was the last occasion that a March story was to appear in either the Foley or O. Henry anthologies. "The Escaped Elephant" was contributed to *The Old Line*, a student magazine of the University of Maryland, in response to a request by Professor Norman MacLeod of the English faculty. This particular number was an International Literary Issue, offered as "a literary challenge to Hitler's threat to wipe out culture in the modern world" and "as living proof that no amount of physical unrest or mental anguish can destroy the imagination." The material for the issue was culled from all sources, not only from the allied nations but also from the Nazi-dominated countries. One poem was smuggled out of Occupied France and another poem was written by a Belgian who had managed to escape to the haven of a free country. None of the contributors—including such poets as Pablo Neruda, William Carlos Williams, and Kenneth Patchen, and such prose writers as James T. Farrell and Albert Halper—was remunerated for his work.[14]

Despite Alistair Cooke's statement that March was able to live a life as untouched by the frenzy of World War II as it is possible to imagine,[15] it would be entirely foolish to suppose that during this period he was in any way living the life of a dedicated hermit, not allowing the war to impinge at all upon his day-to-day existence. He would have found himself unable to ignore it, no matter how deeply he may have wished to do so. For one thing, with the influx of exiles and refugees from Europe, the whole quality, texture, and tempo of life in New York were gradually, sometimes subtly, changing, lending the city a much more cosmopolitan character.

It is noteworthy that in all his fiction March only rarely makes any reference to the World War II scene.[16] Indeed, it would seem that for March there had been only one war—that being the one in which he had served with such honor and bravery a quarter of a century or so before. His attitude might be compared to that of the World War I veteran Corporal Curtain in one of the short stories March wrote during 1943, "I Broke My Back on a Rosebud," who tells his listeners: "I'm talking about the last war, remember—not about this new, fancy one" (*TB*, p. 431). In another short story also written that same year, "It's Your Hard Luck," set in Central Park, March introduces the character of a young World War II sailor who is more interested in seeking likely female company than in listening to the rambling reminiscences of an old World War I veteran, stressing the unbridgeable gulf March obviously felt existed between the two generations of servicemen. Similarly, in "Ballet of the Bowie Knives," written in 1945, the leading character, while having a shoe shine in Grand Central Station, observes the young servicemen of the day descending and ascending the stairs of the men's washroom and begins recalling his own World War I experiences. Yet another story, "Send in Your Answer," written in 1944, is structured around the character of a World War I hero, awarded the Congressional Medal of Honor, who, years later, falsely accused of theft and forced to sell his medal to provide himself with the bare necessities of life, commits suicide when he realizes that he has lost his most precious possession—his dignity as a man.

Even in the final chapter of *The Looking-Glass*, which brings the story up to date in 1942, there are only three brief, almost condescending, references to wartime America. In the first, the authorial narrator visits Reedyville to collect material for the book he is writing and at the station he sees "masses of soldiers in winter khaki from the near-by training camps: soldiers looking undecided and unhappy, not knowing what to do with themselves" (*LG*, p. 325). A little later on, he sees the eighty-year-old Wesley Boutwell telling a group of young soldiers of his exploits in the Spanish-American War (*LG*, p. 328). Some months afterward, in Minnie McInnis McMinn's fabulous New York apartment, he hears a radio commercial urging the womenfolk of America to use a certain brand of beauty preparation to ensure that they will look lovely and radiant when their soldier boys come home from the great battlefields of the world (*LG*, pp. 342–43).

Minnie's apartment is clearly based on March's own, except that it is on Central Park South and not, like March's, on Central Park West. In Joseph St. Joseph's words, Minnie "lives . . . in great magnificence . . . Her living room is papered—if that's the right word—with zebra skins and mirrors. She's thirty stories above street level. Possibly it's fifty. I'm not sure which. Anyway, her view of New York is staggering" (*LG*, p. 330). While one cannot associate zebra skins and mirrors with March himself, the view from March's windows could well have been transferred to the pages of the novel when he describes Minnie's guests looking down upon snow-covered Central Park:

> The snow had stopped at last, and the air was clearing. Below us, the Park was covered with cold, impersonal white, and the buildings on its western side cast delicate shadows across it—shadows tinted blue and pink and lavender which moved forward implacably as the light died out of the sky. Then, as we watched there, the strung, elaborate lights of the Park came on, shining pale and timid on that stretching waste of snow. . . . we stood quietly beside the window . . . watching the lights along Fifth Avenue shine upward, against the buildings there, with a gentle, steady glow: renewing the soft, inherent sheen of the individual stone, accenting, anew, the luster in each weathered and shimmering brick. With the approach of darkness, the frozen Park seemed wasted and shrunken in size. Lights threaded it through with an involved, elaborate preciseness, but they were too small, too distant, for any human need—too pale for service, against the paler expanse of the snow. The whitened trees and the rocks were like toys, and even the roads themselves, with the tiny, desperate automobiles upon them, were things from remembered childhood, as if what stretched before us were not really a park, where people walked, but a consoling toy, a distracting thing designed for the pleasure of a pampered child. [*LG*, pp. 341 and 345]

The overall mood of this striking passage, the atmosphere of rarefied unreality that dominates it, must have mirrored precisely the sense of unreality that was from time to time (and to become increasingly so) part of March's own life at this particular period. The unaccustomed luxury of his surroundings, his almost total isolation from the human swarm in the streets and park below, would have engendered not only a feeling of secure detachment and solitude but also a feeling of intense loneliness on those occasions when, just as desperately as he sought seclusion, the need for company manifested itself.

He continued to keep up correspondence with old friends. Among these was Kay Boyle, who had returned to America in the summer of 1941 with her husband, Laurence Vail, her three children, and her two stepchildren, all of them having recently escaped from the privations of life in Occupied France. By the time of her reunion with March in New York in 1943, Kay Boyle had divorced Laurence Vail and was married to Baron Joseph von Franckenstein, an Austrian, now an American citizen and serving with the U.S. ski troops in Colorado. She lived with her children in an apartment hotel on West 58th Street, and almost every day, taking the children for their walk in Central Park, she would meet March.

> Bill and I would walk and talk together, while I pushed my baby son in his stroller. I felt in a singular way that the children were always an intrusion upon him. He did not want them there. His obsession was then with still another alien world: the bizarre world of sexual, and largely "perverted," encounters which took place in the remote sections of the park. From his window on Central Park West, Bill was able to observe through a pair of binoculars the random encounters and subsequent sexual activities of these lonely wanderers. He would tell me in detail of all he had witnessed, but the stories were never gleefully or viciously recounted, but in something like wild despair, his face tight as a fist with concern. At times, I believed he told me these things out of apprehension, out of the fear of his own loneliness, and that this kind of love was all that was available to those who were alone. At other times, I saw this furious anxiety as part of Bill's acute understanding, as a writer, of the predicament of other men and women. I do not remember him so much as noticing the leaves on the trees, or the ducks and swans on the water, or the polar bears in their stained white coats. But he told me of an old woman, a mad old woman, crazy as a coot, whom he watched through his binoculars from his apartment window. She would station herself at the intersections of the paved walks, he said, and direct the baby-carriage traffic like a cop. She even had a whistle that she blew to halt one line of baby carriages while she waved on a contingent of strollers waiting to cross. I never saw this old woman, but Bill would show me the exact location where she stood, at the converging of four paths, and I have never had any doubt that this was true.[17]

Understandably, to many people, March's obsession with the sexual aberrations he was able to observe from his vantage point on the thirty-second floor and his vicarious study of other forms of abnormal and eccentric human behavior will seem immensely distasteful. Nor, in-

deed, was he confined to making his observations solely from the high
sanctuary of his apartment. At a dinner party shortly after the war, he
told Harry T. Moore that he had become friendly with certain members of the New York Police Department, being allowed to accompany
them on patrols to Times Square and watch them searching for the hair
fetishists who sneaked up behind women to snip off locks of their
hair.[18] Times Square and Central Park, then as now, constituted for
someone with March's interest in human psychology and outré behavior a living laboratory, equally as fascinating as, say, a tidepool would
be to a marine biologist. Those who feel distaste for March's preoccupation with the seamy side of life would be well reminded of Kay
Boyle's description of his face "tight as a fist with concern," almost as if
he were driven by the furies within him to excavate unceasingly the
mysteries of the human psyche, confirming over and over—as though
such confirmation were in any case needed by someone with his
perception and understanding—that side of man's character which is
dominated by his inherent cruelty, moral failings, and lust.

In another sense, the observed life of Central Park was for March a
living sourcebook for his fantasies, in exactly the same way that his
fellow passengers on the London buses and trams had been the main-
springs of the fantasies he had related to Glover.

> In the Central Park walks [Kay Boyle has written], he was in a very
> real sense in control. It gave him a degree of self-assurance. He had
> studied the life of Central Park, sexual, social, criminal and otherwise,
> through his binoculars from his apartment window, and he was familiar
> with the various figures and the various human dramas. He could predict
> the plots and action, and could tell me in precise and imaginative detail
> where the casts of characters had sprung from and where they would go
> in the end. All of them, men and women, the sane and the demented,
> the normal and the perverted, they would all end up in Hell, of course,
> for I do not believe Bill believed in Salvation. All these characters, real
> or fictive, were entrapped in their own corruption, and he saw them as
> beyond redemption.[19]

His gift for analyzing people's handwriting was all part and parcel of
the overall pattern, the continuing quest into the secrets of the human
mind. Kay Boyle recalls that on the occasion of their last walk together
in Central Park she discovered for the first time this interest he had in
handwriting analysis:

> I was leaving with my children to join my husband in Colorado before
> the Mountain Infantry would be going overseas, and Bill brought with

him a short note I had written telling him this. He was intensely absorbed in explaining all he had learned about me, not from the words I had written him, but in the way that they were written. I had written him many times before, and he had never spoken to me of his probing of character in the lines one wrote—or it may have been that this was a new way he was pursuing to reach the inner lives of alien humanity. He was astounded to find, he said, that one of my outstanding characteristics was physical courage; moral courage to a degree, he said, but physical courage to a much greater extent. He was very excited by his discovery and, holding the letter upside down, as the professional writing-analysts do, he pointed out the signs which indicated this.

I was somewhat surprised myself to learn of my exceptional physical courage, but at the moment I was more interested in my son's attempts to get out of his stroller. We had just passed through the tunnel which leads (or once led) in the direction of the elephant and llama houses, when my son became even more determined to undo the harness which held him. As Bill talked with intense concentration about the clues hidden in the signs one made on paper, we stopped beside a bench near the enclosure of the seals and walruses, and I unstrapped my son and lifted him out of the stroller. I set him on his feet, and held him upright under the arms, believing that if I did not he would drop as usual on his hands and knees and start crawling at high speed. But that day he remained standing, pushed my arms away, and then took alone the three or four tottering steps from stroller to bench.

"Look, Bill! He walked!" I cried out in joy, and Bill looked at me in disapproval. "It's the first time he's walked alone!" I said, but Bill was deeply wounded. He looked in grievous despair into my eyes, and the white square of letter-paper shook in agitation in his hand. This scene, so innocent in appearance, so simple to the eye, with the seals barking beyond in the sunlight, has always haunted me—perhaps because it came to seem to me metaphor for the disparateness between Bill's life and mine.[20]

During the summer and early fall of 1943, March continued working on the novella "Bonny May's Dolls." In a letter he sent to Richard Crowder that November, he stated that he wanted to do this short novel "very badly." He also announced that he had another, "more impressive" novel almost finally planned. Crowder had written him a fortnight previously, telling him he wanted to make March's work the subject of his doctoral thesis. March expressed his willingness to assist in whatever way he could. "If," he wrote, "there is one persistent thought or one ineradicable theme which runs through everything I have done, it is this: Man has developed as far as it is possible for him to develop from the outside. If he is to survive, he must turn now and examine his beginnings. He must deny nothing in himself in this appraisal: he must see himself not as the Church or society thinks he should be, but as he is. With this knowledge he must start another painful development—from within this time. If he cannot do this, then he will perish."[21] He expanded on this in a further letter to Crowder the following January, in reply to certain questions Crowder had put to him:

> I did not particuarly have psychoanalysis in mind when I wrote you before. It is certainly an excellent springboard. Any sort of understanding, no matter what the source, is to be desired. I tread warily now, because I know that any writer who attempts to clarify his personal philosophy, particularly in a few lines, is likely to merely make himself ridiculous. I have seen my literary betters do it over and over and I know that I will too, if I'm not careful.
>
> Anyway, I'd like to say that I'm an advocate of any of the "soul searching," as you express it, which is not based on the conventions of any age. My knowledge of the seventeenth century seekers after truth is rather vague, but it seems to me that they sought not so much to discover the truth about themselves as to make their minds and emotions fit into a pattern prearranged for them. In other words, they had accepted for themselves certain barriers and beyond those they could not go. Only the poets seemed to have known the truth by some divine instinct, but of course nobody ever took a poet seriously in any practical sense. This seems unsatisfactory and vague I know, but at the moment I prefer to let my case rest there with no further elaboration.[22]

With regard to the future course he felt his writing would take, he indicated to Crowder that he had found himself becoming more and more enamored with comedy, and noting that many of the already planned fifty stories which he wanted to write were humorous in content, he thought this perhaps surprising, considering the "high average of glumness" of the stories he had already written and published. He mentioned the story "The Borax Bottle," which he had completed in August 1943, as being an example of this new phase in his writing. "The germ of this particular story," he wrote, "has always been present in my work, but it seems now that the accent falls on that particular spot."[23]

In the late fall of 1943, he was forced to abandon work on "Bonny May's Dolls." For some time, he had been having trouble with his vision, and his eyes had occasionally been so painful that he had to rest them. He thought, at first, that the condition was nothing to worry about and that it was simply a matter of eyestrain. But when, with the passing of the weeks, there was no sign of any improvement, he began to believe he was going blind.

There is room for speculation that, like the trouble he had had with his throat when he was in London, the eye condition was hysterical in origin, establishing itself during a period of deep depression. He consulted a doctor, who assured him there was no question of his going blind and who recommended that he should not wear glasses but do eye exercises instead. He carried out the doctor's orders religiously but apparently with little faith. The thought of approaching blindness was so overwhelming that he found it completely impossible to write: as soon as he sat down at his desk, the lines on the sheet of paper before him would blur. He felt unable to discuss his predicament with his friends. He hardly ever went outside the apartment and saw no one for weeks on end, other than the grocery delivery boy. He cooked his own meals, terrified by the idea that if he went to a restaurant and was unable to read the menu he would be reduced to a state of panic in full view of the waiters and the other diners. Some nights, after midnight when most people were abed, he went for long walks, amazed at how quiet and lonely New York could be at these hours. His occulist suggested that another course of psychoanalysis might be the answer. Dr. Glover, however, was several thousand miles away on the other side of the U-boat-infested Atlantic. He made a number of appointments to consult a New York psychiatrist but never kept one of them.

Then, quite suddenly and completely unexpectedly, he looked out of his apartment window early one bright, chilly spring morning and realized he was cured. When he put on his glasses, everything sprang into sharp focus. Years later, he recalled this desperately unhappy and frightening period of his life and the relief he experienced that wonderful morning. "It was over," he said, "but, by God, I came damned near to killing myself that winter. I was a little mad, I think."[24]

What had induced this particular hysterical condition, if such indeed it was? Again, one is reduced to speculation. One answer could be that March subconsciously desired to obliterate the sight of the bleeding humanity he felt compelled to spy upon from his high eyrie in Century Towers. That, however, seems a little too pat an explanation and not somehow in character with the man who had, after all, never shrunk from recognizing and accepting the cruel facts of life. There is an alternative explanation, which would appear more likely. He was, clearly, still suffering from a deeply ingrained residue of guilt, feeling that by resigning from Waterman in order to satisfy his egoistical wish to advance his literary career, he had somehow abrogated his loyalty and responsibility toward the Campbell family and the well-being of its members. The recent financial failure of *The Looking-Glass* would have done nothing to assuage these feelings of guilt. The eye condition could, then, be regarded as a form of self-imposed punishment, a subconscious expression of atonement.

Not long after his recovery, he decided to look for another, less ostentatious apartment, more suitable to his needs. He eventually found the sort of place he wanted and in early May moved to 34 Gramercy Park, a late nineteenth-century building sporting arabesque panels of foliated details, bay windows, and an octagonal turret roofed with a conical cap. From the window of his new apartment, he could, as from the old, look down upon a park. This park, two blocks square, created in 1831 by one of New York's early real estate operators, Samuel B. Ruggles, did not, however, provide the ground for furtive sexual assignations and encounters, for it was private ground, surrounded by an eight-foot iron fence and accessible only to the privileged owners and tenants of the surrounding residences.

With this move to a more genteel environment, March's life-style also underwent a subtle change. No longer did he throw the massive cocktail parties of old. He did, of course, have occasional parties, but these were more in the nature of literary gatherings. He lived fairly simply. He wrote, read, went out for walks. He rarely went to the movies or to the theater. A maid came in and kept the place clean for him, doing the laundry and the shopping and preparing his meals.

The year 1944 saw the publication of three new stories and two new fables, all of them appearing after his move to Gramercy Park. The two fables, "The Prophets and the Mountain" and "The Fat Woman and the Terrier," were the first to come out, being published in the June issue of *Tanager*. The first of the short stories to reach print was "It's Your Hard Luck." It had been rejected by *American Mercury, Coronet, Harper's, Harper's Bazaar, Good Housekeeping, Mademoiselle, New Yorker,* and *Story.* The main criticism leveled against it by the editors concerned was that while it undoubtedly created a mood, it was so diffuse as not to add up to a story. Eventually the story was published in July 1944 in the autumn issue of the literary quarterly *Accent.* The following month, "I Broke My Back on a Rosebud" appeared in *Story,* and in November, "The Slate and the Sorrow" was published in *Esquire,* March's second appearance in that thriving and legendary magazine. These last two stories were both listed by Martha Foley among the distinctive short stories of 1944 in *The Best American Short Stories 1945.*

Ober was continuing to experience some difficulty in placing March's astringent stories in the mass-circulation market. Shortly after the beginning of the new year, the agency returned the story "The Willow Fields," having found it unmarketable. Like "It's Your Hard Luck," it had made the rounds of all the possible homes that might have been found for it: *American Mercury, Cosmopolitan, Esquire, Ladies' Home Journal, Redbook,* and *Story.* March finally placed it himself that fall with the *Rocky Mountain Review.*

Another story, "Dirty Emma," which, to the end of his days, March considered one of the best stories he had ever written, was turned down by *Good Housekeeping* on the grounds that it was "sordid and hopeless." The magazine's editor, Max Wilkinson, who held March's work in the highest regard, even to the extent of opining that there was no better writer in America, pleaded with the author through his agent not to dwell so consistently on the seamy side of life, reminding him that there was hope in humanity. Was it not possible, Wilkinson wanted to know, for March to employ his considerable talents to exploring more optimistic themes?[25] Wilkinson did, however, accept another story, "Whistles," and proved his belief in March's work by publishing in *Good Housekeeping* five of March's ten short stories which appeared in magazines during the two years 1945 and 1946. Another story Wilkinson turned down with great disappointment in December 1944 was "The Static Sisters," a story March had completed the previous month. Wilkinson felt that the story was somehow mechanical and gratuitous, but he offered, if March was unable to place the story elsewhere and was willing to carry out some revisions on it, to reconsider his decision at a later date. The story never achieved magazine publication, making its first appearance in *Trial Balance* the following year.

All in all, had he in the late fall of 1944 looked back over the preceding months, March would not have had any real reason to be displeased with the events of that year—at least, not so far as his literary career was concerned. The prospects looked promising. He was, albeit slowly and painfully, at last establishing a readership in the glossy magazines without compromising his standards in any way. In addition to having three short stories and two fables published, he had written five new stories: "Dirty Emma," "Send in Your Anwer," "She Talks Good Now," "I'm Crying with Relief," and "The Static Sisters." Several of his earlier stories were being reprinted in magazines such as *Encore.* Nelson Olmstead read "The Little Wife" over the WEAF network on January 21, 1944, and the Radio Division of the Coordinator of Inter-American Affairs applied for permission to adapt the story "Bill's Eyes" for radio broadcast. The script was to be translated into Spanish and Portuguese. With March's approval, permission was granted. It did not concern him that, the organization being noncommercial, no fee was to be paid. Then, toward the end of the year, negotiations were commenced to bring out an armed forces overseas edition of *Some Like Them Short*.

Another milestone that year, unfortunately bringing with it some attendant disappointment, was the publication in wartime England of *The Looking-Glass*, the first of his books to appear in that country since *A Song for Harps* eight years before. The book was published by Victor Gollancz on June 26, twenty days after the D-day landings in Normandy, in a slim, war-economy edition with small, closely set type. The disappointment arose from the fact that the British reviewers proved to be on the whole cool toward the book, reserving their main adverse criticism for March's complicated narrative structure. "A huge, untidy book," Kate O'Brien called it in the *Spectator*, adding that "the general effect is of overcrowding and formlessness, and one gets the general effect of having read it all before in many other, better-made novels."[26] The *Times Literary Supplement* expressed the wish that the author "had flung St. Joseph's basting thread technique into the waste-paper basket; for whatever precisely it is meant to be, its results are sadly confused and tedious." The anonymous reviewer went on to observe that life in Reedyville, as seen through the author's eyes, "is almost overwhelmingly insignificant, made up as it is of the dreariest social and domestic commonplaces recorded in the flattest and lengthiest fashion." All the effort that March had put into the book could, in this reviewer's opinion, "well have been directed to less pretentious ends."[27] To Ralph Straus in the *London Sunday Times*, "the jerkiest tricks with time" that March played were "a little irritating" and "wholly unnecessary."[28]

It was the worst critical reception any of March's books had received in England, whose reviewers in the past had, if anything, been more sympathetic and understanding than their American counterparts. Further disappointments came as 1944 drew to its close. For months, March had been unsuccessfully endeavoring to interest a publisher in his book of fables. Several houses had professed initial interest in it— Crown Publishers, Hastings House, and Simon and Schuster among them—but he was at last having to accept that nobody was going to regard the book as a viable commercial proposition. Certainly, his own publisher, Little, Brown and Company, was not prepared to take the risk with such an off-beat work. Another project proposed by March was similarly given the thumbs down by Little, Brown. March had long wanted to bring out an omnibus edition of his collected short stories, comprising all those in *The Little Wife and Other Stories* and

Some Like Them Short, all the stories he had published since the last collection in 1939, as well as some of the stories which had never made their way into print. With this idea in mind, he had gone through all the stories he had written and, destroying those of the unpublished ones he now regarded as worthless, had brought together a total of fifty-five stories, thirty-four of which had already appeared in the two previous collections and twenty-one of which had not appeared in book form. His suggested title for the volume was *In This Order*, the stories being printed in chronological order of composition.

The events of 1938 were being repeated. March had entered into a contract with Little, Brown under which the publishers were to have the first option on his next novel. Because *The Looking-Glass* had not fulfilled its promise in terms of sales, Little, Brown could not offer its author any encouragement for this new collection of stories. Another publishing house, Harcourt, Brace and Company, was interested but did not wish to tread on Little, Brown's territory. While Harcourt was willing to bring out the omnibus collection, it would have preferred to publish a volume consisting solely of the twenty or so uncollected stories rather than to run into possible difficulties over the rights to *Some Like Them Short*, which were, of course, held by the Boston house. March was nevertheless determined that all efforts should be made to ensure that the omnibus was published as he had envisaged it. He sent the manuscript of the fifty-five stories, now collectively titled *Trial Balance*, to Harcourt, Brace on January 15, 1945, and two days later, during the course of an amicable meeting between March, Ray Everitt, and Ivan von Auw of the Harold Ober agency, Everitt agreed to release March from his contract with Little, Brown and, moreover, to release the rights on *Some Like Them Short*. The way was now ostensibly clear for the publication of the omnibus volume so dear to March's heart, but last-minute setbacks were to arise before the book appeared in the bookshops of America.

During the year 1945, March wrote four new stories: "A Great Town for Characters," "Ballet of the Bowie Knives," "First," and "One Way Ticket." Of these, "First" still remains unpublished, although the manuscript is held by the Campbell trustees. "One Way Ticket" was published in December of that same year in *Good Housekeeping*'s January 1946 issue. "One Way Ticket" is a somewhat manufactured and consequently rather unconvincing tale which recounts the first and only—for seemingly it is totally reparative—consultation between a psychoanalyst and an elderly, confused woman. The patient has apparently lost the ability to walk foward. The analyst's diagnosis is somehow too glib and the story reads very much like the closing scene of many a routine murder novel, when the knowledgeable detective gathers all the suspects in one room and then proceeds, ignoring various interpolated protestations, to analyze motives, enumerate opportunities, and uncover the truth. The story concludes in a typically March fashion with the analyst "realizing anew that the thing that astonished him most in his work with others was not that some went under, but that so many survived everything, and were satisfied."[29]

Six other stories appeared in magazines during 1945: "Whistles" (*Good Housekeeping*), "She Talks Good Now" (*Good Housekeeping*), "The Willow Fields" (*Rocky Mountain Review*), "Dirty Emma" (*University of Kansas City Review*), "Send in Your Answer" (*Good Housekeeping*), and "You and Your Sister" (*Encore*). Three of these stories— "Whistles," "She Talks Good Now," and "The Willow Fields"—were listed by Martha Foley as distinctive short stories in the 1946 edition of *The Best American Short Stories*.

It was not always easy for Ober to find publishers for March's work. While Max Wilkinson of *Good Housekeeping* immediately took "One Way Ticket," he returned another story submitted to him that year, "Transcribed Album of Familiar Music," because, he said, the magazine already had too many stories on hand commenting wryly upon life and March's story would not do the magazine much good at the present time. Ober also had one success and one failure with *Esquire*. On March's fifty-second birthday, September 18, 1945, Ober was able to inform him that *Esquire* had bought "A Town Full of Characters," as "A Great Town for Characters" was originally titled, for three hundred dollars. The previous month, however, Ober had returned "Ballet of the Bowie Knives" to March, reasoning that as it had been declined by *Esquire* there was no possible outlet for such a story, based as it was on the quasi-smoking-room anecdote dating from March's marine days and centered on what was in those days, so far as general publication was concerned, an almost unmentionable part of the male anatomy. Even after March had carried out some cosmetic revisions, Ober was similarly unable to place "The Borax Bottle" with its recounting of the extraordinary and embarrassing events which occur when an eight-year-old boy is stung on his penis by a wasp. The agent returned the story to March in January so that the author could, if he so wished, try it himself on some of the literary quarterlies. The story was accepted by the *Harvard Wake*, a new literary magazine being put out by a group of enthusiastic Harvard students with the editorial assistance of José Garcia Villa. The story was scheduled to appear in volume 1, number 4, of the magazine in June 1945, but unfortunately for March, a palace revolution had recently occurred on the editorial board, the editor,

Seabury Quinn, having been deposed and "pushed upstairs" as president. Quinn read March's manuscript and was offended by the story. He maintained that it should not be published, but he was outvoted by the other members of the editorial board. There the matter might have rested but for the obvious sense of injustice and ill-feeling Quinn still nursed following his deposition. Not to be outdone, he presented his objections to the dean of Harvard College, A. Chester Hanford, "a gentle, kindly man of the old school." Seymour Lawrence, Villa's coeditor, has recorded what then transpired:

> The following morning I was summoned to the dean's office in University Hall. Dean Hanford's desk was bare except for the manuscript of "The Borax Bottle." He asked my intentions and I told him that the editors had voted to publish the story. He allowed that he had read the story, found it embarrassing, not in the best of taste, and certainly not appropriate to an undergraduate magazine bearing the name of Harvard. He went on to say that he could not prevent us from publishing the story and he had no intention of being a censor. However, if we persisted, he had no recourse but to suspend the magazine and to suspend me and my associates from Harvard College. We bowed before the crimson glove and scepter, and "The Borax Bottle" did not appear in Volume 1, number 4. And Mr. Seabury Quinn did not appear in number 5 or in any issue thereafter.[30]

March was anxious to include "The Borax Bottle" in *Trial Balance*, so he did not endeavor to place it elsewhere because it would have proved impossible to achieve magazine publication before Harcourt, Brace's tentative publication date of October for the book.

The contract for *Trial Balance* had been signed on March 2. It was necessary then to ensure that all the required permissions to reprint the stories already published were obtained. The copyright of *The Little Wife and Other Stories* had been assigned to March some time previously by Random House. Little, Brown had now released the rights to *Some Like Them Short*. March decided, however, to omit "Nine Prisoners," which had appeared in *Some Like Them Short*, presumably because its text formed part of *Company K*. He also decided, again one assumes because of its connection with a longer work, to omit the uncollected story "The Unploughed Patch." He did, on the other hand, include two early unpublished stories he had not destroyed when going through his papers. These were "Personal Letter" and "Mr. Edwards' Black Eye." It was also time, he thought, for his first published story "The Holly Wreath," omitted from both the two previous collections because they already contained enough war stories, to appear in book form. A problem arose in ascertaining who held the copyright of the story, which had been published by the now defunct *Forum,* but it was duly and satisfactorily resolved. The editors of some magazines holding stories awaiting publication in their pages were unable always to give firm commitments as to dates, and arrangements were entered into that if magazine publication did not precede the book's appearance the magazine would agree to return the story on reciprocal return of its fee.

In the end, all relevant deadlines were met and *Trial Balance,* containing seven previously unpublished stories, was published on October 11, 1945. The book was dedicated to "Finley and Lucille," March's old Mobile friends, Mr. and Mrs. Finley McRae.

eleven

Trial Balance and
the Edge of the Abyss

Trial Balance, like most omnibus volumes, almost overwhelms the reader with a surfeit of riches. The collection does not possess the selectivity of the two earlier books of short stories, but by its very nature it possesses a fascinating and comprehensive unity the two earlier volumes lacked, tracing chronologically the progress of March's work in the genre; the first story, "The Little Wife," dated from 1928, and the final story, "The Static Sisters," was written in 1944, which brought the collection up to date. This chronological pattern is revealing in many ways. To begin with, that very first story impresses one with the quiet assurance of its realization. In this retrospective collection, it still holds its own as one of the best pieces of work March ever did. Significantly, comparison of the original *Midland* text of the story with the text as here reprinted reveals that March was apparently so satisfied with his original that he did not feel the need to revise it for inclusion in either *The Little Wife and Other Stories* or in the omnibus volume.[1]

The chronological presentation of the stories also reveals a slow decline in their quality, particularly obvious in those written after March's resignation from Waterman, perhaps reflecting his efforts to break into the more lucrative market of the mass-circulation glossy magazines. March was far from being a writer of commercial stories. That he may have felt impelled, within his own standards, to attempt to be one could not have been an altogether happy experience for him, although in the better stories of this later period, such as "Whistles" and "She Talks Good Now" (to quote but two examples), he demonstrated that his unique artistry as a short-story writer was as powerful as it had ever been.

Of the fifty-five stories in the volume, seven were appearing for the

first time in print: "Mr. Edwards' Black Eye" and "Personal Letter,"
two early stories dating from 1932 and 1933 respectively; "Not Worthy
of a Wentworth" (1937), "Transcribed Album of Familiar Music"
(1938), "The Borax Bottle" (1943); and the two most recent stories,
written in 1944, "I'm Crying with Relief" and "The Static Sisters."

"Mr. Edwards' Black Eye" is a slight piece, illustrating March's
whimsical sense of humor. It tells of the almost unbelievable innocence of a provincial businessman on a trip to New York. Visiting a
Greenwich Village restaurant with a friend, he notices two girls dancing. Attracted by one of them, he cuts in, whereupon the other girl,
the larger of the two, who is actually a transvestite, savagely attacks
him, telling him in no uncertain terms to get his own girl if he wants
one. The joke is that Edwards is so innocent that he does not appreciate the nature of his assailant and his pride is wounded because he
believes he has been knocked down by a girl.

In "Not Worthy of a Wentworth," Mrs. Kent relates to her guest,
Clark McBride, the story of Carrie, the last in line of the Wentworths,
the aristocratic family of Reedyville. Mrs. Kent chronicles Carrie's
frustrated attempts to find herself a husband in the face of the fierce
opposition of her mother, who never considers any of Carrie's choices
worthy of her. At sixty-two, Carrie has apparently still not given up
hope of marriage, although, her mind gone, forever dominated by her
mother, she dresses up as a little girl and plays with her dolls in the
garden.

The rich financier Martin L. Challett in "Transcribed Album of
Familiar Music" similarly disapproves of his son's choice of marriage
partner. Unlike the Wentworths, Challett had a deprived childhood
but married into wealth and was thus given the opportunity of creating
more and more wealth for himself and his family. He is determined
that his only son, Robert, shall have all the advantages in childhood
which were denied him. Like Scott Fitzgerald, he holds the rich in
awe, believing that their wealth makes them different from other
people. Robert, taught by his mother to despise his father's philosophy, completely rejects the life his father has mapped out for him and
proposes to marry a notorious socialist agitator. Martin is forced to
make the best of a bad situation. He accepts that the marriage will take
place, consoling himself in the knowledge that the woman comes from
an extremely prolific family and that consequently she will, in all
probability, provide him with many grandchildren, each of whom will
be potential material to be molded to his way of thinking. As he tells a
reporter who comes to interview him for his reactions to the coming
wedding: "It seems to me that the generations move in a monotonous

pattern, always a little different on the surface, always the same underneath" (*TB*, p. 412).

When, in "The Borax Bottle," eight-year-old Frankie Kent is stung on his penis by a wasp, six-year-old Cordie's curiosity is such that she spies on him through the bathroom window as he endeavors to soothe his painfully throbbing member by inserting it into a bottle of borax water. Relating the incident many years later to her house guest Clark McBride, Cordie reveals that it was in this way she first discovered the anatomical difference between boys and girls. It is her good sense that solves Frankie's predicament when his swollen member becomes stuck fast in the neck of the bottle. She theorizes that by inserting his penis into the bottle he was typifying "the instinctive reaction of the romantic to frustration" and that he needed "someone practical" like her "to keep him out of trouble." She determines then and there that when she grows up she will marry him. As Dr. Kent gently but pointedly upbraids her at the end of the story: "If you must tell these intimate family secrets, . . . a fiction writer like Clark McBride is the ideal person to confess to. At least you can be sure who he's going to tell afterwards, and that's merely the American reading public" (*TB*, p. 452).

The girl in "I'm Crying with Relief" is standing on a crowded subway platform when a man throws himself under a train. She had heard the man complaining to those standing nearby him of his appalling personal troubles, bemoaning the fact that he had nothing to live for. Like all the other embarrassed people on the platform, it is not until the man jumps into the path of the incoming train that the girl realizes he really did mean everything he said. She runs horrified from the scene. Her subsequent obsession with the man's fate takes such a hold on her that she is compelled to make inquiries, eventually discovering that he was extricated from under the train and taken to a hospital. She is told that he has been blinded, has lost both his legs, and has suffered severe head injuries. She explains to a girl friend: "I'm crying with relief, Jerry! I thought all along that the poor man died!" (*TB*, p. 492). The irony of her genuine but misplaced compassion is very much a March touch.

"The Static Sisters" is a mood poem, recording the demise of a proud family. The two sisters, Miss Adeline and Miss Leila Clayton, living out their days in Mrs. Furness's select boardinghouse, are known as the "static sisters" because their chattering reminds the other boarders of the atmospherics on the newly developed radio. The two sisters live very much in the past, reliving their old glories and constantly recalling their connections with other fine families, as if wanting to reassure themselves over and over again that their whole lives have not been a lie in the same way as, at the backs of their minds, they suspect the origin of their family was a lie. It is the younger sister, Leila, who becomes the eventual reluctant pragmatist, comparing the family with the plant they nurtured in a pot in the cellar when they were children, finding an analogy between Adeline and herself and the "two pale, shriveled little buds at the end of all that growth and foliage" (*TB*, p. 505). Reality leaves her desolate, condemned forever to pander to her sister's continuing fantasies of the past.

The confusion that can arise in the human mind between reality and fantasy is again explored by March in "The Wood Nymph," which is, apart from "The Holly Wreath," the earliest of the previously un-collected stories in the volume. Written in 1930, rejected by *Midland* that same year, and remaining unpublished until 1939, when it ap-peared in the *New Mexico Quarterly*, the story is the study of the mind of a woman verging on the act of suicide. For Miss Innis, life itself has become unreal. She avoids all possible contact with her fellow guests at the country inn where she has come to stay, presumably to recuper-ate after some physical or mental illness, repulsing all tentative ap-proaches by declaring that she is a wood nymph and thus has nothing in common with people. She discovers a nearby pool and there, escaping completely into her fantasy, she meets a beautiful young man, a Pan-like creature, who suggests to her that he is the thing she has always wanted. She admits that this is so. They make love and she allows herself to be enticed into the pool. But as soon as her head goes under the surface of the water, reality intrudes into the fantasy and she struggles back to the bank and to life. The godlike boy is revealed to her as Death in one of his many disguises. Safely back at the inn, she vows never to return to the pool, but her very words imply that her determination is as inconstant as her hold on life itself. She will inevitably return to keep her tryst with Death.

If Miss Innis is cursed with an overactive imagination, the girl Hazel in "Not Very—Subtle" is condemned to see only the superficial surface reality of her dull existence. She works as a counter clerk for a tele-graph company, continually bemoaning the fact that it is unfair that she should be cooped up day after day in the office, where nothing ever happens. She professes to have imagination, but in her view nothing "inneresting" ever occurs during the day. She exists under the illusion that it is only the high life which will provide some stimulus to her dormant imagination, not realizing that the high life for which she yearns is in fact far more superficial than the daily realities of life she encounters while doing her job. She fails to recognize the existence of the sorrows and the ecstasies, the failures and the triumphs of ordinary people's lives revealed in the messages she handles. She accuses all those with whom she comes in contact as being "not very—subtle," whereas, in truth, it is she herself who lacks subtlety.

In "The Female of the Fruit Fly," March once again returns to his own prejudiced view of the sex war, the man inevitably the victim, the woman inevitably the victor. When Dr. Farr, a professor of biology, returns home from a lecture tour, he discovers that his wife has run off with her lover. As a scientific man, he endeavors to rationalize the situation. It is clear that this is not the first time such a thing has occurred during their married life. He realizes that his wife, like the female of the fruit fly, will copulate with whatever male appears on the scene who attracts her. March introduces undeniable sexual imagery into this description of the gift the husband has brought home for his wayward wife: the little jade elephant "whose neck lifted triumphantly in the air and whose trunk curved backward a little" (*TB*, p. 336). He has been in the custom of bringing home one of these little jade elephants each time he has been away lecturing, and they stand, identical except in size, in graduated line on the bedroom mantelshelf. He places the new elephant in its ordered place. The procession of elephants seems to represent not only the succession of his wife's lovers, past and future, but an expression of his own frustrated sexual longing. He lies on the bed, gazing at the mantel, painfully accepting that this is the preordained pattern of his life to come and that there is little, if anything, he can do about it.

"Whistles," which deserves recognition as one of March's most perfectly realized stories, is a moving remembrance of childhood, evoked in a semi-Proustian manner. For Marcel it was the taste of a little cake dipped in tea, for Mr. Ridley it is the off-stage sounding of whistles during the performance of a play in a New York theater. The sound brings vividly to his mind recollections of his boyhood in the sawmill town of Hodgetown and of Mrs. Foley who ran the sawmill boarding-house. He remembers how, with the arrogance of youth, he used to belittle the everyday simplicity of her life and how she had argued with him that she had at least put her life to some practical use, whereas he could only talk about the good deeds he was going to do when he grew up. Thinking back on these things, he realizes now that when the men sounded the sawmill whistles during her funeral they were not acting with cruel thoughtlessness but were giving spontaneous expression of their esteem for this woman who "had known clearly what her work was . . . to wake up the world and wash its face, feed it, and get it to work on time" (*TB*, p. 371). Ridley is given pause to wonder "if his own benign but vastly superior attitude toward others, his earnest efforts to rescue those who did not want to be rescued, to save those who did not even know that they were lost, were not a little juvenile, a little presumptuous" (*TB*, p. 371).

March's constant interest in the more bizarre sexual proclivities of his fellow men is illustrated in "Cinderella's Slipper." The subject of this impressive psychological study is Verne Hollings, a young lawyer who contemplates running for municipal office on an independent ticket. He is assured of the backing of the new reform party, the leading members of which consider him "God's gift to the party," because, despite their having had him under close surveillance, they can find no scandal connected with him. A bachelor, he leads a clean, honest existence: so blameless as to be almost beyond belief. The truth of the matter is that he is a shoe fetishist and the mere thought of normal physical love fills him with disgust:

> It seemed incomprehensible to him . . . that another man would embrace a mass of flesh, stuffed with digesting food, when there were shoes to be loved, shoes as impersonal and as beautiful as the one he now held against his lips; and yet there were: in fact, you couldn't go to the theater or to the movies, or even walk in a public park, without seeing men and women locked in each other's arms, their lips pressed together.
>
> He lifted his head, his eyes burning with the pure, fierce light of a crusader. A shoe was also flesh, in a way, he thought; but it was flesh with the disgusting things taken out. [*TB*, pp. 379–80]

In "The First Sunset," written in 1937, March returns to the theme of "Personal Letter." Although the Nazis and their extreme philosophies are not mentioned as such in the later story, there can be little doubt that the elderly Dr. Albert Erlich of March's story is modeled on Dr. Albert Einstein and that, like Einstein, he is a refugee from Nazi oppression. As in "This Heavy Load," March propounds the theory that the faith every man must have to give reason and purpose to his life need not necessarily be in the normally accepted Christian terms, although in "The First Sunset" the parallels between the mythical boy Surd and Christ are particularly self-evident.

The story immediately following "The First Sunset" in *Trial Balance*, "You and Your Sister," is an example of March in one of his ostensibly lighter moods. The tale recounts the abortive attempts of a New York housewife to pair up her unmarriageable sister Mildred with a friend of her husband's who is on a flying visit to town. She invites the friend to dinner, mentioning that Mildred will also be coming, and is disgusted

when, after not turning up at the appointed hour, the friend tele-
phones late that evening in an obviously drunken state and tells some
cock-and-bull story about having got lost in the city. It is clearly not
the first time such a thing has happened to Mildred. She tells her sister
and brother-in-law: "People always get drunk at the last minute and
don't show up in this town. . . . Either that, or they say 'yes' and then
don't come" (*TB*, p. 401). The pathos of her situation is accentuated by
her attempt to disguise the very real hurt she has sustained by assuming a somewhat aloof attitude toward the whole incident. This Chap-
linesque touch to the comedy is delicately done. Mildred, the reader is
left in no doubt, will end her days as an embittered maiden aunt.
March's so-called lighter touch stands finally revealed as little more
than a patina, thinly covering an underlying human tragedy.

The sixteen-year-old Mamie in "The Slate" is a similarly pathetic
figure. She is hopelessly in love with Dr. Eldridge, a man more than
thirty years her senior, whose wife was killed in a drowning accident
after they had been married only three years. The doctor is totally
unable to reconcile himself to her death. Rumor has it among the
townspeople of Williston, where he carries on his practice, that he
communicates with her through the medium of a slate and slate pencil
which he keeps under his pillow. In order to obtain access to Dr.
Eldridge's bedroom, Mamie offers to take her neighbor's eight-year-
old son Grady to the doctor to get treatment for a persistent scalp rash.
While the doctor and Grady are in the consulting room, she sneaks
into the bedroom, finds the slate under the pillow and writes a message, telling the doctor that if he feels lonely he should seek out
Mamie's company. After they have left the doctor's house, she admits
to the boy what she has done and is desolate when he convinces her
that the doctor will never be deceived into thinking that his dead wife
has written the message and that, even if he were, he would not seek
Mamie out, because, as Grady brutally tells her, "You're too big and
greasy-looking" (*TB*, p. 421). The irony of the story is contained in the
comparison between the doctor's professional and scientific diagnosis
that Grady's scalp condition has been exacerbated by the variety of folk
remedies to which it has been subjected and that if left alone it will
cure itself, and his own emotional irrationality in wanting to believe
that his dead wife will one day be able to contact him, that their love
will prove stronger than the barrier of the grave.

A similar theme is explored in "The Willow Fields," written four
years later. Mrs. Rodney, a widow, lives alone in her New York apartment, still unreconciled to her husband's death which occurred only a
few weeks earlier. Subtly, March brings out the whole history of their

marriage: the remembered happiness being but the illusion of an old woman unable to cope with the loneliness which has been so suddenly thrust upon her.

"I Broke My Back on a Rosebud" tells the story of Corporal Curtain. In 1943, at the age of forty-eight, although looking sixty, he lies immobile on a board, where he has been confined for the past twenty-four years as the result of a ridiculous accident. Having survived all the fighting in France during World War I and returned to the States without a scratch, he is marching in the victory parade along Fifth Avenue when an exuberant lady in the crowd flings a rosebud in his direction. He slips on it, falls, and breaks his back. Over the long years since, his reaction to his ironic fate has gone through the three distinct stages of hope, resentment, and resignation, before eventually he finds compensation and peace of mind. As a result of his visible quiet bravery in coping with his cruel predicament, he has received an immense amount of publicity. Several of the men from his old outfit come to the hospital to visit him. He discovers that for most of them, too, hope has been dashed and that it is even possible, in some instances, for him to consider himself more fortunate than they, exposed as they were to the continuing misfortunes of life. He realizes that he is by no means the only one to have broken his back on a rosebud.

"It's Your Hard Luck" is little more than a vignette, a typical March comment on life. Set in Central Park during World War II, the narrator and his female companion (March himself and Kay Boyle?) observe and listen to the people sitting near them on the benches: a young sailor and an embittered World War I veteran, and a little old crazy man who has come to feed the birds. March's message seems to be that it is hard luck if you attempt to be an individualist in an organized world and that you cannot win if you choose not to conform.

March has revealed that the story immediately following "It's Your Hard Luck" and "The Borax Bottle" in *Trial Balance*, "Dirty Emma," was the story which he thought he liked more than any other he had written. He apparently rued the fact that nobody else agreed with him.[2] The story was written in 1944 and published the following year in the autumn 1945 issue of the *University of Kansas City Review*. As well as appearing in *Trial Balance*, it was selected by Robert Loomis for inclusion in the posthumous *A William March Omnibus*, but it has not been reprinted since.[3]

The action takes place in the fictive town of Williston, the same township that provides the setting for the earlier stories "Geraldette" and "The Slate." The story is told by Jamie Gavin in the form of a reminiscence of his childhood. Williston's "Dirty Emma" is a woman in her early forties who lives with her common-law husband Tom Gunnerson, a man ten years older than she, in a tiny dilapidated shack on the edge of town. Her miserable existence holds no beauty. The townspeople avoid her as much as possible, regarding her station in life as lying "somewhere between that of the Negro, who was so innocent in outlook, so ignorant of the subtleties of good and evil, and that of the barnyard animal, to whom the laws of decency and morality did not, in the eyes of God, apply at all" (*TB*, p. 454). Her relationship with Tom is not a happy one. He is a moronic, physically powerful man who takes pleasure in beating her with brutal refinement, having "perfected his technique over a long period, [so that] he was as familiar with the strains her body could stand as an engineer is with the stresses of the common arch" (*TB*, p. 461).

Emma's life is transformed when Jamie's mother gives her a white hyacinth bulb. It is probably the first time that anyone had gratuitously shown any kindness to her. She takes the bulb home and plants it in an old tomato can, nurturing it carefully, until, to her amazement and delight, the plant blossoms into its pure white flower. It seems like a miracle to her. When, in a fit of drunken anger, Tom beats her yet again and, for added measure, throws her plant to the floor and deliberately crushes it underfoot, she realizes what she must do. As he lies in his drunken stupor on the bed, she locks the kitchen door and shutters the windows so that they cannot be opened from the inside, throws the lighted kerosene lamp against one of the walls and quickly escapes through the front door, locking it from the outside. She remains undeterred by Tom's screams for help and stands watching the blazing shack until the roof falls in.[4] When she tells the townspeople that Tom had locked her out and obviously must have upset the lamp in his drunkenness, it does not occur to anyone to disbelieve her. It is not until, on her deathbed, she confesses to Jamie and his mother what she has done that the truth comes out: she punished him, not because of the way he had ill-treated her, but because he had destroyed the purity of the white hyacinth. She became, as Mrs. Gavin saw her, one of the furies of Greek mythology, "a creature dedicated to the avengeance of those subtle crimes against mankind which pass unnoticed—those most terrible crimes of all, since men, as individuals, are so often unaware that they have been wronged" (*TB*, p. 467). This theme of undetected evil is one that fascinated March and is one to which he was to give full expression in *The Bad Seed*.

"Dirty Emma" certainly ranks among the best dozen or so of March's short stories. What, however, will particularly interest the reader who is somewhat aware of the background of March's life is the all-too-brief insight it provides, by way of the Gavins, into the nature of the family life of the Campbells at the time they were living in Century, Alabama: the educated mother, the father who disguises his own lack of education under a veneer of banter, exuding a casual sexuality against which his wife's fine upbringing ultimately has no defense, so deeply in love is she with her "handsome but illiterate lord" (*TB*, p. 467).

"Send in Your Answer" is a biting satire on the popular radio programs of the day, with their manufactured setups, their manipulated studio audiences, the artificial scripts of the commercials themselves, all made "respectable" by the introduction of incidental classical music, but all carefully designed to pander to the baser instincts of the listener. The story takes us through one such program, which presents the history of a war hero who won the Congressional Medal of Honor. After the war, he is falsely accused of theft and is jailed. He does not allow the experience to embitter him, and on his release from prison, able to find only short-term menial employment, he is at one stage forced to sell his medal to keep body and soul together. Despite his own precarious situation, he is always prepared to assist anyone less fortunate than himself. Eventually, overwhelmed by and disgusted with the superficiality of the life he sees around him, he commits suicide, leaving a note as his legacy to an uncaring world: "Man never had anything except dignity, and now he has lost even that" (*TB*, p. 480). Ironically, of course, the note itself serves to precipitate the sort of superficial, artificial, undignified approach to life which it deplores.

"She Talks Good Now" reveals again the pleasure March always took in deflating pomposity and debunking false pride. Ermintrude is the three-year-old daughter of academicians who are determined to train their child to become a prodigy by continually reciting erudite works to her. As a result, the child does not speak at all. When the disillusioned parents leave for the summer to do research in Mexico, they leave the child in the care of a professional nurse. Their colored cook, Lula, takes charge of the child when the nurse falls mysteriously ill. Before long, Lula has taught the little girl to speak. She anticipates that when her master and mistress return home from their trip and discover the progress "Ermie" has made under her tuition, they will be all too anxious to retain her services as the child's permanent nurse. The sting in the tail is that Ermintrude apes Lula's every gesture and, even worse, talks like her. The unsuspecting parents are in for a considerable shock when they discover that Ermintrude, to use Lula's own words, "talks good now." One almost hopes that the ebullient, good-natured, simple Lula will succeed in her forlorn plan. Perhaps it is as well that March spares us the painful details of the consequences for Lula of her ill-conceived meddling.

Trial Balance, as were March's two previous story collections, was generally praised by the critics, but in what had by now become almost accepted tradition, the praise was tempered with a word of warning for the unwary reader approaching March's work for the first time. As Meridel Le Sueur observed in *New Masses*, some of the stories "have the accuracy, the minutiae, even the certain macabre beauty of an autopsy report."[5]

In the New York *PM*, Ira Wolfert blamed March's World War I experiences for his failure to realize his full potential as a writer. Wolfert saw March, "in common with most men who have been in a war," as being "sensitive to death, . . . chronically conscious of the fact that all living people are under sentence of death." In Wolfert's view, this obsessive consciousness had somehow crippled March and prevented him from writing the novels he might have written.[6]

In a long and perceptive critique in the *Saturday Review*, John Farrar linked March's ever-present fatalistic philosophy with his failure to achieve popularity as a writer. Quoting the thoughts of the old man in "The Eager Mechanic" ("Sooner or later nothing is of any importance. At the end nothing is more important than the shadow of my arm against this wall!"), Farrar noted: "It is this sense, in his method, of the unimportance of life that has kept him from as wide recognition as a half dozen others of his contemporaries."[7]

By far the longest, the most enthusiastic, the most probing, and arguably the most balanced review of *Trial Balance* appeared in the December 1945 issue of *New Republic*. In this review, Alistair Cooke resumed the public championing of the writer he considered to be "the most underrated of all contemporary writers of fiction." The review, which was later to form the basis of Cooke's "Introduction to William March" in the posthumous *A William March Omnibus*, set out to explore the reasons for March's failure to reach the popular as well as the critical top league. Cooke observed that March's reputation was "the rather bleak one of being a minor connoisseur of morbidity." Comparing him with Dickens, who displayed in his art a similar morbidity, Cooke argued that Dickens coated the pill of his morbidity with sugared sentiment and comic invention, so that his readers were beguiled into accepting, as it were without question, the "very raw material" in his works. March, on the other hand, did not attempt to sugar the pill he handed his readers and indeed went out of his way to draw the reader's attention to "the ruthlessness of his observation." Cooke then pointed to what he saw as the main reason for so much reader aversion to March's work: the reader's involuntary identification with March's tortured characters. The disturbing ordinariness of the people the author wrote about suggested to the discomfited reader that their crises could very easily be the reader's. Tragedy and insanity might be just around the corner. Cooke went on to examine and discuss three of the principal elements he saw running through the whole of March's work—colorful salaciousness, evangelical regionalism, and liberal humanitarianism—and admitted that the most frequent charge leveled against March, that he was "too clinical, too obviously a psychiatric-textbook student," could not be lightly dismissed.[8]

If March had good reason to feel satisfied with the general tenor of the reviews, the sales of the book again proved disappointing. Like March's second volume of short stories, no edition of *Trial Balance* was published in England.

At the beginning of November 1945, March again heard from José Garcia Villa. Villa had another proposition to put to him. Villa was still editing the student magazine *Harvard Wake* from his address on West 115th Street, New York. He and the other two editors had been preparing a special e e cummings issue for publication in December. The three of them were so pleased at the way this special issue had turned out that they discussed the possibility of starting up their own independent magazine. Money, however, as always, was the overriding problem. Estimating that the magazine could be produced quarterly for a cost of eight hundred dollars annually, they felt the need for a fourth partner in the venture, so that the individual quarterly financial contribution could be kept down to fifty dollars. Would March be willing to chip in, if only for three issues, to get the magazine off the ground? "I thought of you," Villa wrote, "as being the right spirit we want, not the psuedo-intellectual but the warm, human intelligence. Comprendre? . . . Must hear soon, before the 15th of November, for the Cummings issue comes out in December, and the magazine alas will go back to Harvard if thou say no."[9] March, typically, had no hesitation in answering such a call for help. On the very same day he received Villa's letter, he sent him a check for two hundred dollars.

The speed of March's response clearly took Villa by surprise, for he had not yet finally decided to continue the magazine on the proposed independent basis, and his letter had been designed merely to sound March out. By November 23, Villa had decided against the magazine. Returning the check, he wrote that he had shipped all the Cummings

material for the December issue to Harvard and that the magazine
would be appearing there. He had not, however, entirely abandoned
the idea of having his own magazine once more. He told March that he
was hoping to start such a magazine (over which, presumably, he
would expect to exercise complete editorial control) in the spring. If
March was then in the same mind as now, any financial backing he
might wish to advance would be appreciated. He asked March to hold
"a very excellent story" for the first issue of the magazine and announced that he had already lined up for this number a handful of
distinguished British writers and critics: Edith Sitwell, Stephen
Spender, John Lehmann, and David Daiches. He assured March that
there would be no "censorship" problems, as had happened when
March had sent "The Borax Bottle" to *Wake* earlier that year.[10]

With the war in Europe and the Pacific now ended, many friends
were returning to America after service overseas. Clay Shaw decided
to settle in New Orleans after demobilization, but whenever he made
his occasional trips to New York he would meet March and they would
have dinner together or join the small crowd of old friends who would
gather in someone's apartment and endeavor to recapture the mood of
days gone by, as if the war had never been.

Kay Boyle and her husband had moved into a house in uptown New
York. March was a frequent guest. Baron Joseph von Franckenstein
had only just survived the European war. As a member of the O.S.S.
(Office of Strategic Service), his last assignment had been to go on a
mission behind enemy lines wearing the uniform of either the German
or Austrian Alpine troops. He had eventually been caught by the
gestapo, but fortunately for him they did not realize he was an American spy. With the advancing American army near at hand, the gestapo
men were of two minds what to do with this apparent deserter. One
faction wanted to make use of this last chance they might have of
torturing a prisoner. The other faction decided that it was time to
finish with such brutality. They were still arguing over von Franckenstein's fate when the Americans arrived and he was saved.

Harry T. Moore met March at Kay Boyle's. As Moore recalls that
particular evening, there were about a dozen guests and the evening
was an extremely enjoyable one, "as always at a Kay Boyle party." The
guests sat at a long table in the basement dining room. There was a
bucket of iced oysters to which everyone strayed from time to time.

> Joseph sat at one end of the table and March sat at the other. I had a
> place near March, on his left. He was talking to the whole table, and so
> was Joseph, both of them saying fascinating things, and our heads kept

turning from one side to the other like those people watching a tennis match in some Hitchcock film. Neither was speaking loud or attempting a dominating monologue; all of it was just pleasant talk. . . . Later that evening I had a few friendly words with March, who had just said that psychoanalysis was indispensable for a writer. I agreed that it was very useful, but wondered if its usefulness weren't almost entirely in the area of understanding human behavior rather than in that of healing: were neurotics ever really "cured," or was there just a displacement of one neurosis by another? March said that *he* had been cured of some trouble and proceeded to tell me what it was.[11]

It was then that he related to Moore the account of the difficulty he had experienced with his throat when he was in London, his analysis with Glover, and the subsequent discovery that the throat condition was associated with the buried memory of the young German soldier he had killed.[12]

The writer David Mynders Smythe also met March for the first time shortly after the war. They lived two blocks from each other and March attended several parties at Smythe's apartment. Although March was twenty-two years the senior, the age difference did not, in Smythe's words, "affect our congeniality." For all that, they never became really close friends during that period, and after Smythe left New York in early 1947 to settle in New Orleans, as Clay Shaw had done, they exchanged only two or three brief letters.[13]

Yet another writer, Robert Lowry, who had printed the private edition of "The First Sunset" for March in 1940, came to New York in search of a writing career after war service in Africa and Italy. He was engaged by James Laughlin of *New Directions* as a production manager, book designer, and editor. Lowry got in touch with March and was invited over to the Gramercy Park apartment. March obviously went out of his way to put the up-and-coming young writer at his ease.

Although there were, at this time, new acquaintanceships and possible friendships to be developed, some long-established friends began dropping out of his life. Lombard Jones remembers that it was sometime early in 1946 that March came for the last time to his apartment:

Besides him, Edith had invited David Page, former circulation director of the *Forum;* Richard Sherman, who had become a highly successful fiction writer in New York and screen writer in Hollywood; and Katherine Bourne, fiction editor of *Cosmopolitan* magazine. We hadn't seen each other for a long time, but it didn't take long to exchange what we had to say about our war activities. Then Bill riveted our attention with an ingenious analysis of the Lizzie Borden murder case of 1892, unsolved and famous in the annals of American crime. How the subject came up I don't recall, but it occurred to me afterward that Bill, unbeknownst to any of us, including himself, had been reminding us that the horrors of frenzied individual actions in war were much like the horrors of frenzied individual actions in peacetime. His analysis of how Lizzie Borden had behaved and why was ingenious and quite plausible. It certainly demonstrated his never-ending preoccupation with guilt and innocence, cruelty, crime, the wages of sin, the inexorable pressures of existence, the quivering sensitivity and loneliness of many human beings.[14]

The writing of *The Bad Seed* can, in retrospect, be viewed as the climactic expression of March's researches into the criminal mind and his fascination with true-life murder mysteries. He was, in fact, a minor encyclopedia about such matters and a voracious reader of crime magazines. One of the short stories he wrote in 1946, "The Bird House," was based on the actual murder of an illiterate and obscure immigrant named Isadore Fink, born in a small town in Galicia, who had established a modest laundry business in Harlem. The crime was never solved. Ben Hecht had already written and published in *Collier's* magazine a story on this same theme, which he had titled "The Mystery of the Fabulous Laundryman." An account of the case had also been written by Joseph Gallomb in a volume of true-life murder mysteries. March used these two stories as a springboard for his own tale, following the circumstances of the actual crime with almost complete fidelity. He provided, however, as the other two had not, a solution to the mystery. Indeed, he offered four "solutions." Although a cunningly devised and brilliantly executed piece of work, no editor in 1946 was apparently interested in the story, except for Wilkinson of *Good Housekeeping.* Wilkinson asked that the ending be changed, but March was not prepared to do this, and the story was relegated to his file of unpublished work.

Two other stories March wrote during 1946 also did not find a publisher. These were "First Confession" and "The Red Jacket." The former was apparently later destroyed by March, but "The Red Jacket," a reworking of his unpublished 1932 story "Time Has Taken Her," was found among his papers after his death. It still remains unpublished. According to William T. Going, "The Red Jacket" is "a sensitive account of an adolescent's first awareness of the nature and meaning of love. . . . its approach to love is simple, honest, and almost sentimental instead of ironic and brutal; and Mrs. Madison is one of March's few understanding women and his only successful attempt to draw the equivocal feminine psyche." Based on an incident from

March's boyhood days in Lockhart, the story is, in Going's view, "unique among all March's fiction."[15]

A further two stories written in 1946, "Old Sorority Sister" and "October Island," and one of the 1945 stories, "A Great Town for Characters," were published in 1946. The long short story, or novella, "October Island" eventually formed the basis of March's fifth novel *October Island* and will be discussed later in that context. The novella appeared in the October issue of *Good Housekeeping*. "A Great Town for Characters" appeared in the May issue of *Esquire* and "Old Sorority Sister" in *Collier's* magazine for September 28.

In "A Great Town for Characters" March employs the formula adopted by Ring Lardner in his short story "Haircut" of having a stranger in town being told in lurid detail the events of a past local scandal ending in bloodshed. In the process, we and the stranger (in this instance a writer named Arthur Vincent Boyd) are introduced by the garrulous salesman in the stationery store to many of the town's inhabitants. Maidenhair Falls has, as the story's title implies, more than its fair share of "characters"—in other words, people who are individualistic enough to ignore conformity and set up their own codes of behavior, or whose intellectual outlook on life sets them apart from the majority. "A Great Town for Characters" is, in its implications, a frightening story, illustrating the power of public opinion, which can drive a man, even against his will and against all he regards as his inviolate moral integrity, to commit murder.

"Old Sorority Sister" is a light, humorous anecdote, which in subject matter harkens back for the first and only time in March's work to the author's days as a process server in 1917. Like "One Way Ticket," it is basically a "manufactured" story, although, by not taking itself as seriously, it is not as unconvincing as the earlier story. The satirical portrait of the self-assured writer Melinda Broadfoot Opp is brilliantly drawn; an unexpected final plot twist, almost thrown away, will have most readers going back over the story to satisfy themselves that the author has not been guilty of cheating on them—which, of course, he has not.

The year 1946 marked a watershed in March's literary career, for this was the year in which he abandoned the short story, the genre in which he had so long been regarded as a master. During that year, apart from the four stories already mentioned, March completed only one other piece: a curious item of delicious and ironic brevity titled "History of the Credulous Widow." March boasted that it was the shortest short story ever to have been written. He also began, but did not finish, one other story, "The Long Pursuit." This fragment, like "First" and "The

Red Jacket," still remains unpublished. All his subsequent literary endeavors were concentrated on expanding the novella "October Island" into the novel of the same name; an abortive novel, *The Practiced Hand*, of which he completed only the first third; and the work that was to prove to be his last opus, *The Bad Seed*.

Before he was to embark on this final productive period, however, there was an extended dark period of creative sterility and deep personal depression to be survived. The years 1947 to 1949 were, it seems, completely unproductive for March, although it is possible that at various times he may have worked in a somewhat desultory fashion on the book of fables that meant so much to him and which he was never to see in print. He was still, in 1946, sending the fables out into the world. On May 7, Villa, who appears to have had yet another change of heart and was, after all, continuing his editorial duties on the *Harvard Wake*, wrote to him, asking once more for a new story for the next issue of the magazine. March had sent Villa some fables for consideration, but obviously they had not impressed Villa greatly. It seemed he would not be satisfied with anything less than a new major story. At the time, March had nothing to send him. All the available unpublished stories were with Ober, making the rounds of the mass-circulation magazines.

The year 1946 was a watershed in another way. After years of ill health following her stroke in 1942, Susy March Campbell died at home in Tuscaloosa. March's state of mind at this particular time apparently was somewhat disturbed, for when he received the news his initial reaction was that he could not possibly face the additional emotional stress of attending the funeral. However, he did change his mind. He traveled down to Tuscaloosa from New York by Greyhound bus, rather than by train, giving as his reason for doing so that he had not ridden in a bus for a long time, an explanation his relatives probably found somewhat fanciful in the circumstances, to say the least.

March's psychological problems were becoming more and more evident to his friends. Even those who knew him well were every now and then astonished by the discovery of a previously undetected facet to his character. Kay Boyle, for instance, remembers the Christmas Eve party March attended at her home in 1946:

> In every situation in which I encountered Bill there was always one constant: the agony of his seeking to fit himself into what at that instant was taking place, and never quite—or perhaps never at all—succeeding. That Christmas Eve, my husband and I were putting the last bits of

furniture into place in the doll house we were giving our very small children in the morning, and Bill March, as he had with the Family card game we were playing in London, became obsessively (even irritably) absorbed in that: placing the doll furniture exactly as he wanted it to be in the miniature rooms, worrying if a chair was not at exactly the right angle in relation to the father doll's desk, distressed almost to the point of despair when the other guests who arrived made suggestions about the placing of the doll book cases, or lamps, or chinaware.

We were six or eight at dinner, and I noticed that Bill was becoming obsessed then by one animated woman who had come with her husband. I do not remember Bill ever being particularly interested in drink of any kind, so that his intense preoccupation with this guest could not be explained by his having had too much wine. . . . I believe they argued a bit about books, but his concern was far beyond that. But only when the other guests had left, and Bill, in a state of agitation, lingered on, did I learn the reason for his distress.

She was, Bill insisted, a changeling, a definitely sinister creature, a fact that was borne out by her two long, pointed cuspids, the mark of the super-natural, as unmistakable a sign as the unicorn's single horn. Neither my husband nor I had ever noticed anything unusual about our friend's teeth, and on future occasions when we met I tried desperately to see what Bill March had discerned, but without success. But even more strange, he never forgot her sinister presence, as he called it, and he spoke of it at other times with a kind of inner shuddering.[16]

To what extent March became dominated by such fear of the super-natural must, like so much else, remain essentially a matter for speculation. He undoubtedly did immerse himself in the study of the occult, in the same way that he preoccupied himself with a study of the violence existing in contemporary society. The one obsession can be seen as a logical offshoot of the other. Tess Crager, the proprietor of the Basement Bookshop in New Orleans, had no doubts at all on the matter. "There was," she has written, "a whiff of brimstone about him. Outwardly he appeared ultra-conservative, his behavior was impeccable, his manner courtly—but he unquestionably was intimate with Satan before the present day concern with witches and warlocks. He would have given them lessons."[17] Her view of March is a minority one and one which has been discounted by other of March's friends and acquaintances. That a man is obsessed with the thought of all the evil that is abroad in the world does not automatically indicate that he is himself actively involved in that evil. Nor does the fact that a man is obsessed with the subject of black magic necessarily mean that he is a practitioner of the cult.

Indeed, March has admitted to only one brief brush with "witches, warlocks, and black magic." In an article titled "Warlock," which appeared in the *New Orleans Item* of May 2, 1952, he related how one February day many years before he had gone to a Child's restaurant in New York for lunch. The place was crowded and the only vacant seat was over in one corner at a table for two, at which was already seated "a distinguished-looking gentleman with wide shoulders, ruddy complexion, and gray hair." When the waitress came up, March ordered buckwheat cakes and little-pig-sausages, specifying that if there was any sage in the sausages he did not want them, only the buckwheat cakes. Noting the curious gaze of the other diner at the table, March almost felt constrained to explain that it was not that he disliked sage but that it tended to give him hiccups and that this would be particularly inconvenient that afternoon as he had to go to a meeting. He said nothing, however, and when, after an interval, the waitress brought him his order of buckwheat cakes and sausages, he was aware that the other man was still staring at him. The waitress told him the chef had confirmed that to his knowledge there was no sage in the sausages but that if he found otherwise when he tasted them he should send them back to the kitchen. The other diner seemed to be made strangely uneasy by this item of news. He drew back from the table in a horrified fashion as March cut off a piece of sausage and put it in his mouth. Almost immediately, the stranger relaxed, and commented: "I see there's no sage in it!" March wondered how the man could have known, for he was indeed right. The man then introduced himself as William Seabrook, the famous necromancer. He began talking to March in an animated way, discussing the details of his art. March found much of the conversation above his head and was only able to contribute stories of his own experiences as a boy in rural Alabama of the practice of tree talking. The two men parted amicably at the end of their meal and March never saw Seabrook again. The incident provided him with a talking point at many a subsequent dull dinner party, but it was not until much later that he discovered how Seabrook had been able to state so confidently that the sausage had been free of sage. One evening, after relating his story, March was informed by a strange old lady he had never met before that Seabrook was a warlock and that he had recognized March as being one too. "Witches and warlocks," she added, "can't eat sage, as everybody knows. It's even worse on their constitutions than holy water . . . if there'd been even a smidgen of sage in those little pig sausages, you'd have burst into a million pieces right there before his eyes."[18]

By mid-1947, March's mental state was beginning to give his friends cause for real concern. Lombard and Edith Jones had not seen him for many months and heard via mutual friends that he had more or less isolated himself completely from callers in his Gramercy Park apartment. Peter and Gwen Campbell endeavored to pull him out of the pit of deep depression and utter inertia into which he had apparently descended. On one occasion, after much protestation on March's part, Peter managed to persuade him to visit them in their apartment on Bank Street. Even then, Peter had to go himself and fetch his brother. But no more than ten minutes or so after they had arrived at Bank Street, March told them that he simply could not stay any longer and had to get back home.[19]

Martha Foley lived a few doors away from March, but she never realized how ill he was:

> When we met casually in the neighborhood stores he seemed withdrawn and I assumed that he was immersed in writing and did not want to be interrupted, although at one time, years before, he visited my home frequently. Nearly every night during the Gramercy Park period he raced, not jogged, along nearby streets as if he were being pursued. I did wonder about that, but didn't realize that he was on the verge of a breakdown until I heard that someone had gone to his apartment and found him badly off.[20]

One finds a repetition of pattern here, recalling the overwhelming sense of insecurity March had experienced while living in Hitler's Germany. There was no gestapo now to feed his paranoid fantasies, but perhaps, as partial contribution to his condition, his mind had begun to people the city with all sorts of unspeakable demons. Only in the comparative safety of his apartment could he feel safe.

According to Peter and Gwen Campbell, March did eventually consult a New York psychoanalyst, but it is clear he derived no benefit from the sessions. The only man who might have helped him, as he had done in 1936, was Edward Glover, but it was completely out of the question for March, in the perilous state he was already in, to make the necessary trip to London. In 1971, as has already been noted, Glover speculated in somewhat more prosaic terms on the reason for the breakdown: "I believe that the creative side of his mind . . . didn't entirely satisfy him. . . . Whatever his unconscious conflicts may have been there is no doubt that consciously he was torn between the idea of a successful economic career as a lesser tycoon . . . and a . . . vocation as á writer and poet."[21] The great god Money had failed to smile benevolently on his literary activities. He would have been constantly reminded that he had renounced and lost the financially successful position he had held in the Waterman organization and he must have seriously begun to doubt the wisdom of the course he had chosen to take. When he experienced the first small suspicion that his creative juices were drying up, he had been thrown into despair.

His literary agents were finding it extremely difficult to do any business on behalf of their elusive client. In October, an up-and-coming playwright, Elliott Baker, applied for permission to adapt "The American Diseur" into a play, but letters Ober sent to March concerning the project remained unanswered. Attempts to reach the author by telephone also proved abortive. Someone eventually advised Ober of March's condition. Ober told Baker in December that as March was very ill he could not at the moment consider any business proposals. Ober, however, took it upon himself to arrange permissions for readings of "The Little Wife" and "Old Sorority Sister" by Nelson Olmstead over the National Broadcasting Company network in the new year.

Finally, it had to be faced that something would have to be done to save March from himself. The situation had reached the point where he refused to see anyone, not even his brother Peter or his sister Margaret. He told Alistair Cooke later that he had experienced a loathing of being physically touched and that at one time this feeling had become so intense that he could not even abide wearing clothes. In desperation, Margaret wrote to the two people in Mobile who had over the years been her brother's most constant friends: Ed Roberts and Finley McRae. They acted immediately, traveling to New York and persuading the doorman to let them into March's apartment. They found him in terrible shape, sitting by the window overlooking Gramercy Park in his underwear, several days' growth of beard on his face. He had not, it transpired, slept or eaten for a week or more and was in an almost catatonic state, firmly convinced he was going to die, as undoubtedly he would have but for their intervention. The apartment, too, was in dreadful confusion. Checks, dating back several months, were stuffed away in drawers. He had not paid the rent. Roberts and McRae persuaded him to take some nourishment, cleaned him up, and dressed him, and took him back to the South with them. In fact, he looked so ill that McRae wired ahead for someone to meet them at Bay Minette with a car so that they could avoid bringing him to the station at Mobile, where he might be recognized. The car met them as planned and they drove directly to the fashionable Grand Hotel at Point Clear, across the bay from Mobile. The hotel had recently been completed by Waterman as a subsidiary business venture, and arrangements had been made for March to occupy the lavish suite designed to accommodate the company's rich customers.

March stayed at the hotel for more than six months, visited regularly by his friends. In the beginning, he would not leave the hotel grounds and seemed almost unable to fend for himself. His old friend and business associate J. P. Case heard from someone that March no longer seemed concerned about his appearance, that his clothes were worn and dirty and that he was badly in need of a haircut. At the earliest opportunity, Case went to visit him to see if he might succeed where others had failed in rousing his friend out of his apparent chronic lethargy. When he walked into March's room, he saw immediately that all he had been told was true. He said brusquely: "Bill, your wool needs clipping." March answered like a child. "Do you think so, Jack?" he said. "Do you really think it needs cutting? Will you see that it gets done? Will you take me to a barber?" Case led the way to the hotel barber, March accompanying him unprotestingly.[22] Lucille McRae visited March frequently and similarly did those little things for him which, in the early days of his stay, seemed too immense for him to manage unaided.

Gradually, however, a combination of the warm Gulf climate, the sea breezes, the unhurried and uncomplicated tempo of life, the wise advice of his doctor, and the affectionate concern of his friends, induced in him a growing determination to conquer the mood of deep depression that had so completely overwhelmed him. He began to take an interest in life once more.

twelve

The Move to
New Orleans

On May 1, 1948, March wrote to Harold Ober, giving his agent full authority to deal with whatever matters might arise without initially consulting him. He told Ober that he was feeling greatly improved and that he trusted it would not be too long before he was his old self again. For the time being, he added, he was content to spend the days fishing or just lying in the sun.[1]

By August 16, he was able to report to Ober that he seemed to be almost fully recovered and that he had started work on two new pieces. He said he had no specific plans for the future but did intend traveling up to New York sometime soon to close up the apartment in Gramercy Park and arrange for shipment of his possessions to Mobile. He had it in mind to take an apartment in one of the local Mobile hotels and use that as his base, for the winter at least, until he had decided where he was finally going to settle.[2]

Wake was still endeavoring to solicit a story from him for its autumn number. The magazine was now under the editorship of Seymour Lawrence, Villa having apparently at last departed from the scene. Lawrence was careful to point out that the magazine had severed its connections with Harvard University and was now a totally independent production. He assured March, as Villa had done, that there would be no repetition of the unfortunate fiasco experienced earlier in connection with "The Borax Bottle." This time, there would be no deans with the power to censor the contents of the magazine and overrule the editor. March instructed Ober to send "The Bird House," which, so far as he could recall, was still unplaced on the agent's files. He was anxious to see the story published but recognized that it stood little chance with the glossy, mass-circulation magazines. Although Ober sent the piece to Lawrence on August 18, it never appeared in

Wake; clearly Lawrence did not consider the rather unconventional murder mystery suitable for the issue he was then planning, which was to contain work by e e cummings, Edith Sitwell, Walter de la Mare, and many translations from established French, German, and Italian writers, as well as the work of several new young writers.

Later that month, March journeyed to New York to close up his apartment. Probably he felt little regret at the time, for the rooms must have held many recent unhappy memories for him. The day that the movers came was the hottest day recorded in New York for many a year. By the time the operation was completed, March wanted only to flee from the city and return to the South. He did not even have the time, so he later wrote to his agents, to call in and say hello. Apologetically, he assured Ober he would be visiting New York again that winter and that he would certainly see him then. On September 17 he notified Ober that he was leaving Point Clear that afternoon and that for the next few weeks he would be staying at the Battle House, Mobile. The following day was his fifty-fifth birthday. It was as good a day as any to begin a new phase in his life.

Nothing came of the two pieces he had started the previous month, but in October he wrote to his sister Margaret in New Jersey, asking her to send him copies of all the stories he had written since the publication of *Trial Balance.* He was particularly anxious to have the manuscript of the unfinished story "The Practiced Hand." He aimed to complete it as soon as possible, so that he would have enough stories to make up a new collection. It really did begin to seem that the nightmare was over. He told Clay Shaw that he had "been to the edge of the abyss and looked over" and averred that, having survived, he would never be frightened again. Shaw always considered the statement too boastful.[3] The truth was, of course, that the recovery, although miraculous, was not as complete as March wanted everyone, including himself, to believe.

Possibly thinking that it might assist in the reparative process, the board of the Waterman Steamship Corporation had urged him to return to work for the company. March did not, however, feel that salvation lay in that direction, and money, certainly, was no particular incentive. He politely turned the offer down.

Nevertheless, in his doctor's view it was urgent that he find an interest other than his writing. The question was, What? He seemed, during this postdepression period, to be consumed with some form of inner restlessness. He moved out of the Battle House in early 1949 and took an apartment at 459 Conti Street, Mobile. Using this apartment as a base, as previously he had used the Battle House, he made several trips to New York, where he stayed at the Roosevelt Hotel, close by Grand Central Station. He interspersed these long-distance trips with more frequent visits to New Orleans, whose special atmosphere and charm were exerting an increasingly irresistible spell over him.

He was in Mobile in February at the time of the Mardi Gras. Case, who had joined the huge crowds lining the streets to watch the procession, happened to see March leaning against a wall, away from the crowds, shrinking back as if he wanted no one to see him. Case went over to him and greeted him. March answered him almost apologetically: "Hello, Jack. I just came out for a packet of Tums." This statement seemed to Case to preclude the possibility of any sustained conversation. After a few brief exchanges, Case left him and rejoined the crowd to enjoy the festivities.[4]

Mrs. Ada Broadnax, the black woman March had employed to look after his apartment, always remembered him with affection. He was, she used to say, unlike anyone else in the world. Although she thought him in many respects a peculiar man, she also considered him as surely the sweetest person she had ever known. She had observed how he had suffered from "terrible nerves" after his illness, but as the months went by he (to use her phrase) "quietened down somewhat." She claimed to understand him but doubted that most other people did. He loaned her money from time to time and was extremely generous if there was something she wanted and could not afford. On the other hand, he quite often overlooked paying her wages, but whenever that happened he put the matter right as soon as she reminded him. She maintained that he liked the smell, but not the taste, of coffee and that he always declared that he could not trust her to make it properly. Over his bed he had hung the portrait of a woman with curls and he told her that each curl represented someone the woman had killed. He called the woman in the painting his "girl friend." To Mrs. Broadnax's knowledge, however, March never had a "girl friend" as such, and she had the impression that he was petrified of getting "tangled up" with women. She recalled his having told her that one evening he had seen an old female acquaintance of his at the Battle House and that he had quickly left, so as to avoid having to speak to her.[5]

March's lifelong fear of involvement with other people, particularly if it threatened to become of a committed intimate nature, had, if anything, become more deeply rooted than at any period in the past. Consequently, his social life was limited. This is not to say that he did not cultivate new friends. During his stay at Point Clear, he had met Mr. and Mrs. Nicholas McGowin. They were considerably younger than he was, but McGowin's profession as a lawyer gave them a common interest. March clearly felt relaxed and happy in their company. The McGowins, on their part, found his company stimulating, his stories fascinating, and the strong views he tended to propound, both as to people and contemporary issues, somewhat unusual but never superficial.

His unpredictable movements were beginning to cause problems for his agents, for they seemed never able to make direct contact if anything urgent came up requiring consultation with him. Even on his visits to New York, he never bothered to call or visit them and they always learned too late of his stays at the Roosevelt. A letter they wrote to him on April 20, addressed to Conti Street, followed him around on his travels, missing him wherever he went. It was not until June 28 that he eventually replied to it, suggesting that in future they address all correspondence care of the Trust Department, Merchants National Bank of Mobile, as he always kept the officials there fully informed of his movements. His agents' letter of April 20 was to advise him that because of the recent very small sales of *Trial Balance*, Harcourt, Brace was not proposing to carry the title any longer and had it in mind to remainder the 1,700 copies still in stock and to melt down the plates. Did March want to buy any of these copies or the plates? By the time March replied, he assumed the matter was already a fait accompli, but in any case, he told his agents, he was not interested in acquiring any copies of the book.

Eventually, following his doctor's advice, he discovered a hobby outside his writing: art collecting. Apparently he did not consciously set out to become an art collector but drifted into the role completely by chance. In the opinion of Klaus Perls, the noted New York art dealer, March was merely seeking people with whom he could talk and be at ease and had found that there were some such people among New York art dealers. From this contact, there logically flowed his interest in art. Always, however, the interest in art was of a secondary nature. His primary interest was in the person of the art dealer, and being essentially an extremely generous and understanding person himself, he felt it only right that if he was taking up the art dealer's time he should buy some of the works he had to offer.

March had, in all probability, wandered into a number of art galleries before that day in the spring of 1949 when he walked into Perls's small, quiet, second-floor gallery situated on Madison Avenue and 58th Street. The gallery was a private place, never crowded, except possibly on Saturday afternoons. Usually no more than three or four people visited it in the course of a day, a fact that satisfied March's preference for the more secluded atmosphere. For March the gallery

was, as Perls has expressed it, "a retreat in his mind: a retreat where he
found a resonance in things that preoccupied him, that he was creatively mulling over in his mind."[7]

That first meeting between the author and the art dealer can be seen
in retrospect as one of the turning points in March's life. It was also,
had he but known it at the time, a momentous event for Perls. If Perls
was thinking, as he first began talking to this new visitor to his little
gallery, that this man—conservatively and expensively dressed, well-
groomed, spotlessly clean, and, above all, the epitome of the southern
gentleman—was some member of the board of a large corporation on
the lookout for a likely investment to hang on his dining-room wall or
deposit in a safe vault, he was soon to have his illusions swept away. He
quickly came to realize that March was obviously a highly sensitive and
highly disturbed man, still very worried and very afraid about his
mental health and of his ability not only to write but to discipline
himself sufficiently to see his work through to the end, and wanting
desperately to find someone with whom he could talk about his present and future projects.

Fate could not have been kinder to March than when it introduced
him to the sympathetic and understanding Perls at this time in his
literary career. As well as developing his interest in art and introducing
him to the tortured world of Soutine, Perls was also able, in a strangely
active yet subordinate way, to encourage March in his own creative
work. But for Perls's unobtrusive wisdom, March may never have
found the strength of purpose to believe in himself and begin writing
again. Perls himself has charted the course of their relationship:

> He came to me quite openly and frankly as a sick person trying to find
> mental equilibrium. He told me very quickly that he was sick—I mean,
> maybe not during the first or the second visit, but certainly very quickly
> afterward. As a result of his telling me this and because I was myself very
> psychiatrically oriented in those days, I was especially careful in what-
> ever I would say, so as to keep the things I said on as neutral a level as
> possible and not accidentally increase any of the enormous tensions I felt
> he was struggling with. That is one of the reasons I would sit and listen
> for hours and hours. Bill Campbell was never boring. He was always
> most articulate and most interesting. His flights of fantasy were totally
> fascinating, because one could follow the processes of his mind very
> clearly. It was never a stream-of-consciousness talking. It was always a
> totally structured, disciplined, and grammatically correct and articulate
> kind of sentence-by-sentence procedure of trying to develop an idea.
> There was never any skipping around. There was never any of the talk
> you get from a manic-depressive personality in his manic stage, where

one sentence will follow another, sometimes without any connection. These were always very strictly thought out scenarios of his books, or specific information on specific events. For all intents and purposes, he gave the impression of a very highly organized and responsible and even wholly warm person. But, then, in his flights of fancy, it would come out that there was a side of him which was all the exact opposite of that. This part of him, which I considered was his creative part, was the side of him that, to the extent to which I felt I could safely do it, I tried to encourage by throwing out ideas which I felt would tend to go in the direction of his story lines, his thinking, his feeling, and his particular method. This, I think, encouraged him to come back and do some more of the same, because he felt he could to a large extent let himself go in my presence without fear of going over the border. To that extent, I think our long conversations were of some value to him. Of course, what he was looking for were people who would appreciate his qualities as a creative artist whilst at the same time not being themselves creative artists, because then immediately there is competition. Since he knew, and I emphasized, that I was not a writer and that I was absolutely not going to write, this was marvelous for him, because I was not in any sense a competitor. I was an art dealer, and, to the extent that I was an art dealer, he satisfied that part by buying art. So for the rest we could then go about what interested him. Also, I was not a doctor. Maybe he told the doctor a lot more other things than he told me, and probably more significant things, but with me he could go into all the possible scenarios for his books, which the doctor would have thought highly extraneous to the entire therapeutic situation.[8]

Clearly, in Perls, March had found, for the first time since he had undergone analysis with Glover in London, someone who deeply understood his need not only for fantasy per se but for a person who could act as a sympathetic sounding board, encouraging his particular brand of schizophrenia in its more extreme moments and not attempting to stifle it.

This is the thing that impressed me so much in Bill Campbell—that is, when he found that I had quite a bit of experience with creative people, he was able to loosen up completely and let his creativity come to the surface without fear that I would step on it. That is why creative people wear their masks—because they are extremely sensitive in their creative processes. When they feel naked and vulnerable they therefore wear the social mask, so that when people talk to them about their art they can dismiss it completely—because that's just the game and the theater. The creative aspect is reserved for when they are really creating. But, you see, Bill Campbell, after he had tested me and found that I was willing to accept creative ideas, however much he as a southern gentleman knew that they might be forbidden, taboo, to the normal kind of listener, when he found that I was perfectly happy to let all this pass without criticism and accept it solely as the creative bubbling over of a creative mind, then he felt perfectly safe to go ahead and create in my presence.

Actually, he was a very direct and earthy person, because what he was trying to do was to break down the enormous barriers which socially exist between people. One of the things that struck me in those days as absolutely marvelous was that he told me: "You know, you sit in a train coming up from Mobile to New York, you sit next to somebody and you really don't know who that person is and you want to find out quickly, then you turn to him and you say, 'By the way, how old were you when you first masturbated?'" Now, you must not forget that this was in 1950. In 1950, you simply did not say things like that. It would seem to me that if Bill had lived long enough to be able to use his very direct approach in writing, without being afraid that it would all be immediately censored, couldn't be printed, couldn't be sold and so on, that he would have been a much happier writer. Because he constantly had to try and find ways of expressing thoughts which he could very simply have expressed if it hadn't been for all these many taboos from which he did suffer. It was a tough discipline, and he realized how arbitrary and really ridiculous it was. He would have loved to be able to write as people write today. . . .
As a southern gentleman, he was used to certain forms of behavior and of contact with other people. It was a creative act on his part to break through this and, like the anecdote on the train, to try and get close to people in a hurry, which is one of the things a southern gentleman simply does not do. But rationally he knew that this was wrong, that it was not the way to live. Yet it was so ingrained in him . . . the cultural forces surrounding the power which he tried to deny in *The Bad Seed*. Yet he himself was totally subject to it, and I don't think he could have helped it had he wanted to. It caused enormous conflict. It ended in the tragedy of his having to go in his sexual pursuits into areas where tragedy in those days was bound to follow.[9]

This difficulty March experienced all his life in breaking through the ethical barriers of convention and formality was not wholly a result of his southern roots. There were, in Perls's view, other perfectly valid and understandable reasons for his being, quite correctly, labeled a "loner" by so many of the people who knew him:

Even at a party he was always the loner, in the sense that he was the observer more than he was the participating person. You see, this is not possible once you are the creative artist, the creative writer. You always stand outside of yourself as an observer. While you may do things with other people, at the same time you are watching yourself doing these things with other people. It was very plain that this was again one of the mental difficulties he had. He was trying to enjoy himself occasionally on a more relaxed basis, but it was practically impossible for him to do so. He could never not be a critic of whatever anyone else was doing. He would try out all sorts of things, just to see as a writer, as a critic, the reaction that would follow.[10]

The pattern is, of course, a familiar one. He used Perls in exactly the same way as he had used people before and would continue to use them in the future, throwing at Perls ideas he had for new books and stories, so as to discover from Perls's responses what his chances of writing these novels and stories might be. There was, however, a vast difference between carrying out his sort of exercise amid the hubbub of a party, where his listeners, fascinated though they might be by the things he was saying, were nevertheless in a basically superficial frame of mind, and carrying it out in the quiet intimacy of the little art gallery with a fully attentive, wholly sympathetic, discerning and responsive Perls as sole listener. Perls recalls:

> He would always, in our discussions, throw out ideas of plots and possibilities and we would discuss them at great length, because these ideas fascinated me. A lot of things he was thinking about at the time were very much in line with things that preoccupied me also. . . . When it came to his projects, his books, the kind of things that really preoccupied him at the time, then he was very clear and very sharp. Any kind of thing I would say, he would take seriously, because this mattered to him. There was then absolutely no sign of any illness, mental or otherwise. . . . When I read for the first time the books he wrote after we had met, I found a lot of the ideas we had developed together in our conversations beautifully incorporated in these books.[11]

March's visits to Perls's gallery in New York covered the years 1949 to 1953. He invariably traveled up from the South by train, his stays in New York lasting sometimes several weeks, sometimes only a few days. It was over this period that, with Perls's advice and guidance, he gradually acquired the magnificent collection of modern French paintings that filled his New Orleans house at the time of his death.

> He had no very extensive knowledge of art when he first came to me [Perls has observed]. He did not know what he was looking for. He had absolutely no idea about their investment quality or monetary value. This was done simply on trust. He couldn't have cared less about any of them. The only thing that he cared about was whether or not he could get an emotional response or an emotional stimulus from the work he was

buying. This was quite apparent from the things he bought: Rouault, Picasso, Joseph Glasco, and, above all, Soutine. He bought very little of the so-called classical art. He bought exclusively because a painting did give him some kind of an emotional shock. It *had* to be a shock effect: an emotional shock. That is what he was looking for.

I guided him in the selection of paintings to the simple extent to which I have always guided people. That is, I have shown him and others the type of thing which I would feel would best correspond to their taste direction. Sometimes that works and sometimes it does not work. It is, however, well known that if an art dealer has genuine enthusiasm—the accent here is on *genuine*—for a work, this enthusiasm is apt to transmit itself to the prospective buyer, if the prospective buyer has any kind of emotional relationship to the dealer. You can't do it with salesmanship. You really have to have that feeling. So if I really thought that a picture was a first-class Soutine, then I could be pretty sure that Bill Campbell also would think it was very fine and probably would buy it.[12]

It was Perls who introduced March to the work of Chaim Soutine. The circumstances in which March first heard of Soutine's name, twenty years or so previously, make a rather amusing anecdote which he was not averse to telling against himself. It happened in New York during a period when he was sharing an apartment with a fellow Mobilian, Hilary Lyons. One day, Lyons, who was at the time taking a course in general aesthetics at Columbia University, brought home from the library a book on the history of art. He left it lying around and March began idly reading it. He became fascinated by what he read. Unfortunately, he had the opportunity of reading only the first fifty or so pages before Lyons, ignoring his protestations, returned the book to the library. Even so, March had acquired a smattering of knowledge which encompassed the Byzantine mosaics, Greek vase painting, the early Florentine and Sienna schools, and Cimabue. He had just reached Giotto when his reading was abruptly terminated. Some nights later, at a party of Lyons's intellectual friends, the names of painters began to be bandied about. March, who felt left out of the conversation, had been sitting quietly listening to the strange names being mentioned, when he was suddenly asked what was his opinion of the emotional content of Soutine's paintings. Like so many of the other names that had been mentioned, he had never heard of Soutine, but, loath to display his ignorance, he put a brave face on it and told his questioner, somewhat loftily: "It's a matter I'm not qualified to discuss. You see, Art ends for me with Cimabue." Hilary Lyons collapsed into boisterous laughter and, aware of the reason for March's answer, cried, "He ain't kidding, either!"[13]

March purchased his first Soutine from Perls in June 1949. The following year, he bought six more, three in August, one in September and two in November. One of these paintings, *View of Montmartre,* dating from about 1919, was loaned by its new owner to the Museum of Modern Art for the Soutine Exhibition which ran in New York from October 31, 1950, to January 7, 1951, and then in Cleveland from January 30 to March 18, 1951. Of the twenty-eight paintings in March's collection which were offered for sale after his death in 1954, nine— almost one-third—were Soutines, all of them dating back to the 1920s: *Paris: Montmartre* (c. 1920), *Paysage de Banlieue* (c. 1920), *Jeune homme dans un fauteuil* (c. 1920), *Fleurs et poisson* (c. 1923), *Nature morte aux poissons* (c. 1924), *Le garçon á l'habit bleu* (c. 1925), *L'homme aux Rubans* (c. 1926), *Le poulet* (c. 1926), and *Le boeuf ecorché* (c. 1926). This exceptional accent on Soutine in the collection has been explained by Perls:

> In the paintings of Soutine—because Soutine was indeed a patholog-
> ical character—he found something to which he could really relate. He
> felt a kinship of spirit. It was the general turbulence and also the manic-
> depressive situation in Soutine that attracted him enormously. He saw in
> Soutine all kinds of subject matter which to my mind was certainly there,
> but which may have been there as unknown to Soutine as it felt to Bill
> that it should be known to him.[14]

David Mynders Smythe recalls that March accurately diagnosed himself as "a paranoid type." Smythe thought it hardly surprising that Soutine should be his favorite artist: "Soutine's horrifying (to me) canvases were what the artist saw when he looked on the world, and to an extent that was true of Bill—he saw people preying upon each other, clawing and tearing to pieces and devouring."[15]

Sometime during 1949 or 1950, March moved his Mobile residence from Conti Street to the magnolia- and oak-lined Government Street, using his new apartment, too, as little more than an accommodation address. When he was not visiting New York, he would be staying in New Orleans. It is clear that New Orleans had cast an irresistible spell over him. He began to feel more and more at home in this unique, colorful, beautiful city than anywhere else he had ever been. This empathy extended beyond the mere physical atmosphere of the place to the less puritanical moral climate he discovered there. In New Orleans, he could observe at leisure, without recourse to binoculars or other subterfuge, those human behavior patterns which so fascinated him and which here, if not altogether accepted as the norm, seldom provoked the raised eyebrow. Additionally, as the late New Orleans writer Robert Tallant has observed: "There are many things that make New Orleans desirable, not the least among them being the fact that not only is it not considered disgraceful here to resist working in business or in a trade, but that among certain old families it was until recently unthinkable to do so."[16] This was an attitude of mind, a philosophy, March would have found most attractive, acting as a salve to his conscience, which was still troubling him as a consequence of his family's continuing lack of understanding over his resignation from his lucrative position in the Waterman organization.

In late 1950, March moved permanently from Mobile to New Orleans, although for tax purposes retaining his address at Government Street. He was not among strangers in New Orleans. Even prior to this late period of his life, he had probably visited New Orleans on several occasions, conceivably on Waterman business. Like William Faulkner and Sherwood Anderson and many other writers before him, the Vieux Carré, or French Quarter, would have acted like the candle flame to March's moth. He would have naturally gravitated to this section of the city where artists and writers have traditionally gathered. According to Tess Crager, he had known the writers Lyle Saxon and Roark Bradford, both of whom died before March came to live permanently in New Orleans.[17] Through these two men, he would have been introduced to the artists' colony in the French Quarter and given a taste of what life was like there. It must therefore have been at the back of his mind for many a year that it was here that he would finally settle, not all that distance from the city of his birth and from his family, but far enough away for him to feel free to give unfettered expression to the less conventional side of his nature.

He had reestablished contact with David Mynders Smythe by telephone. It had been three years since the two men had last met in New York, and knowing something of the history of March's recent troubles, Smythe was pleasantly surprised to find him much as he had known him before, perhaps in even better physical condition. It was through Smythe that March and Tallant first met. In his memoir "Poor Pilgrim, Poor Stranger," published two months and two days after March's death, Tallant recalls how, when he and Smythe were on their way to call on March, Tallant asked Smythe what March looked like. Smythe told him "like a preacher with wicked eyes." When they arrived at March's apartment, Tallant discovered that the description was rather apt:

I met a man of medium height, of slim physique and erect carriage, with a thick crop of wavy, graying hair. He looked much younger than what I knew his age to be, and his whole appearance was mild; his voice was soft; his manner gentle. Only his eyes were different. They gleamed from behind his glasses, probing, studying everyone in the room, and, as I came to know later, analyzing everyone. Then, as I became conscious of what the quiet voice was saying, I discovered it was a highly barbed monologue that was pouring out at us, witty, mischievous, brilliant.[18]

March and Tallant became close friends:

. . . Bill March loved to talk, and he talked a great deal about himself, curiously perhaps as if he were another person. He dug deeply into others, too, but mostly, and I think preferably, into himself. As I came to know him better I heard bit by bit the entire story of his life, and nothing was omitted. I believe he had total recall. He would talk of something that had happened when he was three years of age as if it had taken place yesterday. He talked of his childhood, of his parents, of his brothers and sisters, . . . of his service in World War I, of his years with Waterman, of his writing, even of the time when his emotional life got the better of him for a while and suspended his writing, suspended his life.[19]

If it is indeed true that March was as forthcoming about his childhood and his family as Tallant asserts, then he had assuredly made of Tallant a privileged confidante. All his other friends and acquaintances have recorded how circumspect in general he was about his family life, many of them gaining the distinct impression that relations between March and certain members of the Campbell family were strained, to say the least. So far as March was concerned, it was a never-ending source of regret that his family for the most part refused to appreciate why he had chosen his particular mode of life. For some of them, clearly, his taking up residence in the notorious French Quarter of New Orleans was the last straw. In their eyes, he became the proverbial black sheep, possibly beyond redemption. Perhaps in retrospect it can be seen that he was equally to blame for the rift that grew between them, for it would seem that he made little effort to explain himself, almost as if he sensed that, in any case, explanations would solve nothing. For all that, he retained an innate sense of loyalty toward his family and except on rare occasions remained silent rather than utter words of criticism or reveal family secrets.

Smythe, for instance, admits that March told him little about the Campbell family, never once mentioning his father to him. March did, however, relate to Smythe one incident concerning his mother when she was an old lady. One day when he visited her, he found her sitting

in her rocking chair, her long white hair hanging down her back, while
an old male servant was brushing her hair slowly and with deliberate
regularity. To Smythe's way of thinking, this little cameo scene had
been etched indelibly in March's mind. Smythe considered it a vignette straight out of Reedyville and to what extent it was fact or
merely a figment of March's imagination is perhaps unimportant. What
is, however, of interest is that to another New Orleans friend March
told a different and much embellished version of the incident, one that
was clearly pure imagination, although cruelly and pointlessly passed
off as fact. In this version, the three participants are the same—his
mother, the black male servant, and March himself as mere observer.
This time, according to March, the incident occurred during his childhood, when, upon hearing a noise from his mother's room and upon
opening the door to investigate, he was confronted by the extraordinary sight of his mother being strangled with her own long hair by a
massive half-naked Negro. His unexpected entry into the room
brought the bizarre activity to a halt. His mother asked him why he
was not in his room and asleep and then, as if feeling some explanation
was due to her son, told him that the Negro had a "thing" about long
silky hair. To demonstrate this, she proceeded in her turn to use her
hair to strangle the Negro, after which they again reversed roles and
the servant once more began strangling her.[20] March offered no explanation for this totally unbelievable incident, but one can postulate that
he had manufactured the whole preposterous anecdote from the memory of seeing his mother having her hair brushed by the servant and
from his observations when he was out with the New York police
chasing hair fetishists in Times Square, linking the two memories to
produce in his imagination a story he thought would intrigue his
listener. It is not easy to understand why he should wish to despoil his
mother's memory in this way, but what is certain is that his mother was
not the only member of his family to be so used by him. One of March's
cousins, Dillon T. March, has recalled that two of his aunts thought
they recognized themselves as book characters who were presented by
March in an unsympathetic light. According to Dillon T. March, the
aunts were understandably upset and offended.[21]

In relating such anecdotes as this outrageous one concerning his
mother and the Negro, March was obviously, as always, trying out
ideas for stories by passing them off as fact on whoever might be
listening at the time. To those who knew him well, the trick was
transparent, and they came to accept most of the more outré stories
with a grain of salt. Sometimes, however, even they had difficulty in
deciding whether or not the anecdotes were true, for March was

always persuasive and rarely gave any indication whether what he was saying was fact or fiction. However, as Smythe affirms, they were all *good* stories. For example, when he first came to New Orleans, March changed his address several times, each time saying that he had been subjected to annoyance of one sort or another from his immediate neighbors. In one briefly occupied apartment, so he told Smythe, he had been kept awake all night by some Koreans in the apartment above rolling balls back and forth across the floor.[22] The paranoid element in March's personality had obviously not diminished over the years. Here, in New Orleans, if his stories of such experiences are to be believed, it troubled him in the same way as it had done in Hitler's Germany and in postwar New York, although undoubtedly he did not feel this time so deeply disturbed by these imagined or real harassments as he had on previous occasions. In New Orleans he found a very simple, if inconvenient, solution: change his address.

He eventually settled in a tiny apartment at 906 Royal Street, a thoroughfare of antique shops and pretentious houses. His simple tastes in furnishings, which Clay Shaw had remarked upon when he lived in New York, had not changed. "He cared nothing for furniture," Smythe remembers. "He had only necessary pieces, none worth noticing. The two items I did notice in his Mobile apartment, a handsome desk and a Persian rug, he did not bring with him to New Orleans. There was a cold puritan air about his habitations. I never saw a living plant in any of them. Few, if any, books either, and none of his own works."[23]

Besides Robert Tallant, March made other new friends as he settled down contentedly in the French Quarter. Thomas Griffin, the "Lagniappe" columnist of the *New Orleans Item* (later the *States-Item*), recalls how he and March became friends shortly after the author came to live in New Orleans, occasionally having drinks or dinner together. March never allowed Griffin to write a line about his background or his fame. In Griffin's opinion, he was one of the most genuine publicity-shy men he had ever met, never holding an autograph party, never speaking at women's clubs, and steering clear as much as possible from literary teas, preferring his work to speak for itself.[24]

On some evenings when they dined together, it is possible that March and Griffin went to the late Owen Brennan's famous restaurant, then located in the building that used to be the old Vieux Carré Restaurant at Bourbon and Bienville Streets. March and Brennan struck up a very special kind of relationship and the author was invariably treated as an honored customer whenever he visited the establishment, even though he was known among the staff as "a gourmet with a pretty taste in wines, but with a wary eye on the price list, and never a lavish tipper."[25] The friendship that existed between Brennan and March was one of those not unremarkable instances of the attraction of opposites, for the restaurateur was a cheerful, handsome Irish extrovert, the sort of person, in fact, from whom one would have expected March instinctively to have recoiled. The extrovert and introvert personalities of the two men, as so often happens, seemed to counterbalance each other, welding a deep and enduring friendship which was to last until March's death.

Brennan's Restaurant, as well as being a place where he could enjoy exquisite satisfaction for his palate, a congenial atmosphere, and entertaining conversation with its proprietor, was for March a source for picking up the news of people and happenings in the Quarter. Whatever news he failed to pick up at Brennan's he was sure to pick up on his regular nightly visits to LaFitte's Blacksmith Shop at Bourbon and St. Philip Streets. The Blacksmith Shop had always been regarded as a local landmark and, because of its association (though this still remains unauthenticated) with the pirate-patriot Jean LaFitte, a place of national historical interest.[26] Since the end of World War II, however, under the name Café LaFitte, it had been used as a bar. Brennan's friend, Tom Caplinger, who died in 1957, presided over the establishment at the time March went to live in New Orleans, operating the bar on the ground floor and living with his family on the floor above.

Caplinger had done virtually no restoration to the building from the time he had acquired the lease of the premises, so that its atmosphere remained almost undisturbed. Indeed, the principal architectural feature of the place was the old forge. During the period Caplinger ran it, writers, artists, newsmen, visiting celebrities, owners of other Bourbon Street joints, strippers, and what have you, looked upon it almost as a second home. Born in Kentucky, Caplinger ran the place with good-humored casualness. Having lived in Europe during the "lost generation" years of Hemingway, Scott Fitzgerald, Harry Crosby, and the other expatriate writers and artists, he was, in many respects, an extremely good and certainly an extremely articulate critic. He detested phonies of whatever category but was unfailing in his kindness to young artists in every field. His language was frequently ripe and he was by no means averse to uttering a string of forceful four-letter obscenities when he felt occasion warranted it.[27]

Whether Brennan introduced March to Caplinger, or Caplinger introduced March to Brennan, it is not now possible to say. March, however, seemed to have found his precise milieu in New Orleans, and nightly visits to the Café LaFitte for a couple of hours of relaxation

in the company of friends after a day's work at his writing soon became
an established part of his routine. New Orleans and his long talks with
Klaus Perls had at last revived his creative powers, but he was wise
enough to realize he would have to impose a strict discipline upon
himself, keeping to a rigid program, if he were to complete any further
work after this long period of sterility. Accordingly, he split his writing
day into three sessions. He arose early most mornings and breakfasted
at home. He wrote or checked notes until noon. After lunching in one
of the small neighborhood restaurants, he would return home and
work again until five o'clock. He dined early, almost invariably at an
inexpensive place, apart from those days he went to Brennan's, and
then, back in his apartment, would, from seven to ten, go over the
day's written production. This review of the day's output was, in itself,
a creative process. On occasions, he admitted, he had sat staring at a
sentence for a half-hour or more, searching for the precise word, the
precise phrase, he wanted. By ten o'clock, he was more than ready to
unwind in the informal atmosphere of the Café LaFitte.

It was at the Café LaFitte, in the spring of 1952, that March first met
James Clinton ("Clint") Bolton. Bolton had recently arrived in New
Orleans on a newspaper assignment and, through the good offices of a
mutual friend of Brennan's, had been fixed up by the restaurateur with
a room in his apartment over the Old Absinthe House. On the evening
of his arrival in town, Bolton went over to Brennan's Restaurant for
dinner. Brennan joined him as he was finishing coffee, and over co-
gnacs Brennan imparted all the current news and gossip concerning
the denizens of the Quarter. The two men went out into Bourbon
Street and worked their way along the bars until they reached the Café
LaFitte. Here, Bolton was introduced to Caplinger and made to feel so
at home that he returned alone the following evening. Just before ten
o'clock, Caplinger asked him if he had read any books by "a guy named
William March." Bolton mentioned *Company K* and Caplinger confirmed that that was the man.[28]

"At exactly ten o'clock, he'll come in," Caplinger told Bolton. "I'll
introduce you. He doesn't dig strangers much. But I think you might
get along with him. For Christ's sake, don't ask him about writing—
don't mention style or anything like that. He sits and talks with a
couple of us, stretches a couple of scotches till about midnight and
goes home. Don't talk too much and leave it to me." It was not, to be
sure, an altogether reassuring briefing.[29]

March came into the bar at exactly ten o'clock, just as Caplinger had
predicted, "looking for all the world like a business man who had some
paperwork to finish up at the office and was going to have a quick one

before returning home."[30] After Caplinger had greeted him, the two men retired to the remotest corner of the bar, where, although the place had been steadily filling up during the course of the evening, one stool had remained significantly unoccupied. March perched himself on this, and the man already sitting on the stool alongside greeted him like an old friend. A few minutes later, Caplinger beckoned to Bolton and, drink in hand, he joined the trio. Another stool was produced almost miraculously from nowhere. The man who had greeted March so warmly proved to be Robert Tallant. Caplinger said to Bolton: "We're talking about voodoo—an old New Orleans occupation. You used to live here. Did it ever interest you?"[31]

In such manner, then, was Bolton accepted into the select March circle at the Café LaFitte. March was clearly fascinated by the stories Bolton had to tell of his experiences in Haiti. The four men conversed animatedly about black and white magic until midnight, when March went home. Caplinger, Tallant, and Bolton carried on talking and drinking well into the small hours.

A day or two after that first meeting, March telephoned Bolton and invited him to have lunch with him. It happened to be only eleven o'clock in the morning and Bolton was just partaking of his first cup of coffee of the day, but being a newspaperman he had long grown accustomed to irregular hours and meals—breakfast, lunch, it made little difference to him—so it did not occur to him to think there was anything untoward about the early hour March had set for their appointment. They met at a small restaurant in the French Quarter. It was a day of brilliant sunshine. There was a mild breeze blowing and cool shadows dappled the ancient stones of the restaurant patio.

> It was a pleasant, informal place [Bolton has recalled], and I wore slacks and a sports shirt. March had arrived ahead of me, and waved from a corner table. He was wearing a lightweight business suit, white shirt, and a characteristically neutral tie. I recall this clearly after the many years that have passed, for it accented the banker-like impression. I do not think that on more than three occasions did I ever see March informally turned out. Allowing for seasonal changes in clothing weight, the quiet business suit was uniform. In deep summer, he wore starched, old-fashioned seersucker suits, and once or twice he appeared in a white suit and panama hat. The overall impression was of a Southern business executive, circa 1900.
>
> Our brunch was the beginning of a friendship that might better be termed a "good acquaintance." Bill's sense of privacy was so strong that it was better to let him make the first move on every occasion. On that first person-to-person session, I had a curious feeling that I was under a

benign but searching microscope. I had known that the restaurant where we sat did not serve drinks, so I had taken an eye-opening Bloody Mary at the Absinthe House and a second one en route to the rendezvous. Although I had been in New Orleans only a few days then, I was "the writer guy stayin' in Owen's pad over the Absinthe House," and over each Bloody Mary had picked up some gossip of the night before. Bill was intrigued that I had so rapidly acquired a small bag of odds and ends of information. I explained to him how most newspaper reporters get all sorts of news from barside chats and chance encounters.[32]

Again, as during that evening at the Café LaFitte, March was quite evidently intrigued by what Bolton had to say, this time enumerating the various methods he had employed from time to time to obtain his news stories. They sat long over coffee and it was not until about three o'clock that they parted. "Walking back to the Absinthe House," Bolton concludes, "I realized that Bill had found out a great deal more about me than I had found out about him."[33]

March's love of gossip was given full opportunity to blossom in the intimate environment of the French Quarter. He was always ready to discuss his own foibles, as well as those of others, but he inflexibly stipulated those areas of his life he was prepared to bring into the conversation. There was, it was made very clear, a well-defined boundary line over which his friends stepped only at their peril. He could be uproariously funny when he had some choice tidbit to share. He reveled in playing games with people. For instance, when passing on a piece of gossip, he would tell his listener in whispered confidentiality, "This is for your ears only." It would not be long, however, before the recipient of this piece of news would hear at the Café LaFitte the selfsame story March had ostensibly so secretively told him.

In some ways, it seems extraordinary how easily and happily the reclusive March had adapted to the ribald, noisy atmosphere of Caplinger's bar. As Bolton has put it:

> Bill was a very nice guy who, when he got to know a few of us, probably enjoyed watching us clown about. That some of us could switch from the usual brouhaha of Tom's lively place to some thoughtful consideration of writing and how to go about it, I am sure Bill appreciated. We did not "lionize" Bill. We did not light candles to him. We liked him and were, to a degree, somewhat protective. Bill's corner was his. We grouped around him, mostly for give and take discussions of many matters, but also in a never spoken desire to shield him from the

occasional interloper who wanted to impose himself on what was the man's basic privacy.[34]

The atmosphere at the Café LaFitte was as intellectual as at any bar in New Orleans. In the "corner," conversation would range from local politics to abstract art, jazz as an art form, and the reality of dreams. It was invariably left to March to bring up any literary subject. This he seldom did, but when it happened that Bolton became involved in producing a series of half-hour scripts for a TV series called "NOPD," based on cases from the files of the New Orleans Police Department, March displayed great interest in the mechanics of writing to a deadline, as Bolton was obliged to do. He was astonished when Bolton told him that he was able to turn out one of these half-hour scripts in anything between six to eight hours.

Bolton had originally joined the "NOPD" unit as assistant director. In those days, the scripts were written by Frank Phares from synopses supplied by Benjamin Franklin Hay, then crime reporter for the *New Orleans Item,* who enjoyed privileged access to the police department's files. Phares, however, found himself unable to maintain the writing pace of one script a week and at Caplinger's suggestion approached Bolton, asking him to take over as script writer. Bolton agreed to ghost for Phares, while still retaining his assistant directorship.

Bolton spent each Saturday, which was the day when the "NOPD" unit as a whole took a rest, in writing the scripts. As each one was finished, he passed it over to Caplinger and March to read before handing it over to Phares the following Wednesday. Caplinger was always ready with suggestions, most of them good, for improving the scripts in small detail here and there, particularly where local speech patterns were concerned. March, on the other hand, seemed to read them solely for his own entertainment, certainly never suggesting any changes or criticizing them in any way. The "NOPD" unit frequently filmed interior scenes in the Café LaFitte, and occasionally March would join the Caplinger "in" crowds on the fringe of the set. He would sit or stand quietly to one side while the scene was being shot, a script in his hand, closely following the action.

I think [Bolton admits] that Bill's interest in "NOPD" stemmed largely from his overall interest in violence in man, rather from any actual interest in my writing ability. I recall that in one episode we had a completely brutal and needless murder. Two hoods followed an old man from a bar. He carried the receipts in a paper bag, and placed them in a bank night deposit drop. He was a cinch to rob once his routine was

established. Jumped from behind, he was knocked to the pavement of
Pirates Alley, hard by St. Louis Cathedral. One thug grabbed the brown
paper sack and the other carefully shot the old man. . . . I consider this a
completely heinous act of murder, and as the old man had been slugged
from behind and was unconscious there was no danger of his later
identifying his assailants. It was cold-blooded, wanton, and a very evil
deed. Yet it actually happened, and, aside from changing names and
locations, it was direct from the NOPD files. Bill questioned me closely
on this scene. Did I make it up? No. It had actually happened that way.
The subsequent inquest showed that the old man was out cold when he
was shot. Indeed, he might never have recovered from the crashing blow
of the gun butt. To shoot him had just been one guy's form of kicks.

I don't believe Bill ever committed anything more violent than swat-
ting a fly, but this was the sort of evil, needless violence which continually preoccupied him. . . . A gangland killing, for instance, did not
intrigue him. There was a logic in such killing. A death resulting from a
hold-up shooting did not interest him. But the old lady killed by a
passing tramp for the grocery money, young adults and minors wantonly
killing, was his meat. Bill had a collection of news clippings along these
lines, and from time to time he would show me one of special interest.
Through all of them were trace-lines of true evil, of "planned evilness,"
to recall his phrase. To planned evilness we would also add the truly
violent man who, in a barroom brawl, would not only batter an adversary
into unconsciousness, but stomp or kick him to death. Such saloon
killings happen almost anywhere, and in New Orleans, especially on the
waterfront, the weekend police blotter would have a couple. Bill's con-
tention was that men who killed under such circumstances were truly
evil and had within them the same wickedness that produced the Jewish
gas chambers in Hitler's Germany, and other massive crimes, including
the atomic bombing of Hiroshima and Nagasaki. . . .

His concern with good and evil was a very real thing. At the time, I felt
that his attitude was that of a writer using his skill to make eight-year-old
Rhoda Penmark [in *The Bad Seed*] a symbol. Only in after years have I
become convinced that he actually believed in true deviltry. I know now
that Bill saw the face of evil as clearly as he saw the face of the clock on the
spire of St. Louis Cathedral. Today, were he alive, he would certainly have
pursued the actuality of evil with growing intensity. . . . On several occasions, he would draw me out. Did I believe in "white" and "black" magic?
Did I think some persons actually could cast spells for good and evil? In
these conversations, I would try to explain that primitives the world over
still have old beliefs and superstitions. But in the end, Bill would narrow it
down to "good" and "evil" in actual people. Some nights I would say, "Bill,
we've all got devils and saints in us. Sometimes one is up and the other is
down." This was not a good answer for him. In his very quiet voice, he
would insist, "But some people are truly evil." . . . I recall at one time he
talked (but I doubt if he ever wrote) about a neighboring female whom, he

somewhat jestingly (though when he jested he sometimes meant exactly what he said) suggested, practised witchcraft. He told me, "I don't mind seeing her around, or even saying good day to her, in broad daylight. But I think she is possessed by some kind of rat demon." "What do you mean?" I asked him. He explained, "Every time I see her after dark, I can win bets that I will wake up that night with a nightmare that rats are all over the room, and they all look like her." . . .

Bill once commented that my own experience as a reporter on a police beat and a correspondent abroad had, along with "getting by in the Depression," given me a very keen sense of survival and had calloused me. "You were more ready for Hitler's war on a personal basis," he once said to me, "than I was for the Kaiser's war." I had seen bullet-riddled bodies of gangsters, riots in India, and, in a sense, violent death was part of my trade. Bill, on the other hand, entered the service as a young man with little or no experience in man's true brutality, and possibly without ever really having seen violent death. Actually, he seldom mentioned his participation in World War I, and only a handful of us really knew he had a "combat record." I don't think he ever mentioned decorations and other matters. So we seldom discussed personal war experiences, and, on those rare occasions when the subject did arise, I, more freshly from combat and fifteen years the younger, probably made the more frequent references to my own experiences. But I had read *Company K*, in which, with dreadful clarity, Bill had recorded the savagery and the utter waste in war. With the passing of the years, I had inevitably come to share—in part, at least—some of Bill's conviction that man is inherently violent, evil and wicked. From World War I until now is a hell of a long time. But the twenty-four-year-old Bill Campbell saw then and knew that forever we humans are truly violent people.[35]

March's long-established life-style was not, as has already been noted, unduly disrupted by his residence in New Orleans and his involvement with some of the more ribald characters of the French Quarter. He continued to live an essentially frugal existence, although none of his friends and acquaintances was under any illusion that this was in any way because of lack of ready cash. The existence of his growing art collection was well known to his intimates. It was simply that, remembering the financial restraints of his childhood, he was loath to waste money on what he considered nonessentials—as demonstrated by the somewhat mundane furnishings in his various apartments. He never owned an automobile, radio, or television. He shopped daily for whatever food he prepared for eating at home. Nothing extra was stored in the cupboard. He would, when it was his turn, buy a round of drinks in the "corner" at Caplinger's, but there was never any extravagant call by him for drinks all round. New acquaintances quickly discovered they could not butter him up in the hope that the "famous author" would buy them a drink. He frequently dined at a cafeteria across Canal Street in the commercial district, maintaining that the cafeteria's roast beef was "the best buy" in the whole of New Orleans. This frugality can be contrasted with his occasional meals at Brennan's, which, even in those days, was not a place for those who lived on a careful budget. Bolton has recalled that March invited him more than once to dine at Brennan's and was always an extremely generous host, "from the pre-dinner cocktails to an excellent post-prandial cognac and a pre-Castro cigar as the final grace note."[36]

Certainly, March was never ungenerous when he felt the occasion demanded. Indeed, as he had been many times in the past, he was capable of frequent acts of unsolicited generosity. One evening in the Café LaFitte, he heard from the bartender of the distress of a young man in the Quarter who, from poverty or from love, had attempted suicide and was recovering in Charity Hospital. March did not know the would-be suicide at all, but, typically, he drew the bartender to one side and handed him a sum of money to transmit to the young man, stipulating that its source remain secret. The bartender was so loyal to March's wishes that it was only after March's death that this particular story was revealed.

March avoided, whenever possible, any kind of official literary function. On another evening at the Café LaFitte, Robert Tallant, who was conducting a course in writing at Sophie Newcomb, the women's college at Tulane University, asked March in front of Bolton and Caplinger if he would come along and lecture to the young ladies. March's refusal was immediate and emphatic. He swiftly changed the subject, giving no one a chance, even mildly, to second Tallant's request. After he had left that night, Tallant told the others: "I didn't mean to upset him. But I did tell the students that from time to time I would have guests come to talk to them."[37] March's reaction had been such as to make Tallant fear that his innocent request had seriously damaged their friendship. Both Bolton and Caplinger reassured him that March would forgive and forget. They were right, but the possibility of March's lecturing to the girl students was never broached again.

Smythe had introduced March to Tess Crager and the Basement Bookshop. Mrs. Crager, as well as being a renowned bookseller, also acted as a literary agent and publisher. She held frequent autographing parties at her shop and every now and then March, obviously against his better judgment, was persuaded to attend one. After *October*

Island came out, Mrs. Crager suggested that he might like to auto-graph copies of his book in her shop. This was something he had never contemplated before and it was not without great difficulty that she eventually squeezed agreement from him. Finally, he told her: "I'll do it for you, if you think anybody cares." He did not endear himself to the customers, for he made no attempt to disguise his indifference, not only about signing the books but also whether or not the customers bought them, so distasteful was he finding the experience of this face-to-face encounter with his potential reading public.[38]

There is, all the same, little doubt that the unique literary atmo-sphere of New Orleans, from which—no matter how much he may have wished—he could not entirely divorce himself, was to prove beneficial overall. He decided that to get himself back into the public eye as an author he would have to write another full-length novel. Remembering the frequent criticism leveled against his work in the past that it amounted to little more than fictionalized casebook psy-chology, he determined to attempt something in a comparatively lighter vein. Searching around for a subject, he happened upon his novella "October Island," published in 1946 in *Good Housekeeping*. He decided that this story was exactly what he was looking for. So, just as the unpublished short stories "The History of a Tic," "The Man with a Mark on His Heart," and "Come in at the Door" were expanded into the novel *Come in at the Door,* and the published story "The Un-ploughed Patch" was expanded into the novel *The Tallons,* the novella "October Island" was expanded into the novel of the same name.

The writing of the book progressed more or less concurrently with his increasingly active interest in the world of art, so that art objects were very much on his mind at the time. He discussed the book with Perls, who has pointed out that the art objects March describes in *October Island* are not, of course, the kind of thing March had in his collection:

> The art objects he introduced into the book were more in the line of what one might call Freudian symbols than actual art objects. But it seems to me that if, instead of being a dealer in modern French art, I had been a dealer in primitive art, South Seas Island art, African art, which, to begin with, very few people bought in those days, Bill Campbell might have related to these objects even more than he related to French art. Of course, this is an "iffy" question. It didn't happen. But in *October Island* he obviously showed a greater interest in what is referred to as primitive art, folk art, than the very sophisticated art of the School of Paris that he collected, although the kind of art of the School of Paris he

collected, like Soutine especially, is less sophisticated than artists such as Braque or Picasso or even more classical people. He would never have been interested in surrealist art, because that would have been too literary for him to consider. He was himself a super-sophisticated person. He was looking for the immediate emotional shock treatment and not sophisticated stimulus.[39]

October Island was completed in late 1951 and the typescript despatched to Ober. Several U.S. publishers turned it down, including Alfred A. Knopf and Scribner's, although March's British publisher Victor Gollancz accepted it before the year's end. His agents were eventually able to place the book with Little, Brown and Company in the new year and it was scheduled for U.S. publication in the fall. By the time contracts had been signed, March was already engaged on another project. He wrote to Ivan von Auw at Ober on January 27, announcing that he was getting to work in earnest on a new novel called *The Bad Seed*, which, he considered, should be exciting, if nothing else, adding that he thought the subject matter was "fairly fresh."[40]

William T. Going has provided an interesting history of the genesis of *The Bad Seed*, which traces the later evolution, at least, of the book:

> The extant papers of March suggest that this novel is partly an outgrowth of a projected story, "Presbyterian Picnic"; the sweetly feminine Rhoda attends a Presbyterian Sunday School where she always wins awards of "golden butterfly" stickers for her piety in memorizing "the bloodier precepts of the Old Testament." March also abandoned an earlier novel on this theme of "congenital evil," tentatively called *The Practiced Hand*, in which the "hero" was to be a young boy, the son of a policeman. Irony is March's weapon against the temptation of sentimentality. . . . the shift to the female for "heroine" probably won out because to March the female was more deadly than the male—the praying mantis and the female of the fruit fly are recurrent figures in his stories and fables. March's concern with inherited tendencies and psychoanalysis is never pushed beyond the bounds of presently acceptable reality.[41]

The Bad Seed, then, is probably yet another example of March's following the "short story into novel" formula. Unfortunately, there is no indication as to when March first embarked on the projected "Presbyterian Picnic" story, but according to Clay Shaw and another New Orleans friend, the painter Joseph Dickinson, the novel's beginnings originated much further back in time than Going's account would suggest. Clay Shaw has recorded his very clear memories, going back to 1938 or 1939, of March's discussing *The Bad Seed* with him at the time March was living in the apartment on 54th Street in New York. He had been doing some research on the subject of mass-murderers and told Shaw that he was going to write a book about a homicidal little girl. He planned it to be his really great work, the summit of his literary career. Each time he and Shaw met, he would tell Shaw about some new development in the story. "That woman upstairs," he would say, "I think I'm going to call her Monica Breedlove and she will have been analyzed by Freud. What do you think about that?" Eventually, realizing that March had committed nothing to paper, Shaw became convinced that March had talked the book away and consequently would never write it. March persistently assured him that he would. When he settled in New Orleans and he and Shaw were seeing more of each other again, he continued relating the latest developments he had devised for the story, and Shaw continued to maintain that it would never be written. Shaw truly believed that after so long a gestation period, during which time March had apparently discussed the plot with all and sundry, the creative urge to complete the book must now have been destroyed. But March went on assuring him that he *would* write it.[42]

On the other hand, March confessed to Dickinson that he had in fact never planned to write *The Bad Seed*. He revealed that its genesis was not only unusual but completely accidental, beginning as nothing more than a sort of hoax on his part. To what extent March's version can be accepted as the truth is, as always, a matter for conjecture, but taking all the circumstances into account, there does seem to be a certain strange credibility about March's explanation. As March told it to Dickinson, he was at a cocktail party in New York when Shaw asked him what he was currently working on. At that time, as it happened, March was not working on anything, but not wishing to admit this he improvised, on the spur of the moment, the outline of *The Bad Seed*. Subsequently, whenever Shaw pursued his inquiries as to the progress of the novel, March was obliged, of course, to tell him that it was still at the stage of a verbal sketch. He would then proceed extemporaneously to embellish the basic plot, secretly amused by Shaw's almost frantic urgings that he should get it all written down before it was too late.[43]

The joke, if indeed it was a joke, backfired on March, for the story of the evil eight-year-old Rhoda Penmark took hold of his imagination. He discovered that having so lightheartedly created her, he was forced to take her seriously. One evening, when he arrived as usual at the

Café LaFitte, someone remarked that he looked tired. "I've had a frightening day," he explained. "I'm writing the story of a very wicked little girl, and she is beginning to terrify me."[44] Perls recalls that he and March had long talks about the girl and that March purchased a small Bombois painting of a girl child that seemed to him to incarnate some of the aura of evil associated with the child he had created in his imagination.[45] He even telephoned Tess Crager one day to ask her advice on a small matter which, with his penchant for accurate detail, was of vital importance so far as he was concerned. "Would it be likely," he wanted to know, "that Rhoda would wear a dotted Swiss dress to a picnic?" Mrs. Crager was able to tell him No, that gingham or calico would be de rigueur. "That," she has recalled, "was my sole contribution to his most successful book."[46]

By April 1952, plans were going well ahead for the British and U.S. publications of *October Island*. March advised von Auw that he had had some publicity photographs taken by a local photographer, Myles De Russy, and that he was intending to send copies of all six poses to Gollancz and Little, Brown, leaving the publishers to make their own choice as to which one, if any, they used. He also enclosed some biographical data about himself, which he hoped would meet Gollancz's needs.[47] The photographs were ready less than a week later and on the eighteenth he sent a complete set direct to Gollancz in London and another complete set to John Woodburn, Little, Brown's New York editor. On April 23, von Auw acknowledged yet another set which March had sent to his agents "in the event the need for a photograph should turn up"[48] and revealed to March that Rita Smith,[49] the fiction editor of *Mademoiselle*, had telephoned him to sound out the possibility of the magazine's using some extracts from the new novel. Because of the previous publication of the novella version in *Good Housekeeping*, however, the arrangement could not be made. Nevertheless, the news must have given March a deal of encouragement and satisfaction, indicating as it did that interest was being widely generated in his forthcoming book. Was this, he might have been forgiven for wondering, to be the big breakthrough for him?

Such hopes could well have been additionally fed by a telephone call he received from Robert Tallant. Tallant told him that he had been commissioned by the *Saturday Review* to write an article on March, perhaps in interview form, for one of the forthcoming issues. The editors were further planning to run a cover drawing of March in conjunction with it. Unfortunately, for one reason or another, the projected piece never materialized and it was not until after March's death and the success of his subsequent book had made him news that

Tallant's article, by then sadly in the form of an extended obituary, appeared in the magazine.

As with *The Tallons*, the British publication of *October Island* preceded the American. Gollancz brought the book out on June 9 and the first review clippings from the British press were encouraging. Everything really did seem to be pointing to the success March so badly desired.

It was about this time that March read a copy of *Ellery Queen's Mystery Magazine* and noticed that the editors ran a story contest each year, the first prize being two thousand dollars. He was surprised at the quality of some of the winners, many of the stories having only the remotest connection with the solution of crime. It occurred to him that the unplaced story "The Bird House" might stand a chance in the following year's contest. Reading through the story again, he remembered that Max Wilkinson, although interested in it, had finally rejected the piece for *Good Housekeeping* when he had been unwilling to change the ending. Realizing now that Wilkinson had been right, March revised the last two pages of the typescript and sent them to Harold Ober, asking him to substitute them for the last two pages of the ribbon copy in the agent's files and then to enter the story for the contest on his behalf, provided that, as he put it, "this sort of affair is consonant with your dignity in the community."[50] Ober replied that he would be glad to submit the revised story and assured March that there was nothing "undignified" in this, adding that in his role as agent he usually submitted several entries each year to this particular contest.[51]

Meanwhile, John Woodburn, who had probably initiated the proposed *Saturday Review* project, was continuing to do all in his power to promote *October Island* prior to its U.S. publication. On July 14, he wrote to Kip Fadiman, a regular columnist in the magazine *Holiday*, telling him how excited he and all his colleagues at Little, Brown were at the prospect of the publication of March's new novel. He reminded Fadiman of what Alistair Cooke had said in the *Manchester Guardian* the previous year when writing about the award of the Nobel Prize to William Faulkner. "I dare to go on believing," Cooke wrote, "that William March is a whole ionosphere above Faulkner, and is still the unrecognized genius of our time." It was an assessment with which Woodburn, so he told Fadiman, found himself unequivocally in agreement.[52]

October Island was published by Little, Brown on September 20, 1952. The book's dedication, "To Dolly and Klaus," acknowledged March's debt to the role played by Perls and, to a lesser extent, his wife in its creation. The dedication in the British edition had read "To

Klaus and Dolly." Perls has offered this explanation for the two deliberately different versions:

> He sensed that my wife was very much what today would be called a feminist—which, of course, didn't exist in those days—and, of course, in the South especially, the little woman had to stay in the background all the time, a situation which my wife didn't like at all, although she did it in those days. He sensed that this was a difficult thing for her to do, so he felt that he should reverse the dedication. This is typical of him. As a southern gentleman, he would have said, "To Dolly and Klaus," but he felt that since most of his conversations, most of his relationships, had been with me, rather than with her, as a writer he should say, "To Klaus and Dolly."[53]

Here, then, is again demonstrated the dilemma with which March had so often been faced in the past—the choice to be made, as it were, between the conventional world and the artistic or bohemian world, and the psychological conflict inherent in the situation. It must have given him great pleasure that he was, on this occasion, able to solve this particular problem so satisfactorily by way of so convenient a compromise.

thirteen

October Island and
New Roots Established

The long short story, or novella, version of "October Island," which was written by March in 1946 and published in *Good Housekeeping* that same year, recounts the story of two ardent missionaries, the Reverend Samuel Barnfield and his wife, Irma, who take up residence on October Island, somewhere in the South Seas, in the early 1900s and live there for the next quarter century or so, leaving only when the Board of Missions back home in America runs into financial difficulties and finds it no longer possible to provide the necessary funds to maintain them in their distant and somewhat obscure station. By the time they leave the island, Samuel is sixty-four years of age and a dying man, pining for the cold climate of his native Vermont, fearful that he will not survive the long journey back to the land of his birth. He comforts himself with the knowledge that he and his wife, with a degree of success of which they had never dared to dream, have achieved God's work among these heathen people by bringing about a mass conversion of the island's population. Both he and Irma are, however, blissfully unaware that the miraculous conversion was the direct consequence of Irma's elevation in the eyes of the islanders to the status of a pagan goddess. Samuel survives the journey but dies soon after they reach Vermont. Irma, alone now in the world, realizes that she has come to look upon October Island as her true home. The half million dollars she inherits from a cousin enables her to return to the island, where she receives a rapturous welcome from the inhabitants. Although herself completely ignorant of what is going on, she is at last ritually established to the islanders' satisfaction both as a goddess and the divine concubine of the great god Raybaat, the founder of the cult of Shurabast, who dwells in Min-Raybaat, the twin-coned volcano which dominates the island. She is also happily ignorant of the fact

249

that, in accordance with custom, she will be worshipped to excess for precisely one year and then thrown into the sacred crater to rejoin Raybaat. Captain Hansen, the half-breed master of the schooner that is the island's only link with the outside world, acts as a sort of chorus to the story, giving it an added depth, and he is used by March as the medium through whom much of the significance of the events which occur is revealed to the reader.

When he came to write the novel, March antedated the year of the Barnfields' arrival on October Island to 1895 and telescoped the length of their stay from twenty-five to nine years. He also elaborated the basic story line of the shorter work, introducing a number of additional characters as well as a completely new subplot, which, from one point of view, could be considered an overextended and irrelevant diversification and possibly an artistic mistake on March's part. This subplot does, however, provide undeniable potent and ironic comment in many respects, as well as leading the reader to a more colorful explanation of how Irma came by the windfall which allowed her to return to October Island after her husband's death, and there is a strong case for maintaining that the book would be the poorer without it.

In the longer work, we meet Axel Hansen's fun-loving mother Toppateeter, who bears her painful terminal illness with remarkable stoicism, braving the ludicrous, violent, supposedly curative administrations of the *brunga-brungas,* the local medicine men. We meet the Radja, the island headman who treats all white intruders, be they anthropologists or missionaries, with immense, far-seeing tolerance, striving, though not altogether successfully, to understand their many puzzling ways. Above all, we meet Irma's wayward elder sister Lurline, the principal protagonist of the subplot, a richly realized character, the justification for whose recurring and frequently dominating presence is not revealed until after the account of her death in the penultimate chapter of the book.

With the looser structure of the novel, March is able to indulge his imagination by considerably expanding the brief reference he makes in "October Island" to the origins and history of Shurabast. The whole cult, as he tells it, is based on the belief of its followers that the world was created during a period of sexual dalliance between Raha (the Sun) and Baat (the Moon) and that, as a result of their divine copulation beneath October Island (a corruption of the name Ok-tur-baat, said variously to mean "Garden of the Eternal Breast," "Garden of the Final Redemption," "Place of the Beginning and Ending," or simply "The Earth"), the hermaphrodite god Rahabaat (Sun-and-Moon-in-One) is conceived and after his birth is placed by his mother for safety in the crater of Min-Rahabaat (the place of conception), the twin cones of the volcano having been formed when, in the throes of her sexual union with Raha, Baat had pressed her body upward against the underside of the land. In the course of their rather wild lovemaking, some of Raha's seed spills into the sea and onto the land, creating the life from which all the creatures of the earth and the oceans have their beginning. Two of his seeds fall on the newly formed twin cones of the volcano and become Kaplinja and Ellomeat (the Shurabast equivalent of Adam and Eve). In time, Rahabaat grows and acquires the combined power of his parents, fertilizes himself, and produces a wife, Kallapaaga.

According to the findings of the nineteenth-century anthropologists who had visited the island some years before the Barnfields arrive, the cult of Shurabast had come into being ten or twelve thousand years before Christ and thus could reasonably lay claim to being the first of all the known great cultures, being at its height worldwide in scope and arguably having an influence on all the cultures and religions that were to follow and supplant it. In 9000 B.C., the barbarians sacked Ok-tur-baat, torturing and putting to death all the Shurabast priests. The strength of the cult became dissipated, its area of influence shrinking to the ever-faithful October Island alone, its surviving rituals observed now, at the time of the Barnfields' coming, merely in "a rudimentary and inconclusive form" (*OI*, p. 69). The islanders nevertheless believe deeply in the prophecy handed down through the ages that a virgin priestess would appear among them on two occasions: on the first occasion in the company of others, on the second occasion unaccompanied. It is part of the prophecy that this priestess will provide them with evidence of her identity and, restoring the power of Shurabast, lead her worshippers into a thousand years of happiness.

All this is, of course, immensely good fun and is set down by March with a certain deadpan humor. But in direct contrast to this pagan religion which allows its followers to lead a carefree and permissive life, he invents the Church of the Gospel Prophets, of which the Barnfields are members. This somewhat obscure Christian sect, according to March, was founded in Pennsylvania in the mid-nineteenth century by one Horace L. Huhner, from whom the Gospel Prophets derive their more commonly known name of Huhnerites. The mainspring of the Huhnerite faith is a rigid Calvinist code of conduct:

Drinking, profanity, gambling, smoking, and those usual sins resulting from lust—being transgressions obvious enough for even the decadent

religions to condemn—were forbidden as a matter of course. So was the
use of perfume, feathers, ornamental buttons, dotted veiling, and a host
of other things that would take too long to enumerate. [*OI*, p. 21]

As a child, Irma had gladly accepted the teachings of the Gospel
Prophets, regarding her cruel, bigoted father as "a regular saint on
earth" (*OI*, p. 19). March is able to expend all his old venom for the
Gosepl Prophets and their factual ilk in the portrait of Irma's father,
Brother Huffstetter, who, having destroyed the lives of his wife and his
two daughters with his religious fanaticism, is granted God's sanction
to die peacefully in bed at the ripe old age of eighty-two.

When, at the age of nineteen, Irma marries a man fifteen years older
than herself, Samuel Barnfield, pastor of a Huhnerite congregation,
she accepts that she is entering upon "a marriage of the spirit only"
(*OI*, p. 30), so that when she arrives on October Island at the age of
forty-two she is still a virgin, a fact which causes the islanders much
amusement and astonishment when it becomes known to them. Behind her back, they call her Luala Mananola ("The One Too Slippery
To Be Caught"). Later, her virginity is to assume a more significant
meaning for them.

It is interesting to compare March's treatment of Irma in the two
versions. Whereas in the novella she retains a firm hold on her
Huhnerite convictions to the very end, apparently remaining totally
ignorant of the true meaning of the islanders' momentous regard for
her, in the book her character changes as gradually the realization
dawns upon her that her dedication to the Huhnerite creed has ad-
versely affected her life. She begins to accept and enjoy her new role
as a pagan goddess. Unlike the Irma of the shorter work, she is shown
in the novel to be full of human frailties after all.

In the beginning, these frailties are not apparent. She is shocked by
the nakedness of the natives who come to greet her and her husband
when they first arrive on the island. Both the men and the women are
wearing nothing more elaborate than inadequate breechclouts and tiny
fiber aprons. There is, nevertheless, nothing sexual in her sense of
shock. The nudity of the women with their ample breasts hanging
down almost to their waists offends her eye the most, but purely on
aesthetic grounds, the nakedness of the men being somehow more
tidy, less obtrusive. She reminds herself, rather primly: "I, too, have
breasts . . . not human breasts of corrupting flesh, but the larger
breasts of faith and duty" (*OI*, p. 5). Her immediate reaction to the
situation is a predictable one: "We must get clothes on them somehow.
That is clearly our first task" (*OI*, p. 4). She discovers that to be easier

said than done, and although she sets about with a will, machining up a supply of shifts, it is not until many months later that she persuades Toppateeter to don one. Soon Irma is deluged with requests for the no longer disdained shifts and she is obliged to step up production. The islanders have the final word, even then, for the women cut large holes in the fronts of the garments to allow their enormous breasts to hang through in all their glory. After a short while, the novelty wears off, the shifts are discarded and the women go around once more in their unrestricted, happy nakedness. Nine years later, when she leaves the island to take Sam home to die, Irma recalls these attempts of hers to encourage the women to observe the proprieties and she wonders "at her tourist earnestness of those remote days, her concern with such trivial matters" (*OI*, p. 210).

Irma's more liberated viewpoint can be seen to date from the moment she receives the news of her father's death. Instead of feeling the overwhelming sense of grief she had always expected she would feel, she experiences an all-pervading sense of relief. She realizes that "her life had been arranged thus far not for her own happiness, but to spare Papa's sensibilities, and to avoid the quick penalties of his wrath" (*OI*, p. 87) and that she had over the years denied herself so many things she should have had and known, just because her father wanted her "sweet and 'unspoiled'" (*OI*, p. 87). In more recent years, believing herself not nearly so mean and narrow-minded as she had once been, she rationalizes her sister Lurline's outrageous behavior toward their father by trying to convince herself that "Lurline loved Papa, in her way, and wanted his love and affection in return; but since her disposition was what it was, of course Papa could never give those things to her" (*OI*, p. 31). Now that Papa is no more, however, she can confess to herself that because she did not have Lurline's courage in standing up to their father and refusing to bend to his will, she had simply taken what had then seemed the easy, hypocritical way out, suppressing the fact that "in her own whining way, she had always hated Papa as much as Lurline had" (*OI*, p. 88).

Irma rejects the past so fiercely that, at the age of fifty-one, she has gradually become aware, rather uneasily at first, of her own sexuality, so that she is able at last to admit to herself, "Shapely young men are my weakness" (*OI*, p. 171). After she has buried her husband under the gray January Vermont sky, she weeps "not for the happiness she had lost, but the happiness he might have given, but had denied her" (*OI*, p. 224). She finds that she misses Sam no more than she would have missed a familiar piece of furniture that had long been a part of her life. Returning to October Island, she can even wonder curiously if carnal love is all it is said to be, but her good sense warns her that although there would be ample opportunity for her to have the pick of those young male islanders who attracted her so, such things are too late for her now and she should live out her life a virgin.

In the transition from novella to novel, Irma thus ceases to be merely a detailed caricature of the archetypal missionary wife and becomes a rounded, living, and finally sympathetic character. In the same way, Sam Barnfield is developed from the somewhat shadowy personality he is in "October Island" into a fully realized character in the novel. Unlike Irma, on the other hand, he never unbends, rigorously repressing all his natural emotions whenever they tend to overwhelm him. Given to uttering such platitudes as, "Here is a field that awaits the plow of the Lord" (*OI*, p. 3) and "I am God's creature. I exist only in His love" (*OI*, p. 36), it is certain that he never comes anywhere near to really understanding the islanders. He is convinced that his lack of success in winning them over to the Huhnerite creed is due to the fact that they have no sense of guilt, the essential require-ment, as he sees it, in the potential convert. It is certain, too, that, as in the novella, he never fully comprehends the true significance of the sudden and totally unexpected mass conversion of the islanders when it eventually takes place. He is simply grateful that, after so many frustrating years, the miracle has occurred and that the Huhnerite Governing Board of Ordained Bishops gives him full credit for it. He saps his remaining strength in working all hours of the day instructing and baptizing the natives, until, inevitably, he collapses completely under the strain.

Sam's impotence against the irresistible force of Shurabast is fore-shadowed at the very beginning of the book. When, approaching the island for the first time on the schooner *Mattie B. Powell* and already a sick man, he sees the twin-coned volcano Min-Rahabaat, he experi-ences a sense of deep unease. Even though Irma assures him there is nothing to be afraid of, he cannot help but visualize all the power that lies bottled up in the craters, waiting to explode. Even more specifi-cally, the dominating cones remind him of immense female breasts and stir in him the sexuality he has always fought to deny. He, like Irma, finds the nudity of the natives disturbing, being particularly troubled by the sight of the women running, lifting their large pendulant breasts with one arm and holding them outward as if displaying "a basket of ripe tropical fruit for others to view and admire" (*OI*, p. 7). He is painfully aware of his secret weakness, dreading the possibility that he might someday break the vow of chastity he took when he entered the Huhnerite ministry, thankful for his marriage to Irma, knowing "that one of its blessings was the fact that this rather masculine, aggressive, literal woman would never, with her skinny body, her flat chest, and her freckled hands, tempt him from that vow" (*OI*, p. 78).

Almost as if they were knowingly testing to the ultimate his moral strength and his faith, the Governing Body of Ordained Bishops consistently ignores his requests to be assigned to missionary stations in the far North, where, so hard and hazardous would be the life, there would be little opportunity or desire to contemplate sin. Every one of his assignments had taken him to the South Seas, stretching him continually on the rack of temptation:

> He was sick of these hot and easy places, these corroding lands where everything was a seduction of the senses, a trickery of the flesh. Here even the fruits and flowers, those innocent things, were designed to divert and entice the unwary—the phallic fruit, the yonic orchid—for they felt and smelled, not as vegetation should feel and smell, but as warm, excited flesh.
>
> There were, in these places, flowers that closed their petals or drew back with human coquettishness as you stretched your hand forward to touch them; there were plants that bled as you stripped their leaves; there were vines that caressed the lonely who passed through the forest, seducing his flesh with a touch as delicate as the touch of a woman, and winding about his throat and waist in an embrace so passionate that unless he moved at once he never moved again; there were those plants with narcotic juices and sweet smells that lay in wait, as though themselves sentient and aware of the evil of their intentions, to trap the insect with their lures, to destroy him, to digest his juices with their juices. [*OI*, pp. 32–33]

He witnesses with dismay and a certain amount of disgust his wife's continuing and increasing interest in the Shurabast religion and its rituals. When she is asked by the islanders to preside over one of their pagan ceremonies, he forbids her to go. She rounds on him bitterly and cruelly taunts him for the ineffectiveness of his work, informing him that the islanders laugh at him behind his back, calling him Nupoona dool Palladole ("Old Dried-up Talking-bone"), ridiculing his sermons and running away whenever they see him coming. When he tells her she is a lost woman, she retorts: "And you, Reverend Barnfield, are a dirty-minded old man" (*OI*, p. 168). Even when he cannot avoid the knowledge that he is dying and longs only for the recompense of ending his days in his beloved Vermont, he steadfastly refuses to take any action to bring about his departure from the island he hates so much, telling Irma "that he was a soldier in the service of the Lord, and that soldiers remained at their posts until they perished, or were recalled" (*OI*, p. 183). Unbeknown to him, Irma writes to the Governing Board, explaining the situation, and in due course the letter she has asked for arrives, requesting them to return to America for conference and possible reassignment.

In the end, it seems, even the comfort of his religion is denied Sam, for he has for some months prior to their departure been given to contemplating eternity, "trying to measure it with thought" (*OI*, p. 160). Unloving and unloved, his body is symbolically laid to rest in the frozen earth. If Sam Barnfield is presented in these pages as a somewhat foolish man, he is also presented as a man who recognizes his own human weaknesses, deliberately taking for his wife a woman who holds no physical attraction for him and firmly turning away from all the easily accessible erotic pleasures of the South Seas, dedicating his life to the service of his intractable God, without joy, possibly without hope of ultimate reward in heaven. In an extraordinary passage toward the end of the book, during the voyage to Honolulu on the schooner, the first stage of his long journey to his grave in New England, he tortures himself with thoughts of what he considers has been his general incompetence in carrying out God's work on earth. He feels the nearness of death and becomes terrified with the idea that he will die before they reach land:

> he passed his hands roughly across his face, as if to brush something away from him. He had read somewhere that men buried at sea did not sink to the bottom: instead, they found the particular level in the bed of the ocean where the weight of their bodies coincided with some intricate displacement of water, and thus remained suspended there, neither buried nor unburied, for all time. He shuddered. [*OI*, p. 204]

This, of course, is the concept of eternity he has always dreaded, his body and his soul suspended in an everlasting limbo.

For Axel Hansen, the mate (later captain) of the schooner *Mattie B. Powell*, the sense of being in a sort of limbo is a living reality. He is the most fascinating, and in many ways the most tortured, character in the book. Son of Toppateeter and Professor Hans Axel Hansen, an eminent Danish anthropologist who had lived for a time on October Island "to investigate the customs of its people, and who, plainly enough, had done so with some success" (*OI*, p. 48), Axel Hansen's emotions are continually torn asunder by the mixed blood flowing in his veins. He is unsure of his true place in either of the two societies to which by birth he belongs, unable to settle and establish a permanent home for himself with the wife and family he desires, condemned like the legendary Flying Dutchman to rove the world forever in a fruitless search for peace. He is regarded by both his peoples with suspicion and unease. When, for instance, on the Barnfields' arrival he acts as interpreter, translating the Radja's speech of welcome, the Radja is quick to note how

> Mate Hansen—who had even repudiated his musical, native name for the coarse name of his foreign father—had occasionally smiled and raised an eyebrow in a significant and most amusing way. Perhaps at such times he had also commented humorously on the text of his ruler's welcome, or had interpolated little explanatory jokes on his, the Radja's appearance, or on his known foibles. The shape of a face, or the color of a skin, was easy enough to determine: he, and all others, could estimate by glancing at Mate Hansen what part of his blood belonged to October Island, and what part belonged to the outside world; but who could determine the shape of a mind, or the color of a thought? [*OI*, pp. 10–11]

Educated at his mother's behest by the missionaries and scientists who visited the island after his father left, he determines when he is old enough to seek his father out and effect a joyful reunion with him. When, as a seafaring lad of sixteen, he finds himself in a port quite near to his father's home, he seizes the opportunity of making his dream come true. He writes to his father, announcing that he will call at a certain time on a certain day, but when he arrives at the house he is met by policemen who accuse him of attempted blackmail. The experience is a trauma from which he never really recovers:

> It had not occurred to him before in his fantasies, but all at once he knew his father was ashamed of him and of the episode that had resulted in his existence—that he had canceled both from his mind with cold and efficient calculation. . . . The memory of that bitter day remained with him all his life. When it was fresh in his mind, he would often stop what he was doing, stand still, and shudder; but now, eight years afterwards, he only felt shame, and a little regret, as he recalled the senseless, unnecessary humiliation. . . . he did not blame his father for what he had done: his father had married again, and had other children whose lives must be considered, along with his own. Who, under those conditions, would welcome a forgotten half-breed bastard? [*OI*, pp. 57–58]

In later life, he suffers yet another humiliating rejection, when, attempting to give up life at sea, he teams up with Miss Carmen

Dilustra, a dancer of Sicilian descent, to form a novelty singing-and-dancing act called The Blond Hawaiians, falls in love with her, asks for her hand in marriage, and is refused on account of his native blood. After she has left him, he learns that she has undergone an abortion to rid herself of their unborn child. He comes to realize that

> his was the melancholy of those who are neither one thing nor the other. Once, long ago, he had lived with some assurance; but as the years receded, and the cleavage in his nature became more and more apparent, he saw nothing about him but sadness, as if a deep pathos, for his kind, was the essence of life itself, the background against which we are born, and struggle, and live out our lives to their ends. . . . In the years since he had left October Island, he had become familiar with every vice, he had participated in every depravity known to man; and he had rejected them all at length, not because he considered them wrong, but because he found them tiresome, so that now, as he approached his middle thirties, he had achieved not corruption, but a kind of impervious and monstrous purity. [*OI*, pp. 201, 207–208]

Although all his life he hankers for unconditional acceptance by white society, he is nevertheless unable to throw off entirely the inescapable reality of his October Island origins. When he visits his mother, he is quite willing to discard his Western clothes and adopt the tiny apron worn by the islanders to cover his nudity. He indulges in the easy sexual games of the native girls, observing the carefree but ritualistic customs which lead to congress. When his mother dies, it is to Rahabaat he prays for comfort, not the god of Christianity.

It is he, from his unique vantage of having one foot in each cultural and spiritual camp, who is able to observe with clear objectivity the effect that the Barnfields have on the islanders and the effect that the islanders have on the Barnfields. He can appreciate the ambivalence of the situation that develops, where it becomes by no means clear "if the missionaries had actually converted the people of October Island, as they imagined, or if they, themselves, had not unwittingly embraced Shurabast" (*OI*, p. 190). He, unlike the Barnfields and the islanders, can understand how each side has mistakenly interpreted the other's actions. When Irma tells him how she has been digging up obscene prayer stones, washing them and throwing them into the crater of Min-Rahabaat to prevent them falling into the hands of the anthropologists, he knows that the islanders will have observed her and, while puzzled a little by her behavior, will have been greatly impressed by her piety in returning all these objects to their rightful owner, Rahabaat. He knows that once the seed has been self-planted in the minds of the islanders, Irma's virginity will soon assume new significance. He knows that when she survives the apparent sacrilege of eating food left on a wayside altar for Rahabaat, the islanders' suspicion that she is a goddess will become more firmly founded. He knows, too, that when she finds the rock crystal cup and spoon and uses them to dispense condensed milk to a sick man, thus provoking an instant miraculous cure, this will be the final piece of evidence the islanders require to establish her deity, for he is aware of the ancient legend of the cup Rahabaat made from the skull of his divine mother and from which he and Shurabast had drawn all their power, the cup the islanders had always prayed would one day be restored to them.

The cup, which is immediately recognized by the islanders, is indeed the instrument of the mass conversion. So eager are the islanders to take milk from it that they form a great congregation around the Barnfields. To Sam and Irma, it seems that they are celebrating a form of holy communion and when Sam preaches and exhorts the islanders to enter the ranks of the Gospel Prophets not one of them runs away.

As the days go by, Sam innocently and enthusiastically continues conducting pagan rituals under the guise of Christian ceremony. Irma is not so naive. She realizes that it has been her good fortune to be given the power to influence the islanders and takes the view that the ends justify the means, suspect though they may be. Providing that Sam and the Governing Board do not know the truth, then no one will be hurt. Certainly she revels in her own elevated status in the eyes of the islanders, for the first time in her life experiencing the adulation she had, ever since a child, wanted more than anything else—mere admiration would not have been enough—so that when she has to leave October Island to accompany her husband back to their homeland, as it is her wifely duty to do, she experiences a nagging sense of loss. Almost from the moment she leaves the shores of the island, she lives and prays for the day when she will return.

Although she promises the islanders that she will come back to them, they are distraught at her departure. They feel lonely and abandoned by their so recently found goddess. Remembering her exhortations that they should pray for her return, they abase themselves in the hope of impressing the god Jehovah, even becoming celibate in accordance with Huhnerite doctrine. When, however, their prayers appear to remain unanswered, they decide that the situation calls for extreme measures. They buttress their piety by falling back on the more reliable Shurabast ways.

Aware that Shurabast is partial to the flesh of young children, they persuade themselves that if they sacrifice their children by throwing them into the crater of the volcano, Rahabaat will express his gratitude by heeding their prayers and bring back Mrs. Barnfield, so that she may lead them toward the promised Golden Age. Initially, the islanders balk at the idea of actually sacrificing their beloved children, even for the best of causes, and, in one of the book's most richly comic passages, using the most elaborate and pliable logic, they convince themselves that Rahabaat will not notice the difference between a child and a pig, provided the pig is shaved, stained the light brown of human bodies, and dressed in a child's breechclout. But when their prayers continue to remain unanswered, they are ultimately obliged to realize that Rahabaat has not been deceived by their trickery. They are left with no alternative but to commence a daily sacrifice of the children.

Just when the supply of children is about exhausted and the islanders are all but overwhelmed with despair that their prayers and the sacrifices they have made have all been in vain, Irma returns on the schooner, this time, of course, alone, thus fulfilling the prophecy in every detail. She dresses herself up in priestly robes before the schooner enters the lagoon and as soon as they set eyes upon her the islanders are transported with joy. She is overcome by the ecstatic fervor of their greeting. Her puzzled inquiries as to why there are no children to greet her go unanswered in the exuberance of the occasion. She tells them that "October Island [is] her true home . . . and not the silly, terrifying world that lay outside it" (*OI*, p. 243) and freely abandons herself to all the administrations and adulations heaped upon her. In contrast to the novella, her ultimate fate is not touched upon in the novel, and the reader is left with the final memory of her being carried off in reverential triumph, seated on a throne borne on the strong naked shoulders of the islanders. Irma Barnfield, March would have us believe, has at last found her true haven and state of enduring happiness.

The last chain in the link is Irma's elder sister Lurline. Effectively, she is little more than a deus ex machina, the whole point of her existence in the book being to provide the means by which Irma is enabled to return to the island when she is left, for all purposes, destitute after Sam's death. Whereas in the novella we are simply and very briefly told that Irma has become the surprised sole beneficiary of "a certain Miss Amelia Goodpasture," a cousin of hers she has not seen since childhood, and receives a legacy of more than a half million dollars, in the longer work March recounts in piecemeal fashion the whole rambunctious, hilarious, and finally pathetic history of Lurline. Condemned by her tyrannical father as "vain, sly, scheming and pleasure-loving" (*OI*, p. 20), she is whipped again and again by him for disobeying the code of behavior he has laid down for her. One is reminded here of the terrible childhood Ira Graley endured at the hands of his grandparents in *The Looking-Glass*. Like Ira, Lurline eventually rebels and leaves the family home in New Orleans at the age of twenty, but not before thrashing her father with his own strap and promising to bring disgrace on him as often as possible by her behavior. She lives up to her word, ensuring that every newspaper report of her misdeeds and of her activities as a hooker in a Basin Street brothel carries mention of the fact that she is the daughter of Brother Huffstetter, the prominent Gospel Prophet.

In course of time, she marries a river gambler, but he is shot and killed a few weeks later. She next marries a little crooked-backed photographer named Vetter, who runs a studio on St. Peter Street, New Orleans. The few years she has with him are the happiest she is ever to know. She is content to devote herself to looking after him and is prostrate with grief when he dies. With the small amount of money he leaves her, she opens a bar on Decatur Street. There, at the age of forty-five, she meets Charles Goodpasture, an alcoholic and a compulsive liar, a young man whose eyes "bulged outward a little, as though pressure were applied to his throat" (*OI*, p. 130). She feels a certain degree of sympathy for him and helps him live through a number of attacks of the "horrors." When he asks her to marry him, she agrees, even though she has no idea of his background and will have to sell the bar so as to keep temptation out of his immediate reach. It is not until he takes her to his home in Philadelphia that she discovers he is the scion of an extremely wealthy family. His relatives are predictably antagonistic toward her, taking it for granted that she has married him simply to get her hands on his money. She persuades him to take a cure. When, his brain at last cleared of alcoholic fuddle, he sees her in the cold light of day, he realizes what sort of woman he has married and recoils from her in horror. Lurline readily agrees to divorce, accepting that in the arrangement she will act as the guilty party, and receives a settlement of $100,000.

She decides to return to New Orleans for sentimental reasons, but when the train reaches Mobile, she is seduced by the smell of bananas that pervades the atmosphere and, on an impulse, leaves the train, assumes the name of Mrs. Bessie Pigg and buys a small, out-of-the-way brick house. After nailing up all the windows and all the doors but one, she settles down to live the life of a virtual recluse. She becomes a local "character," becoming more and more withdrawn until finally she ventures out only at night, scavenging from the garbage pails for her food, collecting old newspapers, tin cans, and other useless bric-a-brac, filling the rooms of her house to the ceilings with the rubbish, spending her days pointlessly cataloguing it and moving it about from one place to another. She dies alone among the piles of accumulated debris, succumbing to starvation, all her money intact, the one letter Irma had written her when she first arrived on October Island eleven years previously tucked away in a large telescope bag, the envelope still unopened.

This letter is the only communication to have passed between the two sisters since Lurline left the family home when Irma was fourteen years old. Irma, who had betrayed her sister to their father and provoked the momentous row which had culminated in Lurline's departure, writes to her from a vague sense of guilt, to ask her forgiveness for the wrongs she has done her in the past. Not knowing Lurline's current address, she sends the letter care of the New Orleans Police Department, asking them to forward it. Aware of the sort of life Lurline had been leading the last time she had had news of her, Irma imagines her sister as an unlovely, middle-aged drab in need of both financial and spiritual help. Lurline, however, has just divorced Charles Goodpasture and she jumps to the conclusion that Irma has heard that she has "made money on the Goodpasture deal, and . . . wants part of it" (*OI*, p. 138). She throws the letter, unopened, into the telescope bag and apparently forgets all about it. When it is found among her effects after her death, her lawyers get in touch with Irma, informing her that she is the sole heir of her sister's estate. Not only is Irma given the means to return to October Island, but she is also able to realize the ambition of Captain Hansen, for whom she has developed a deep and potentially sexual affection, to own his own vessel. She buys him the *Mattie B. Powell*, on the understanding that he will rename it the *Irma H. Barnfield*. As she explains to him: "It isn't all vanity on my part . . . although there's vanity in it" (*OI*, p. 236). Discussing the unexpected turn of her fortunes with Captain Hansen, Irma observes wonderingly that "the *good* people she'd known, who'd loved her, had done little for her; but Lurline, who'd hated her so openly, had made her dreams come true with her *badness*" (*OI*, p. 237).

The irony of the Irma-Lurline relationship goes beyond the mere final application of Lurline's fortune, for Lurline herself, by treating her sister's letter so disdainfully, is alone instrumental in ensuring that Irma inherits her money. Had she torn the letter up or thrown it away, there would have been nothing to connect Mrs. Bessie Pigg with Mrs. Irma Barnfield. There is irony, too, in the fact that Lurline, the lover of life, ends her days in desperate, pathetic solitude, pitied only by the Negroes in the neighborhood where she lives, whereas Irma, the virgin puritan, discovers her sexuality and a life-giving purpose to her previously unfulfilled existence, glorying in the sensual and atavistic rituals of the pagan religion to which she surrenders herself. That other puritan virgin, Sam, on the other hand, is not so fortunate. The irony of his destiny is that, righteous and clean-living though he has always been, he contracts the ills of the dissolute: an enlarged liver and prostate. Also, an inept missionary, he is acclaimed for achieving a mass conversion of the islanders, a mass conversion for which he is not responsible and which occurs because of an almost farcical misunderstanding on the part of the natives. Irony, too, is the fate of the islanders themselves, for they embark on the "Golden Age" having misguidedly eliminated one whole generation of their race. Their "Golden Age" can almost be equated with the Golden Age that our own Western politicians promised us as justification for the mass slaughter that was perpetrated in France and Belgium during World War I.

One is struck by the apparent care with which March has chosen the names of his characters. They have a singular appropriateness which cannot have been merely accidental. The name Barnfield, for instance, suggests the very dichotomy of the lives of Sam and Irma: the barnlike enclosed and oppressive world of their religion in which, to begin with at least, they feel safe, and the wide world of the field in which they carry out their duties as missionaries. Charles Goodpasture is the one who, by devious and haphazard circumstance, provides the bounty which enables Irma and Captain Hansen to reap the harvest of their desires. The pseudonymous Bessie Pigg can be seen as counterpoint to the pigs who are abortively sacrificed by the islanders, for it is she, not the children as they imagine, who is immediately responsible for making the islanders' prayers come true. And Axel Hansen is the character who stands at the still center of the whole work and around whom everyone else seems to revolve.

Additionally, it can be seen that March has playfully and under only light disguise purloined the names of some of his New Orleans friends for use in his narrative. Kaplinja and Ellomeat, the first man and woman according to the Shurabast religion, clearly derive their names from Tom Caplinger and his wife. The Radja's young, good-looking nephew, the guardian of Kaplinja's "old moldy thighbone," as Irma thinks of it, is named Brenan-Oan, after Owen Brennan. Even the name Rahabaat is a fair enough phonetic approximation, and certainly a closer approximation than the original Raybaat, of the name Robert to allow speculation that March was perhaps jokingly identifying the pagan god with his friend Robert Tallant.

This tongue-in-cheek use of the names of his principal New Orleans friends gives a clue to one possible interpretation that can be imposed on *October Island,* particularly when one recalls the circumstances in which the book was written and the changes of emphasis March introduced when transforming the novella, written before his breakdown, into the full-length work. It is possible that the book is a sort of personal statement, October Island being a metaphor for New Orleans itself, the place where, like Irma, March felt he had found his true home, escaping from "the silly, terrifying world that lay outside it." It is not without significance that when Axel Hansen has his photograph taken in Mobile, he poses before "a wide, eerie backdrop painted to resemble a jail" (*OI,* p. 73). There is, of course, some confusion of character identification here, but there are elements of March in both Irma Barnfield and Axel Hansen. Irma wishes to leave something tangible behind, so that she will be remembered (the renamed schooner) and she secretly hankers for the adulation of others, just as March, like every author, desired the kudos of critical acclaim for his literary output. Axel Hansen, however, is the principal March alter ego. Like March, he is torn between the two sides of his character, in his case the conflicting mixture of his blood, in March's case the opposing factions of conventional and bohemian life, his loyalties divided between his family and his art.

Although on the surface *October Island* may seem a more light-hearted work than any of March's previous novels and thus more attractive to the general reader, the whole book is permeated with a very real and very potent underlying seriousness. Some of the critics of the day, obviously delighted to have a book from March which was apparently so unashamedly humorous and blatantly satirical, tended to overlook its darker side, extolling its virtues to their readers and, in some instances, almost ruefully commenting upon what they regarded as its uncharacteristic superficiality. Like all good comedy, however, *October Island* contains a generous helping of tragedy, as has been demonstrated, and implicit in those figures of fun who perform their perambulations through the pages of the book is the dominating shadow of suffering mankind. It would not be March's book were it not so.

There can be little doubt that March gained a great deal of pleasure in writing the book: that is clear from every one of its 244 pages of text. But it is also clear that he was setting down a summation of all those thoughts and ideas he had discussed during his long, liberating conversations with Klaus Perls on the subject of the nature of man—his behavior, his beliefs, his fears, and his sexuality—which he had garnered and pondered over during the course of his life. If the book reveals a March more mellow in his attitudes with the passing of the years, it also reveals a March who was perhaps at last coming to terms with his own personal conflicts. As Axel Hansen reflects in the very last paragraph of the book:

> if we desire greatly enough, if we seek with a proper diligence, all strange things—even happiness, the strangest of all—become true to life at the end. Perhaps that was the meaning the divided ones like himself, who have peace nowhere in the world, seek with such desperation, and rarely find. [*OI*, p. 246]

Possibly March too was beginning to believe that he may have become one of the rare ones and had found *his* peace in the congenial atmosphere of New Orleans.

Unlike any of his other full-length works in either mood or setting, certainly not so intricately accomplished as *The Looking-Glass* or as historically important as *Company K, October Island*, being the most personal of all his novels, is a key work in the March canon and undoubtedly one of the most interesting.

The British reviews of the book, following its publication by Gollancz on June 9, 1952, seemed equally divided between an almost unqualified enthusiasm and a puzzled indifference. The first of the reviews to appear in the quality papers and journals was that of Lionel Hale. Writing in the *Observer* on the day before publication, he declared: "This, for fiction and me, is a rich week, for *October Island* is one of those gently poised novels that do not often come from the United States, and are the more welcome when they arrive. . . . Wise, ironic, and sensible-sensitive, *October Island* might not reach a large public, until the larger public became more discriminating."[1] Hale's sentiments were echoed precisely a week later in C. P. Snow's review in the *Sunday Times* (London). "It is," Snow wrote, "a witty, experienced, readable and intelligent fantasy. . . . I find Anglo-American literary interchange increasingly mysterious, when I think of the dimwits whose work I have been asked to admire, and then compare them with this delightful writer. If you miss *October Island*, you miss one of the civilized enjoyments of the year."[2] March's old friend Arthur Calder-Marshall, writing in the *Listener*, professed himself defeated in his attempts to "convey the flavour of this mellow novel," and went on to observe that "it is witty and satirical, but at the same time wise and sympathetic. It is beautifully written, but the delicacy of style is unobtrusive. If it would appear blasphemous to a fanatic sectarian, to a rationalist it would appear a work of faith. In a word, *October Island* is universal."[3]

The anonymous critic for the *Times Literary Supplement* began rather ominously: "*October Island* is a strange book, and it is not entirely easy to see the point of its story." After providing a précis of the plot, the review concluded on a note of what might perhaps be termed as diplomatic ambivalence: "Mr. William March has been highly praised as a writer. There can be no doubt that his narrative is unfolded with remarkable smoothness. At the same time the air of simplicity, seeming to suggest some deep inner meaning, sometimes raises doubts in the reader's mind about its final effectiveness."[4] Paul Bloomfield in the *Manchester Guardian* also had difficulties: "*October Island* is hard to review in a few words. However, I have got to try." He, too, was perplexed in much the same way as the *Times Literary Supplement* critic. "But what is it really all about?" he asked. "Mr. March is a very intelligent and able writer, and one can read the book without bothering much about 'meaning.' Still, one wants to know." Unlike the *Times Literary Supplement* critic, however, Bloomfield did offer a possible interpretation: "The answer may be that if the South Sea Island and South North American Ways of Life are juxtaposed, neither (in the author's view) is more irrational than the other."[5] The *Times* (London) reviewer, on the other hand, did not seem overconcerned to discover meaning, but, then, he could fairly be accused of damning with faint praise: "*October Island* is a lighthearted farce . . . entertaining if slightly bawdy, [it] has no particular individuality and might have been tossed off by any good serious writer in a relaxed mood."[6]

The American critics were on the whole more enthusiastic than were their British counterparts, but whereas the worst British reviews were merely indifferent the bad reviews the book received in the United States were, in some instances, undisguisedly hostile. This hostility probably stemmed from a recognition of March's satirical attack, both direct and oblique, on the American Way of Life, including the manner in which, comparing American civilization and South Seas mores, he seemed, uncomfortably to some readers, to find so many areas of identity. As Charles Rollo expressed it in the *Atlantic Monthly*, the point of the book seemed to him to be "that man, civilized or uncivilized, is ultimately governed by the irrational."[7] In this respect, of course, the book's blatant satirization of certain types of religious sects, together with its overall and underlying sense of agnosticism, surely upset and enraged many people. March's old publisher and friend

Harrison Smith, writing in the *Saturday Review*, put the matter succinctly and possibly a little conservatively, when he noted that the author "reveals a philosophy that would hardly be acceptable to Christian creeds."[8]

Donald Barr of the *New York Times Book Review* was not impressed, maintaining: "There are two books here, one the novel that *October Island* nearly was, and one the novel it is. The first is a cheerful, clever book about the biological contours of religion. The second is indifferent and obvious. . . . if you have a good idea for a novel you should be very chary about writing it; because when you are done, unless you have a genius for doing things the hard way, your readers will all exclaim: 'Oh, what a good idea for a novel!' *October Island* is a good idea for a novel."[9]

It was to be expected that with the publication of *October Island* March should find himself regarded as something of a local celebrity in New Orleans. This was not a state of affairs he was likely to relish. The social and commercial pressures it imposed upon him were definitely not welcomed, as demonstrated by his churlishness when at Mrs. Crager's urgings he reluctantly committed himself to signing copies of the book in the Basement Bookshop. There was, of course, a certain amount of speculation among the New Orleans community as to which local characters, if any, may have been transplanted into the South Seas setting of the book. People who had previously been unaware of his existence now sought him out. Whenever he visited Brennan's Restaurant, he resorted to the sanctuary of the kitchen until such time as Brennan could assure him that there was a quiet corner table available and that no one was likely to bother him. One day, when he and Bolton were strolling peacefully along Royal Street, a matron from the Garden District espied him, immediately approached and launched into effusive speech. March simply fled, leaving Bolton to concoct on the spur of the moment the explanation that the author had just paid a visit to his eye doctor, that the effect of the drops put in his eyes had not yet worn off and that he could still not see properly. It was rather a lame excuse, particularly considering the manner in which March had taken to his heels as soon as the lady opened her mouth. Bolton caught up with March and walked home with him. The incident had clearly upset March. He told Bolton, "I'll see you later." It was obvious to Bolton that March just wanted, at that moment, to be left alone.[10] On another occasion, while all this initial postpublication excitement was still at its peak, a Sunday feature writer for one of the local newspapers heard about March's collection of paintings and wanted to write an article about it. Caplinger and Bolton thought it an excellent idea, arguing that it would be an additional boost for the book. March would have nothing of it. In retrospect, his friends came to realize he was right. As someone put it: "Bill doesn't want some idiot who wouldn't know a Soutine from a Monet prowling around his house. The book will ride on its own merits. The other reason is that Bill has never sought publicity, and he is prudent, to say the least." This last remark implied that March, knowing full well the worth of the paintings on the walls of his apartment, did not intend to invite burglary by broadcasting the existence of his valuable collection.[11]

Early in September, March had received a letter from the screenwriter Dudley Nichols in which Nichols had mentioned the story "This Heavy Load." With his reply of September 11, March sent Nichols a prepublication copy of *October Island*. He assured Nichols he was not thinking of a movie adaptation, for he knew it would not be possible. He was sending the book solely in the hope that it would give Nichols pleasure. Nichols obviously did enjoy reading the book, for in another letter, a week or so later, March wrote: "I can't tell you how delighted I am that you liked *October Island*. The customs and legends and folklore are all made up: the names of the palms and the other vegetation is [*sic*] accurate. (I got it [*sic*] from travel books and encyclopedias.) Poor Toppateeter's name bothered me too. I experimented with a number of names, but none semed right. I called her originally "Tettertopper" but that sounded too much like your own columnist." He added that in the book he was currently writing he had a character named "Monica Breedlove," a name which, he confessed, "for some reason I cherish."[12]

In this same letter, March, in his turn, explained what he found so much to admire in Nichols's own work. The following extract from this letter demonstrates the unqualified respect March, as a true artist, could feel for someone he considered a master of his craft in his own rather specialized field:

> The more I see of your prose style, the more clearly I understand why your position in your particular profession is both distinguished, and, in a sense, unique: many people have the capacity for depth of feeling where they alone are concerned; a much smaller group have the ability to understand the emotions of others, and to fit those emotions, without conflict, into the depths of their own feelings: but almost nobody has the gift of sifting and combining the two and bringing the result to the surface in words of sincerity and freshness, as you do so spontaneously. I think that is the great gift which enables you to transcend all the irksome limitations that are put on you, to achieve, in spite of all handicaps in

your medium, a sense of life and of that strange quality, which can't be defined, which is a sense of the material meaning more than it says on the surface. *I* can't do it, as you will see from the inadequacies of the above paragraph.[13]

The appearance of *October Island* had, it seems, awakened interest in March's work in more than one quarter and, during the months of October and November, Ober was able to advise him that his agents were involved in negotiating paperback reprints of his four previous novels. This was encouraging news indeed for an author who only a year or so before had come to believe that his literary career might be at an end. There was vague talk of "The Little Wife," to be adapted by Philo Higley, being produced on the stage, even of being sold to the movies. In late November, von Auw broke the news that "The Bird House" had won a special prize in the Ellery Queen contest. Although the monetary value of the prize was small ($200), von Auw predicted that the publicity value would be considerable. He requested that March keep the news to himself for the time being as the official announcement of the prize would not be made until shortly after Christmas. Suddenly, everything seemed to be coming together for March. Thomas Griffin advised him that the *Hollywood Reporter* had carried a notice about *October Island*. March understood that this was entirely the result of the efforts of Dudley Nichols and, in a letter to the screenwriter on November 29, he whimsically promised: "I'll burn a candle for you in one of the little blue cups—the best *grade* of cup, naturally—the next time I find myself in St. Louis Cathedral—the oldest church in the United States, if we can believe the guides."[14]

There were, on the other hand, some disappointments and setbacks. He was puzzled by the reviews of *October Island* that had appeared in the United States. Obviously, he felt that most of the critics had missed the whole point of the book, dismissing it as "a wholesome, tropical romp: a gay fantasy without interior meaning."[15] If some of the British critics had been unable to appreciate the book's underlying meaning, he felt that they had at least recognized that a message was there. He remained convinced to the end of his days that, in the matter of *October Island,* he had received a fairer deal from the British than he had from his fellow countrymen.

The biggest blow, and one that hit March very hard, was the sudden and totally unexpected death from a heart attack in November of Little, Brown's New York editor John Woodburn. He was greatly distressed by the news, which he heard in a roundabout way, for he knew he had much to thank Woodburn for. Woodburn had believed in

October Island, had promoted it with all his energy, and had been as responsible as anyone else in encouraging March's reawakened belief in himself as a writer.

Throughout September and October, March worked somewhat fitfully on *The Bad Seed.* The initial creative drive which had launched him upon the writing of the book at the beginning of the year was beginning to fade. In his letter of September 11 to Nichols, he reported that he had just completed another three pages of the new novel. On September 25, he wrote to Nicholas McGowin: "I've been working with fair regularity on a new book, and despite my laziness and chronic despair I manage to accomplish a little something. I can still have it ready for publication next year if I can put on a little burst of speed for the next few months. I work on the theory that that is better than running down the street wild-eyed and screaming, although I could be wrong."[16]

He continued to discuss the work in progress with Klaus Perls on his occasional visits to New York. Perls has recalled:

> *The Bad Seed* was really the topic of many, many conversations we had during that year. He was delighted, I think, that I was not shocked by the idea of an intrinsically bad child. This was before Tennessee Williams' "Cat on a Hot Tin Roof," where children are described as "little no-neck monsters." To him, the idea of the "little no-neck monsters" would have appealed very much. He felt very strongly that he had personally encountered such human beings as Rhoda in real life. It went actually to a basic question of how much of a person's character is due to education and cultural climate and how much is due to heredity. As far as he was concerned, it was practically all heredity and very little of it cultural planning. So in that respect, although he was not particularly interested in politics, he was discussing the discrepancy between the American idea and the Russian idea. This had not come so much out in the open in those days, but he felt very strongly about it.[17]

In mid-November, he wrote to von Auw, telling his agent that although he had done a "fair amount" of work on the book, he was currently experiencing one of those spells (a mild spell on this occasion, he assured von Auw) when nothing, least of all the writing of books, seemed of the slightest importance. "I can still have it ready, I think," March added, "for fall publication next year if I can find a little spurt of energy. It is entirely different from *October Island,* and, to my surprise, harder to do."[18] The patient and long-suffering von Auw could be forgiven if he wondered, reading this letter, if his unpredictable client was teetering on the verge of another breakdown.

The truth was much less ominous than that. March had simply encountered a writing block. The new book was not working out the way he wanted. He knew he would have to put it to one side for a while and this was a prospect he clearly, at that time, did not find unwelcome. Although he wrote to McGowin that his social life was "the skimpiest imaginable," he was speaking only in the general sense. He continued to enjoy the company of his small circle of intimates and was content to let the life he had chosen for himself wash over him and gently carry him along on its current. "I suffer," he admitted to Nichols, "from what the psychiatrists call initial inertia, or in the language of the laity, 'plain laziness.' I've answered your letters several times in the way I usually answer letters—at night, with my head on my rubberfoam pillow just before I go to sleep. I seem to be so clever, so capable, at such times, and I finally cork off, comforted by my well-turned (or so they seem at such times) phrases."[19] He interested himself in observing the occasional visits of Hollywood personalities to New Orleans. He was at Brennan's one night at the same time as the producer Walter Wagner, his beautiful film star wife, Joan Bennett, and their young daughter. "Owen was holding the little girl," he reported to Nichols, "a most attractive child, while the severed parents ate their Chicken livers St. Pierre. Wagner has the pure, tortured face of an early Christian martyr."[20] Very occasionally, he visited the cinema. Again writing to Nichols, he admitted that he had missed the screenwriter's latest film, *The Big Sky*, when it was running in New Orleans. "The last movie I saw was 'The Greatest Show on Earth,' which was a bit on the silly side, although I did enjoy the photography. Betty Hutton surprised me. I had a feeling that nobody knew what was going to happen until just a few minutes before they started doing it. I went on the recommendation of my lady grocer, a Mrs. Joe Nepolitano. She said the whole thing had been one of the greatest inspirations of her life."[21] He went to a "crab boil" (which he described as "something like a wienie roast, or a clam bake" but nothing at all like a marshmallow toast) one night out at Lake Pontchartrain and ended up the following morning with "a hangover of classic proportions."[22]

Once or twice he accompanied Bolton to the Bourbon House on Bourbon and St. Peter Streets, a bar catering to street people of a somewhat lesser social breed than those who frequented Tom Caplinger's establishment. Predictably, the atmosphere of the Bourbon House was decidedly more rowdy and clamorous than that of the Café LaFitte. Bolton had the impression that on these visits March always adopted the analytical eye: that this, and this alone, was his justification for entering the place. He would almost shrink into a corner seat and, from that comparative seclusion, survey the company. He drank nothing stronger than coffee on these occasions and was always visibly relieved when the time came to leave.[23]

His solitary wanderings about the French Quarter were on a more sedate level. He might enjoy a midmorning coffee and Creole doughnuts seated at a table outside the Café du Monde, just across the road from Jackson Square, or in the Morning Call in the French Market area. He frequently sampled the impressive Creole cuisine at the Gumbo Shop on St. Peter Street and shopped for his groceries at the local A & P store on the corner of Royal and St. Peter.

There were the almost regular book-launching parties at the Basement Bookshop, which, when he could find no suitable excuse, he attended with reluctance. He even joined, of all institutions, the New Orleans Athletic Club, so that he would have a place in downtown New Orleans where he could drop in from time to time to read the papers. From the moment he joined, he told McGowin, the athletic director had been bombarding him with letters, urging him to make more use of the various sporting facilities available, such as squash, handball, and tennis. He simply ignored these exhortations.

It was about this time, in the late fall of 1952 or the early spring of 1953, that March's frequently expressed prediction that he would one day be murdered, or, at the very least, violently robbed, came uncomfortably close to being realized. On the particular evening concerned, he left his friends in the Café LaFitte about midnight and set out for his usual quiet stroll home, a mere three blocks from the Blacksmith Shop. He had gone no further than half a block when he was set upon by two young muggers, who, thankfully, did nothing more violent than to slam him against a wall and hold him powerless while they went through his pockets, relieving him of the thirty or forty dollars he was carrying in his billfold. He suffered no injuries, his face was unmarked and his spectacles not even broken. After the two men had run off into the night, he continued, understandably somewhat shaken and angry, on his way home. As soon as he had recovered sufficiently, he telephoned the police and reported the incident. By then, it was too late for anything to be done and the police could do little more than take down the descriptions March gave them of the two men.

When, the following evening, March told the Café LaFitte circle what had befallen him, he was severely chastised for not having returned to the Blacksmith Shop immediately after the mugging had occurred. The street people who were friends of his friends operated a very effective bush-telegraph system for this sort of situation and it was a fifty-fifty chance that, had action been taken swiftly, not only would March have recovered his money but his two young assailants would have been taught the lesson of rough vigilante justice.[24]

After this experience, March never carried more than five one-dollar bills in his wallet on his evening visits to the Café LaFitte, just sufficient, in fact, to see him through the evening, to pay for his regular couple of drinks and to take his turn in paying for a round. He did, however, being still the cautious businessman of old, make due provision for emergencies in the form of a twenty-dollar bill he secreted in his shoe. If, as did happen on occasion, the corner talk became particularly engrossing and March, loath to leave the fun, exceeded his normal quota of drinks, he would surreptitiously fish in his shoe for the twenty-dollar bill. After the existence of this standby note became common knowledge among the members of the circle, it became a sort of game to get March launched upon a line of conversation or immersed in deep and jovial discussion, so that he would be tempted into ordering another round or two to keep the talk flowing and thus be obliged to resort to his emergency fund. It was all done in good-humored and affectionate conspiracy and it is more than likely that he never did realize how he was being gently tricked by his friends.[25]

In March 1953, the lease of the Blacksmith Shop expired and Caplinger was unsuccessful in obtaining a renewal. He was not a person to give in easily. He simply moved his business one block up Bourbon to the corner of Dumaine and there established the Café LaFitte-in-Exile, which still exists, more than twenty-five years after Caplinger's death.

With the move safely and satisfactorily accomplished, all the old crowd settled happily in their new surroundings and, without difficulty, created the unique atmosphere of the Blacksmith Shop, even though the physical character of the new bar bore no resemblance to that of the old. Caplinger covered the walls with brown fireproof burlap. The lighting was low-key. There were a few small tables and chairs around the edges of the room, but the main feature was the magnificent centrally sited bar, designed and constructed by Enrique Alferez, a Mexican sculptor friend of Caplinger. The bar was shaped in a free-form version of the curve the Mississippi River makes around New Orleans, giving it the "Crescent City" name. In the middle of the serving area, behind the continuous counter, display shelving boasted such concoctions as green and yellow chartreuse and Cherry Heering. There was very little call for these sort of drinks from the regular habitués, who, for the most part, confined their drinking to the bourbon, scotch, gin, and vodka kept in the well, which, together with the ice boxes, was deployed strategically under the counter around the inner side of the bar. Caplinger would preside over all, moving around and saying hello to favored patrons. Most of the time, he would be with the group clustered around March at that end of the bar farthest from the double-doored entrance. He would stand, leaning against the pillar almost alongside the bar stool March always occupied and, being a tall man, he could, from this vantage point, survey the whole room, keeping an eye on the bar and every one of his customers, ready to move in on any potential disturbance his eagle eye might detect.

Once March was settled in, access to him was effectively blocked, as it had been at the Blacksmith Shop, by those of the crowd who gathered around him, casually screening him from unwelcome strangers. Occasionally, someone whom one of them knew would approach the group and March would have to be introduced. He was always introduced as "Bill Campbell," which enabled him to preserve a certain degree of anonymity, provided the outsider was not aware of his true identity as the author of *October Island.* On these occasions, the atmosphere would become very formal. March would acknowledge the introduction, but this would be his only social gesture. Certainly, he would not be in the least forthcoming while the outsider was around. Very infrequently, the defenses would be breached, and some complete stranger would attempt to engage him in conversation. Bolton has recalled: "Peering out from behind the loom of Caplinger's shoulders, March would hiss angry invectives, at complete variance from his polished prose. One night, after such an episode, I remarked with admiration on his use of the barracks' idiom. He beamed through his glasses and said, 'Hell, son, you forget I was a Marine.'"[26]

By now, the temporary writing block conquered, he was again observing the disciplined routine he had instituted for himself when he was at work on a book. Very deeply involved in *The Bad Seed*, he was determined to finish it, no matter how arbitrary the work's origins may have been. The book was the subject of a great deal of conversation in the bar and it was not until the book was finally published the following year that many of those who had sat almost nightly with him, as he relaxed after a long creative day, realized that matters he had related to them he had put down on paper only hours before. Bolton has recalled that when he first read the book he experienced an overwhelming sense of déjà vu. Time and time again he would discover passages which were almost word for word what March had told them over drinks in Caplinger's many months previously.

During those evenings at the Café LaFitte-in-Exile, March continued to sound people out on details he wished to incorporate into the book. In the same way that he had asked Tess Crager about Rhoda's picnic dress, so one evening he asked David Mynders Smythe, "Do you think Rhoda should be eating a peanut butter and jelly sandwich or an eskimo pie when she burns Leroy up?" He was half-smiling when he posed the question and yet he made Smythe feel as if the whole world were awaiting his answer. Smythe told him that he thought eskimo pie would be the more appropriate. March chuckled, obviously pleased by the reply, and said, "Yes, you're right."[27]

Smythe discovered, as had many others before him, that March's sudden changes of mood could be rather disconcerting, even embarrassing. In the spring of 1953, the poet W. H. Auden was on a lecture tour in America and, arriving in New Orleans, had been met by Smythe on the suggestion of a mutual friend. The two men were strangers to each other, but it had been arranged that Smythe would put Auden up for the length of his stay in the city. Wishing to show his eminent guest the sights, Smythe took him to the Café LaFitte-in-Exile during the course of the first evening and while they were there March arrived at his customary hour. To begin with, March was friendly and his conversation was as entertaining as usual, but, after a while, for no apparent reason, he suddenly rounded on Smythe and then stormed out of the bar. Smythe was flabbergasted and totally mystified by this behavior. The only explanation that came to his mind was that perhaps March resented the fact that Smythe had not informed him Auden was coming. The following day, which happened to be a Sunday, Auden and Smythe were taking a slow sightseeing walk through the Quarter when they met March, also out for a stroll. Smythe wondered what would happen, but March had clearly recovered from the puzzling fit of pique. He was his old self again, just as if nothing untoward had ever occurred. He invited the two men to his apartment. The three of them spent a pleasant evening drinking and conversing.[28]

The Bad Seed did not, naturally, entirely dominate the conversations at the Café LaFitte-in-Exile. Bolton has recalled one night when the conversation ranged over the disparate subjects of mutual funds, the possibility of the nation's merchant marine being "priced out" of world competition by top-heavy union demands, Bonnard as sculptor and painter, Degas, and witchcraft. They did not discuss writing that evening, as March clearly did not want to, making his point by ignoring any leading remarks and questions in that direction. By the same token, he steered the conversation, via art and ocean-going steamship rates, to yet another discussion of witchcraft, a subject which continued to fascinate him.[29]

March rarely allowed the subject of religion to enter into the conversations at Caplinger's, yet there is little doubt that despite his more satirical and less virulent treatment of the subject in *October Island,* he still held the very strong views concerning organized religion that he had promulgated so effectively and so mercilessly twenty years before in *Company K.* Smythe recalls one incident which squarely places March's true feelings into perspective. Smythe and a friend were watching Eisenhower's first inauguration on television, when March arrived. He sat watching the ceremony until the moment came for the minister, rabbi, and priest to perform their invocations, when he turned to Smythe's guest and asked: "Do you believe in all that stuff?" The answer was: "If you mean 'Do I believe in God?'—yes, I do." March clapped his hand to his forehead, announced quietly, "I have a terrible headache," and rising abruptly from his chair, left the apartment.[30]

If the years had not mellowed him, they had made him increasingly aware of his own mortality. He was approaching his sixtieth birthday and his concern about his general health was becoming a sort of minor obsession. He had always been something of a hypochondriac and had frequently told his friends that he was convinced—presumably if he were not murdered first—he would either go blind or die of cancer. He had radically cut down on the number of cigarettes he smoked each day and, if his nightly consumption at Caplinger's was anything to go by, he was no more than a very moderate drinker. During 1953, he had a very thorough checkup at a clinic and was relieved when the doctors reported that they could find nothing of a serious nature wrong with him. He subsequently gained great delight in telling his friends about the rectal examination he had undergone during the course of the checkup, describing with a certain relish how, stark naked, he had been spreadeagled on the examination table. He made the indignity of the situation seem excruciatingly funny, particularly when he introduced the punchline of the story, as the nurse, who was peering between his legs, called out: "Oh, doctor! Come and see what a classical rectum Mr. March has!"[31]

For some time now, March had felt the need to buy a home of his own in the French Quarter. He wanted a place within easy walking distance of Caplinger's, large enough for him to display the whole of his growing art collection, a place in which his privacy would be assured. He was, it seems, attracted to certain properties in Dumaine Street and with typical thoroughness he went in search on foot for the ideal home. At 627 Dumaine Street, the tenant, Charles Warner, and his house guest, Joseph Dickinson, were sunbathing one day in deckchairs on the patio at the rear of the house, when March walked in upon them unannounced. After apologizing for his intrusion, he explained the purpose of his quest, adding that he understood that this particular house was on the market. With Dickinson's help, Warner, who did not want to give up his tenancy, discouraged March from even thinking of making a bid for the place, devising as many reasons as possible on the spur of the moment to demonstrate that the house was virtually uninhabitable. March listened to what they had to say and then, apologizing once again for intruding on their privacy, left. After he had gone, Warner told Dickinson who March was and informed him of the fabulous collection of paintings the author was reputed to have on the walls of his apartment in Royal Street.

A few days later, Dickinson encountered March in the street. March assured him that he had given up any thought he may have had of acquiring 627 Dumaine Street as he had found an almost identical property, number 613, a hundred yards or so along the road, and was now negotiating for its purchase. During the course of their brief conversation, Dickinson mentioned March's art collection and suggested that he was qualified to move the collection, if March so wished, as until recently he had been employed as assistant to the director of the Guggenheim Museum in New York. March politely declined Dickinson's offer, explaining that for insurance requirements it was necessary for him to engage the services of professional movers. He did invite Dickinson up to his apartment to view his collection. Dickinson recalls that of all the paintings he saw that day the Rouaults made the greatest impression on him, possibly because they were the ones hung in the most favorable light, nearest the window. Later, he realized that March had room in the Royal Street apartment to display only part of his collection.[32]

By the beginning of June, March was installed in his new home. He had made an excellent choice. A pure Creole cottage, standing more or less midway between Royal and Chartres Streets, opposite Mrs. John's Legacy (the only existing prototype of the French Colonial raised house), it was flanked by houses hidden from the street by high walls. The brick facade was covered with the traditional thick coat of plaster cement, painted a faded beige in March's day, a bold flat molding serving as a simple cornice, under which (and March would have been delighted with this touch) one of the rare remaining fire plaques recorded that one of the original owners was thrifty enough to insure his property. The steep-pitched roof had gabled ends and was topped by twin chimney pots. The classic French casement doors, each with six large panes of glass held in place by wooden muntins, through which one could gain entrance directly from the street, were protected by heavy batten shutters with faded green-painted boards on the outside and deep paneling within. There were two wrought iron gates, one to the main alley which led to the slave quarters at the back of the main house, the other from the street to a wooden stairway which led to the attic room. March also had an inside stairwell constructed leading from the bedroom he ordinarily used to the attic when the Vieux Carré Commission, which oversees all exterior structural changes in the Quarter, refused him permission to have the outside stairs rebuilt.

The main house was square, all the rooms being of approximately equal size, roughly twelve feet by twelve feet, with a "family room," floored in black and white marble, which doubled as a dining room and which had been added to the original structure. Downstairs, the original house consisted of a living room, a dinette, a kitchen, and a laundry room. On the second story were two bedrooms and two bathrooms. The attic had been converted into a living area. The front attic room, which had two dormer windows affording both light and breeze, was used by March as his study. It was paneled in pine and the floor was of wood covered with durable but inexpensive rugs. The bedroom to the rear apparently also served the previous occupant as a dining room, for the bed could be slid away into the wall under the slope of the roof when it was not in use. At one end of the attic space was a tiny kitchen, so small that movement was severely restricted. Despite the cramped conditions of the attic area, someone had nevertheless installed an immense bathtub, large enough for two people to bathe in together quite comfortably.

Between the main house and the slave quarters was a red brick patio, measuring approximately forty-two feet by fifteen feet. It was quiet, shady, and completely secluded. There was a palm tree in the center of the patio and a little fountain against one wall. The little flowerbeds contained a datura bush, camellia, azalea, and hibiscus.

The slave quarters became March's favorite part of the property. In the large, forty-two-foot long living room, one had on even the hottest of days the agreeable illusion of a breeze. Next to the living room was a dining room. The kitchen was upstairs, together with a bedroom, which had its own miniature balcony overlooking the main area downstairs, and a bathroom.

"The furniture," a friend remembers, "was dark mahogany stain, of the usual 'good department store' variety, contemporary of period. Some of the cocktail and night tables were leather-topped, and the couch in the slave quarter was excellent leather, terribly expensive. I think Bill's house was a portrait of himself, really. It was quiet, firm, infinitely liveable, totally lacking in ostentation."[33]

"I expect," March wrote to his agents, "to be [here] most of the time until they take me out in my coffin. When I think of the years I wasted in dull places like London, Hamburg, and New York, I sigh with regret."[34] Much sooner than he or anyone else could have imagined, his words were to prove tragically prophetic.

March's confidence, or at least the insurance company's confidence in the efficiency of professional movers was shown to be misplaced. One of the paintings, Utrillo's *Une rue à Sannois*, had been hung on an insecure nail and had fallen onto an andiron, making an L-shaped puncture in the center of the picture. Remembering Dickinson's offer, March wrote to him at his home in Brownsville, Tennessee, ruefully admitting that he had possibly made a mistake in not availing himself of Dickinson's services to see the move through and asking him if he would use his expertise and skill in patching the painting. Dickinson, because of his Guggenheim Museum background, was versed in the art of restoration and gladly accepted March's invitation to carry out the repair work, for which March was to pay a fee of $150. Although, obviously, March could have provided Dickinson with accommodation at 613 Dumaine while he was completing the repair, the artist chose to stay with his friend Charles Warner, going along to 613 each morning at ten o'clock. March served lunch, which usually consisted of heated-up ready-prepared packaged dinners, and they ate without ceremony.

For the first time, Dickinson was able to see and appreciate the full extent of March's collection. There were twenty-eight paintings in all, hanging in five or six of the property's many rooms. In the large living room in the slave quarters alone, there were Picasso's *Femme assise*, Soutine's *L'homme aux Rubans*, Modigliani's *Portrait of Mme. Czechowska*, a Modigliani gouache, *Nu accroupi*, Rouault's *Le Christ et les Pêcheurs*, Klee's *Danseuse*, and Braque's *Nature morte aux cerises*. In the bedroom were two Vlamincks, *Nature morte fauve* and *Nature morte aux fruits*, and Soutine's *Jeune homme dans un fauteuil*, a painting which, according to March, could be interpreted as depicting a young man masturbating. The remainder of the collection was in the main house.

Dickinson was shaken by March's apparent complacency regarding the safety of the collection. He referred to the ease with which a robbery could be accomplished. March told Dickinson that he did not worry. Visitors could not, of course, avoid noticing the paintings and there was nothing he could do to hide them from the curious gaze of anyone who called at the house. Without fail, he said, these casual visitors would comment on the profusion of canvases on the walls and would ask him if he had painted them himself. He always told them he had. Then the visitors would remark on the excellence of the frames, to which March would reply, "I made them all myself." When he told Dickinson this, Dickinson smiled and said, "You got a lot of help from Heydenrik, I would guess." This observation clearly impressed March, for he had indeed purchased the frames from Heydenrik, a noted New York firm, and in later conversation with Warner he mentioned that he thought Dickinson may have been the only visitor to the house to have identified the framemakers.

One day March asked Dickinson, "If you could have any painting from the collection, which one would you choose?" Dickinson replied that he would choose Modigliani's *Portrait of Mme. Czechowska*. When March asked why, Dickinson said that portraiture was his particular metier. March later commissioned him to paint his portrait.[35]

During an official visit to New Orleans in the late 1940s, the mayor of Paris had made a semiformal call at the Blacksmith Shop, favorably compared the ambience of the Vieux Carré with that of the bohemian quarter of Paris and presented Caplinger with a large scroll conferring upon him the title of honorary mayor of Montmartre. Caplinger had the scroll framed and displayed on a wall in his bar. Shortly afterward, he decided to follow the practice of various bistro owners in Paris who hung the work of their artist clientele on their café walls. This served two purposes: a continuing change of paintings for the patrons to look at and possible sales for the artists concerned. Caplinger continued the practice even after the move to the Café LaFitte-in-Exile, and March vigorously supported him, although he was known to admit on occasions to one or the other of the Caplinger regulars: "I may not come back here until this exhibition ends. I can't bear it." Nevertheless, however much he might dislike some of the works on show, he was always quick to defend Caplinger's generosity. When one day some stranger not familiar with the establishment noted that all the paintings had price tags and remarked in a loud voice that "the management probably takes a big cut," March discarded his unobtrusive stance and retorted in a voice dripping acid: "I'll have you know that every penny of every purchase goes direct to the artist. Tom Caplinger obviously does not have your cheapness of mind!"[36] When, in late 1953, Caplinger invited Dickinson to show some of his portraits on the bar walls, Dickinson's first reaction was to decline, feeling that the place was unsuitable. March persuaded him otherwise and, as a result, Dickinson was pleased to find that he sold several of his canvases.

March himself purchased three of them to use as presents that coming Christmas.[37]

In November, March loaned five of his Soutines to Klaus Perls for the Soutine Exhibition Perls held at his New York gallery from November 2 to December 5.[38] March never wished nor intended that he should be remembered principally as an art collector. This is why he directed in his will that after his death his collection should be sold by auction and thus cease to exist as an identifiable entity. Even so, at one time, when he was still living in Royal Street, he had it in mind that he would like to leave substantially the whole of his collection to the Delgardo Museum (now the New Orleans Museum of Art). At a cocktail party he attended during one of his trips to New York, he chanced to meet Alfonzo Lansford, who was then director of the Delgardo Museum. He invited Lansford to come to his apartment to see his paintings. Lansford, imagining that March was merely an amateur artist eager to show off his own work, thought nothing more about it. When he returned to New Orleans, March telephoned Lansford at the museum, suggesting a date and time a few weeks hence for the viewing. Lansford accepted the invitation but then presumably forgot all about it, for he failed to keep the arranged appointment. March, understandably, was greatly incensed by what he assumed was the museum's undeniable lack of interest, and any idea he may have entertained of being the generous benefactor seemed immediately less appealing. Lansford, on the other hand, was soon to realize the blunder he had made. On another trip to New York, someone asked him what he was doing to secure the March collection for the museum. "What collection?" Lansford queried. Upon learning that the collection was possibly one of the finest private collections of modern French masterpieces in America, Lansford hurried back to New Orleans and contacted March without further ado. But by then it was too late. March did eventually relent to the extent of donating six paintings to the museum. "They could have had the whole collection," he told Dickinson, "if they'd had a director rather than a jackass." By then, Lansford had resigned his post with the museum.[39]

March did not allow the move to Dumaine Street to interrupt work on *The Bad Seed.* Two or three weeks before the move, he wrote to his agents, apologizing for his long silence. He advised them that after two false starts, he had been forced to destroy all the work he had done on the new novel and begin again from scratch in another manner. He had been working on the new version for approximately two months and was anticipating having the book completed by mid-June. The worst part was behind him. He felt that the book was now going along "under its own momentum." He also revealed that he had done some work on another novel, but that he had put this aside for the time being with the idea of having it ready sometime the following year. On the same day he wrote this letter, May 14, he sent von Auw the first 137 pages of *The Bad Seed*, together with a carbon copy for his British publisher, Victor Gollancz. This section of the typescript, according to March, was in final form and represented about 43,000 of the book's planned 70,000 words.[40]

Within a week, von Auw had written back, praising the new novel, although he was doubtful about the title, which he thought sounded a little like a book for a child rather than a book about a child. He had already passed the partially completed typescript on to Ned Bradford, who had arrived from Boston to take over as Little, Brown's New York editor after John Woodburn's death. Victor Gollancz, then on a visit to New York, was pleased to learn that March had a new novel almost finished. He had not been shown the incomplete typescript, as von Auw felt him to be too distracted on his brief trip to the States and thought it advisable to wait until the book was finished before letting him see it.[41] Five days later, von Auw reported that Bradford had read the typescript, was very excited about it, and was eager to see the rest of it. Stanley Salmen, the director of Little, Brown, saw the typescript on Bradford's desk while he was on a visit to the New York office and requested that it be sent up to Boston so that he could read it. He was, so it was said, wild about the book and sent a letter to March to this effect.[42]

In the meantime, March had written to his agents, asking for the return of both the ribbon and carbon copies of chapter 7 so that he could make a few minor changes.[43] As the typescript was by then in Stanley Salmen's hands in Boston, it was not possible for von Auw to comply immediately with March's wishes. On June 13, March sent von Auw the remainder of the typescript, together with a completely redrafted chapter 7. He asked his agents to ensure that both copies of the old chapter 7 were destroyed. The 230-page typescript ran to a total of between 68,000 and 70,000 words.[44]

Dickinson was restoring the damaged Utrillo during the two weeks March was putting the finishing touches on *The Bad Seed*. March regaled him with interesting snippets he had discovered in the course of his crime research for the book. He told Dickinson several times one story which, in a macabre way, seemed to amuse him greatly. This concerned a nurse who murdered her niece for the insurance proceeds and who, when caught and convicted, declared: "If I had known that tiny pinch of arsenic would have shown up in the test, I never would have done it!" March intimated to Dickinson that he had introduced some of the artist's mannerisms into the book. For example, when Rhoda determines she has to kill Leroy, she goes into the kitchen and takes three matches from the box above the stove, decides three is too many, and returns one to the box. According to March, Dickinson did that one day when he was fixing their lunch. Dickinson helped March pack up the typescript and send it off to Ober. March gave him his typewriter, saying, "If I write anything more, I'll go electric."[45]

A fortnight later, von Auw gave his verdict. He thought that the whole book stood up beautifully and suggested that it could be turned into an effective play, if someone could contrive to bring all the action onstage rather than partly offstage. He had only one minor criticism. On page 157 of the typescript there was a reference to the Eisenhower-Stevenson presidential election campaign. He felt there was a danger that this might date the book in a few years' time. He thought the reference should come out. No word had yet come through as to Little, Brown's reaction to the book, but he promised to let March know as soon as it did.[46] Von Auw went on vacation on August 7 and it was not until he returned to the office on September 1 that he learned the unbelievable news that Little, Brown had rejected the book. Bradford was distressed by the decision, for he liked the book considerably, as apparently did most of the other people at Little, Brown, including Salmen himself. Salmen, however, had some preconceived idea that the book would not sell, and his word was final in the matter. He respected the author enough to send him a personal letter, setting out his reasons for declining the book. To von Auw, March professed himself not unduly perturbed, particularly as he was aware that another publishing house was already interested. Theodore Amussen, a long-time admirer of March's work, had recently joined Rinehart and Company as vice-president and editor-in-chief and, hearing through the grapevine of Little, Brown's decision, got in touch with von Auw on his return from vacation. That very same day von Auw dispatched the typescript to Rinehart. Dudley Frasier, who was previously Little, Brown's promotion man, was now also at Rinehart, and von Auw predicted, when writing to March, that Amussen and Frasier between them would ensure the book's acceptance and a first-class publication.[47]

Due to the temporary uncertainty concerning the fate of *The Bad Seed,* March decided not to continue work immediately on the novel he had partly completed but to concentrate instead on producing a few new short stories. One of his "trivial ambitions," as he put it, was to write one hundred stories, so that he could eventually publish a companion volume to *Trial Balance,* which he proposed to call *Century Mark.* At the present time, so he informed von Auw, he had done "about sixty-seven." There had been considerably more than that, but he had destroyed all the others as not being "quite up to par."[48] He had once told Robert Tallant that he did not possess a single old manuscript, nor had he kept any files or records. Although patently he was somewhat dramatizing the situation, he must, nevertheless, during that terrible time of deep black depression in New York, have been incredibly ruthless in his desperation and despair, consigning countless manuscripts and papers to the furnace.[49]

By mid-September, Rinehart had made the decision to publish *The Bad Seed.* The editorial and sales departments were wholeheartedly behind the book. Robert D. Loomis, March's editor, requested that a small amount of revision be carried out to reduce the length of the actual and fictional case histories which elaborated on Christine Penmark's background and origins. Writing to von Auw on September 17, Loomis expressed the opinion, shared by his colleagues, that, although the case histories served to give a frame to the book and to give depth to the action, March had tended to use too many of them and had even continued using them after their purpose had been achieved, with the result that they ultimately slowed up the narrative. Loomis accepted that it was difficult to be precise as to how many of these case histories should profitably be omitted. The more pertinent question to be asked, he suggested was: "How many are needed to create the effect wanted?" The book could only be weakened, as at the moment he felt it was, if that number was exceeded. The general consensus at Rinehart was also that as March had written it the central history of the fictional Denker case was too long, so that it almost became a self-contained story in its own right and threatened to destroy the unity of the rest of the book. These suggested revisions affected approximately a dozen pages or so of March's typescript. Loomis hoped the author could accept the publishers' reasoning as sound and would agree to make the revisions.[50] There was, on the other hand, no question of Rinehart's declining to take the book if March was not prepared to carry out the changes, and when, on September 18, von Auw sent March a copy of Loomis's letter he stressed that it was entirely the free choice of the author whether or not he followed Loomis's suggestions. As if further to make the point that the final decision regarding the revisions rested solely with March, von Auw enclosed three signed copies of the agreement with Rinehart for March's signature and return.[51]

When he sent back the copies of the contract, March indicated his willingness to make the changes Loomis had recommended. To enable him to do this, he asked von Auw to arrange for chapter 7 onward of the typescript to be returned to him. A week later, both copies of the last six chapters arrived at Dumaine Street and March set to work. By October 5, he had completed the revisions, exactly as Loomis had suggested, by cutting approximately 3,500 words from the typescript. March also deleted the topical allusion to the presidential campaign that von Auw had mentioned earlier. Loomis was naturally delighted by the manner in which March had followed his editorial suggestions. He told von Auw that everyone at Rinehart considered that the author had done an excellent job on the revision, and he requested that the agent should convey Rinehart's appreciation to March for his cooperation.[52]

It occurred to von Auw that *The Bad Seed* might be suitable for serialization in one of the glossy national magazines. He submitted it to *Good Housekeeping* and *Collier's*, but for various reasons both editors thought it too "strong" for their magazines. The *Collier's* fiction editor thought it a "tremendously exciting novel," but the magazine had just run a very unconventional serial which had caused something of a stir among its readers and she felt it essential that the magazine's next few serials present more wholesome characters and activities than did *The Bad Seed*.

One project which still remained dear to March's heart was the publication of his book of fables. He wrote to von Auw, mentioning that he had come across the manuscript while going through his files and wondered if anything could be done with it. Originally, he told von Auw, there had been 125 fables, but he had discarded all but 99 of them and these comprised a manuscript of approximately 40,000 words. He felt it was too good to destroy, yet he accepted that, so far as any publisher was concerned, it was not a commercial proposition. Could von Auw explore the possibility of his having it published at his own expense? He added that it would mean much to him to have it published during his lifetime.[54] Von Auw submitted the manuscript of *Ninety-nine Fables* to Rinehart on December 3, making it clear that he was not submitting it as an option book and implying that if the cost factor was a problem he had certain suggestions to propose which might make the idea of publishing the book more attractive to the firm.[55]

Meanwhile, plans for the publication of *The Bad Seed* in the following spring were going ahead. Amussen wrote to March on December 11, telling him how delighted Rinehart was to have him on its list,

reiterating his enthusiasm for the novel and trusting that their association would be "a long, happy and prosperous one."[56] March reciprocated Amussen's good wishes and conveyed his own pleasure at being
with Rinehart. He assured Amussen that he had a new novel "fairly
well planned," tentatively titled *Poor Pilgrim, Poor Stranger,* and that
he was hoping to begin work on it in earnest on New Year's Day. If all
went well, he was aiming to finish it in four or five months.[57] This was
presumably the book March had earlier mentioned to von Auw, a story
which was to take place between the years 1917 and 1920 and be told in
the first person. As he planned it, it would run to less than 60,000
words. He was, he explained to von Auw, "getting more and more to
dislike the long, padded novel where everything is said at least six
times."[58]

"The Bird House" was published in *Ellery Queen's Mystery Magazine*
on December 24, 1953. On that same day, March was invited by the
lady who lived next door to come into her walled garden to listen to a
group of children singing Christmas carols. The neighbor knew something of March's views on religion and so had at first hesitated to ask
him. She need not have worried. He stood with the rest of the invited
audience in the garden, listening while the children sang through their
repertoire. When eventually the little concert ended, his neighbor was
astonished and touched to observe that there were tears in his eyes.[59]

Toward the end of January 1954, March received the not altogether
unexpected news that Rinehart had returned the *Ninety-nine Fables*
manuscript to von Auw, regretting that they could not see their way
clear to taking the book and suggesting that one of the smaller private
presses, such as the Levee Press, might be able to help. March gave
von Auw the go-ahead to approach Hodding Carter, the proprietor of
the Levee Press, on the basis that it could do no harm to ascertain
Carter's views on the project. He repeated to von Auw that he wanted
to bring out the book of fables as soon as possible, sensing with
increasing certainty that the fables had a higher survival value than
anything else he had done.[60]

In February, March commissioned Dickinson to paint his portrait.
Dickinson had by then moved into an apartment of his own on St. Ann
Street, which he was sharing with a young artist friend, Robert Clark.
March went to Dickinson's apartment for the sittings, stipulating,
however, that Clark should not be present at these sessions, presumably because he thought he would find a stranger's presence about the
place distracting. As always, he insisted that he, and he alone, choose
his friends: he did not wish friends thrust upon him. During these
sittings, he revealed to Dickinson what seemed to be a developing

awareness of agoraphobia. He predicted that, as time went by, his journeys would become shorter and shorter in length until he would not go beyond the boundaries of the state, then never beyond the city limits, then never out of the French Quarter, then never into any other street and finally never outside the house. If March did suffer to some degree with a form of agoraphobia, it never manifested itself in a way that was obvious to most of his friends. Perhaps he was simply trying out another of his stories on Dickinson to while away the sittings (there are, after all, some unmistakable parallels with Lurline's last years in *October Island*), or perhaps he was again simply overdramatizing. March was pleased with the portrait when it was finished and hung it in his house among the French masterpieces.[61]

February ended on a note of puzzled disappointment. Gollancz had returned the typescript of *The Bad Seed* to March's British literary agents, Hughes Massie, saying the firm did not wish to publish it. The final decision, apparently, had been that of Victor Gollancz himself. His daughter, Livia Gollancz, present head of the firm, has explained:

> My father very much disliked, personally, the idea of a child murderer. But he did not want to break a relationship with an esteemed author for what he realized might have been his personal whim. He himself took the book to read when it first came in, but found himself able to read only parts of it; and then it was read by the firm's two chief readers, two of the firm's (then) directors, his secretary, and finally myself, who had at that time only recently joined the staff. He thought the book brilliant, and probably very saleable. But he felt that it was shot through with horror and evil, with at the same time no purgative catharsis, and therefore he could find no real purpose in publishing it.[62]

It was a sad end to a long literary association spanning more than twenty years and it was a personal blow to March, who commented: "I'd thought I'd turned the wick too low, but apparently not."[63] Even so, he could not resist exaggerating Gollancz's reaction, telling Dickinson that his erstwhile British publisher had termed *The Bad Seed* a demonic book which should be bought in manuscript by some philanthropic organization and burned.[64]

Mardi Gras was celebrated in New Orleans on March 2 that year. March had always disliked the festivities, possibly because they converted the atmospheric uniqueness of the city into a noisy, exuberant, stereotyped turmoil, the familiar streets becoming swamped with carousing strangers, many of whom cast inhibitions aside, the familiar haunts becoming crowded and unbearable. When Dickinson was standing that day in Royal Street, waiting for the parade to pass by, March came up behind him and commented: "Oh, there's nothing so depressing as an Anglo-Saxon trying to get into the carnival spirit!" Writing to von Auw a few days later, March gave thanks for the fact that Mardi Gras was over for another year.[66] As it happened, he would not have to tolerate another one.

During the first week of that month, the advance and complimentary copies of *The Bad Seed* were distributed by Rinehart. The author gave his verdict that the book looked "rather handsome."[67] Rinehart advised him that it was sending him a further copy under separate cover, with the request that he sign it and return it to the jacket artist, Lawrence S. Kamp, who was a member of the Rinehart staff. Dudley Frasier assured March that everyone at Rinehart was convinced that the book was going to sell well and that they were all looking forward to publication day, fixed for April 8.[68]

About this time, there was some interest in making *October Island* into a play. It was not the first time that March had received a proposition for the book to be adapted for another medium. Little more than twelve months before, an independent film producer, Henry F. Ehrlich, had made approaches for an option on *October Island*. Ehrlich, an attorney and counselor-at-law, had formed an association with Oscar Dancigers, the head of Ultramar Films, one of the leading film companies of Mexico, which also handled all Hollywood productions made in that country. Ehrlich and Dancigers had coproduced a film version of Defoe's *Robinson Crusoe*, directed by the notable exiled Spanish director Luis Bunuel. Although the film had not been released at the time Ehrlich made his initial approaches, H. N. Swanson, the Hollywood agent who acted for Ober, recommended that if Ehrlich was prepared to make an offer for a six-month option on the screen rights of the book, then Ober should accept on March's behalf. As it turned out, no offer did materialize. In March 1954, the Hollywood screenwriter Ketti Frings, whose credits included *Come Back, Little Sheba* and *The Shrike* and who had the previous year also made inquiries regarding the availability of the book, again expressed interest, saying she would like to adapt *October Island* into a musical play for the stage. Would March, von Auw wanted to know, be interested in collaborating with Miss Frings on such a project? Although March gave von Auw carte blanche to do whatever he thought best in other respects, always assuming the project got off the ground to begin with, he wanted no part of working with Miss Frings on writing a script for such a venture.[69]

He was more concerned, at that particular moment, to arrange the printing of his book of fables. It is conceivable that he subconsciously sensed that the sands of time were running out for him. An author friend, Harnett T. Kane, suggested to him that Hanover House, a subsidiary of Doubleday and Company, might be interested, and March wrote to von Auw, asking him if he would pursue this possibility.[70] The agent, however, pointed out that Hanover House was interested only in books which would appeal to a mass audience. *Ninety-nine Fables* certainly did not fall within this category. Von Auw was still awaiting a reply from Hodding Carter of the Levee Press. He had also written to Lambert Davis, director of the University of North Carolina Press and one-time editor of *Virginia Quarterly Review*, asking him if he would like to see the fables. Remembering how, twenty or more years ago, he had consistently been unable to place his short stories with Davis, March was probably not unduly optimistic upon receiving this piece of news from von Auw. Later that month, von Auw was able to report that not only had he sent the manuscript to Davis, after having received a letter from Davis expressing both his eagerness to see the book of fables and his hope that it would be something the University of North Carolina Press could publish, but that he had also received Carter's long-delayed reply, asking if he, too, could see the manuscript. In the same letter, von Auw informed March that *The Bad Seed* had been sold to the British publishing house of Hamish Hamilton, that Hamilton himself, unlike Victor Gollancz, was very enthusiastic about the book and was promising to promote it heavily.[71]

On March 24, March wrote to Dudley Frasier, telling him that he thought Rinehart had done "a very fine job" on the book and approving Frasier's promotional campaign of sending three "teaser" cards to booksellers and reviewers at staggered intervals prior to the date of the book's publication. He also informed Frasier that Lawrence S. Kamp's copy of *The Bad Seed* had arrived two days before and that he had autographed it and returned it the same day.[72]

On the day after writing that letter to Frasier, March suffered what was termed at the time a mild heart attack. He was rushed, ironically enough, considering his religious views, to Hotel Dieu, one of the oldest private hospitals in Louisiana, and directed by the Catholic Order, the Sisters of Charity. The first object his eyes focused upon when he regained consciousness was a painting of the Sacred Heart, framed in red, on the wall opposite the foot of the bed. The story goes that in very clear and measured tone he left no doubt in the minds of the mother superior and the nuns who were attending him that he wanted the picture out of the room forthwith. To avoid exciting him and worsening his condition, his wish was immediately granted.[73]

To those who came to see him during the following days, it was evident that March was extremely frightened by what had befallen him. His fear showed clearly in his eyes. When Dickinson first visited him, March told him: "Joseph, they have a system here for reducing a man of all his dignity."[74] It would not have been surprising had he proved to be a bad patient, but, strangely enough, the opposite was the case. His friends were astonished and moved when they detected the sense of warm rapport that had grown between patient and nursing sisters.[75]

He was still in the hospital when *The Bad Seed* was published on April 8. It was, perhaps prophetically, the first of his books to carry no dedication.

fourteen

The Bad Seed and
Posthumous Success

Although, by no means the intensely personal work that *October Island*
had been, *The Bad Seed* nevertheless contains several brief and mainly
rather obscure allusions to March's personal life. For example, although the city in which the action of the novel takes place is unnamed, it is, as William T. Going has observed, "unmistakably . . . the
Mobile March knew," the centrally situated square to which Christine
Penmark takes her daughter, Rhoda, being an atmospherically accurate description of Mobile's Bienville Square and the house where the
Penmarks have their apartment being "typical of many small-unit
dwellings on Government Street and its side avenues."[1] The red-brick
house itself, with its "three floors of ponderous, Victorian elegance
. . . and its turrets, oriel windows, spires and ornamental spouts
[which] balanced and matched one another in a sort of impressive
architectural madness" (*BS*, p. 11), is reminiscent not only of the
apartment house in which March had resided on Government Street
but also of the house in Gramercy Park where he had lived in New
York and where he had experienced his disastrous breakdown. Indeed,
before her marriage, Christine Penmark herself had lived for a while
with her invalid mother in Gramercy Park. She had also been employed for a while in a New York art gallery, very similar, one assumes,
to the gallery owned by Klaus Perls. When she first meets her hus-
band-to-be, Kenneth, at a dinner party, they discuss at some length
the painters of the Paris school. He visits the art gallery and tells her
he is going to buy a Modigliani drawing for the girl he is going to
marry. He asks her if she thinks the girl will like it. Christine tells him
that if the girl does not like it, then he should not waste any further
time on her. A few days later, Kenneth gives Christine the drawing as
an unspoken proposal of marriage.

March uses to good effect the knowledge he had recently acquired about modern French art. The physical appearance of the book's central character, the monstrous eight-year-old Rhoda, was partly influenced by the Bombois portrait of a young girl he had purchased from Perls. A reference to this artist is made by Miss Claudia Fern, Rhoda's art teacher, on the second page of the book, when she rhapsodizes to her pupils about the beauties of *Benedict,* the old Fern summer place at Pelican Bay, where the annual school picnic is to take place:

> "*Benedict* is such a beautiful spot. . . . Little Lost River bounds our property on the Gulf side, and flows into the bay there. . . . The landscape at that point reminds me so much of those charming river scenes by Bombois." Then, feeling that some of her pupils might not know who Bombois was, she went on, "For the sake of some of the younger groups, Bombois is a modern French primitive. Oh, he is so *cunning* in his artlessness! So right in his composition. . . . You'll learn much about Bombois later on." [*BS,* p. 4]

As the reader is also to learn, March himself is cunning in his apparent artlessness. The opening paragraph of the book, for instance, seems designed to lull the less wary reader into a false sense of security by implying a continuity to Christine's life which does not in fact occur in the subsequent narrative. When Christine does die, such a reader will experience the same sense of disbelieving shock and outrage many people felt by the totally unexpected and unprecedented murder of the leading lady midway through Alfred Hitchcock's film *Psycho.* Yet nothing in this first paragraph of *The Bad Seed* is essentially false or misleading. Indeed, the implication is there—and very explicitly—that Christine will commit suicide. On the first page, character and circumstance have not yet been established, and as the plot begins to unfold, the first-time reader, with this opening paragraph constantly but imperfectly hovering in mind, is likely to impose a prejudged ending to the book, with Good (Christine) triumphing and Evil (Rhoda) being suitably eliminated. Not only does Rhoda survive, but March provides us with no immediate comfort: the eventual outcome of Rhoda's history being, with perfect artistry, left in midair, although March does speculate, through Christine's chaotic thoughts, what Rhoda's possible fate will be:

> unless something were done, [Rhoda] would repeat the idiotic pattern of her grandmother's life, making the necessary allowance for time and circumstances. She, too, for Rhoda was very clever indeed, would escape for a long time; but she would be caught and destroyed at last. [*BS,* p. 236]

Christine's maternal instincts, overpowering her repugnance, rule that she should save Rhoda from what she regards as the inevitability of the electric chair. She can see only one solution to her dilemma. She therefore administers an overdose of sleeping tablets to her child—and then shoots herself. The one thing she does not provide for is the concern of her neighbors. Rhoda is found in time, before the tablets have taken full effect.

It was certainly not an ending that pleased all the book's readers. The lady who wrote to Rinehart in 1955, complaining that March had not finished his story and urging the publishers to persuade their author to write a sequel, had plainly failed to appreciate the final irony of the novel's ending. But March had known precisely what he wanted to achieve. He had not been planning and orally writing the book all those years (even if for a time in fun) for nothing. Through the crime writer Reginald Trasker and his conversations with the distraught Christine, March is able to propound his theories concerning the criminal mind and, by so doing, induces us to accept unquestioningly the character of Rhoda and the motivation for her appalling actions.

Like March himself, Trasker has a particular interest in one type of criminal:

> In this sort of criminal, which seemed different from all others, there seemed to be as many women as men, which was unusual to begin with. His type, if they weren't too stupid or too unlucky, ended up as murderers on a grand scale. They never killed for those reasons that so often sway warm but foolish humans: they never killed for passion, since they seemed incapable of feeling it, or jealousy, or thwarted love, or even revenge. There seemed to be no element of sexual cruelty in them. They killed for two reasons only: for profit, since they all had an unconquerable desire for possessions, and for the elimination of danger when their safety was threatened. [*BS*, p. 142]

Trasker's researches have also shown him that such criminals do not always delay commencing their lives of crime until after they have reached adulthood:

> children quite often committed murders, and clever ones, too, at times. Some murderers, particularly the distinguished ones who were going to make great names for themselves, usually started in childhood; they showed their genius early, just as outstanding poets, mathematicians and musicians did. [*BS*, p. 83]

Detection of these criminal monsters, Trasker tells Christine, is frequently made more difficult because of the face they show to the world:

> the normal are inclined to visualize the multiple killer as one who's as monstrous in appearance as he is in mind, which is about as far from the truth as one could well get. . . . these monsters of real life usually looked and behaved in a more normal manner than their actually normal brothers and sisters: they presented a more convincing picture of virtue than virtue presented of itself—just as the wax rosebud or the plastic peach seemed more perfect to the eye, more what the mind thought a rosebud or a peach should be, than the imperfect original from which it had been modeled. [*BS*, p. 182]

Rhoda fits perfectly into the pattern, as March's initial description of her demonstrates:

> The child half turned, so that her mother could inspect her hair, which was straight, finespun, and of a dark, dull brown: her hair was plaited precisely in two narrow braids which were looped back into two thin hangman-nooses, and were secured, in turn, with two small bows of ribbon. . . . Rhoda sat down at the table, her face fixed in an expression of solemn innocence; then she smiled at some secret thought of her own, and at once there was a shallow dimple in her left cheek. She lowered her chin and raised it thoughtfully; she smiled again, but very softly, an odd, hesitant smile that parted her lips this time and showed the small, natural gap between her front teeth. [*BS*, pp. 6–7]

The patina of innocence and sweetness masking the evil personality is thus beautifully conveyed from the very beginning. As one of Rhoda's teachers perceptively remarks to Christine: "The child lives in her own particular world, and I'm sure it isn't anything at all like the world you and I live in" (*BS*, p. 29). Most adults, however, untroubled by the sort of unformulated insight Miss Octavia Fern possesses and recognizing nothing sinister in Rhoda's obsessive, indeed pathological, neatness and cleanliness and her compulsive desire for acquisitions, are completely wooed by the exterior child: "When speaking of [Rhoda], the adjectives that others most often used were 'quaint,' or 'modest,' or 'old-fashioned'" [*BS*, p. 6]. Children, on the other hand, are quite certain of their feelings toward Rhoda. We are told that at school "the other pupils both feared and detested" her (*BS*, p. 31). Eventually, the Fern sisters advise Christine that they feel Rhoda is not a good influence on the other children and pointedly suggest that it would be better if she were to withdraw her daughter from the school.

It is obvious to Christine that the Fern sisters are intimating more than they wish to reveal.

A similar situation had occurred the previous year when Rhoda was at school in Baltimore, where the Penmarks then lived. Her teachers had found her to be both "a fluent and a most convincing liar" and "an ordinary, but quite accomplished, little thief" (*BS*, p. 40) and she had been expelled. According to the school psychiatrist, Rhoda was "like a charming little animal that can never be trained to fit into the conventional patterns of existence," possessing, as she did, a remarkable quality of shrewd and mature calculation, none of the guilts and anxieties of a child and no capacity for affection in her overweening self-centeredness (*BS*, p. 41).

By the age of eight, Rhoda has four victims to her credit, not counting the unfortunate pet dog she throws from an upstairs window because she has become bored with having to look after it. She claims her first victim at the age of seven. An old lady, a neighbor of the Penmarks in Baltimore, possesses a crystal ball which Rhoda covets. The old lady promises Rhoda she will leave the trinket to her in her will. One day, Rhoda is left alone in the house with the old lady, who, in unexplained circumstances, falls to her death down a flight of stairs. Rhoda promptly asks the old lady's daughter for the crystal ball. She claims all three other victims during the two-month time span of the novel. Her second victim is her classmate Claude Daigle who has won at school the gold penmanship medal Rhoda believes is rightly hers. The boy is drowned when, trapping him on a disused wharf during the school picnic, Rhoda intimidates him into handing over the medal to her, then hits him with her metal-cleated shoes until he falls into the water. Her penultimate victim is Leroy Jessup, the moronic, paranoid janitor of the apartment house. She kills Leroy by setting fire to the basement room where he is taking his afternoon nap when she mistakenly believes he has retrieved from the incinerator the one piece of evidence which will incriminate her in little Claude's death—her cleated shoes. Her final victim, as it were by proxy, is her mother.

Even if, considered dispassionately, the plot of *The Bad Seed* creaks rather ominously in places, March weaves his narrative spell so persuasively that we accept it all as we read. Only later do we perhaps begin to question. Although we are occasionally admitted to the obscene and envious thoughts of Leroy, most of the action of the book is viewed through the eyes and keyed to the emotions of Christine, she being the only one of the characters aware of all the facts and implications surrounding the horrifying discoveries she makes, both concerning her own past and her child's current activities. This single viewpoint is possibly the book's principal defect, for it imposes upon the structure of the work a certain rigidity which, in its turn, produces a certain sense of artificiality. But one is hard put to see how March could have written the book in any other way not only to give as great a credibility as possible to the basic premise of the plot but also to bring out to the full the psychological pressures which force Christine to act in the manner she does, ultimately choosing an emotional and irrational, but very human, solution to her problem. Indeed, the artificiality of the plot becomes even more evident in Maxwell Anderson's subsequent dramatic adaption when, by reason of the medium, the story is presented in more objective terms.

March's extremely suspect theory that hereditary evil can be transmitted from generation to generation, perhaps remaining quiescent for a generation but never being eradicated, is the book's central theme and its principal rationale. The failure by default of two generations of mothers to kill their female offspring—Bessie Denker failing to kill Christine, and Christine in her turn failing to kill, but for completely different motives, Rhoda—ensures the perpetuation of "the bad seed." As the appalled Christine slowly but inevitably learns of her true origins and realizes that the two people she had always regarded as her mother and father were not, in fact, her true parents, she tortures herself with the thought of her own responsibility in creating the monster that is her child: "How can I blame Rhoda for the things she's done? I carried the bad seed that made her what she is. If anybody is guilty, I'm the guilty one, not Rhoda. . . . I'm the guilty one. . . . I was the carrier of the bad seed" (*BS*, pp. 189–90).

With her husband away from home on business for the whole summer, Christine endeavors to cope with the crisis alone. But she finds herself unable to find any means of escaping from the hideous reality in which she is enmeshed, other than the extreme action to which she ultimately resorts. She takes her secret to the grave, incapable of bringing herself to share with anyone, not even her husband, not even her sympathetic and garrulous neighbor Monica Breedlove, the truth she has discovered.

Monica, an elderly divorcee who lives with her younger bachelor brother Emory in the upstairs apartment, is perhaps March's most outrageously amusing character, acting in contrapuntal role to the diabolical Rhoda and providing the book with much welcome light relief. She is an extremely well-known and respected figure locally, even though she had once achieved some notoriety as the first woman in town to bob her hair and the first woman to smoke in public. When she divorced her husband, she astutely invested all the money he settled upon her in real estate and watched it grow in value with the steady growth of the town. The author of a best-selling cookbook, she devotes herself unstintingly to voluntary social work and fund-raising on behalf of various charities. A year or two before, she won the Civic Association award as the most valuable citizen of the year.

The breakup of her marriage occurred in the late 1920s after a three-year sojourn in Europe and England. Her husband, "not knowing what else to do with her" (*BS*, p. 43), had, at her request, paid for her to take a trip to Vienna, so that she could be analyzed by Sigmund Freud himself. Unfortunately, as she proudly was to tell her friends and acquaintances, the great man had been forced to admit that "her particular temperament was beyond his skill" (*BS*, p. 43) and, at his suggestion, she had undergone a course of analysis with one of his pupils, a Dr. Aaron Kettlebaum, who practiced in London. Kettlebaum, apparently something of a mystic, believed in "the power of the individual soul, and . . . considered sex of only trivial interest" (*BS*, p. 43). As a result of his indoctrination, Monica decided she was unable to resume her married life and, on her return to America, began divorce proceedings, a course of action her husband did not see fit to oppose.

Through Monica, it almost seems, March is taking a wry, light-hearted dig at himself. For, like him, Monica is a "party psychiatrist," forever analyzing other people's actions in Freudian (or Kettlebaumian) terms. In this analyzing, the sexual aspect plays a prominent part, just as it did in March's own pronouncements. She regards her brother as a "larvated homosexual," an opinion she broadcasts freely to everyone's embarrassment but her own. Her reasons for this diagnosis are simple enough: her brother is fifty-two years old and a bachelor and has never, to her knowledge, had a love affair. His interests are all male oriented. He gains a great amount of satisfaction from reading mysteries in which the bodies of housewives are gorily dismembered. She is just as forthcoming about her own sexual hang-ups, professing an incestuous fixation for her brother. She nevertheless dismisses the idea of incest as "trite," averring that her fixation is not more than latent penis hostility and penis envy. She concludes that she married her husband Norman only because she was subconsciously attracted by the implication of his two names: "Norman" having a strong association with the reassuring word "normal" and the two syllables of his surname "Breedlove" suggesting a state of growing affection.

For all her ostensible wisdom in matters psychological, she is basically one of life's innocents. Against a child like Rhoda she has no defenses at all. She showers the child with gifts, completely oblivious of the fact that by so doing she is in all probability preserving her life only temporarily, choosing to ignore the warning signs of the child's undisguised greed for possessions. One is left with the terrible suspicion that just as the old lady in Baltimore, Claude Daigle, and Leroy were destroyed by Rhoda because they had something the little girl could not obtain in any other way, so will Monica also assuredly be destroyed when it serves Rhoda's purpose to destroy her.

The depth of Monica's infatuation, the extent of her ignorance of Rhoda's true nature, is demonstrated at the very beginning of the novel when she gives the child a locket given to her when she herself was eight. The locket is decorated with a garnet, which is Monica's birthstone. When she tells the child she will have the garnet changed for a turquoise, which is Rhoda's birthstone, Rhoda quickly, and much to her mother's discomfiture, asks Monica if, in that case, she can also keep the garnet. Monica is entranced and amused by Rhoda's forthrightness, commenting: "How wonderful it is to meet such a *natural* little girl" (*BS*, p. 13). Christine, even before she begins making her traumatic discoveries, can view Monica's infatuation with perceptive objectivity: "Monica loves Rhoda, and she loves me, too. When she loves anybody, she can never see any wrong in them. She's completely loyal. She's a wonderful friend to have" (*BS*, p. 71).

But when Christine needs her most, Monica proves to be ineffective. She is naturally aware that Christine is greatly troubled and almost out of her mind, but she is unable to employ her muddled psychological expertise to break through the barrier of her friend's reticence. Although she urges Christine to trust her, she can do no more than comfort her and suggest that what she needs is a good night's sleep. She gives Christine the sleeping tablets which Christine uses in her abortive attempt to kill Rhoda. Indeed, it is Monica, by her very friendship, loyalty, and concern, who finally foils Christine's agonized plan to eliminate the bad seed for once and for all. She becomes worried when she does not receive an expected telephone call from Christine and induces a neighbor to break into the Penmark apartment, thus discovering the still-breathing Rhoda and the body of her dead mother.

To the very last, then, Rhoda fools them all. Monica's comment early on in the book, when referring to Rhoda, that a "child's mind is so wonderfully innocent. So lacking in guile or deceit" (*BS*, p. 27) is echoed by another well-meaning neighbor at the end of the book, misinterpreting completely Rhoda's cool unconcern over her mother's death: "She's too young as yet to understand what happened. She's such an innocent child in many ways" (*BS*, p. 246). Comforting the grief-stricken Kenneth, she tells him: "You must not despair, Mr. Penmark, and become bitter. We cannot always understand God's wisdom, but we must accept it. Everything was not taken from you as you think: At least Rhoda was spared. You still have Rhoda to be thankful for" (*BS*, p. 247). With these chilling words, the book ends.

On one level, *The Bad Seed* is an extremely effective spine-tingling thriller. But March is never merely an entertainer. Like all major writers, he uses his fiction to provide an outlet for the dissemination of his ideas and beliefs. The book can also be read as March's final (as it transpired) and definitive statement on the subject of violence in contemporary society, the inherent violence in man that March had recognized, observed, and feared all his life.

Near the beginning of the book, Christine overhears two men talking in the street:

> "I was reading the other day," said the taller of the two, "that the age we live in is an age of anxiety. You know what? I thought that was pretty good—a pretty fair judgment. I told Ruth about it when I got home, and she said, 'You can say *that* again!'"
>
> "Every age that people live in is an age of anxiety," said the other man. "If anybody asks me, I'd say the age we live in is an age of violence. It looks to me like violence is in everybody's mind these days. It looks like we're just going to keep on until there's nothing left to ruin. If you stop and think about it, it scares you."
>
> "Well, maybe we live in an age of anxiety *and* violence."
>
> "Now, that sounds more like it. Come to think about it, I guess that's what our age is really like." [*BS*, p. 33]

When, the following day, Rhoda asks her mother to assist her with her Sunday school lessons, Christine is dismayed to find that the Old Testament text on which Rhoda is to be tested is one in which a massacre of innocents is described in all its gory detail. She asks herself: "Is there nothing but violence anywhere? Is there no real peace anywhere in the world?" (*BS*, p. 66). With an exquisite turn of irony, Rhoda comes out top in her Sunday school class and returns home that afternoon with a copy of *Elsie Dinsmore*, which she has been awarded as a prize.

Rhoda herself can be seen as a metaphor for all the violence and greed that is a part of every one of us, lying dormant, as it did in Christine, subconsciously or even unconsciously suppressed, awaiting the opportunity, the extreme situation, to be released and manifest itself. In a more general sense, March, it seems, is endeavoring to warn us against our complacency, reminding us that monsters such as

Rhoda, who have cast aside the basic humanities, do indeed live among us, that we should be continually on our guard against the false face of innocence, the treacherously beguiling smile and the convincing lies, not only in our purely personal relationships but also, and perhaps more pertinently, in the wider context of national and international politics.

Even before the appearance of *The Bad Seed* in the bookshops, there were clear indications that March may have written a winner. The February 15, 1954, edition of *Kirkus*, noting the book's forthcoming publication on April 8, reported: "William March's virulent talent is thoroughly at ease in a quietly horrifying little story. . . . A caustic entertainment, in which March, along with his little fiend, consummates more than one kind of wicked retaliation."[2]

In one of the first reviews after publication, the *New Yorker* critic compared Rhoda with the child monster in Lillian Hellman's 1934 play: "Mr. March writes with fine, cold restraint, and his baby Gorgon might easily be the envy and despair of [Hellman's] rather less accomplished prototype in 'The Children's Hour.' Undoubtedly one of the year's best."[3] James Kelly in the *New York Times Book Review* agreed: "It's pleasant to report that *The Bad Seed* scores a direct hit, either as an exposition of a problem or as work of art. Venturing a prediction and a glance over the shoulder: no more satisfactory novel will be written in 1954 or has turned up in recent memory."[4] Like Kelly, there were other reviewers who were not content to consider *The Bad Seed* on a single level. In a perceptive review in the *New York Herald Tribune Book Review*, Dan Wickenden suspected that March's purpose was not simply to write a pure horror story, but he confessed himself somewhat puzzled as to what was the author's ultimate message and intention. "It is possible," he suggested, "to read *The Bad Seed* as an allegory of our violent times, as a commentary upon the bewilderment and helplessness of all men and women of average good will who find themselves face to face with pure evil, which is incomprehensible."[5]

Rinehart celebrated the publication of *The Bad Seed* by arranging for a magnificent basket of flowers to be delivered to March's sick room at Hotel Dieu. Amussen also wrote, sending March his good wishes for a speedy recovery, offering his felicitations on the book's publication and saying how delighted everyone at Rinehart was by the ecstatic reviews which had so far appeared. He additionally gave the sick author the news that Rinehart had had an advanced sale of more than 5,000 copies before publication day.[6]

The news probably did March much good. On April 9, the day he received Amussen's letter, he was allowed to sit up for the first time.

Dickinson had been visiting March each day at the hospital, taking him his mail and doing his errands, and it was he who wrote to Rinehart on March's behalf, thanking Amussen and the rest of the staff for the flowers, telling them that March's health seemed to be improving each day, and indicating how encouraged March had been by the reviews he had read.[7]

Frederick R. Rinehart himself wrote to Dickinson on April 13, sympathizing with "Mr. March's present situation" and recalling that nine years previously he too had suffered a heart attack, from which, although—like March's—it had been only a "mild" one, it had taken him a long time to recover fully. The tone of his letter offered hope and countenanced patience. He was able to pass on yet a further piece of good news. This was that a telegram had arrived the previous day at Rinehart from Maurice Evans, the actor-producer, expressing interest in the stage and film rights of *The Bad Seed*. Evans admitted that he had not yet read the book himself but stated that he had been convinced by the reviews that here was likely material for dramatization.[8]

Evans was not the only one to express such an interest. Robert Breen, vice-president of the nonprofit New York corporation Everyman Opera, the man who had taken George Gershwin's *Porgy and Bess* on international tour, also inquired as to the possibility of acquiring the dramatic and film rights, as did two other top producers, Leland Hayward and Courtney Burr. Three Hollywood studios asked Swanson to quote a price for the movie rights, and James Wong Howe, the distinguished cameraman, proposed an independently produced film based on the book. Swanson, realizing he was holding a really hot property, set his sights high, fixing the initial asking price for the motion picture rights at $65,000. On April 27, William Fields, the press representative of the Playwrights' Company (whose members included playwrights Maxwell Anderson, Robert Anderson, Elmer Rice, and Robert E. Sherwood), wrote to March in care of Rinehart, offering his opinion that *The Bad Seed* would make an excellent play and wondering if the author had ever thought of trying his hand at a dramatization. Fields expressed his willingness to discuss the matter with March. All this news was, of course, imparted to March by his delighted agents and publishers.[9]

What March did not know was that there were moves afoot to give him recognition for his services to literature. José Garcia Villa has recalled that that April, shortly after *The Bad Seed* came out, he was having dinner with Kay Boyle, Malcolm Cowley, and some other writers at the annual ceremonial of the American Academy of Art and Letters. Villa asked Cowley, who was president of the National

Institute of Art and Letters, the junior body of the academy, why it was that March had never been selected as a member. Cowley made what was for Villa the astonishing statement that he had never heard of March, but, following Villa's representations, undoubtedly supported by Kay Boyle, Cowley promised to look into the matter. He was as good as his word, for on April 22 the institute advised Rinehart that March had been recommended as a candidate for one of the 1955 Arts and Letters Grants and requested six copies of *The Bad Seed* for distribution to the institute committee. Rinehart was enjoined to keep this information in strictest confidence and there is, indeed, no evidence that either March or his agents were ever told.

It is, then, fairly certain that March died unaware of the proposed honor that might have been bestowed upon him. He would assuredly have been deeply proud to have received this recognition, for he had never altogether regarded himself as a professional writer in the accepted sense of the word. And yet, although he was comparatively little known outside his small circle of admirers, he felt his position secure among his peers. When *The Bad Seed* appeared, he received a number of letters from other writers, including Hemingway, Dos Passos, and Eudora Welty, congratulating him on the book's success. He also received a letter from Carson McCullers, who was at that time staying with friends in Charlotte, North Carolina. She had found *The Bad Seed* particularly gripping and told her friends that she thought it "marvellously creepy." She wished, she added, that she had written it herself.[11] She was still recovering from the effects of her first stroke and although she had not attempted to write any letters since the onset of her disabling illness, she determined to write to her old sponsor and friend herself. She was obliged to draw each letter painfully with a pencil clutched uncertainly in her left hand. After a page of congratulations and expressions of enthusiasm for the book, she began the second page with a reference to her late husband Reeves, who had died by his own hand in Paris the previous November, recalling that it was March who had first warned her that Reeves was suicidal.

There is a certain irony in the fact that March considered *The Bad Seed* the worst book he had ever written. To his brother Peter, he referred to it as being little more than a potboiler. His reaction to the book's success was one of incredulity. On one occasion he confided that he thought it an almost vulgar work, one which he regarded even with some embarrassment. His main purpose in writing the book, so he averred, was for its shock value and its controversial elements. In this respect, it is of passing interest to note that *The Bad Seed* was March's sixth published novel, just as *Sanctuary* was Faulkner's sixth published novel. Faulkner, like March, had attracted only a small readership with his five previous novels and he had resolved to write a novel which would make him money by inventing "the most horrific tale I could imagine." Thus, there is a faint parallel to be drawn between *Sanctuary* and *The Bad Seed*, except that March had probably not been motivated, as Faulkner had been, by the desire to make money. At the time *Sanctuary* appeared, Faulkner was practically indigent. By no stretch of the imagination could March be said to have been desperately in need of funds in 1953–54. What undoubtedly was of overwhelming importance to him, as Robert Tallant has pointed out, was the fact that with *October Island* and *The Bad Seed* he had accomplished an artistic comeback after too long a silence. The commercial success the new book was enjoying, although exceedingly pleasing, was of secondary moment.

On May 5, von Auw sent March the contract with Hamish Hamilton. By then, March was back home, having been discharged from the hospital on April 24. Shortly before March left the Hotel Dieu, Dickinson was obliged to make an extended visit to Nashville in connection with a painting commission. He was unhappy over leaving March at this time and he also sensed that March, who had obviously come to depend a great deal on his services, even to the extent of taking them somewhat for granted, resented his departure for Tennessee. Dickinson, however, felt he had no option but to go. He had his own career to consider. March, after all, was in good hands and almost anyone could assume Dickinson's not very onerous duties, essentially nothing more or less than those of a superior errand boy. Dickinson accordingly completed his plans to leave New Orleans, arranging that after he had gone a neighbor would pick up March's mail from 613 Dumaine Street, deliver it to March's hospital room, and get any minor items of shopping March might from time to time desire to need. This arrangement never got off the ground, for the neighbor contracted influenza.

Even before the day of Dickinson's departure, it had become apparent that there was every likelihood that March would be leaving the hospital in the near future. Clearly, the invalid would require a temporary companion to be with him at home, until a more permanent arrangement could be made. Dickinson therefore suggested that his young artist friend Robert Clark, who was still sharing his apartment, should, in addition to acting as errand boy while March was in hospital, move into 613 Dumaine Street when March went home. March was patently not attracted by the idea, which would entail an encroachment upon the privacy he had always so jealously guarded, but he conceded that it would not be wise for him to be entirely alone in the house. So he asked Clark if he would be willing to occupy the upstairs apartment in the main house and act as his factotum. Clark agreed.

Clark took March home from the hospital a few days after Dickinson had left for Nashville. When Dickinson returned briefly to New Orleans to close up his apartment, he called at Dumaine Street and found both March and Clark looking very unwell. March, it seems, had been a hard taskmaster since his arrival back home and had kept Clark, in his capacity as a sort of unpracticed nurse, on virtually twenty-four-hour duty for several days. March told Dickinson: "Bob's been kind. I don't know how I could have managed without him." Dickinson made it clear that he thought too much responsibility was being placed on Clark's young shoulders and that March could well afford proper professional help. He obtained March's agreement to hire a cook and a relief nurse. During the next few days, in between attending to his own affairs, he attempted to organize the household into some degree of working order, thus giving March's young companion some much-needed rest and a chance to recover.

Dickinson was in New Orleans for only a week. During this period he read *The Bad Seed* for the first time. March showed some interest in his friend's reaction to the book, frequently interrupting Dickinson in his reading to ask, "Where are you reading now?" Dickinson would read out a passage and March would then proceed to tell him how the passage had been written in an earlier version, or what had been deleted in arriving at the final text. Dickinson preferred *October Island* to *The Bad Seed*, and he helped to pass the hours for March by reading the book aloud to him. March seemed to enjoy the reading, as if he were hearing his own prose for the first time. Dickinson recited the Edna St. Vincent Millay poem "To the Calvinist on Bali," and March's comment was that he regretted not having known of the poem when he had been writing the novel.

At the end of the week, Dickinson felt more than ever unhappy, even guilty, about carrying out his plans and leaving for Nashville. He offered to stay on, only to be told: "No, indeed. You have your profession, and it takes you to middle Tennessee." It was not until later that he learned how deeply March had felt let down at his time of need.[13]

According to Clark, the first days at home were fearful ones for March. "It was his habit," Clark has recalled, "to sit resignedly, clutching at his chest and throat, not untheatrically. Bill seemed suddenly to have achieved a diminished size. I think he felt an overwhelming sense of defeat in his illness. . . . He would have me answer the door and the telephone, with instructions to tell whoever was calling, 'Mr. March is not in,' or 'Mr. March is napping.'"[14]

On May 7, March returned the Hamish Hamilton contracts, duly signed. He appended a little note to his agents, observing that this was the first writing he had done since he had been stricken with his heart attack. He gave von Auw authority to handle any stage or movie offers for *The Bad Seed* in any way he thought fit. He told von Auw that he was just embarking on the seventh week of his illness and noted, with some element of assurance as to his future, that the first six weeks were regarded as being the crucial ones. He admitted to spells of unreasoning anxiety, but he considered that, apart from this human failing on his part, his physical recovery was proceeding very satisfactorily along conventional lines. He was, he added, looking forward to commencing work on a new book.[15]

As the seventh week progressed and March's confidence in his ultimate full recovery became more established in his mind, the depressing atmosphere he had created around himself began slowly to disappear. He was undoubtedly comforted by the thought that every day that passed must signify an increasingly hopeful prognosis. His doctor, after all, had promised him that he was good for another ten years, if he was careful.[16]

There were, in fact, occasional moments of pure humor. March had taken a great interest in Clark's progress as a painter and he frequently suggested compositions to the young artist. One of the canvases Clark had executed as a result of one of these suggestions caught March's fancy and he bought it, placing it, while it was still drying, on the mantel of the fireplace in the slave-quarters living room, surrounded by the august company of Picasso, Modigliani, Soutine, Rouault, and Braque. His day nurse came in the following morning, espied Clark's little painting and, dismissing, as it were, the works of the masters that graced the walls, announced in an assumed "professional" voice: "Now, *that's* what I call a purty picture!" March, as Clark puts it, was "ecstatic with glee."[17]

These days, one can speculate, were for March a period during which he began to reassess a number of long-held values. He certainly seems to have regretted, and not for the first time, that he had never married and achieved the stability of a permanent emotional relationship with another human being. He told Clark: "This love thing: I'm beginning to think I may have been missing something."[18] But it is unlikely, had events turned out differently, that he would have been able to shake off a lifetime's aversion to the establishment of deep and enduring ties. He was certainly unwilling to die, not solely because of his natural fear of death but, as much as anything else, because he wanted to survive long enough to see his fables in print, to write five more novels and to complete the "century mark" of short stories which had long been his goal.

He had discussed with several of his friends and members of the Campbell family the plots or random details of these novels and stories he planned to write. Some months earlier, he had outlined to Bolton the central episode of a further thriller-type novel, to be called *The Ragged Stranger*, in which he proposed to continue his insistent exploration into the interrelated themes of crime and evil that so fascinated him. As Bolton recalls it, *The Ragged Stranger*

> concerned a man who wished to get rid of his unwanted but wealthy wife, and who hired a nameless drifter to enter the house while the couple were out. When they returned, the drifter was to shoot the wife. But—and here's the kicker—the husband would double-cross the killer by shooting him. A perfect crime, and in Bill's view a very evil deed. Over several years, he had given this idea more than passing thought. It originated, I think, in actual form in one of those newspaper clippings he had collected, in which something very like the above happened, but the "ragged stranger," suspecting the double-cross, also shot the husband. Of course, as Bill observed when he showed me the clipping, "He should have shot the tramp first. Then shot the wife with the tramp's gun. He couldn't let the tramp live. He would have been blackmailed." I think that's the way it would have been done in Bill's book had he lived to write it. The wife would certainly not suspect her husband as he bent over the dead intruder. Even as he scooped up the gun, shot her, and returned the gun to the dead man's hand, death and recognition of treachery would have come together.[19]

Robert Tallant has recorded how, when he went to visit his friend in the hospital, March mentioned to him the new book he was planning, which was to be titled *Poor Pilgrim, Poor Stranger* or *The Gift*. Clay Shaw also remembered March speaking of a projected work called *Poor Pilgrim, Poor Stranger* and how once March described the ending of the book to him: "the man going off into this sort of pink snow—pink snow falling. It was a great thing in his mind."[20] March apparently never revealed to Shaw what this pink snow was, nor what it was supposed to represent, but it brings to mind the traumatic execution scene in *Come in at the Door*, when the peach blossoms fall "like pink, intermittent snow" around Baptiste's dead body. Dickinson does not recall March telling him about the pink snow, but he remembers a detail from a short story March said he wanted to write in which a middle-aged couple make token love, the man being impotent, the woman loving "his penis, small and pink and unthreatening."[21]

To Robert Clark, March expressed a desire, perhaps uncharacteristically, to write his autobiography, whereas his brother Peter and his sister-in-law Gwen understood that the book he wanted the most to write was one based on the story of the Campbell family. He told them, however, that he would never contemplate publishing such a work so long as any member of the family was alive. So far as Peter and Gwen were aware, he never even started writing the book.[22]

By mid-May, *The Bad Seed* had been on the *New York Herald Tribune's* best-seller list for three weeks and had just moved up again to thirteenth place. On May 13, Anne Gustavson, of the Rinehart publicity department, sent March another batch of the "enthusiastic reviews" that were still "pouring in." On the same day, Dudley Frasier also wrote to him, announcing that sales were "hovering around 10,000" and that another round of advertising had been scheduled in the quality newspapers and journals. Frasier added that all at Rinehart were looking forward to the new William March novel and expressed the hope that it was going well.[23]

March would have received these letters the following day, Friday the fourteenth, the day on which, for the first time since his heart attack, he was able to leave the house to visit his doctor. Clearly, he was reassured by whatever it was the doctor told him. Sometime, after he returned home, he went, unbeknown to Clark, up to his study, sat down at his desk and inserted a clean sheet of paper in his typewriter. For the last time, fantasy and reality were, briefly, to intermingle. He typed the title *Poor Pilgrim, Poor Stranger* and then the following single paragraph:

> The time comes in the life of each of us when we realize that death awaits us as it awaits others, that we will receive at the end neither preference nor exemption. It is then, in that disturbed moment, that we know life is an adventure with an ending, not a succession of bright days that go on forever. Sometimes the knowledge comes with repudiation and quick revolt that such injustice awaits us, sometimes with fear that dries the mouth and closes the eyes for an instant, sometimes with servile weariness, an acquiescence more dreadful than fear. The knowledge that my own end was near came with pain, and afterwards astonishment, with the conventional heart attack, from which, I've been told, I've made an excellent recovery.[24]

That evening, he sat with Clark in the slave quarters. Clark was reading *Company K*. He came to one passage that moved him so greatly that tears came into his eyes. March noticed and asked what it was that had touched him so. Clark reread to March the words he had written almost a quarter of a century before, describing how Private Theodore Irvine, dying slowly and in unbearable agony from the wounds he had received in the war, is silently offered and fiercely rejects the opportunity of ending his suffering with a self-administered overdose of morphine, telling himself: "I'm going to live as long as I can and fight for my last breath. . . . Better to suffer the ultimate pains of hell than to achieve freedom in nothingness!" March gazed quietly out at the patio for a few moments and then said sadly, "Thank you." Later, the two men chatted for a while, discussing, among other things, the possibility of Clark's eventually going to Paris to study art.[25]

When he retired that night, March must have felt comforted by the thought that the worst of his illness was behind him. There would surely have been the double satisfaction for him, too, in the knowledge that not only at long last had the praises of the reviewers for one of his books been reflected and matched by its sales but that he had also set down on paper the opening words of the work that was to succeed *The Bad Seed*.

Clark awoke momentarily at five-thirty the following morning. He slept in the room immediately above March's bedroom. The doors of both bedrooms were left open, so that Clark could hear if March called him during the night. He was not sure what had disturbed him, but he heard March turn over in his bed. Clark went back to sleep, happy that everything was as it should be. But when, shortly after nine o'clock, he came downstairs and went into March's room to awaken him, he discovered March lying there in bed, his eyes open, his face, clearly showing pain, half-buried in the pillow.[26] Clark endeavored to rouse him, but to no avail. He summoned a neighbor, Dr. Robert P. Cameron, a staff doctor at Charity Hospital. Upon examining March, Cameron pronounced the author dead.

Shortly afterward, the police arrived. After the police, came the coroner and his men. Under the law, an autopsy was necessary, as it is in every case where the deceased has died "unattended" at home without the presence of a physician, nurse, or other qualified medical person. The coroner's men removed the body from the bed, placing it rather unceremoniously in a large oblong basket. They were even careless about covering the body properly before carrying it out of the house. Tallant has recorded how the curious neighbors, who had gathered outside, could see "a naked white foot protruding from beneath the white sheet."[27] It was, in its macabre way, the final insult to March and his innate sense of privacy.

Clark, as he had been instructed to do in the event of any crisis, contacted Bannister Slaughter, vice-president of the Merchants National Bank of Mobile, and informed him of March's death. Slaughter called the Campbell family and then traveled to New Orleans to make the necessary funeral arrangements.

News of March's death was passed swiftly around the Quarter. Bolton recalls that it was about noon on that Saturday when he heard. He was in the Café LaFitte-in-Exile, talking to Tom Caplinger and drinking a Bloody Mary, when someone came in and announced that Bill March had died early that morning in his sleep. "We all sat there, silently looking out into the bright glare of noon on Bourbon Street. Caplinger said, 'Ah, Jesus.' Ted Reed, Tom's bartender and able assistant, poured the drinks."[28]

The autopsy at the coroner's office established the time of death as 8:15 A.M. and the cause of death as acute myocardial infarction. One doctor told Clark later that it had been a massive coronary, the clot large enough to have killed a number of horses. March had, in fact, been living on borrowed time for quite a while, for the records show that certainly since he had first come to live in New Orleans, he had been suffering from coronary sclerosis and hypersensitive heart disease. Once the autopsy was completed to the coroner's satisfaction, March's body was placed in the hands of the undertakers, who arranged for its immediate transportation that same evening to Tuscaloosa.

Tallant was at Caplinger's that Saturday night. "Everyone was talking about Bill March," he has recalled. "They both discussed him and argued about him. Someone would say it was a good way to die and a good time to die, and someone else would say it was not. They talked of his writing and things he had said, and why certain ways of his had been as they were, and why others were not so. Accounts of his passing were clipped from the newspapers and tacked on the walls. At least two people wept. In a way this was his wake. I think it all would have pleased Bill."[29]

March was buried in Evergreen Cemetery, Tuscaloosa, on May 17. Finley McRae, John P. Case, and other old Mobilian friends acted as pallbearers. Clark and Dr. Cameron were, from all accounts, the only two of March's New Orleans friends to be invited to the funeral.

Clark was asked by Bannister Slaughter and March's sister Patty if he would stay on at 613 Dumaine Street as caretaker, until such time as March's effects were sorted through and disposed of and arrangements made for the sale of the property. This Clark readily agreed to do. So, while the house was being slowly stripped of March's possessions, Clark stayed in residence, moving into the small attic apartment March had used as his office, receiving a regular check of fifty dollars a week, until, just before the eventual and unsuccessful (as it transpired) attempt was made to auction the house, he had to move out. By that time, apart from the few pieces of essential furniture in the rooms Clark occupied, the house was quite denuded. When Clark finally vacated the premises, Patty presented him with March's desk as an additional token of the family's gratitude.

It was a condition of March's will that his art collection should be sold. Before it was disposed of, however, the collection was exhibited at the newly opened Perls Galleries at 1016 Madison Avenue, New York. The exhibition, which ran from October 4 to November 13, 1954, showed twenty-eight items. All who visited it remarked to Perls on the excellent and remarkable quality of the paintings March had collected. When Perls subsequently arranged the sale of the collection, March's estate received many times the total of the sums he had paid for the paintings only five or so years before.[30]

Three days before the opening of the exhibition, *The Bad Seed* was published in London by Hamish Hamilton. Like their American counterparts, the majority of the British reviewers hailed the book as a superb piece of storytelling, although, echoing the views of the American critics, they voiced their reservations concerning the validity of March's central thesis. "*The Bad Seed* is terrifyingly good," L. A. G. Strong wrote in the *Spectator*, "not only because its theme is worked out so powerfully, but because every character is convincing. One has to believe that these appalling things took place exactly as the author says they did."[31] In the *New Statesman and Nation*, Walter Allen considered the book "the most terrifying novel I have read for a long time. . . . " The heredity theory of the transmission of evil from one generation to another was, on the other hand, a matter Allen felt incompetent to comment on, but he felt "that it was mechanical and, being so, reduced a terrifying novel to a neat horror story." The moral issue raised by the novel had, he thought, been evaded.[32]

On December 8, 1954, Maxwell Anderson's adaptation of *The Bad Seed* was premiered on Broadway. The play, presented by the Playwright's Company at the Forty-Sixth Street Theatre, had completed a successful out-of-town run and had promoted further sales of the novel. These had reached by mid-November a satisfying 17,000 copies. For Maxwell Anderson, who had decided to make the adaptation after reading March's book while convalescing from a prostate operation in

July of that year at the Cedars of Lebanon Hospital, Los Angeles, *The Bad Seed* was to be his last successful Broadway play. Anderson had finished the first draft of the play by late August and in early September he had traveled to New York to arrange its production. He always considered the play as something of a potboiler, as did March his novel. Like the novel, it proved to be a hit. Starring Nancy Kelly in the role of Christine and the remarkable Patty McCormack as Rhoda, the play ran for 332 performances.

The whole audience sat enthralled through the first performance. It was immediately apparent to the playwright, the cast, and the members of the Campbell family who attended the occasion that they had a success on their hands. This impression was confirmed the following day when the notices appeared in the New York newspapers. In the *New York Herald Tribune*, Walter Kerr wrote: "A genuine fourteen-carat, fifteen-below chiller . . . thrilling entertainment. As a work of purely theatrical excitement, it is beautifully carpentered, suspensefully acted, craftily sustained. *Bad Seed* is an ingenious piece of straight showmanship."[33] Brooks Atkinson in the *New York Times* called it an "extraordinarily literate horror story and a superior bit of theatre."[34] Under the heading "'Shocker' Proves a Hit," John McClain proclaimed in the *New York Journal-American*: "I think everybody agrees that we need a good shocker this season, and for my money this is it."[35]

A British production of the play, presented at the Aldwych Theatre, London, on April 14, 1955, did not prove so successful. According to the critic Kenneth Tynan, what was needed from the cast and director was "the strictest Hitchcock realism," whereas from Diana Wynyard's Christine and Frith Banbury's direction all the London audiences got was "amateur operatics." Tynan conceded that "Carol Wolveridge brought a transfixing purity of attack to the part of the eight-year-old murderess, a Wordsworthian child rejoicing in intimations of mortality."[36]

The first posthumous publication of March's own work appeared in the spring 1955 issue of the *University of Kansas City Review*. This was the fable "The Bretts." Four more previously unpublished fables ("The Woodchuck and the Old Bones," "The Cock and the Capon," "The Doctor and the Hippopotamus," and "The Unspeakable Words"), as well as eight others which had been printed in little magazines over a decade before, appeared for the first time between hard covers in *A William March Omnibus*, which Rinehart brought out on February 6, 1956. The selections were chosen by Robert Loomis. The volume contained a glowing introduction by Alistair Cooke and reprinted the whole of *Company K*, twenty-one short stories and the novella "October Island." In his tribute, Cooke wrote:

> William March lived and died without much acclaim, except for the two books he cared least about: his first and his last. He won a few prizes for short stories. He is not mentioned in the 2,239 pages of the Spiller-Thorp-Johnson-Canby *Literary History of the United States*. Among the professional critics who remembered him for anything later than *Company K*, he was thought of, but not for long, as a journeyman realist, a third-rate Sherwood Anderson. When he was singled out, it was as a minor connoisseur of morbidity.[37]

The publication of the omnibus provided the critics of the day with the opportunity of reaffirming or reassessing March's place in modern American literature. In the *New Yorker*, Anthony West referred to Alistair Cooke's closing statement in his introduction that March was one of the most underrated of contemporary American writers of fiction. "It would be fairer to say," West observed, "that he was an intelligent, scrupulous storyteller, with a respect for the truth, who set himself moderate goals and usually achieved them, saying what he wished to say interestingly, calmly, and without breach of literary convention."[38] In the *New York Times Book Review*, Maxwell Geismar pondered on the dangers and vagaries of literary fashion, noting that "William March was one of these gifted artists who never quite achieved his due during the Nineteen Thirties and Forties. . . ."[39] Under the hopeful heading "Toward a Restoration of William March," John Hutchens in the *New York Herald Tribune Book Review* reminded his readers that when the omnibus came along to rescue March from oblivion, only two of his books, *October Island* and *The Bad Seed*, were in print. Hutchens hoped that it was not too late to see justice done and March's name restored. He concluded a long and balanced review of the omnibus with the following words:

> [March] would not fake, or "heighten," or pile on local color. He was a true writer who had mastered the simple declarative sentence. And it would be good to think that, by a happier irony than some of those he experienced in his lifetime, his deep, straight stories will outlive the showier writing that has tended to shade his own.[40]

The movie rights of *The Bad Seed* had been purchased by Warner Brothers approximately one month after the play version opened on Broadway, the screenwriter John Lee Mahin being signed to write the screenplay based on Maxwell Anderson's stage play. Mervyn LeRoy produced and directed the movie. Six of the original New York cast repeated their roles on the screen: Nancy Kelly, Patty McCormack, Henry Jones (Leroy), Evelyn Varden (Monica Breedlove), Joan Croyden (Miss Fern) and Eileen Heckart (Mrs. Daigle). Much publicity was given to the fact that the film was to have a secret ending, different from that of both the book and the play. With typical Hollywood ballyhoo, it was announced that even the stars themselves had not been told of the nature of the climax and that special police guards had been thrown around the studio's Stage 7 on the evening that Mervyn LeRoy shot the ending. As an added safeguard against the public's discovering the ending during production, LeRoy commissioned Mahin to write three different but equally dramatic and surprising final scenes, any one of which could be used, as the publicity handouts proclaimed, "without harming the overall emotional impact of the story."[41] When revealed, it was found that the "secret ending" totally destroyed the ironic horror implicit in the final denouement of March's book, for in the film Christine survives her suicide attempt and Rhoda (possibly at the behest of the Breen Office) is exterminated by a convenient bolt of lightning. As if this were not sacrilege enough, a cozy little postscript is tacked to the end of the film, in which, one after the other, the principal members of the cast, all smiles, take a good-humored "curtain-call," presumably to reassure the ostensibly terrified audiences that all they had been witnessing had been nothing more nor less than pure charade, that Leroy had not in fact been horribly burned to death in his cellar, that Christine had only been pretending to have been driven out of her mind with the knowledge of the monster she had spawned, and that the little monster herself was, after all, only a clever and persuasive child actress, certainly no naughtier than any other child of her age and perfectly willing to enter into the spirit of these final proceedings by being stretched across Miss Kelly's knees and subjected to a well-deserved (but clearly also make-believe) spanking.

Most knowledgeable critics railed at this cheap farrago, which ruined completely everything that had gone before, some (like Hollis Alpert in the *Saturday Review*) advising their readers to walk out of the cinema three minutes before the film ended. The *New York Times* critic Bosley Crowther felt that "as a consequence of looking too closely at its basically melodramatic characters" the film tended "to appear synthetic . . . at times . . . downright droll."[42]

Perhaps, in the less violent and less permissive climate of those days, the producer-director was well-advised to alter March's inconclusive ending. The audience then possibly *did* want all the loose ends tied up for them, everything neat and tidy, even if the subsequent "curtain-call" was psychologically ruinous. In the same way, the lady reader from Alexander, Louisiana, had expressed the wish the year before that March should write a sequel to *The Bad Seed*, so that she and all the other readers of the novel could know what happened when Mr. Penmark discovered for himself Rhoda's true nature and the truth concerning his wife's family history and the circumstances of her death. "I won't," this lady wrote to Rinehart and Company in August 1955, "have any peace of mind until Mr. March completes the story. I will appreciate it very much if you will pass this message along to Mr. March."[43]

March's wish to have his *Ninety-nine Fables* published was eventually realized six years after his death when The University of Alabama Press brought out an elegant illustrated edition under the title *99 Fables*. The extent to which March had revised, polished, and repolished the collection is attested to by the fact that in editing the volume William T. Going had available three quite separate typescripts, two of which were in the possession of March's sisters Patty and Margaret and the third in the possession of Paul Strickland of Mobile.[44]

The fables are astringent little prose pieces, expressing infallible truths, or, more frequently, half-truths. In three of the fables March introduces the character of Aesop himself, representing him as a man who is unable to converse except by reducing everything to the level of a fable. As March authorially comments, the fable "is, and always has been, the platitude's natural frame" (*99F*, p. 2). This habit of Aesop's to talk continually in fabular terms causes the direct-thinking Delphians to lose patience with him at last and to throw him over a cliff to his death. With typical March irony, Aesop's grandson, who is paid damages by the Delphians in recompense for killing his grandfather, contemplates the fate that has brought him unexpected fortune and, rather than feeling animosity toward the murderers, excuses them, telling himself, as he jingles in his pocket the gold coins he has received, that the Delphians could not have acted otherwise than they did.

Many of the fables, unlike the classical ones, introduce human beings. All the fables, despite their frequently platitudinous nature and despite the half-truths masquerading as truths, make valid and wise comment on the human condition. Many of the themes March explored in his novels and short stories are here restated in more simplistic form. In "Man and His Natural Enemy," for example, the natural enemy is shown to be man's own intolerance and cruelty toward his fellowmen, just as it is in, among other works, *Company K* and "Happy Jack." The old hen in "The Fishermen and the Hen," willing to bear the cruelty others show toward her provided she is given a little affection every so often, is reminiscent of Dirty Emma, who endures much at the hands of Tom Gunnerson. "The Pious Mantis" demonstrates, as does Sister Cotton again and again, that "there is no creature more cruel in her heart than a pious woman" (*99F*, p. 189). In "The Sheep and the Soldiers," as in *Company K*, the soldiers in their blind stupidity do not realize that they will more than likely end as willing sheep to the slaughter, urged on by the military and political leaders who will regard their suffering and their deaths of little consequence ("The Philosophical Lead Ram") and by the religious leaders who persuade them of the justification of the cause for which they fight and become willing to lay down their lives ("The World and Its Redeemers"). And, in "Cowards and Fearless Men," March makes the extremely pertinent point that many a soldier in war must have felt that "there's no companion more dangerous than one without fear" (*99F*, p. 147). Our reluctance to recognize evil in those of our own kind, even when it is staring us in the face (as in *The Bad Seed*), is again the subject of March's warning in "The Doubting Ducks." Conversely, the eagerness of some to believe in false miracles, as did the islanders in *October Island*, is the subject of "The Miracle," March even introducing the same "faraway island" and the people who "worshipped the god of the volcano that lifted itself above them" (*99F*, p. 163).

Delightful and thought-provoking though they are to read, it is doubtful that these beautifully composed, sparse fables have added much to March's overall reputation. As is the case with most books from university presses, the audience was a limited one, which is a pity, for the fables do provide in a terse form an illuminating insight into March's troubled vision of the world. Each fable makes its point not only with a directness and simplicity which cannot be open to misinterpretation but also, through March's lightness of touch, in a manner which, unlike so many of the novels and short stories, avoids the danger of repelling the more sensitive reader.

An act of homage on Going's part, *99 Fables* completed the publication of virtually the whole of the March canon, only a handful of sonnets, the unfinished novel *The Practiced Hand* and three short stories, "First," "The Red Jacket," and "The Long Pursuit," still remaining unpublished. Going planned to edit a further volume consisting of March's uncollected stories, including the three which have never appeared in print, which he proposed to title *Some in Addition*, but because of copyright and other difficulties the project was unfortunately never realized.[45]

Afterword

The novelist John Gardner, discussing the mysteries of the creative processes, considered the nature and extent of bibliotherapy, explaining in the following terms what it means so far as he is concerned:

> You really do ground your nightmares, you *name* them. When you write a story, you have to play that image, no matter how painful, over and over until you've got all the sharp details so you know exactly how to put it down on paper. By the time you've run your mind through it a hundred times, relentlessly worked every tic of your terror, it's lost its power over you. That's what bibliotherapy is all about, I guess. You take crazy people and have them write their story, better and better, and soon it's just a story on a page, or, more precisely, everybody's story on a page. It's a wonderful thing. Which isn't to say that I think writing is done for the health of the writer, though it certainly does incidentally have that effect.[1]

There is, in one respect, a marked similarity between Gardner's exposition and March's own approach to his writing, in that he also used his literary work as a means of exorcising his own particular devils by putting them down on paper and displaying them for the world to see, like esoteric objects laid out in a glass exhibition case. The psychic scars which were imprinted on his mind as a result of his experiences in France during World War I were, to a large degree, exorcised through the process of writing *Company K*, although it seems likely that despite the detailed no-holds-barred retelling of the incident in the Private Manuel Burt section of that book, he was never able to expunge the memory of one young German soldier's face. When he first returned to America from France in 1919, it is possible that he

316

invented his somewhat spectacular physical war wounds (the silver plate in his skull, the lungs destroyed by gas) simply because he found, as did Private Paul Waite in *Company K*, that people back home would not accept or take seriously the fact that a man could have been wounded psychologically just as badly as if he had lost an arm or a leg. By the time he underwent analysis with Glover in the mid-1930s, his war experiences no longer posed an overriding problem, as Glover was quick to discern. By then, the emotionally crippling nature of his childhood, stemming possibly from his relationship with his father, together with the conscious and subconscious conflict arising from the duality of his nature, manifesting itself in the two personalities of Campbell the business tycoon and March the author, had assumed a far greater importance as the fulcrum of his analysis. These new devils, once identified, had also to be exorcised. To an extent, he dealt with the landscape of his childhood in *The Tallons* and in the short stories set in Hodgetown and Williston. But apart from that one tantalizing glimpse of the Campbell-Gavin family at home in "Dirty Emma," there is no other clear and identifiable portrait of his family anywhere else in his works.

In addition to providing him with this therapeutic outlet, March's writing gave him a means of escape into fantasy from the cares and problems of the day, without the danger of his losing grip on the solid reality of life. According to Alistair Cooke, March once quoted to him a remark of Salvador Dali's: "The only difference between me and a schizophrenic is that I am not a schizophrenic." Cooke comments: "March could savor this rather horrible truth because he had the advantage here over Dali: he had been there and back. When he could let loose and tame his fantasies on paper, he remained a fairly contented social animal. When he could not, the abyss was never far away" (*WMO*, p. vi). March needed his fantasies, in exactly the same way an underwater swimmer needs periodically to break the surface to replenish his lungs with life-giving air. In *Ways of Escape*, the second volume of his "autobiography," Graham Greene, after observing that writing is "a form of therapy," goes on to wonder "how all those who do not write, compose or paint can manage to escape the madness, the melancholia, the panic fear which is inherent in the human situation."[2] It is not without significance that March's major breakdown in 1947 followed a long period of creative sterility.

One has only to recall the portrait of Roy Newberry in the story "Upon the Dull Earth Dwelling" to appreciate the sort of mental yearning for release March must often have experienced while he was performing the more mundane or socially onerous of his duties for

Waterman. Unlike Roy Newberry, whose fantasies progressed no further than impotent daydreaming, March, fortunately for us, possessed the exceptional talent—and the occasional touch of genius—which enabled him to transmute his fantasies into enduring works of art. Another part of him, surely, was very much like Bob Decker in "A Haircut in Toulouse," in that he too would have liked the courage to break loose and pursue a more bohemian way of life. This desire was only partially satisfied when he went to live in the French Quarter of New Orleans, for he discovered, even while he was soaking up the atmosphere where the outlandish is almost considered the norm, that he was still unable to discard completely the restrictive corsets of conformity and thus continued to preserve the outward image of the orthodox business type, obviously made uneasy if he found himself in markedly unconventional surroundings. Always, as during his visits to the Bourbon House with Bolton, he would hold back, erecting an invisible wall between himself and the rest of the company, and assume the role of an interested, but wary, passive spectator.

There is little doubt that for all his outspokenness on the tangled subject of sex, March's makeup included a very broad streak of the puritan. As a child, it will be recalled, he had been made to feel "depraved," or so he maintained. His letter to Richard Crowder, in which he made this statement, provides no details, but there is every likelihood that he was overreacting, as many a child will do, to normal adult admonitions, transposing his inherent puritan self-guilt into a guilt he believed had been imposed on him by others. The fact that by legend and tradition the bohemian life-style to which he aspired was notorious for its sexual permissiveness would not have helped to assuage the underlying guilt he was already experiencing when he made the decision, or had the decision made for him, that he should resign from Waterman. Shortly after his move to New Orleans, he did at long last come to terms, at least in part, with the duality of his character—and, to a lesser extent, his feeling of sexual guilt—through the writing of *October Island*. In that book, too, he endeavored, successfully or not, to rationalize his relationship with his father. One has the suspicion that had he lived long enough to write the story of the Campbell family—the book, according to his brother Peter, he had always wanted to write—the portrait he would have drawn of his father would have been a surprisingly affectionate and sympathetic one. It is again significant that among the not extensive collection of books March had on his shelves at 613 Dumaine Street at the time of his death was a copy of the Raven edition of *The Works of Edgar Allan Poe*, bearing John Leonard's signature and the inscription "Century, Florida, 1903."[3]

There was no deep sense of alienation between March and the other members of his immediate family. It was just that, as with relationships outside the family circle, he regarded ties as constricting, only very occasionally allowing himself to become intimately involved and then on no one else's terms but his own. Although he did, in the main, tend to keep his siblings at arm's length, there was still mutual love and respect. To most of his relatives, however, he was an enigma and, from time to time, very much a source of embarrassment, particularly so far as the March side of the family was concerned. The scholar Richebourg Gaillard McWilliams, who knew March briefly during the early and middle Waterman years, had occasion to mention March in a lecture he gave, five months or so after the author's death. When the lecture was over, a young man came up to him, introduced himself as a cousin of March's and expressed surprise at the number of times McWilliams had seen fit to mention March's work and at the way he had praised March's literary style. The young man volunteered the information that his father had always looked upon his author-nephew as the black sheep of the family. Having made that comment, the young man did not offer any explanation as to why his father should hold such an opinion, and McWilliams did not feel inclined to probe further.[4] That two of his aunts had been severely upset by the way they had seen themselves portrayed in one of March's books indicates that the young man's father was probably not alone in his opinion.

It could be, of course, that the two ladies concerned were merely being unduly sensitive, but it is more than likely that the portraits to which they took exception were either satirical or unsympathetic. Despite his statement that he would never write about his family while its members were alive, March undoubtedly did introduce his relatives now and then into his fiction. Peter Campbell, for instance, has suggested that their sister Margaret is in *The Looking-Glass*, and there is also that little vignette of the readily identifiable John Leonard and Susy Campbell in "Dirty Emma."

As has been noted, many of the women who appear in the pages of March's fiction are the villains of the piece; it is they who bring disaster to the menfolk. In a considerable number of instances, it would be fairer to say that they do what they do without really being aware of the profound havoc they are inflicting on the lives of others. They are like dark birds of fate, strangely incapable of controlling the events they have set in motion. Ruby and Abbie in *Come in at the Door* and Myrtle in *The Tallons* are prime examples. They are not basically evil women, but the results of their actions are the same sort of results that would flow from conscious evil-doing. There is substantial evil in Mitty in *Come in at the Door*, inasmuch as she is willing to do almost anything to gain her own ends. She stops short of murder, however. Baptiste's death is the evil outcome of her machinations, an outcome for which she is only indirectly responsible but which, to her discredit, she savors to the full as she witnesses Baptiste's passion on the hangman's noose, forcing Chester to observe the death agonies of his erstwhile friend and tutor. The obsessive preoccupation with evil and violence that runs like a steel thread through all of March's work, reaches its ultimate expression in the portrait of the child Rhoda Penmark. Tess Crager has recalled that she and her husband were in New York shortly before the publication of *The Bad Seed* and were invited to have drinks with Theodore Amussen at the Rinehart office. The prepublication reviews of the book had just come in and Amussen was wildly happy about them. Mrs. Crager thought he was treating the book with far more reverence than it deserved and when he asked her if she did not see it as a powerful study of the struggle between good and evil she replied: "You do not know your author as well as I do. . . . He is much more fascinated by evil."[5]

Had he lived, March would undoubtedly have found himself in sympathy with some of the subsequent fashionable teachings of Dr. R. D. Laing. Laing's thesis, developed in *The Politics of Experience*, of human alienation created by outrageous violence and resulting in the escape into so-called madness is vividly explicated in March's very first book.[6] The principal theme of *Company K* demonstrates how the collective madness of war—engendered by the vicious propaganda spewed out by political and religious leaders alike, by the rigid and frequently inhuman codes of discipline imposed by the military establishment, by the horrific, senseless slaughter on the battlefield, and by the terrible sense of isolation experienced in moments of extreme stress—reacts upon the individual soldier, driving him into insanity or an unbearable sense of guilt.

March lived during a violent and turbulent age, an age that saw two world wars and a dozen or so lesser wars, Prohibition and the rise of gangsterism, the depression, and extreme political and social unrest. Much of all this he witnessed firsthand, not only in America but also in France, Germany, and England. Although his novels and stories reflect the general tenor of the era, he rarely published—as it was fashionable to do in the 1930s and 1940s—an overt sociopolitical tract dressed up as fiction. With the possible exceptions of *Company K* and the short stories "Senator Upjohn" and "Personal Letter," March did not choose to make explicit political statements in his work. This is not to say, on the other hand, that he did not write about the conditions prevailing during the years between the two world wars. Stories such as "The First Dime," "A Snowstorm in the Alps," "The Pattern That Gulls Weave," "Runagate Niggers," and "A Short History of England" are powerful, unrelenting social studies, presented entirely without authorial comment but nonetheless vibrant with anger and full of compassion for the underdog. March's overwhelming interest, after all, was not in events but in people and what made them tick—not only how they reacted to the external pressures imposed upon them but how they coped or did not cope with the interior pressures of their own natures.

March's obsession with violence was not entirely concerned with the more recognizable physical destruction. He was also fascinated by the controlled violence of the creative mind which could produce magnificent and powerful works of art, like the Soutines he hung on the walls of his home. Robert Clark remembers being particularly impressed by the Soutines: "I think Bill lived to some extent for the horror elicited by the paintings. . . . He delighted in telling me what he knew of the artist: which was considerable. He apparently felt a kinship with some of the artists whose works found themselves on his walls."[7] As March once told Clark: "No man can be really creative until he has suffered enough."[8]

That March suffered from a series of emotional problems of varying degrees of intensity throughout much of his life cannot be denied. Only toward the end did he achieve some sort of uneasy peace within himself. His underlying attitude toward life, the uncertainties he always felt, can perhaps best be summed up in a passage from *Come in at the Door*. When Chester Hurry returns to the family home to bury his father, from whom he has been estranged for many years, he goes for a walk alone by the river where he had spent numerous hours as a child:

A feeling of despair, unreasoning and deep, came over him: an understanding of the cold cruelty which underlies everything and which will outlast everything that lives. These things came to him less definitely than thought, deeper than thought or reason, with the overwhelming sadness of music. He sat upright on the bank and looked again at the trees, the gray sky and the ceaseless river, as if to fix them in his mind forever. "What is it I want?" he asked over and over. . . . "What is it?" [*CIATD*, p. 338]

In one of his 1943 letters to Richard Crowder, March stated: "With the exception of one or two short stories, nothing that I have done has the faintest autobiographical connotation, a thing that may surprise you a little."[9] But there can be little doubt that, if not directly autobiographical, much of his material was culled from his own immediate experiences of life and his direct observations of people and events. In this respect, a large proportion of his work can perhaps be said to be *emotionally* autobiographical, rather than *factually* autobiographical: the basic situation which has been experienced in real life and the locale in which the situation existed being transposed into fictive form and intertwined with and blurred by invented detail. There is, of course, nothing in the least remarkable about this: it is a form of creative process as old as the hills and practiced in varying degrees by a great number of writers and artists. Its more obvious manifestations in the March canon appear in *Company K*, "The Little Wife," and "Personal Letter," to name but three examples.

That March fulfilled his early promise there can be no argument. Why then—and the question must be posed—is it that he has not received the ultimate recognition he so richly deserves? The failure of March's art for many of his readers lies in the fact that the style does not communicate the content. March employs a fine, workmanlike prose style, very seldom indulging in verbal pyrotechnics of any description. Consequently, the emotion and the turmoil that is the basis of all his work is so completely submerged beneath the veneer of this almost prosaic literary style that the superficial, unwary reader can perhaps be forgiven for frequently missing the point the author is making. In fact, for all his measured, often dry, and sometimes uninspired prose style, March is one of the most exciting of modern writers. He was not an innovator like Sherwood Anderson or Gertrude Stein, a stylist like Ernest Hemingway, or an experimentalist like William Faulkner, but his work provides startling, often terrifying insights into human nature, plumbing depths of the human psyche remaining totally unexplored by most other writers.

Those of his readers perceptive enough to realize and appreciate his full purpose often find themselves repelled by his subject matter and do not wish to identify, even by proxy through the printed page, with his characters. He is by no means a cozy or reassuring writer to live with. His is the voice of a rational man who possesses an uncomfortable insight into the human mind, who understands human nature to such a degree that he is capable of relating the most horrifying events and behavior patterns in quiet, even tones and with the unhurried and meticulous detail of professorial exposition.

Wally Dennis, the young aspiring novelist in James Jones's *Some Came Running*, poses the question: "I wonder if a guy could really write a book about people as they really are and still make it interesting enough to read?"[10] March's characters are certainly, in the general sense, ordinary enough. They display no Faulknerian grotesqueries or excessively flamboyant modes of behavior to keep the fantasy of fiction at one remove from the reality of life. Indeed, it is this very ordinariness of March's characters which is so disturbing, making their psychological troubles and their private hells seem frighteningly identifiable with the reader's own secret experiences of life, forcing him against his will to realize certain undeniable truths about himself he would have preferred to evade.

In this respect, March is the realistic writer par excellence, a master not only in his realistic depiction of the *external* nature of things but also in his realistic examination of the *inner* life of man—his emotions, his desires, his fears, his guilts, even his fantasies. As Alistair Cooke has expressed it:

> His art is so direct, so patently engaging, and its symbols so familiar, that the reader unwittingly recognizes his own world and gladly becomes part of it, until the line between it and the swarming pit of the unconscious is seen to be disturbingly thin. Not many people are grateful for being asked to sink themselves in a mess of human tragedy where but for the grace of God or the comforts of Mammon go they. The audience for tragedy, when its subjects are contemporary, is greatly overestimated."
> [*WMO*, p. ix]

What he observed of his fellowmen, what he discovered buried deep in their souls and in his own soul, March committed fearlessly to paper. He held no brief for those readers whom he equated with the rich and ostensibly public-spirited Mrs. Steiner in *Company K*, who is willing to entertain soldiers wounded in action, provided she does not have to endure the unpleasantness of coming face to face with anything "really revolting or gruesome" (*CK*, p. 198). March unflinchingly shows his readers the worst of life when he is convinced that this is what has to be shown, not allowing them to avert their gaze for even an instant from all the ugliness and cruelty and rending heartache that is the human condition as he so often saw it. He felt it no concern of his if, in writing truthfully about these things, he upset his readers' sensibilities. It is an unfortunate result of this ruthlessly truthful, if somewhat subjective, aspect of his art, that many readers were driven away from his books.

For all that, it must not be forgotten that while, inescapably, most of his work is devoted to an exploration of the darker areas of human behavior, this exploration is sometimes conducted with more than a glimmer of wicked humor. He is, indeed, when he wishes to be, a master of black comedy, although he tends perhaps to be a little too adept at thrusting home the knife and twisting it, in what must seem, if one did not know him better, an almost apologetic fashion, in the vitals of his unsuspecting reader. Humor does not predominate in March's work. On the other hand, he does not particularly set out to preach, nor does he set himself up as the authorial paragon with the unquestionable right to condemn. He is too aware of his own human frailty. Possessing a very deep understanding of the pressures which drive people into patterns of extreme aberrational behavior, he can consequently sympathize with and even identify with the outcasts of society. His authorial attitude is rather: "This, reader, is the way it is. Nothing will change it. All one can do is endeavor to understand. And, above all, feel compassion." He can deride and despise the social do-gooders among his characters, like Sister Joe Cotton and Mr. Hubert Palmiller of the Reedyville Vice Society, not so much because of what they do but because never, never do they show any sense of compassion for their victims. But the grief of such people in times of family tragedy evokes his compassion in exactly the same way as does, for example, the character of Ella in the short story "Tune the Old Cow Died To." The concept of retribution, divine or otherwise, was not, one suspects, one he would likely have admired, although he accepted its moral and legal justification.

That his work is full of compassion and tenderness, understanding and tolerance, often tends to be overlooked by those who prefer to criticize him for the pessimistic and, for many, unedifying content of his novels and short stories. In many ways, he was an author in advance of his time. Had he been writing now, his books surely would have received a different reception from the one they received in the 1930s and 1940s, for it is a sad fact that the cruel, unthinking, and unnecessary violence of our times has laid its hand, in one way or another, on all of us and is taken more for granted as an ingredient of life than it was even during the turbulent two decades from 1919 to 1939. The general permissiveness of our present age would also have made the sexual content of his work more readily acceptable, enabling him to treat such matters in a franker manner than he was ever allowed.

It is, of course, in many respects, a pointless exercise to attempt a prediction as to how his work would have developed, or in what direction it would have gone, had he survived that second heart attack. One can, however, speculate that he would have been urged by his publishers to follow up the success of *The Bad Seed* with a similar work, but it is unlikely that he would have agreed to be "type cast" in this fashion. He would surely have had a momentous contribution to make to the recent spate of novels about the paranormal and the supernatural. Indeed, it is not beyond the bounds of probability that he would have spearheaded the genre. We may have been given another masterpiece on the order of *The Turn of the Screw.* It would have been of great interest to see how he would have developed his gifts as a novelist. The indications are that he was already moving away from the somewhat sprawling and diffuse narratives of the past and concentrating on the shorter and more tightly structured form he had successfully achieved for the first time in *The Bad Seed.*

Even more important, he may have been given the time to complete his grand design of one hundred short stories and to publish the projected collection *Century Mark.* He was essentially a short-story writer and it is not too great a claim to make that in that genre his talent was more than once touched with genius. The best of his novels, *Company K* and *The Looking-Glass,* are each really no more than a series of related short stories welded into an integrated structure. In the less successful *Come in at the Door,* the structure remains incomplete and the relationship between the narratives is fractured by the somewhat baffling introduction of the Whisperer episodes. *The Tallons,* perhaps the least successful of the longer works, gains little from its transition and elaboration from the novella "The Unploughed Patch," the shorter work being far less labored and far more vital in its telling. The same criticism that nothing has been gained in the transition from shorter to longer work may possibly also be leveled at *October Island,* except that here the novel cannot be faulted for being in any manner labored or lacking in vitality.[11]

The cruel irony of his death, coming at the moment it did, deprived him of the immense satisfaction of the worldwide recognition he would have enjoyed following the success of *The Bad Seed.* Now March has been almost forgotten. His reputation, however, if little known at present, remains established and secure. Those of us who know, love, and admire his work live in the belief that one day March will be recognized as one of the most remarkable, talented, and shamefully neglected writers that America has produced in this or in any other century.

Notes

All interviews were conducted by the author unless otherwise noted. After the first citation of each, only the last name of the person interviewed and the date are given. For published works not included in the bibliography, full citations appear at the first mention of each one; thereafter shortened forms are used. Abbreviations of the works of William March are listed in the front of the book. Abbreviations of collections of papers follow.

DePauw Archives	DePauw University Archives, Greencastle, Indiana.
Editorial Corres., *VQR*	Editorial Correspondence of the *Virginia Quarterly Review*. No. 292, box 31. University Archives, University of Virginia Library.
GH Collection	Granville Hicks Collection, George Arents Research Library for Special Collections at Syracuse University.
H and H Collection	*Hound and Horn* Collection, Collection of American Literature, Beinecke Rare Book and Manuscript Library, Yale University.
HO Archives	Archives of Harold Ober Associates. AM 21623, boxes 4, 7, 11, 13, and 16. Princeton University Library.
Millett Collection	Fred B. Millett Collection, Collection of American Literature, Beinecke Rare Book and Manuscript Library, Yale University.
Nichols Collection	Dudley Nichols Collection, Collection of American Literature, Beinecke Rare Book and Manuscript Library, Yale University.
Notre Dame	University of Notre Dame, University Libraries, Department of Rare Books and Special Collections.
Pagany Archive	*Pagany* Archive, Special Collections, University of Delaware Library.

RH Papers   Random House Papers, Rare Book and Manuscript Library, Columbia University.

Sensabaugh Papers   Private research papers held by Mary Holmes Sensabaugh, Lexington, Virginia.

Waterman Papers   Waterman Collection, Mobile Public Library, Mobile, Alabama.

WMC Papers   William March Campbell Papers, William Stanley Hoole Special Collections Library, University of Alabama.

YR Papers   *Yale Review* Papers, Beinecke Rare Book and Manuscript Library, Yale University.

Chapter 1

1. There has always been some element of doubt regarding the correct year of March's birth, for in those days no registration of birth was required in Alabama. The family bible shows the year as 1894 and this is the year recorded not only in his university records, on his Phi Kappa Sigma initiation card, his official Marine records, but even on the memorial stone marking his grave. In 1937, when supplying biographical data to Fred B. Millett for Millett's *Contemporary American Authors* (1944), March stated that the year of his birth was 1893. When, two years later, Millett queried the date, March insisted that the earlier year was the correct one. He confirmed this in a letter he wrote to Richard Crowder on November 24, 1943, and again in the background information he provided for the entry in *Twentieth Century Authors*, edited by Stanley J. Kunitz, and published in 1955, after March's death.

2. Details regarding March's family background are unfortunately not easy to come by. Very little information has found its way into print and the small amount of unpublished information available to the researcher is not altogether reliable, depending, as so much of it does, on family reminiscences passed down from generation to generation. It has not therefore proved possible to reconcile certain discrepancies both in names and dates, nor to account satisfactorily for minor variations in accounts of family events. Much of the information concerning March's antecedents is drawn from a letter dated June 7, 1937, which March sent to Millett. I am indebted to Donald Gallup, Curator, Collection of American Literature, Beinecke Rare Book and Manuscript Library, Yale University, for providing me with a Xerox copy of this letter. For further elucidating information regarding the March and Campbell families, I am also indebted to Homer W. Jones, Jr., the son of March's elder sister Margaret, and to March's younger brother Peter Campbell and his wife Gwen. William T. Going's essays, "Some in Addition: The Uncollected Stories of William March" and "William March: Regional Perspective and Beyond" (both cited in full elsewhere), have also provided rich source material.

3. Gwen Campbell, interview with Preston C. Beyer, New York, July 30, 1976.

4. This school report is among the WMC Papers.

5. Alistair Cooke, *WMO*, p. vi.

6. Lincoln Kirstein to Roy S. Simmonds (hereafter, RSS), Sept. 4, 1978.

7. Nicholas S. McGowin, interview, London, Feb. 27, 1972.

8. Dr. Edward Glover, interview, London, Aug. 3, 1971.

9. Glover, Aug. 3, 1971.

10. McGowin, Feb. 27, 1972.

11. Robert Clark to RSS, May 10, 1976.

12. J. Finley McRae, Sensabaugh Papers.

13. March to Dudley Nichols, Nov. 29, 1952, Nichols Collection.

14. Going, "William March," p. 432.

15. *Wilson Library Bulletin* 17 (June 1943): 786.

16. Margaret's scrapbooks form part of the WMC Papers.

17. I am indebted to the late Mrs. Ruth Warren, Special Collections, Mobile Public Library, for her assistance in providing information relating to the organization of the lumber industry in Alabama and of the social life in the mill towns.

18. "The Gulf Coast Country," *Alabama's New Era: A Magazine of Progress and Development* (Alabama State Board of Immigration, 1911), pp. 94–95.

19. *Wilson Library Bulletin* 17 (June 1943): 786.

20. *Forum* 82 (Oct. 1929): lxiv.

21. March to Millett, June 7, 1937, Millett Collection.

22. Sensabaugh Papers. According to Margaret, William's romantic feelings toward Bessie Riles lasted at least up to the time he was attending Valparaiso University during the years 1913 and 1914. In his essay "William March: Regional Perspective and Beyond," William T. Going records that March's roommate at Valparaiso, Yulee Mann, was also in love with Bessie and that "March actually wrote Mann's love letters back to Miss Riles, whom Mann later married" (p. 437). Margaret claimed to have sung at the wedding of Yulee Mann and Bessie Riles.

23. Peak, "William March and His Short Stories," p. 4.

24. Lombard Jones to RSS, Oct. 18, 1976.

25. March to Marie Campbell, May 22, 1917, copy in Sensabaugh Papers.

Chapter 2

1. U.S. Marine Corps records, Department of the Navy, Headquarters United States Marine Corps, Washington. I am indebted to Brigadier General E. H. Simmons, director of Marine Corps History and Museums for his invaluable assistance in making Marine Corps records available to me.

2. March to Marie Campbell, Aug. 18, 1917, copy in Sensabaugh Papers.

3. The war letters March sent to his sister Margaret are unfortunately no

longer extant. He subsequently used them as the basis for his novel *Company K*. Once the novel was completed, he apparently destroyed the letters, possibly feeling that the immediacy of the emotions they expressed ran counter to his retrospective attitudes toward the war. No personal record of March's service overseas is accordingly available, other than those he fictionalized in *Company K*. The course and nature of March's war experiences can, however, be reconstructed, albeit inadequately, by drawing on U.S. Marine Corps archives, various official and unofficial histories of the war, and the memoirs of the men who fought. Most of the material in this chapter was gleaned from the following sources: Major James M. Yingling, U.S.M.C., *A Brief History of the 5th Marines* (Washington: Historical Branch, G-3 Division Headquarters, U.S. Marine Corps, 1963; revised 1968); Laurence Stallings, *The Doughboys: The Story of the AEF, 1917–1918* (New York: Harper & Row, 1963); John Dos Passos, *Mr. Wilson's War* (London: Hamish Hamilton, 1963); and John W. Thomason, Jr., *Fix Bayonets!* (New York: Scribner's, 1927).

4. *Forum* 82 (Oct. 1929): lxiv.

5. U.S. Marine Corps records.

6. Yingling, *A Brief History of the 5th Marines*, pp. 11–12.

7. See Going, "William March," p. 433.

8. Edmund Wilson, *A Prelude* (New York: Farrar, Straus & Giroux, 1967), p. 269.

9. U.S. Marine Corps records.

Chapter 3

1. J. P. Case, Sensabaugh Papers.

2. Arthur Calder-Marshall to RSS, June 3, 1976.

3. J. P. Case, Sensabaugh Papers; Lombard Jones to RSS, Oct. 18, 1976; Harry T. Moore to RSS, Nov. 14, 1976.

4. J. Finley McRae and Mrs. Robert Pratt, Sensabaugh Papers.

5. J. Finley McRae, Sensabaugh Papers.

6. Mrs. Robert Pratt, Sensabaugh Papers.

7. March to Millett, June 7, 1937.

8. Paul Engle to Ellen Fay Peak, Jan. 19, 1962.

9. Hugh Ford, *Published in Paris* (London: Garnstone Press, 1975), p. 175; Malcolm Cowley, *Exile's Return* (London: Faber & Faber, 1961), pp. 249–50.

10. Alistair Cooke, *WMO*, p. vi.

11. Peter Campbell, interview with Preston C. Beyer, New York, July 30, 1976.

12. Attested statement by E. Herdon Smith of a conversation with Harry Hardy Smith, Dec. 26, 1972.

13. Joseph Dickinson to RSS, Aug. 10, 1976.

14. J. Finley McRae, Sensabaugh Papers.

15. J. Finley McRae, Sensabaugh Papers.

16. J. P. Case, Sensabaugh Papers.

17. *Wilson Library Bulletin* 17 (June 1943): 786.

18. Margaret Deland to March, Jan. 19, 1931, WMC Papers.

19. Lombard Jones, who was to join *Forum* in 1931 and to marry the magazine's fiction editor in September 1933, has recalled in a letter to RSS dated October 18, 1976, that Edith Walton considered March's "The Holly Wreath" to be a superior story to Faulkner's "A Rose for Emily." "Faulkner's was a contrived horror story, via Edgar Allen Poe out of Grand Guignol. March's, on the other hand, came out of an experience that anguished his soul from the day it happened in World War I until the day he died." What exactly that experience was, however, is not at all clear.

20. Quoted in Michael S. Reynold's *Hemingway's First War* (Princeton, N.J.: Princeton University Press, 1976), p. 83.

21. "Our Rostrum," *Forum* 82 (Dec. 1929): 1.

Chapter 4

1. Lombard Jones to RSS, Oct. 18, 1976.

2. March to Waterman, April 7, 1930, Waterman Papers.

3. J. P. Case, Sensabaugh Papers.

4. March to Kirstein, March 26, 1930, *H and H* Collection.

5. March to Frederick, May 30, 1930, Notre Dame.

6. Frederick to March, Aug. 17, 1930, Notre Dame.

7. March to Frederick, Aug. 29, 1930, Notre Dame.

8. Those of Somerville, Terwilliger, Frankel, Romano, Calhoun, Keith, and Howie.

9. Frederick to March, Dec. 3, 1930, Notre Dame.

10. March to Frederick, Dec. 26, 1930, Notre Dame.

11. March to Frederick, June 16, 1930, Notre Dame.

12. March to Frederick, Sept. 6, 1930, Notre Dame.

13. The reaction to "Flight to Confusion" was a foretaste of the frequent reaction March was to receive in the future to what were, for their time, regarded as unacceptably outrageous stories. Magazine editors simply would not touch them. In the following year, the somewhat innocuous story "Woolen Underwear" was rejected by the editor of *Virginia Quarterly Review* on the grounds that it made "hot reading for July in Virginia." Unlike "Woolen Underwear" (to be published in 1934 in *Esquire* under the title "Mrs. Joe Cotton" and again in 1935 under the title "The Woolen Drawers" in *Golden Book Magazine*), three stories—"The Shoe Drummer" (as "Flight to Confusion" was eventually to be called), "A Memorial to the Slain," and "The Borax Bottle," which he was to write in 1937 and 1943 respectively—never in fact attained magazine publication and did not appear in print until March included them in short-story collections: "The Shoe Drummer" and "A Memorial to the Slain" in *Some Like Them Short* and "The Borax Bottle" in *Trial*

Balance. In contrast to "The Shoe Drummer," which typifies March's morbid interest in mental and sexual aberration, the latter two deliciously lighthearted stories provide perfect examples of the delight March always derived from giving expression to his wicked sense of humor and shocking people. It is not difficult to appreciate that in the moral climate of those days these stories, while they would cause little stir if they were to be published for the first time in magazines today, dealt with what were then regarded as "forbidden subjects." In publishing them, editors would have undoubtedly upset the sensibilities of many of their readers and, indeed, even run the risk of possible legal action. In this respect, March was far ahead of his time. He would have led a happier life as a writer had he been publishing his work in the 1960s and 1970s, enjoying the freedom of expression that a more permissive age allowed its artists.

14. March to Lambert Davis, Aug. 25, 1930, Editorial Corres., *VQR*.

15. March to Johns, Dec. 7, 1930, *Pagany* Archive.

16. March to Frederick, Oct. 28, 1930, Notre Dame.

17. "George and Charlie," "The Monument," "Raise in Pay," and "The Unploughed Patch." "Raise in Pay" may possibly have been an earlier version of the story eventually published under the title "Upon the Dull Earth Dwelling."

18. March to Frederick, Oct. 18, 1930, Notre Dame.

19. Waterman to March, Oct. 8, 1931, Waterman Papers.

20. March to Waterman, Oct. 9, 1931, Waterman Papers.

21. March to Waterman, Oct. 20, 1931, Waterman Papers.

22. Frederick to March, Jan. 27, 1931, Notre Dame.

23. José Garcia Villa, interview with Preston C. Beyer, New York, Oct. 7, 1976.

24. Villa to March, Aug. 5, 1931, in the possession of Mrs. Cameron Plummer, Mobile, Ala.

25. These stories were "He Sits There All Day Long" and "Nine Prisoners."

26. March to Hicks, Nov. 17, 1931, GH Collection.

27. "Our Rostrum," *Forum* 87 (Feb. 1932): xx, xxii–xxiii.

28. Villa, Oct. 7, 1976.

29. Lombard Jones to RSS, Oct. 18, 1976.

30. Granville Hicks to RSS, Sept. 20, 1976.

31. Lombard Jones to RSS, Oct. 18, 1976.

32. Ibid.

33. J. P. Case, Sensabaugh Papers.

34. Lombard Jones to RSS, Oct. 18, 1976.

35. Lois Cole Taylor to RSS, Nov. 11, 1976.

36. Kirstein to RSS, Sept. 4, 1978.

37. Halper to RSS, Nov. 12, 1976.

38. Villa to March, June 11, 1932, in the possession of Mrs. Cameron Plummer.

39. Villa, Oct. 7, 1976.

40. Villa to March, June 20, 1932, in the possession of Mrs. Cameron Plummer.

41. The stories Villa discussed were "The Eager Mechanic," "I've Baked My Bread," "Come in at the Door," "Light," and "It Will Be Nice to Be Old."

42. Villa to March, Aug. 1, 1932, in the possession of Mrs. Cameron Plummer.

43. Villa to March, Aug. 19, 1932, in the possession of Mrs. Cameron Plummer.

44. Villa to March, Aug. 22, 1932, in the possession of Mrs. Cameron Plummer.

45. Villa to March, Aug. 24, 1932, in the possession of Mrs. Cameron Plummer.

46. Villa to March, Aug. 27, 1932, in the possession of Mrs. Cameron Plummer.

47. March to Hicks, March 7, 1932, GH Collection.

48. March to Johns, Jan. 13, 1932, *Pagany* Archive.

49. March to Hicks, March 7, 1932, GH Collection.

50. Kirstein to March, May 27, 1932, *H and H* Collection.

51. These stories were "George and Charlie," "Sixteen and the Unknown Soldier," "Two Soldiers," "The American Diseur," "The Arrogant Shoat," and "Happy Jack." Had it not been for the unfortunate demise of *Clay* and *Contact* that year and the editorial rescheduling imposed by Johns by the impending demise of *Pagany*, March would probably have had at least a dozen stories published during 1932.

52. *O. Henry Memorial Award Prize Stories of 1932* (Garden City, N.Y.: Doubleday, Doran, 1932), pp. xviii–xix.

53. March to Frederick, Sept. 11, 1932, Notre Dame.

54. March to Frederick, Sept. 19, 1932, Notre Dame.

55. March to Hicks, Nov. 22, 1932, GH Collection.

56. March to Miss Louise Bonino, Jan. 13, 1933, RH Papers.

Chapter 5

1. Kirstein to RSS, Sept. 4, 1978. In a letter Kirstein wrote to March, shortly after the publication of *Company K*, he regretted "very much the exclusion of several passages which would have made it that much more unbearable" (Kirstein to March, February 6, 1933, *H and H* Collection).

2. The Private Charles Upson section.

3. The Private Leo Brogan section.

4. L. P. Hartley, supplement to the *Week-End Review* 7 (March 25, 1933): 336.

5. Bolton, "Bill March." Unpublished memoir. Ribbon copy in possession of Bolton's widow, carbon copy in possession of RSS.

6. Glover, Aug. 3, 1971.

7. Dickinson to RSS, Aug. 10, 1976.

8. Haas to March, Jan. 26, 1933, RH Papers.

9. Arthur Ruhl, "As It Was," *Saturday Review* 9 (Jan. 28, 1933): 399.

10. Smith to March, Jan. 31, 1933, RH Papers.

11. "New Books," *Catholic World*, June 1933, p. 370.

12. In the first and second printings of the first U.S. edition, the passage reads: "I was lying in the wheat near Captain Matlock when he got hit and I was the first man to reach him. One machine gun bullet had hit him squarely between the eyes, plowing through his head and coming out at the base of his skull." In the third printing, it reads: "I was lying in the wheat not far from an officer when he got hit and I was the first man to reach him. One machine gun bullet had hit him squarely between the eyes, plowing through his head and coming out at the base of his skull. It was getting dark and his face was covered with blood. I thought it was Captain Matlock."

13. March to Haas, Feb. 4, 1933, RH Papers.

14. March to Smith, Feb. 27, 1933, RH Papers.

15. Quoted by Sheila Hodges in *Gollancz: The Story of a Publishing House 1928–1978* (London: Victor Gollancz, 1978), p. 117.

16. Gollancz to Hughes Massie, records of Victor Gollancz Ltd.

17. Phyllis Bentley, "The War and Company K Through American Eyes," *Evening Chronicle*, March 21, 1933, p. 14.

18. E. M. Delafield, "Miss E. M. Delafield Discovers a Masterpiece," *Morning Post*, March 21, 1933, p. 14.

19. Gerald Gould, "Aspects of War and Peace," *Observer,* March 19, 1933, p. 6.

20. H. L. Morrow, *John O'London's Weekly* 28 (April 1, 1933): 1057.

21. Eric Gillett, "New Fiction," *Time and Tide* 14 (March 25, 1933): 362.

22. March to Waterman, n.d., Waterman Papers.

23. March to Waterman, Feb. 18, 1933, Waterman Papers.

24. Smith to March, March 7, 1933, RH Papers.

25. March to Roberts, March 23, 1933, Waterman Papers.

26. March to Roberts, May 30, 1933, Waterman Papers.

27. For the complete text of March's letter of March 23, 1933, to Roberts, see Simmonds, "William March's 'Personal Letter.'"

28. March to Smith & Haas, April 29, 1933, RH Papers.

29. "The Eager Mechanic" in the January-February 1933 issue of *Midland*; "The Unploughed Patch" in the final issue of *Pagany*; "This Heavy Load" in the December 1933 *Forum*; and "The Pattern That Gulls Weave" (the only short story he wrote that year other than "Personal Letter") in the December 1933 *Story*.

30. "The American Diseur," "The Arrogant Shoat," "Happy Jack," and "Two Soldiers."

31. March to Smith & Haas, Oct. 21, 1933, RH Papers.

32. March to Smith & Haas, Dec. 2, 1933, RH Papers.

33. Smith & Haas to March, Dec. 23, 1933, RH Papers.

34. Bonino to March, Jan. 9, 1934, RH Papers.

Chapter 6

1. March to Millett, June 7, 1937, Millett Collection.

2. Ibid.

3. In a letter to the novelist Evelyn Scott dated May 12, 1934, March blamed his German secretary for the excessive printing and grammatical errors in the American proofs of the novel. Evelyn Scott Collection, Humanities Research Center, The University of Texas at Austin.

4. March to Crowder, Nov. 24, 1943, DePauw Archives.

5. Lucas Stanford, "Come in at the Door," *Atlantic Journal*, April 15, 1934.

6. Charles Clayton, *St. Louis Globe Democrat*, March 17, 1934.

7. Fred T. Marsh, "'Come in at the Door' and Other Recent Works of Fiction," *New York Times Book Review*, Feb. 25, 1934, p. 8.

8. Francis Iles, "New Fiction," *Daily Telegraph*, Aug. 17, 1934.

9. Graham Greene, "Fiction," *Spectator* 153 (Aug. 24, 1934): 264.

10. March to Crowder, Nov. 24, 1943, DePauw Archives.

11. Marie Campbell, Sensabaugh Papers.

12. See Christopher Isherwood, *Christopher and His Kind* (New York: Farrar, Straus & Giroux, 1976), p. 122.

13. Engle to RSS, May 24, 1976.

14. Finley McRae, Sensabaugh Papers.

15. Calder-Marshall to RSS, June 3, 1976.

16. Going, "William March," p. 436.

17. Kay Boyle to RSS, March 8, 1976.

18. These stories were "The Eager Mechanic," "The Pattern That Gulls Weave," "This Heavy Load," and "The Unploughed Patch."

19. Smith to March, Aug. 28, 1934, RH Papers. "The First Sunset" had not at that date been published and was probably an early and subsequently discarded version of the story bearing the same title which was eventually published, in an obviously much longer version, in *American Prefaces* in 1940. According to the date of composition given it by March in *Trial Balance*, this final version was written in 1938. March thought sufficiently well of the story to have it privately printed after its appearance in *American Prefaces* and distributed as 1940 Christmas cards to friends and relatives.

20. March to Haas, Oct. 19, 1934, RH Papers.

21. Glover, Aug. 3, 1971.

22. Glover, Aug. 3, 1971; Miss Lillian Jackson to RSS, Dec. 11, 1972.

23. Halper to RSS, Nov. 12, 1976.

24. Albert Halper, *Good-bye, Union Square* (Chicago: Quadrangle Books, 1970), p. 207.

25. Engle to March, Dec. 21, 1942, WMC Papers.

26. Engle to Nicholas McGowin, Sept. 18, 1954, WMC Papers.

27. Engle to Ellen Fay Peak, Jan. 19, 1962.

28. W. J. Bedding to RSS, May 17, 1976.

Chapter 7

1. Robert Clark to RSS, May 10, 1976.

2. March to Nichols, Nov. 29, 1952, Nichols Collection.

3. Cooke, *WMO*, p. ix.

4. Fred T. Marsh, "The Fine Tales of William March," *New York Times Book Review*, Feb. 17, 1935, p. 2.

5. Elizabeth Hart, "Unforgettable and Disturbing Tales," *New York Herald Tribune Book Review*, Feb. 10, 1935, p. 3.

6. Cyril Connolly, "The Little Wife and Other Stories," *New Statesman*, March 30, 1935, p. 462.

7. Anon., "The Little Wife," *Times Literary Supplement*, May 16, 1935, p. 312.

8. Clay Shaw, interview, London, Aug. 31, 1972.

9. Glover, who died in 1972 at the age of eighty-four, was a recognized authority on the works of Sigmund Freud and was regarded as one of the leading psychoanalysts of his day. Born in Lesmahagow, Scotland, in 1888, he was educated at the University of Glasgow, graduating in 1915. For a time, he held the post of house physician and house surgeon at the Glasgow Royal Infirmary and at the Royal Hospital for Sick Children. He subsequently became superintendent of the Birmingham Municipal Sanatorium. In 1923, however, he decided to concentrate on the subject which was to constitute his true life's work—medical psychology—and he began practicing as a consultant in London. The author of many books and a well-known broadcaster on psychoanalysis, he held office as secretary of the International Psycho-Analytic Association and the British Psycho-Analytic Society and as chairman of the Medical Section of the British Psychological Society.

10. Glover, Aug. 3, 1971.

11. Moore to RSS, Sept. 8, 1977.

12. Glover to RSS, Sept. 8, 1971.

13. Going, "William March," p. 438.

14. Glover, Aug. 3, 1971.

15. March to Crowder, Jan. 18, 1944, DePauw Archives.

16. Engle to Peak, Jan. 19, 1962.

17. William M. Beasley to RSS, Nov. 6, 1972.

18. Calder-Marshall to RSS, June 7, 1976.

19. Dickinson to RSS, Aug. 10, 1976.

20. O'Loughlin to RSS, Oct. 14, 1978.

21. Kay Boyle to RSS, May 23, 1976.

22. The Rich & Cowan edition uses the English spelling "grey."

Chapter 8

1. March to Crowder, Nov. 23, 1943, DePauw Archives.

2. Clark to RSS, May 10, 1976.

3. March to Millett, June 7, 1937, Millett Collection.

4. Going, "Some in Addition," p. 88.

5. Going, "William March," p. 437.

6. T. S. Eliot, *Elizabethan Essays* (London: Faber & Faber, 1934), p. 61.

7. March to Millett, June 7, 1937, Millett Collection.

8. Ibid.

9. Anon., "A Captive World," *Times Literary Supplement*, Sept. 5, 1936, p. 711.

10. Charles Hanson Towne, "Books," *New York American*, Oct. 21, 1936.

11. Harold Strauss, "A Strange Triangle," *New York Times Book Review*, Oct. 25, 1936, pp. 22–23.

12. Mark Schorer, "Books in Brief," *New Republic* 89 (Nov. 25, 1936): 126.

13. Helen Neville, "Craftsmanship," *Nation* 143 (Nov. 14, 1936): 582.

14. Mary Colum, "Tragedy of Inadequacy," *Forum* 97 (Jan. 1937): 34–35.

15. Lawrence E. Spivak to Haas, May 14, 1937; Haas to Spivak, June 14, 1937; Random House to Spivak, Aug. 26, 1937, RH Papers. (Spivak was the business manager of the *American Mercury*.)

16. March to Millett, June 7, 1937, Millett Collection.

17. These stories were "The Listening Post," "A Short History of England," "Time and Leigh Brothers," "Not Worthy of a Wentworth," "A Memorial to the Slain," "Tune the Old Cow Died To," "Not Very—Subtle," "Runagate Niggers," "The Female of the Fruit Fly," "The Funeral," "A Haircut in Toulouse," "Whistles," and "Cinderella's Slipper."

18. "The Last Meeting," "Maybe the Sun Will Shine" ("Bill's Eyes"), "Geraldette," and "Sweet, Who Was the Armourer's Maid?"

19. The exact circumstances surrounding March's resignation from Waterman are something of a mystery. According to a statement made by Paul Strickland (a friend of March's later years) to William M. Beasley, March was requested by Ed Roberts to resign when he failed to answer letters and to keep the company's head office in Mobile informed about what was going on in London. Both Nicholas McGowin and Miss Lillian Jackson doubt the veracity of this. However, the Evelyn Scott Collection, Humanities Research Center, The University of Texas at Austin, holds a letter March wrote to Evelyn Scott on April 17, 1939, in which he refers to having been ousted from office, despite what may have been stated publicly. The letter gives no details of the reasons for his being required to terminate his employment with the company.

20. March to Margaret Jones, Dec. 29, 1937, quoted in a letter from Homer W. Jones, Jr., to RSS, July 10, 1972. Both the *New Yorker* and March's literary agents, Harold Ober Associates, confirm that there is no record of any sale of March's work to the magazine, *New Yorker* to RSS, Oct. 17, 1972; Patricia Powell to RSS, Nov. 14, 1972.

21. Carson McCullers to March, April 22, 1938, WMC Papers.

22. Shaw was to acquire unwanted fame in March 1967 when he was arrested by the New Orleans district attorney, Jim Garrison, and accused of involvement in an alleged conspiracy resulting in President John F. Kennedy's

assassination in November 1963. The subsequent trial in 1969 ended with Shaw's complete exoneration, the jury unanimously returning a verdict of not guilty.

23. Shaw, Aug. 31, 1972.

24. Smythe to RSS, Feb. 17, 1976.

25. Going, "William March," p. 440.

26. Shaw, Aug. 31, 1972.

27. Ibid.

28. Edith Roberts, "The Devious Labyrinth of the Mind," *Chicago Sun*, Jan. 24, 1943.

29. William Du Bois, "Alabama Townfolk," *New York Times Book Review*, Jan. 10, 1943, pp. 4–5.

30. Smythe to RSS, Feb. 17, 1976.

31. It is perhaps possible to include in this category March's story of his escapade in penetrating the German lines during World War I, the "Ballad of the Bowie Knives" episode, and even the story of his bayoneting the young German soldier.

32. J. P. Case, Sensabaugh Papers; McGowin to RSS, Feb. 20, 1976.

33. Going, "Some in Addition," p. 84.

34. Shaw, Aug. 31, 1972.

35. Cooke, *WMO*, p. viii.

36. Glover, Aug. 3, 1971.

37. These were "The First Sunset," "You and Your Sister," and "Transcribed Album of Familiar Music."

38. March to McAfee, July 19, 1938, *YR* Papers.

39. March to McAfee, July 23, 1938, *YR* Papers.

40. March to Crowder, Jan. 18, 1944, DePauw Archives.

41. March to Everitt, Oct. 28, 1938, Little, Brown & Company records.

42. Everitt to March, Nov. 1, 1938, quoted in a letter dated April 10, 1945, from Little, Brown & Company to Harold Ober Associates, HO Archives.

43. March to McAfee, Nov. 2, 1938, *YR* Papers.

44. March to McAfee, Nov. 8, 1938, *YR* Papers.

Chapter 9

1. *Columbia Workshop Plays: Fourteen Radio Dramas*, selected and ed. Douglas Coulter (New York: Whittlesley House, 1939), p. 272.

2. March to Crowder, Jan. 18, 1944, DePauw Archives; Marion Davenport to Lawrence William Jones, July 8, 1970.

3. March to Nichols, Nov. 29, 1952, Nichols Collection.

4. N. L. Rotham, "A Developing Talent," *Saturday Review* 19 (March 18, 1939): 10.

5. Harry Hansen, "The First Reader," *New York World-Telegram*, April 29, 1939.

6. James Gray, "Brevity Carried to Inane Degree by William March," *St. Paul* (Minn.) *Dispatch*, March 21, 1939.

7. Villa to March, May 24, 1939, in the possession of Mrs. Cameron Plummer.

8. Peter and Gwen Campbell, July 30, 1976.

9. Ibid.

10. March to Crowder, Nov. 24, 1943, DePauw Archives.

11. Going, "Some in Addition," p. 89.

12. Lowry achieved national and international fame in later years as the author of the terse war novel *Casualty*, as well as many other distinguished novels and short stories. He founded *The Little Man Magazine* in 1937 on campus at the University of Cincinnati. The magazine folded when Lowry left the campus in March 1938, but after touring America he recommended publishing the magazine off-campus. All of these activities developed into the founding of the Little Man Press, which specialized in publishing modest limited editions of works by celebrated writers of the day.

13. Lowry to RSS, Sept. 25, 1976.

14. Villa to March, March 17, 1941, in the possession of Mrs. Cameron Plummer.

15. Hardwick to March, Aug. 19, 1941, WMC Papers.

16. March to Everitt, April 11, 1942, Little, Brown & Company records.

17. Engle to Peak, Jan. 19, 1962.

18. Finley McRae, Sensabaugh Papers.

19. Clay Shaw, Aug. 31, 1972.

20. Halper to RSS, Nov. 12, 1976. See also Halper's *Good-bye, Union Square*, pp. 208–209, for an amusing account of the goings-on at one of March's parties.

21. March to Everitt, Aug. 9, 1942, Little, Brown & Co. records.

22. March to Everitt, Sept. 1, 1942, Little, Brown & Co. records.

23. Everitt to March, Sept. 3, 1942, Little, Brown & Co. records.

24. March to Everitt, Sept. 10, 1942, Little, Brown & Co. records.

25. March to Everitt, Sept. 22, 1942, Little, Brown & Co. records.

26. March to Everitt, Oct. 2, 1942, Little, Brown & Co. records.

Chapter 10

1. Cooke, *WMO*, p. vii.

2. March to Crowder, Nov. 24, 1943, DePauw Archives.

3. Stanley Edgar Hyman, "Alabama Faulkner," *New Republic* 108 (1943): 187–88.

4. March to Crowder, Nov. 24, 1943, and Jan. 18, 1944, DePauw Archives.

5. Crowder, "The Novels of William March," p. 125.

6. M.M., "Segments of World Aflame Pictured in Three Books," *Los Angeles Times*, March 7, 1943.

7. William Du Bois, "Alabama Townfolk," *New York Times Book Review*, Jan. 10, 1943, pp. 4–5.

8. Diana Trilling, "Fiction in Review," *Nation* 156 (Jan. 30, 1943): 172.

9. Helen B. Cole, "Reflection of Life as seen in a Coney Island Distorting Glass," *New York Daily Worker*, Jan. 31, 1943.

10. Iris Barry, "Books and Things," *New York Herald Tribune*, Jan. 16, 1943, p. 11.

11. Anon., *Wilson Library Bulletin* 17 (June 1943): 786.

12. *Saturday Review*, May 1, 1943, back cover.

13. Everitt to March, May 4, 1943, Little, Brown & Co. records.

14. See "Editor's Note," *Old Line* 12 (April 1943): 1. Further information regarding the magazine and Professor MacLeod's work in soliciting material for this special issue was kindly provided by Robert E. L. Hall, McKeldin Library, University of Maryland, in a letter to RSS, April 6, 1976.

15. Cooke, *WMO*, p. vii.

16. Only one story in the whole of the March canon contains any direct reference to the fighting in World War II. This is "One Way Ticket," published in the January 1946 issue of *Good Housekeeping*. Gazing into a gilt-framed mirror in a shop window, a mother sees an image of her dead son, killed in the Pacific war: "There was a little island with palm trees on it. There was a beach of white sand, too, and Martin lying there alone, his feet in the direction of the trees, his head toward the water; and every now and then a small wave came up and washed over his pitiful dead face."

17. Boyle to RSS, May 23, 1976.

18. Moore to RSS, Nov. 14, 1976.

19. Boyle to RSS, June 24, 1977.

20. Boyle to RSS, May 23, 1976.

21. March to Crowder, Nov. 24, 1943, DePauw Archives.

22. March to Crowder, Jan. 18, 1944, DePauw Archives.

23. Ibid.

24. Details regarding March's hysterical eye condition have been culled from the following sources: Bolton, "Bill March"; Clark to RSS, April 26, 1976; Gwen Campbell, New York, July 30, 1976.

25. Wilkinson to Ober Aug. 4, 1944, box 4, HO Archives.

26. Kate O'Brien, "Fiction," *Spectator* 173 (July 7, 1944): 20.

27. Anon., *Times Literary Supplement*, July 8, 1944, p. 329.

28. Ralph Straus, "New Novels," *Sunday Times* (London), Aug. 6, 1944, p. 3.

29. "One Way Ticket," *Good Housekeeping* 122 (January 1946).

30. Seymour Lawrence, "Memoir of a 50-year-old Publisher on His Voyage to Outer Space," in *The Little Magazine in America: A Modern Documentary History*, ed. Elliott Anderson and Mary Kinzie (New York: Pushcart Press, 1978), pp. 146–47.

Chapter 11

1. March was not, on the other hand, as has already been mentioned, satisfied with the original version of "The Holly Wreath," as a comparison of the opening paragraphs of the *Forum* and *Trial Balance* texts will demonstrate. First, the *Forum* text:

To the left of the village square, a dead mule lay on a manure heap. Its stiff legs were stretched to the June sky and its glazed eyes, wide open and rolled backward, were like two pieces of dirty mica. Its yellow teeth were bared in a fixed snarl. From between its teeth there hung a swollen purple tongue, and over it flies crawled and disputed and lived amorously.

Corporal Reagan and his water detail surveyed the wrecked village with interest. After a moment they saw the well at which they were to fill their canteens: it was in the center of the ruined square.

"The Germans sure gave this place hell!" said Reagan.

"You said it!" agreed Private Bouton. [*Forum* 82 (Oct. 1929): 235]

Now the *Trial Balance* text:

To the left of the village square, a dead mule lay on a manure heap. Its legs were stretched to the June sky and its glazed eyes, wide open and rolled backward, were like pieces of dirty mica. Its yellow teeth were bared in a snarl. From between its teeth there hung a swollen purple tongue, and over it flies crawled and disputed and lived amorously.

Corporal Reagan and his water detail stood silent and surveyed the wrecked village. After a moment they saw the well at which they were to fill their canteens. It was in the center of the ruined square. "They really put the bee on this place," said Bouton mildly. "They did for a fact." He turned, as if for confirmation, to Keeney—but Keeney said nothing at all. [*TB*, p. 16]

In the later version, one can see at work the hand of the master who has learned his craft over the years: the deletion, in the first paragraph, of the wholly superfluous adjectives "stiff," "two," and "fixed"; the substitution of the phrase "stood silent" for the phrase "with interest" in the opening sentence of the second paragraph conveying more tellingly the feeling of awe the three men experience as they enter the devastated village; and the transfer of the initial comment from Reagan to Bouton, allowing March to introduce immediately and unobtrusively the third member of the water detail.

2. March to Nichols, Sept. 11, 1952, Nichols Collection.

3. In a further letter, dated October 7, 1952, to Nichols (Nichols Collection), March discussed a comment Nichols had made in a previous letter about "the indefinable significance" of names he had seen in the past, or of happenings he had experienced. March admitted having had himself a number of experiences which ostensibly had meant "so much more than they could mean" and, as an example, he related an incident which he had witnessed as a child of eight, when the Campbell family had been living in Century, Florida, an incident which undoubtedly provided one of the germs of the story "Dirty Emma":

There was an old woman, the Widow Winkler, who, although white, was so poor that she "took in washing," an unforgivable offense in the South at that time for a white woman. One night the shack of the Widow Winkler (she had a big, silly daughter named Emma who went to school with me) caught fire and the whole town turned out. The whites stood on one side and the negroes on the other, watching the conflagration with fascination, but nobody tried to put it out. Emma came rushing out of the house with a plain white cup in her hands. She showed it to everybody alike and kept saying, "Well, anyway, they didn't burn up my cup!"

4. This method of murder was also to be used by Rhoda Penmark to dispose of the janitor Leroy Jessup in *The Bad Seed*.

5. Meridel Le Sueur, "No Easy Handshake," *New Masses*, Jan. 22, 1946.

6. Ira Wolfert, "William March's short stories: 'fine, yet heartbreaking,'" *PM*, Oct. 28, 1945.

7. John Farrar, "The Unimportance of Life," *Saturday Review* 28 (Oct. 28, 1945): 44.

8. Alistair Cooke, "The World of William March," *New Republic* 113 (Dec. 1945).

9. Villa to March, Nov. 5, 1945, in the possession of Mrs. Cameron Plummer.

10. Villa to March, Nov. 23 and Nov. 29, 1945, in the possession of Mrs. Cameron Plummer.

11. Moore to RSS, Nov. 14, 1976.

12. Ibid.

13. Smythe to RSS, Feb. 17, 1976.

14. Lombard Jones to RSS, Oct. 18, 1976. March, apparently, was in no doubt that Lizzie Borden was guilty of the double murder of her parents and was convinced that no blood had been discovered on her clothing simply because she had been stark naked when she had wielded the axe. It is a theory that has been postulated and accepted in many quarters. A recent TV film of the Lizzie Borden case, with Elizabeth Montgomery in the leading role, showed the murder of the father being committed in such manner.

15. Going, "Some in Addition," p. 90.

16. Boyle to RSS, June 24, 1977.

17. Crager to Hamblen, March 5, 1971.

18. "Warlock," *New Orleans Item*, May 2, 1952.

19. Gwen Campbell, July 30, 1976.

20. Foley to RSS, Dec. 3, 1976.

21. Glover, Aug. 3, 1971.

22. J. P. Case, Sensabaugh Papers.

Chapter 12

1. March to Ober, May 1, 1948, box 7, HO Archives.

2. March to Ober, Aug. 16, 1948, box 7, HO Archives.

3. Shaw, Aug. 31, 1972.

4. J. P. Case, Sensabaugh Papers.

5. Mrs. Ada Broadnax, Sensabaugh Papers.

6. Mr. and Mrs. Nicholas S. McGowin, interview, London, Sept. 27, 1972.

7. Klaus Perls, interview with Preston C. Beyer, New York, Sept. 28, 1976.

8. Ibid.

9. Ibid.

10. Ibid.

11. Ibid.

12. Ibid.

13. March to Nichols, Nov. 7, 1952, Nichols Collection.

14. Perls, Sept. 28, 1976.

15. Smythe to RSS, Feb. 17, 1976.

16. Robert Tallant, "Where Shall John Go? XIII: New Orleans," *Horizon* 17 (Jan. 1948), p. 63. Tallant, a newspaperman turned author, was, like Lyle Saxon and Roark Bradford, essentially a regional author. He was a protégé of Saxon's and began his literary career with Saxon when both writers worked on the WPA Writers project. Never widely acclaimed, he was little known outside the South even at his peak. Possibly his first book is his most enduring work, if not his best, *Voodoo in New Orleans* (1946), a compilation of voodoo legend and myth, as well as fact. As a treatise, it is not as good as Seabrook's writings, which are mainly about Haitian voodoo. Tallant, however, never claimed to be an authority, merely setting out to make entertaining reading from the voodoo legends which form part of the overall New Orleans mystique. In 1947 he published *Mrs. Candy and Saturday Night*, a novel, and *Mardi Gras*, a most readable history of what is perhaps New Orleans' most internationally famous institution. The following year, 1948, he published another novel, *Angel in the Wardrobe*. Yet another novel, *Mr. Preen's Salon*, followed a year later. In 1952, his children's book *The Pirate Lafitte and the Battle of New Orleans* received the award of the Louisiana Library Association as the most outstanding book written in 1951 about Louisiana. His creative powers declined at a tragically early age. He was dogged by ill health during the last few years of his life and had to contend with a demanding invalid mother. He produced other books, including two sequels about Mrs. Candy—*Love and Mrs. Candy* and *Mrs. Candy Strikes It Rich*—but they were not up to the standard of the original. Eventually, he returned to writing feature stories for the *New Orleans Item*, but even this he found difficult to do. He died in April 1957 at the age of forty-seven, a burnt-out case.

17. Saxon, familiarly known as "the dean of New Orleans writers," died in 1946. Bradford, author of *Ol' Man Adam an' His Chillun*, from which Marc Connolly adapted the highly successful and award-winning play *The Green Pastures*, died in 1948.

18. Robert Tallant, "Poor Pilgrim, Poor Stranger," *Saturday Review* 37 (July 17, 1954).

19. Tallant, "Poor Pilgrim, Poor Stranger," pp. 33–34.

20. Smythe to RSS, March 4, 1976; Dickinson to RSS, Aug. 27, 1976.

21. Dillon T. March to RSS, Jan. 4, 1971.

22. Smythe to RSS, Feb. 17, 1976.

23. Smythe to RSS, Feb. 17, 1976.

24. Thomas Griffin, "Memoriam," Lagniappe Column, *New Orleans Item*, May 18, 1954; Griffin to RSS, Jan. 25, 1976.

25. Bolton, "In Memoriam Bill March."

26. The Blacksmith Shop, so legend has it, was originally owned by Jean LaFitte and his brother Pierre when they came to Louisiana in 1806 and was used by them, in conjunction with a store they purchased on Royal Street, as a "blind" to cover their smuggling activities. On the abolition of the slave trade in 1808, Jean left the business in New Orleans in his brother's hands. He formed a pirate band, initially to enter the trade of smuggling slaves, but he eventually became so powerful that he took command of the privateer colony on the island of Grand Terre at the entrance to Barataria Bay. At one time, he reputedly had 50 ships and 1,000 men under his command. He received a full pardon from President Madison when, in 1815, he threw his men into battle under the victorious Andrew Jackson against the British in the Battle of New Orleans.

27. Bolton, "Bill March."

28. Ibid.

29. Ibid.

30. Ibid.

31. Ibid.

32. Ibid.

33. Ibid.

34. Bolton to RSS, Feb. 8, 1976.

35. Bolton, "Bill March."

36. Ibid.

37. Bolton to Lawrence William Jones, Aug. 11, 1970.

38. Crager to Hamblen, March 5, 1971.

39. Perls, Sept. 28, 1976.

40. March to von Auw, Jan. 27, 1952, box 11, HO Archives.

41. Going, "A Footnote to *The Bad Seed*."

42. Shaw, Aug. 31, 1972.

43. Dickinson to RSS, Aug. 10, 1976.

44. Bolton, "Bill March."

45. Perls to RSS, Sept. 13, 1972.

46. Crager to Hamblen, March 5, 1971.

47. March to von Auw, April 12, 1952, box 11, HO Archives.

48. March to von Auw, April 17, 1952, box 11, HO Archives.

49. Rita Smith (Margarita G. Smith) is, incidentally, the sister of Carson McCullers.

50. March to Ober, June 10, 1952, box 11, HO Archives.

51. Ober to March, June 17, 1952, box 11, HO Archives.

52. Woodburn to Fadiman, July 14, 1952, Little, Brown & Co. records.

53. Perls, Sept. 28, 1976.

Chapter 13

1. Lionel Hale, "New Novels," *Observer*, June 8, 1952, p. 7.
2. C. P. Snow, "Facts as Well as Fiction," *Sunday Times* (London), June 15, 1952, p. 11.
3. Arthur Calder-Marshall, "New Novels," *Listener* 42 (June 19, 1952): 1015.
4. Anon., "Changes of Climate," *Times Literary Supplement*, June 13, 1952, p. 389.
5. Paul Bloomfield, "New Novels," *Manchester Guardian*, June 13, 1952, p. 4.
6. Anon., "New Fiction," *Times* (London), June 14, 1952, p. 3.
7. Charles Rollo, *Atlantic* 190 (Nov. 1952): 110.
8. Harrison Smith, "When Vermont Thaws in the South Seas," *Saturday Review* 35 (Oct. 4, 1952), 34.
9. Donald Barr, "A Tale of Morality and Fulfillment," *New York Times Book Review*, Oct. 19, 1952, p. 44.
10. Bolton, "Bill March."
11. Bolton to RSS, Sept. 12, 1977.
12. March to Nichols, Sept. 20, 1952, Nichols Collection.
13. Ibid.
14. March to Nichols, Nov. 29, 1952, Nichols Collection.
15. March to Nichols, Nov. 25, 1952, Nichols Collection.
16. March to McGowin, Sept. 25, 1952, WMC Papers.
17. Perls, Sept. 28, 1976.
18. March to von Auw, Nov. 14, 1952, box 11, HO Archives.
19. March to Nichols, Oct. 7, 1952, Nichols Collection.
20. March to Nichols, Nov. 29, 1952, Nichols Collection.
21. March to Nichols, Sept. 20, 1952, Nichols Collection.
22. March to Nichols, Sept. 11, 1952, Nichols Collection.
23. Bolton to RSS, Aug. 10, 1979.
24. Bolton to RSS, June 8 and June 12, 1976.
25. Bolton, "Those Were the Days: The Shoes That Laid Twenty Dollar Bills," *New Orleans Magazine* 5 (Dec. 1970): 64.
26. Bolton, "In Memoriam Bill March," p. 4.
27. Smythe to RSS, Feb. 17, 1976.
28. Ibid.
29. Bolton, "Bill March."
30. Smythe to RSS, Feb. 17, 1976.
31. Ibid.
32. Dickinson to RSS, Aug. 10, 1976.
33. The description of 613 Dumaine Street has been garnered from the following sources: letter from March to von Auw, May 14, 1953 (box 13, HO

Archives); letter from Robert Clark to RSS, May 28, 1976; and Edith E. Long, "Home, Sweet Home in Historic New Pad for Courier," *Vieux Carré Courier*, Aug. 16, 1968.

34. March to von Auw, May 14, 1953, box 13, HO Archives.

35. Dickinson to RSS, Aug. 10, 1976. On March's death, the portrait Dickinson had painted passed to March's favorite sister, Patty.

36. Bolton to RSS, Oct. 4, 1979.

37. Dickinson to RSS, Aug. 10, 1976.

38. The paintings were *Nature morte*, *Nature morte aux poissons*, *Le garçon à l'habit bleu*, *L'homme aux Rubans*, and *Le boeuf ecorché*.

39. Dickinson to RSS, Aug. 10, 1976. March donated *Dream* by Adolph Gottlieb and *Child's Bed* by Henry Koerner to the Delgardo Museum in 1951; *Paysage au lac* by Andre Derain and *Crucifixion* by Georges Rouault in 1953; and *La Bella Agnes en bleu* by Marie Laurencin and *Deauville* by Raoul Dufy in 1954 (Charles L. Mo, Registrar, New Orleans Museum of Art, to RSS, May 21, 1976).

40. March to von Auw, May 14, 1953, box 13, HO Archives.

41. Von Auw to March, May 21, 1953, box 13, HO Archives.

42. Von Auw to March, June 10, 1953, box 13, HO Archives.

43. March to Ober, June 5, 1953, box 13, HO Archives.

44. March to von Auw, July 13, 1953, box 13, HO Archives.

45. Dickinson to RSS, Aug. 10, 1976.

46. Von Auw to March, July 28, 1953, box 13, HO Archives.

47. Von Auw to March, Sept. 2, 1953, box 13, HO Archives.

48. March to von Auw, Sept. 3, 1953, box 13, HO Archives.

49. Tallant, "Poor Pilgrim, Poor Stranger," p. 34.

50. Loomis to von Auw, Sept. 17, 1953, Holt, Rinehart & Winston records.

51. Von Auw to March, Sept. 18, 1953, box 13, HO Archives.

52. March to von Auw, Oct. 5, 1953, box 13, HO Archives.

53. Letter from *Collier's* fiction editor, Eleanor Stierhem MacMannis, to Ober, Nov. 19, 1953; and von Auw to March, Dec. 3, 1953, HO Archives.

54. March to von Auw, Nov. 17, 1953, box 13, HO Archives.

55. Von Auw to Amussen, Dec. 3, 1953, Holt, Rinehart & Winston records.

56. Amussen to March, Dec. 11, 1953, Holt, Rinehart & Winston records.

57. March to Amussen, Dec. 21, 1953, Holt, Rinehart & Winston records.

58. March to von Auw, Sept. 3, 1953, box 13, HO Archives.

59. Smythe to RSS, March 4, 1976.

60. Amussen to von Auw, Jan. 21, 1954, Holt, Rinehart & Winston records; von Auw to March, Jan. 26, 1954, and March to von Auw, Jan. 31, 1954, box 16, HO Archives.

61. Dickinson to RSS, Aug. 6 and Aug. 10, 1976.

62. Livia Gollancz to RSS, July 1, 1976.

63. March to von Auw, March 10, 1954, box 16, HO Archives.

64. Dickinson to RSS, Aug. 10, 1976.

65. Ibid.

66. March to von Auw, March 10, 1954, box 16, HO Archives.

67. Ibid.

68. Frasier to March, March 11, 1954, Holt, Rinehart & Winston records.

69. The correspondence relating to these two abortive projects is filed among the HO Archives. The letters relating to the proposed 1953 project are: Ehrlich to Little, Brown, Feb. 19, 1953; Ober to Ehrlich, March 10, 1953; von Auw to Swanson, March 12, 1953; von Auw to March, March 12, 1953; Slaughter to von Auw, March 16, 1953; Swanson to von Auw, March 16, 1953; Ehrlich to von Auw, March 24, 1953; von Auw to Ehrlich, April 9, 1953; and von Auw to Ehrlich, Sept. 2, 1953. Von Auw advised March of the possibility of the musical play version of *October Island* in a letter dated March 5, 1954, and March's reaction is contained in his reply to von Auw on March 10, 1954.

70. March to von Auw, March 10, 1954, box 16, HO Archives.

71. Von Auw to March, March 23, 1954, box 16, HO Archives.

72. March to Frasier, March 24, 1954, Holt, Rinehart & Winston records.

73. Clark to RSS, April 26, 1954.

74. Dickinson to RSS, Aug. 10, 1976.

75. Smythe to RSS, March 4, 1976.

Chapter 14

1. Going, "March's Alabama," *Essays on Alabama Literature*, pp. 111–12.

2. Anon., *Kirkus* 22 (Feb. 15, 1954): 130.

3. Anon., *New Yorker* 30 (April 10, 1954): 151.

4. James Kelly, "The Portrait of a Coldly Evil Child," *New York Times Book Review*, April 11, 1954, pp. 4–5.

5. Dan Wickenden, *New York Herald Tribune Book Review*, April 11, 1954, p. 4.

6. Amussen to March, April 8, 1954, Holt, Rinehart & Winston records.

7. Dickinson to Rinehart, April 9, 1954, Holt, Rinehart & Winston records.

8. Rinehart to Dickinson, April 13, 1954, Holt, Rinehart & Winston records.

9. Fields to March, April 27, 1954, box 16, HO Archives.

10. Villa to RSS, Aug. 5, 1976; Geffen to Rinehart, April 22, 1954, Holt, Rinehart & Winston records.

11. Virginia Spencer Carr, *The Lonely Hunter: A Biography of Carson McCullers* (Garden City, N.Y.: Doubleday & Company, 1975), p. 426.

12. Dickinson to RSS, Aug. 10, 1976.

13. Ibid.

14. Clark to RSS, Nov. 17, 1976.

15. March to von Auw, May 7, 1954, box 16, HO Archives.

16. Thomas Griffin, "Memoriam."

17. Clark to RSS, April 26, 1976.

18. As reported by Smythe in his letter to RSS, Feb. 17, 1976.

19. Bolton, "Bill March."

20. Shaw, Aug. 31, 1972.

21. Dickinson to RSS, Aug. 27, 1976.

22. Gwen Campbell, July 30, 1976.

23. Gustavson to March, Frasier to March, May 13, 1954, Holt, Rinehart & Winston records.

24. Quoted in Tallant's essay "Poor Pilgrim, Poor Stranger," p. 9.

25. Clark to RSS, April 26, 1976.

26. Clark to RSS, May 28, 1976.

27. Tallant, "Poor Pilgrim, Poor Stranger," p. 9.

28. Bolton, "Bill March."

29. Tallant, "Poor Pilgrim, Poor Stranger," p. 34.

30. Perls, Sept. 28, 1976.

31. L. A. G. Strong, "New Novels," *Spectator* 193 (Oct. 15, 1954): 478.

32. Walter Allen, "New Novels," *New Statesman* 48 (Oct. 23, 1954): 513.

33. Walter Kerr, quoted in *Best Mystery and Suspense Plays of the Modern Theatre*, ed. Stanley Richards (New York: Dodd, Mead & Company, 1971), p. 591.

34. Brooks Atkinson, "Theatre: 'Bad Seed,'" *New York Times*, Dec. 9, 1954.

35. John McClain, " 'Shocker' Proves a Hit," *New York Journal-American*, Dec. 9, 1954.

36. Kenneth Tynan, "The Season in London," *The Best Plays of 1954–1955*, ed. Louis Kronenburger (New York: Dodd, Mead & Company, 1955), p. 31.

37. Cooke, *WMO*, p. vii.

38. Anthony West, *New Yorker* 32 (March 31, 1956): 105–107.

39. Maxwell Geismar, "Pathos Is the Essence," *New York Times Book Review*, Feb. 26, 1956, p. 5.

40. John Hutchens, "Toward a Restoration of William March," *New York Herald Tribune Book Review*, March 4, 1956, p. 2.

41. Warner Bros. Pictures, mimeographed production notes on *The Bad Seed*.

42. Bosley Crowther, *New York Times*, Sept. 13, 1956, p. 39.

43. Dorothy D. MacGregory to Rinehart, Aug. 18, 1955, Holt, Rinehart & Winston records.

44. Going, in *99F*, p. v.

45. Going's proposed introduction to the book of uncollected stories has been published under the title "Some in Addition: The Uncollected Stories of William March," in *Essays on Alabama Literature*, pp. 80–96.

Afterword

1. John Gardner, "The Art of Fiction LXXIII," *Paris Review* 75 (1979): 65.

2. Graham Greene, *Ways of Escape* (London: Bodley Head, 1980), p. 9.

3. This information is taken from a list Going transcribed from notes made by him on a visit to Mrs. Patty Campbell Maxwell's home two or three years after March's death and was kindly made available to RSS on March 31, 1977.

4. McWilliams to RSS, Nov. 5, 1976.

5. Crager to Hamblen, March 5, 1971.

6. R. D. Laing, *The Politics of Experience & The Bird of Paradise* (Harmondsworth: Penguin Books, 1967), pp. 11–12.

7. Clark to RSS, Nov. 17, 1976.

8. Clark to RSS, May 28, 1976.

9. March to Crowder, Nov. 24, 1943, DePauw Archives.

10. James Jones, *Some Came Running* (New York: Scribner's, 1957), p. 639.

11. See also the comments of Going in "Some in Addition," pp. 88–89.

Selected Bibliography

The following listing includes March's books, uncollected short stories, and a selection of the more important biographical and critical studies that have appeared both during his lifetime and after his death. For a more comprehensive list, the reader is referred to my "A William March Checklist," *Mississippi Quarterly* 28 (Fall 1975): 461–88.

Primary Sources

Books

Company K. New York: Harrison Smith & Robert Haas, 1933; London: Victor Gollancz, 1933.

Come in at the Door. New York: Harrison Smith & Robert Haas, 1934; London: Rich & Cowan, 1934.

The Little Wife and Other Stories. New York: Harrison Smith & Robert Haas, 1935; London: Rich & Cowan, 1935.

The Tallons. New York: Random House, 1936; London (under the title *A Song for Harps*): Rich & Cowan, 1936.

Some Like Them Short. Boston: Little, Brown, 1939.

The Looking-Glass. Boston: Little, Brown, 1943; London: Victor Gollancz, 1944.

Trial Balance. New York: Harcourt, Brace, 1945.

October Island. Boston: Little, Brown, 1952; London: Victor Gollancz, 1952.

The Bad Seed. New York: Rinehart & Company, 1954; London: Hamish Hamilton, 1954.

A William March Omnibus. With an introduction by Alistair Cooke. New York: Rinehart & Company, 1954.

99 Fables. Edited and with an introduction by William T. Going. University: University of Alabama Press, 1960.

Uncollected Stories

"The Unploughed Patch." *Pagany* 3 (October– December 1932, January– March 1933): 1– 55.

"The Marriage of the Bishops." *Accent* 1 (Autumn 1940): 15– 19.

"One Way Ticket." *Good Housekeeping* 122 (January 1946): 24– 15, 123, 125– 27.

"A Great Town for Characters." *Esquire* 25 (May 1946): 86, 143– 44, 146.

"Old Sorority Sister." *Collier's* 118 (September 28, 1946): 16, 63, 65, 67– 69.

"Ballet of the Bowie Knives." In *Cross Section, 1947*, edited by Edwin Seaver. New York: Simon & Schuster, 1947, pp. 20– 27.

"An Untitled Story." *Ladies' Home Journal* (October 1948): 8.

"The Bird House." *Ellery Queen's Mystery Magazine* 23 (February 1954): 27– 38.

Secondary Sources

Bader, Arno L. "The Structure of the Modern Short Story." *College English* 7 (November 1954): 86– 92. Reprinted in *Discussions of the Short Story*, edited and with an introduction by Hollis Summers. Boston: D. C. Heath, 1963, pp. 40– 45.

Beasley, William Madison. "The New South and Five Southern Novelists (1920– 1950)." Ph.D. dissertation, Vanderbilt University, 1957.

Bolton, Clint. "In Memoriam Bill March." *Vieux Carré Courier*, August 16, 1968, pp. 6– 7.

Cooperman, Stanley. *World War I and the American Novel*. Baltimore: Johns Hopkins Press, 1967.

Crowder, Richard. "The Novels of William March." *University of Kansas City Review* 15 (Winter 1948): 111– 29.

Emerson, O. B. "William March and Southern Literature." *Carson-Newman College Faculty Studies* 1 (1968): 3– 10.

Going, William T. Introduction to *99 Fables*. University, Alabama: University of Alabama Press, 1960, pp. xiii– xxii.

——. "March's *The Little Wife*." *Explicator* 20 (April 1962): Item 66.

——. "William March's Alabama." *Alabama Review*, October 1963, 243– 59. Reprinted in *Essays on Alabama Literature*, by William T. Going. University: University of Alabama Press, 1975, pp. 97– 113.

——. "A Footnote to '*The Bad Seed*: A Modern Elsie Venner.'" *Western Humanities Review* 18 (Spring 1964): 175.

——. "Some in Addition: The Uncollected Stories of William March." In *Essays on Alabama Literature*. University: University of Alabama Press, 1975, pp. 80– 96.

——. "William March: Regional Perspective and Beyond." *Papers on Language and Literature* 13 (Fall 1977): 430– 43.

Hamblen, Abigail Ann. "*The Bad Seed*: A Modern Elsie Venner." *Western Humanities Review* 17 (Autumn 1963): 361–63.

Medlicott, Alexander, Jr. "Soldiers Are Citizens of Death's Gray Land: William March's *Company K*." *Arizona Quarterly* 28 (Autumn 1972): 209–24.

Peak, Ellen Fay. "William March and His Short Stories, Containing Some Disparate Materials Helpful to the Biographer." Master's Thesis, Birmingham-Southern College, 1962.

Routh, Michael. "The Fiction of Pressure: William March's Short Stories." *Mississippi Quarterly* 36 (Spring 1983): 105–15.

Silva, Frederick E. "The Cracked Looking Glass: A Critical Study of the Novels of William March (1894–1954)." Ph.D. dissertation, Indiana University, 1967.

Simmonds, Roy S. "William March's *Company K*: A Short Textual Study." *Studies in American Fiction* 2 (Spring 1974): 105–13.

———. "An Unending Circle of Pain: William March's *Company K*." *Ball State University Forum* 16 (Spring 1975): 33–46.

———. "William March's 'Personal Letter': Fact into Fiction." *Mississippi Quarterly* 30 (Fall 1977): 625–37.

———. "William March." *Dictionary of Literary Biography, Volume Nine (American Novelists, 1910–1945. Part 2: F. Scott Fitzgerald–O. E. Rölvaag),* edited by James J. Martine. Detroit: Gale Research Company, 1981, pp. 190–93.

Tallant, Robert. "Poor Pilgrim, Poor Stranger." *Saturday Review* 37 (July 17, 1954): 9, 33–34.

Index

352